The Ultimate Guide to Freshwater Fishing

Dick Sternberg has combined his skills as a biologist and multi-species angler to write over 20 books on freshwater fishing.

The Ultimate Guide to Freshwater Fishing

Tom Carpenter
Creative Director

Michele Teigen
Senior Book Development Coordinator

Bill Lindner, Tom Heck, Mike Hehner, Pete Cozad, Jason Lund, Dick Sternberg, Phil Aarrestad, Christopher M. Batin, Tom Carpenter/NAMG, Dan Kennedy/NAMG, Animals, Animals: ©Robert Maier; ©LSF, OSF; ©Joe McDonald; ©Carroll W. Perkins; ©Bill Beatty; ©OSF; ©James H. Robinson; ©Stephen Dalton; ©Zig Leszczynski; ©Ralph Reinhold; ©Leonard Lee Rue III; ©Allen Blake Sheldon; ©Fred G. Whitehead; ©Breck P. Kent/Animals, Animals; ©Bertram G. Murray Jr., Keith Sutton, Brook Martin, John Beath, Walt Jennings.
Photography

Dave Schelitzche, Joe Tomelleri, Dave Rottinghaus
Illustration

Julie Cisler, Dave Schelitzche, Jenya Prosmitsky
Book Design & Production

Gina Germ
Photo Editor

Greg Schwieters
Cover Design

Dedication:

This book is dedicated in memory of Jack and Lois Knapp. At their home on State Street in Mason City, Iowa, where they lived for 40 years, they raised a family of ten children that has grown to include nine spouses and 30 grandchildren. Jack and Lois's love of family, community, faith and each other provided inspiration to many. They nurtured dreams in their children. This book is the culmination of just one of those dreams.

Jim Knapp, President
Publishing Solutions, LLC

Acknowledgements:

The publisher would like to thank the terrific team at North American Membership Group, led by Nancy Evensen and Tom Carpenter, for all of their hard work in making this book a reality. Special thanks to Greg Schwieters and Michele Teigen for their significant contributions. Jim Bindas, Book Productions, LLC, provided valuable help in the production of this book. The direction and support of Julie Hughes and Matt Dillon of R. R. Donnelley is especially appreciated.

Published by
Publishing Solutions, LLC
1107 Hazeltine Boulevard
Suite 470
Chaska, MN 55318
952-361-4902
James L. Knapp, President

Production Management
Book Productions, LLC

Printed in China

2 3 4 5 6 / 07 06 05 04 03
ISBN 0-9725580-0-4

CONTENTS
PART I — CATCH FISH ANYWHERE, ANYTIME

CONTENTS
PART II — ARTIFICIAL LURES

Contents
PART III — LIVE BAIT

The Ultimate Guide to Freshwater Fishing

Whether you're pursuing bass of the largemouth or smallmouth variety, panfish from crappies to bluegills, catfish of any type, walleye or perch, pike and muskie,  members of the trout and salmon family, or any other freshwater gamefish for that matter, one factor will make *the* difference in your fishing success.

What is this magic secret? Well, it's not magic. And it's not really a secret. But it is easily attainable.

It is knowledge. And that's what *The Ultimate Guide to Freshwater Fishing* brings you.

Here, in concise and straightforward words combined with photographs from the stunning to the instructive, is the knowledge you need to become an even better fisherman or woman.

Whether you're a seasoned angling veteran, a newcomer to the ranks of the fishing addicted, or just an occasional angler who wants to find a little more success out on the water, this book offers insights and information that will help you catch more fish, bigger fish, more often.

Part I, Catch Fish Anywhere Anytime, helps you understand freshwater gamefish and the places they live, select and use fishing tackle and gear, master important fishing skills, figure out where to find the fish, then put all the knowledge to work when you're on the water.

Part II, Artificial Lures, immerses you in the world of topwaters, plugs, spinners, spinnerbaits, soft plastics, spoons, jigging lures and flies. You'll see exactly how, when and where to use each one to maximize your fishing success.

Part III, Live Bait, takes you into the world of baitfish, nightcrawlers, worms, leeches, insects, frogs, salamanders, crustaceans and more. You'll discover how to fish with live bait most effectively, catching more fish when times are good and learning that live bait is often the answer you need when fishing is tough.

Never before has a fishing book like this been created. That's why it is *The Ultimate Guide to Freshwater Fishing.* And that's why it will put more fish onto your line every time you hit the water.

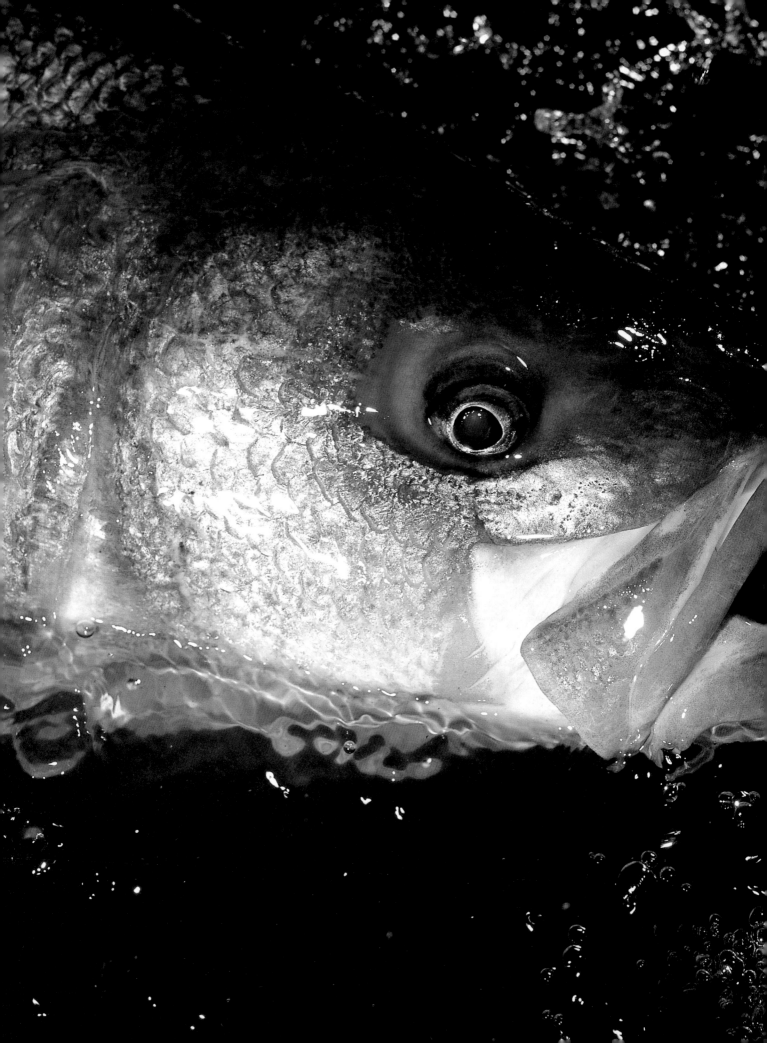

PART I

CATCH FISH ANYWHERE, ANYTIME

INTRODUCTION

*P*art I, *Catch Fish Anywhere, Anytime,* will help you become a better angler, and not because it focuses on the hottest new lure or the latest breakthroughs in fishing electronics. Rather, it highlights the habits of the gamefish you target in the waters you fish. After all, the key to consistently successful angling is finding fish. Even the best lure made can't catch a fish that isn't there!

No matter if you fish bass, salmon, walleye or any other species of fish, or if you are a beginning angler or an expert, *Catch Fish Anywhere, Anytime* contains the information you need to plan a successful fishing strategy. Its clear, concise text and easy-to-understand color photographs are sure to make you a more versatile, more successful angler.

UNDERSTANDING FRESHWATER GAMEFISH

*T*he first step to becoming a successful angler is developing a basic understanding of the fish you're trying to catch. Without this knowledge, even the most expensive equipment will do you no good.

GAMEFISH SENSES

Walleyes and other gamefish can detect prey that they cannot see by picking up vibrations with their lateral line (dotted line).

Every gamefish species is equipped with a set of senses that enables it to survive in an ever-changing aquatic world. When the water is clear, for example, most fish rely heavily on vision to find food and avoid predators, including fishermen. But, when the water suddenly turns muddy from a heavy rain, they depend mainly on hearing and their lateral-line system.

Although every gamefish species has each of the senses we are about to discuss, the acuity of specific senses varies considerably among species. Although there have been no

broad-scope studies to quantify these differences, there have been some studies on particular fish. And, from visual observation, we also know which senses are important to many species. These differences will be discussed in the chapter on "Fishing Techniques" (p. 80).

Vision

In all gamefish, the retina of the eye is equipped with both rods (intensity receptors) and cones (color receptors). The cone-to-rod ratio is highest in shallow-water species, such

as bass and sunfish, meaning that they have better color vision than deep-water species. Researchers believe that most shallow-water fish see the same range of colors as humans.

Good color vision would be virtually meaningless to fish in deep water, because water acts as a color filter. Red is filtered out at a depth of only 10 feet and yellow disappears at about 20. Blue may be visible at depths of 50 feet or more, assuming there is adequate light penetration. But even if fish can't see the color of an object, they may recognize it as a shade of gray. This explains why most veteran anglers place more importance on the flash, action and size of a lure than on the exact color.

Fish that have good color vision may not have good night vision, however, because the retina does not have enough rods. The northern pike falls into this category. Some gamefish, like Pacific salmon, are capable of switching from cone to rod vision as light levels fade.

How far and how clearly a fish can see depends more on water clarity than visual acuity. In very clear water, most gamefish can easily see 75 feet or more. In highly turbid

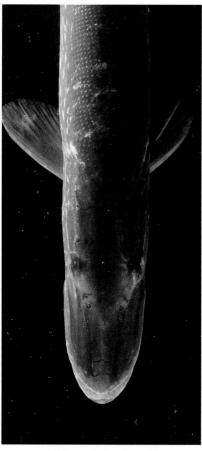

Eyes positioned on the side of the head and toward the top make it possible for fish to see in every direction, except straight behind them and below them.

water, they would be hard-pressed to see a foot.

Lateral Line

This sense, not present in humans, enables fish to pick up vibrations in the water that help them detect predators, prey and even anglers' lures.

The lateral line consists of a row of pores along each side of the fish, extending from the gill to the base of the tail. The pores are connected to a network of nerve endings that sense the slightest vibrations and transmit them to receptors in the inner ear.

Using its lateral line, a fish can determine not only if predators or prey are present, but how big they are, how fast they're moving and in what direction. The lateral line also helps schools of fish swim in unison.

Hearing

Fish do not have external ears, but they have inner ears, which consist of tiny bones that pick up sound and semi-circular canals that help maintain equilibrium. They do not have an ear drum, however, so vibrations are sent to the ear through body tissues.

Many anglers, knowing that gamefish can detect underwater sounds, use lures with rattles when fishing after dark or in murky water.

Smell/Taste

Most gamefish have an acute sense of smell and are

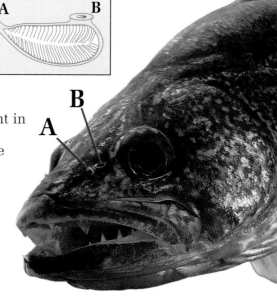

*To detect odors, fish take in water through **(A)** incurrent nares. It passes through the nasal capsule where odors are picked up by folds of sensory tissue (cutaway). The water is then expelled through **(B)** excurrent nares.*

able to detect the odor of nearby predators and prey, assuming the current is favorable. But some gamefish rely on scent much more than others. Scent is most important in catfish, trout, salmon and sunfish, and least important in bass, walleyes and pike.

This explains why catfish anglers have so much success with "stinkbait," why fresh spawn works so well for trout and salmon, and why scented soft-plastics catch so many sunfish. Scented baits are much less effective on other gamefish.

In most gamefish, the sense of taste is much less significant than the sense of smell. But bullheads and catfish do use their sense of taste, especially in muddy water. They comb the bottom, using taste buds in their whiskers and on their skin to find food.

FOOD & FEEDING HABITS

Anglers are constantly trying to determine why gamefish behave the way they do. Practically everyone who wets a line has a theory involving wind direction, cloud cover, water temperature, water pH, moon phase or dozens of other factors. But the number-one factor influencing the daily lives of gamefish is food.

A gamefish will endure water well outside its preferred temperature or pH range, and even will venture into water with practically no dissolved oxygen, if that water holds the food it wants.

Although every fish has a preference for certain foods, those foods may not be available at all times. If a gamefish is to survive, it must learn to be an opportunist.

This explains why the diet of most gamefish changes several times over the course of a year, depending on the abundance of particular food items. To catch fish consistently, you must learn how food availability can affect gamefish behavior.

If bass are busting into schools of shad in open water, for example, you may be able to catch them on topwaters. But when they're rooting crayfish out of the rocks, a jig would be a much better choice.

In most cases, it is not necessary to use a lure that looks precisely like the food the fish are eating. But it helps to select a lure of about the same size with a similar type of action.

Differences in food availability also explain why gamefish in one body of water can behave much differently than those in another. For instance, walleyes in a lake where perch are the primary food do most of their feeding on deep structure, because that's where most of the perch are found. But where shad or ciscoes are the main food, walleyes spend much more time cruising open water.

Common Feeding Behaviors

Ambush predators, such as muskies, lie in wait in dense cover, waiting for baitfish or other foods to make a mistake and come too close. Then, they attack with a burst of speed and return to their resting spot to digest their meal.

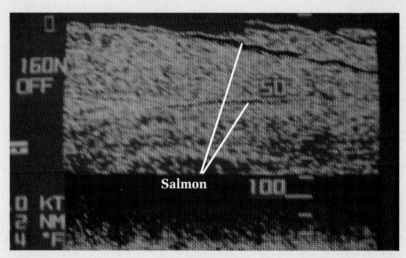

Open water feeders, such as chinook salmon, go wherever they must to find schools of baitfish. This video screen shows a cloud of alewives with several chinooks in its midst.

Scavengers, such as channel catfish, comb the bottom for any kind of food they can find. They will take live crayfish, mussels, insect larvae and baitfish, but will also eat dead or rotting organic material.

Larval aquatic insects are one of the most important foods for young gamefish and, in some cases, adults. During a heavy insect hatch, gamefish like trout and walleyes may feed exclusively on a particular kind of insect larvae.

Tiny mollusks (snails and clams) are food for many kinds of juvenile gamefish. Larger mollusks are food for bottom feeders like catfish. Snails make up a large part of the diet of redear sunfish, accounting for their common name, shellcracker.

Crustaceans are an important food source for all sizes of gamefish. Young fish graze on tiny crustaceans called scuds (shown), while larger fish eat crustaceans like grass shrimp and crayfish.

Small fish make up the majority of the diet of adult bass, walleye, pike and other large predators. As a rule, long, thin fish like shiners make better forage than deep-bodied fish like sunfish, because they slide down easier.

Large fish like adult suckers, whitefish and even rainbow trout are the preferred food of big pike, muskies, lake trout, bass and other good-sized predators. By eating one large fish instead of several small ones, they conserve energy. This 6-pound lake trout has battle scars from a previous encounter with a 40-pound-plus laker.

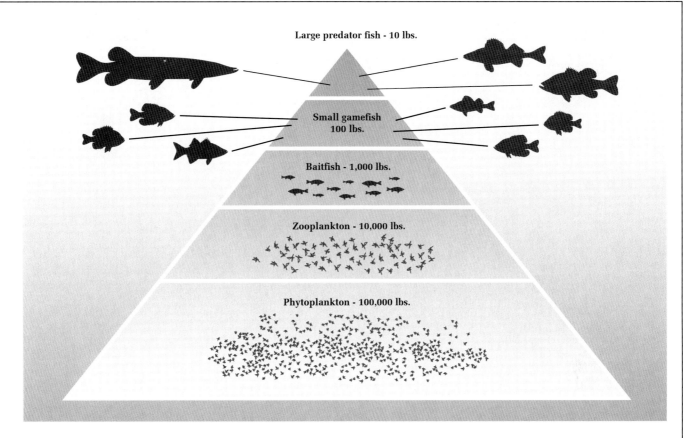

Large predator fish - 10 lbs.

Small gamefish
100 lbs.

Baitfish - 1,000 lbs.

Zooplankton - 10,000 lbs.

Phytoplankton - 100,000 lbs.

Understanding the Food Pyramid

The abundance of gamefish in any body of water is dependent on the abundance of plankton. Without enough phytoplankton, for instance, there wouldn't be enough zooplankton to feed the baitfish, and without enough baitfish, there would be a shortage of gamefish.

Many biologists talk about these food relationships in terms of a food chain, which basically shows what eats what.

But a food pyramid is a more meaningful concept, because it shows how much of each type of food is needed to produce how many pounds of top-rung predators. Although the exact percentage varies greatly depending on the situation, the poundage produced at each level of the pyramid is only about 10 percent of the level below it. In the above example, 100,000 pounds of phytoplankton produce only 10 pounds of large predator fish.

Feeding Triggers

Insect hatches may cause fish to suddenly start feeding. Fish know that a hatch lasts only for a short time, and they must move quickly to get an easy meal.

Approaching storms cause a rapid decrease in light level and a drop in barometric pressure, which may initiate a feeding spree.

Wind pounding into a shoreline creates a mudline. Windblown plankton draws baitfish and, in turn, gamefish that can feed comfortably in low-light conditions.

FISH HABITAT

Walleyes deposit their eggs along windswept rubble shorelines. The eggs slip into crevices in the rocks where wave action keeps them aerated and prevents them from silting over and suffocating.

Every kind of gamefish has its own unique habitat requirements. Even closely related species, like smallmouth and largemouth bass, have a slightly different set of habitat preferences. In order to target a particular species of fish, you must understand its habitat needs.

The term, habitat, means the combination of environmental elements that a fish needs to survive. For gamefish, that combination includes the right kind of cover, good conditions for spawning, the proper range of water temperature, adequate dissolved oxygen and a reliable supply of food. Without any one of these elements, long-term survival would be impossible.

If you take time to study the habitat needs of gamefish, catching them becomes much easier. You'll not only know where to look, but where not to look.

Spawning Habitat

The spawning habits of gamefish vary greatly and so does their spawning-habitat needs. Northern pike, for instance, can spawn successfully in shallow, marshy bays, but if walleyes attempted to spawn there, the eggs would probably not survive.

Shown on this page are a few of the many habitats used by spawning gamefish. You'll learn more details in the chapter, "Fishing Techniques" (p. 80).

Types of Spawning Habitat

A hard, sandy bottom with emergent vegetation, such as bulrushes, for cover, makes ideal spawning habitat for sunfish, crappies and other panfish, especially when it is in a bay or along a sheltered shoreline.

Trout and salmon dig their redds in gravel beds in flowing water. The eggs are deposited in the depression, then covered with gravel. Water flowing through the gravel keeps the eggs oxygenated.

Hiding cover provides young fish protection from a host of aquatic and avian predators. Common types of hiding cover include dense weeds and brush, crevices between rocks, docks, piers and other man-made cover.

Gamefish Cover

Without some type of cover, the life expectancy of a newly hatched fish could be measured in minutes. The tiny hatchling, or fry, would soon become an easy meal for an aquatic predator, such as a minnow, a crayfish or, possibly, an insect. If it is lucky enough to survive for a few weeks and grow a little larger, it attracts predators like bass, herons, grebes and turtles that are looking for a more sub-stantial meal. This intense predation explains why less than one percent of the fish that hatch ever see adulthood.

All but the largest gamefish are also subject to predation, but they need cover for other reasons, as well. Cover provides shade, protection from the current and a hiding spot from which to ambush prey. And, in the heat of summer, overhead cover keeps the water a little cooler.

Ambush cover conceals predator fish so they can dart out and grab unsuspecting prey. Most predators avoid thick weeds or other dense cover because they cannot maneuver well enough.

Overhead cover protects fish from avian predators, provides shade and may keep the water slightly cooler. Common types include undercut banks, root wads and beds of float-ing-leaf vegetation.

Nesting cover, such as boulders and logs, makes it easier for nesting fish to guard their eggs and newly hatched fry, because the nest is protected on at least one side.

Shelter from current is a must for most fish that live in moving water. This explains why they seek cover in eddies that form downstream of boulders, log jams, bridge piers, islands and points.

Water Temperature

Although fish are cold-blooded, different species have distinctly different water-temperature preferences. Biologists place gamefish in three temperature categories. Coldwater fish (trout and salmon), prefer water temperatures in the 50s; coolwater fish (pike, muskie, walleye, sauger and perch), in the 60s; and warmwater fish (bass, crappies, sunfish, catfish), 70 to 80.

But just because a fish prefers a certain temperature doesn't mean it will always be found in water of that temperature. Fish go where they must to find food, and even a major difference in water temperature won't stop them.

In summer, when oxygen levels sag in deep water, coldwater fish are forced into shallower water, where oxygen levels are higher. They are under some stress, but they can usually endure it until the water starts to cool in fall.

Some coldwater fish can tolerate water well above their preferred temperature range. Brown trout, for example, prefer water of about 58 to 62°F, but they're sometimes found in the lower reaches of streams where the water is in the upper 70s.

Conversely, most warmwater fish can tolerate very cold water. Sunfish, crappies and bass live in many waters that ice over in winter, and they continue to feed at near-freezing temperatures.

But, as a rule, the greater the difference between a fish's preferred temperature range and the actual water temperature, the less active it is likely to be. The brown trout in the warm stream, for instance, will be difficult to catch because it is feeding very little. The same

holds true for the bass in the frozen lake.

As gamefish grow older, they generally prefer cooler water. This pattern is most evident in northern pike. Small pike like water in the 67- to 72-degree range, but

once they reach 30 inches in length (about 7 pounds), they prefer 50- to 55-degree water. Their preference for cooler water explains why large fish are generally found in deeper water than small ones.

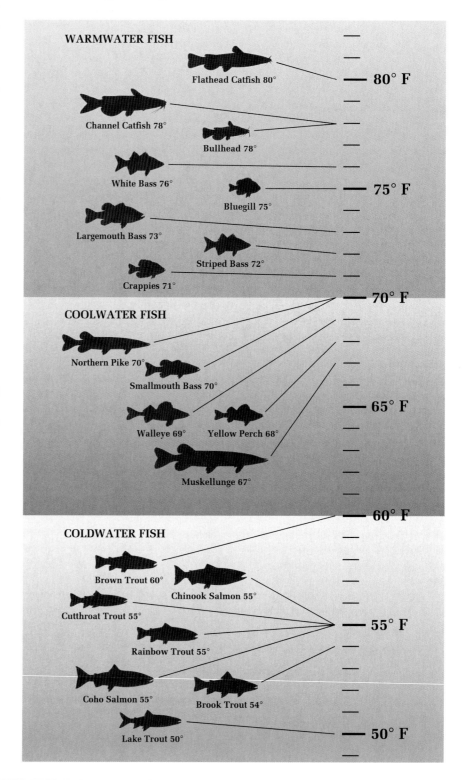

The Fall Turnover

Early Fall	Mid-Fall
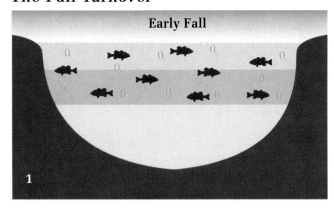	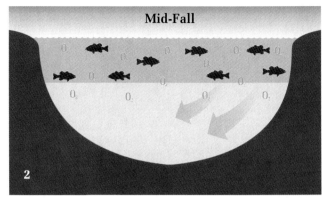

Turnover	Late Fall
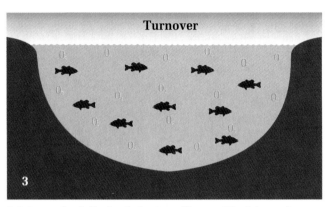	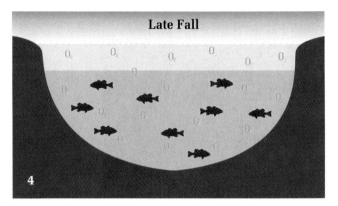

(1) In early fall, the lake is still stratified into three temperature layers. Fish are found only in the upper two layers, because oxygen levels are too low in the hypolimnion. (2) As the upper layer cools in mid-fall, the surface water starts to sink and (3) the turnover begins, scattering fish to all depths. (4) By late fall, the surface water is cooler than the water on the bottom, so practically all of the fish are deep.

Stratification & Turnover

Water is densest at a temperature of 39.2°F. As it gets warmer or colder, it becomes less dense. This density difference causes most lakes to stratify into temperature layers. The deepest, coldest, densest layer is called the *hypolimnion;* the shallowest, warmest, lightest layer, the *epilimnion*. Between the two is a zone called the *thermocline,* where the temperature changes rapidly.

The warmer, lighter water in the epilimnion floats on top of the cooler, heavier water in the depths. And because the water is lighter, it is more easily circulated by the wind. The thermocline may have slight water circulation, but the water below it circulates very little.

After a lake stratifies in early summer, a stagnation process begins. Decaying organic material on the lake bottom, along with living organisms in the water, consume dissolved oxygen. With no circulation to restore it and no aquatic plants to produce it, oxygen levels in the hypolimnion begin to decline. Just how fast they decline depends on the water fertility (p. 22).

The temperature layers remain intact through the summer, as long as the weather is warm enough to keep the surface water several degrees warmer than the water in the depths. But when the weather cools enough that the shallows reach the same temperature as the depths, the fall turnover begins. Because all of the water in the lake is now at the same temperature and density, the wind can circulate the entire water mass. As the surface continues to cool, the water becomes denser than that in the depths so it sinks vertically, bolstering the mixing process.

Mixing from top to bottom continues through the fall. In the North, the surface freezes, but the water on the bottom stays several degrees above freezing. If water did not have the unusual property of being densest at a temperature slightly above freezing, lakes would freeze completely to the bottom.

Eutrophic lakes are shallow and weedy, with highly fertile water. A heavy algae bloom usually develops in summer. These lakes are best suited for warmwater gamefish and roughfish.

Water Fertility

The term "water fertility" refers to the amount of nutrients, such as nitrogen and phosphorus, dissolved in the water. A body of water with high fertility is said to be *eutrophic;* moderate fertility, *mesotrophic;* and low fertility, *oligotrophic.*

Fertility, in itself, has little effect on the daily lives of gamefish. If all of their other habitat requirements are met, they can live in water of most any fertility level.

But fertility is the major determinant of how many pounds of fish a body of water can produce. Just as the amount of fertilizer you spread on your lawn determines how fast your grass will grow, the level of dissolved nutrients in the water determines how much phytoplankton (p. 17) is produced and, thus, how much food is available to gamefish. That, in turn, affects their growth rate and, ultimately, the poundage of fish the body of water can support.

Mesotrophic lakes usually have moderate depth, water clarity, water fertility and weed growth. These lakes often support warmwater and coolwater gamefish.

Oligotrophic lakes are generally deep, clear and infertile, with sparse weed growth. They are best suited for coolwater and coldwater gamefish, although shallow bays may hold warmwater species.

Fertility has yet another indirect influence on gamefish. It is the primary factor determining the level of dissolved oxygen in the water (opposite) so it controls where fish can live and where they cannot.

Dissolved Oxygen

Fish vary greatly in their dissolved oxygen (D.O.) needs. While some species, like bullheads, can get by with practically no oxygen, others, such as trout, require a great deal.

Oxygen levels are measured in parts per million (ppm). When water is fully saturated with oxygen, the D.O. level is about 10 ppm, depending on the water temperature.

You may have noticed that fish are much easier to keep alive in your livewell when the water is cold. There are two reasons for this: Fish in cold water require less oxygen, and the water can hold more oxygen.

Oxygen gets into the water through contact with the air and photosynthesis by aquatic plants. It is consumed by respiration of aquatic organisms ranging from bacteria to gamefish.

In fertile lakes, organic matter is so plentiful that oxygen is consumed faster than it is replenished. In summer, when a lake stratifies, the layer of decaying organic ooze on the bottom rapidly consumes oxygen and, with no circulation to replace it, oxygen levels wane, forcing fish into shallower water.

The fall turnover replenishes oxygen levels, but they begin to dip again in winter. If snow and ice cover are heavy enough to prevent sunlight penetration, plants cannot produce oxygen through photosynthesis, so oxygen levels plummet. If they plummet far enough, fish begin to die and the lake is said to freeze out, or *winterkill.*

Summer oxygen depletion or winterkill are not a problem in infertile lakes, because oxygen is consumed much more slowly.

Minimum Wintertime Oxygen Tolerances of Freshwater Fish Species	
Trout	3ppm
Bass	2ppm
Catfish	2ppm
Sunfish	2ppm
Walleye	2ppm
Muskies	2ppm
White Bass/Stripers	1.5ppm
Crappies	1.5ppm
Perch	1.5ppm
Northern pike	1ppm
Carp	1ppm
Bullheads	.5ppm

How Dissolved Oxygen is Replenished

Oxygen enters the water through contact with the air. Wind circulates the water, carrying oxygen to fish in the depths. In summer, however, the lower layer does not circulate, so no oxygen is added.

When the leaves of plants are exposed to sunlight, oxygen is produced through the process of photosynthesis. When sunlight cannot reach the plants, no oxygen is produced.

FISHING WATERS

*T*o become a successful angler, you must learn what kind of waters hold what kind of fish and why.

Natural Lakes

The Great Lakes, because of their huge size and great depth, stay cold throughout the year, so they support a variety of trout and salmon. But there are many shallow bays and some shallower basins, such as the western basin of Lake Erie, that are warm enough to support warmwater and coolwater fish, like small-mouth bass and walleyes.

Natural lakes include everything from sink holes covering only a few acres to the vast inland seas called the Great Lakes. But these waters have one thing in common: practically all of them hold gamefish.

Scientists who study natural lakes do not agree on how many different types there are or how they should be categorized. Some say there are more than 100 kinds of lakes. But none of this means much to freshwater anglers; they're more concerned about the species and number of fish a lake produces.

From a fisherman's standpoint, there are really only three main categories of freshwater lakes: warmwater lakes, which support warmwater gamefish; coldwater lakes, which support trout, salmon and other coldwater species, like ciscoes and whitefish; and two-story lakes, which support both warmwater and coldwater species. Within each of these categories are lakes of different sizes, shapes and fertility levels.

Warmwater lakes, by far the most numerous type, are found throughout North America, with the exception of the Far North. There, the summers are so short that the water never gets much above 60°F.

Coldwater lakes, the rarest type, exist only in the Far North, in mountainous regions, or where there is enough spring flow to keep the water cold in summer.

Many warmwater lakes have a layer of deep, cold water but, in most cases, this water lacks sufficient dissolved oxygen, so they are not considered two-story lakes. Only those whose depths contain adequate oxygen in summer qualify as two-story lakes.

On these pages are a few of the wide variety of natural lakes found in North America.

Arctic lakes, because of the short summers, stay cold throughout the year. Primarily lake trout producers, many of these lakes also have good numbers of pike and grayling.

Alpine lakes are fed by snowmelt and, because they are at high altitudes, stay cold throughout the year. They support a variety of trout species.

Walleye lakes have sandy shorelines with moderate weed growth. They support a variety of species including bass, panfish, perch, walleyes, pike and, quite often, muskies.

Bass-panfish lakes have mucky shorelines with a few sandy areas and heavy weed growth. They hold largemouth bass, sunfish, crappies, northern pike and numerous kinds of roughfish.

Canadian-shield lakes, because of their bedrock basins, usually have low fertility levels. Many are true two-story lakes, with walleyes, pike and smallmouth in the shallows and lake trout in the depths.

Freeze-out lakes periodically winterkill. They usually hold large numbers of bullheads and other roughfish that are tolerant of low oxygen. But, when there are several years between winterkills, they produce largemouth bass, panfish and pike.

MAN-MADE LAKES

Man-made lakes, also called *reservoirs* or *impoundments,* are created by damming creeks, streams or big rivers. They serve several purposes, including flood control, supplying water for municipalities, irrigating crops and generating electric power.

The size, shape and depth of the lake that is formed depends on the terrain and the height of the dam.

Man-made lakes differ from natural lakes in that the water level usually fluctuates much more. In many reservoirs, the water is drawn down in fall to make room for spring runoff. Some reservoirs fluctuate more than 50 feet over the course of the year.

With the water level changing this much, fish are forced to move much more than they would in a natural lake. A creek arm that held good numbers of bass in spring, for instance, may be completely dry in fall, so the fish have no choice but to move out. The changing water level also makes it difficult for aquatic plants to gain a foothold.

Man-made lakes, like natural lakes, usually stratify into temperature layers. But, in bottom-draw reservoirs,

Lowland reservoirs, often located in swampy areas, are seldom more than 25 feet deep. These highly fertile, low-clarity waters lack distinct creek arms. They usually hold largemouth bass, sunfish, crappies and catfish.

the layer of cold water on the bottom is thinner, because of the deep-water discharge. The coldwater draw may allow trout to live in the river downstream of the reservoir.

Unlike natural lakes, reservoirs seldom winterkill, because the inflow maintains adequate oxygen levels.

The life of a reservoir is considerably shorter than that of a natural lake. The silt load carried by the river is deposited in the reservoir basin, filling it in at a rapid rate. A small reservoir may fill in at a rate of 2 percent per year, meaning that sediment will fill the reservoir within 50 years.

Shown on these pages are the most common types of reservoirs found in North America.

Canyon reservoirs are deep, cold, clear and infertile. The main body is long and narrow and the creek arms may be half as long as the main lake. The shoreline slopes rapidly into depths that sometimes exceed 200 feet. Canyon reservoirs are best suited for rainbow trout, brown trout and lake trout, although some have decent largemouth bass and striper populations.

Highland and hill-land reservoirs are found in mountainous or hilly terrain. The main body of the reservoir is usually more than 100 feet deep, the shoreline slopes quite rapidly and the creek arms may be one-fourth as long as the main lake. These reservoirs support largemouth, smallmouth, white and striped bass, crappies and sunfish. A few have been stocked with muskies and some deeper ones hold trout.

Flatland reservoirs are located on flat or rolling terrain, so most of the basin is less than 50 feet deep. The main lake is wide and the creek arms, short. The fertile water supports largemouth and white bass, crappies, sunfish and catfish.

Prairie reservoirs may be more than 100 miles long and 100 feet deep, with short creek arms. The upper end is warm and shallow and has good numbers of walleyes and saugers. The lower end is cold and deep and may hold trout and salmon.

Desert reservoirs may be more than 100 feet deep, but they are usually located on fairly flat terrain, so the creek arms are short. Generally quite fertile, these lakes produce largemouth, smallmouth, white and striped bass, crappies and catfish.

MAN-MADE PONDS &PITS

Gravel pits and quarries vary greatly in size and depth. They have steep banks with no vegetation, so there is little gamefish cover. Adding brush piles often improves the fishing.

Farm ponds, also called "stock tanks" or just "tanks," are constructed for watering livestock, irrigating crops or controlling erosion. There are an estimated 3 million farm ponds in the United States, alone. Many of these ponds are stocked with fish, usually a combination of largemouth bass and bluegills, and provide excellent fishing.

Some ponds, however, are constructed for the sole purpose of sportfishing. Most of these are private, but there are many "fee-fishing" ponds where you pay by the pound or by the inch for what you catch. These waters are usually well-stocked with catfish or trout.

Pits are nothing more than holes in the ground that fill with water after being mined or excavated for gravel, rock or fill.

Abandoned strip-mining pits are common in the East and Midwest. After filling, they are usually stocked with bass and bluegills, catfish or trout. New pits may be too acidic to support fish but, within a few years, the acidity starts to decline.

Gravel pits, borrow pits and rock quarries are found throughout the country. Their

Farm ponds are made by damming a creek or bulldozing or blasting a depression. Many ponds have to be sealed with a fine clay so they will hold water. Farm ponds usually measure from a fraction of an acre to 5 acres in surface area. In the North, ponds often need to be aerated to prevent winterkill.

water is usually quite clear and infertile, so they do not produce large fish crops. Some are cold enough to support trout, but most are stocked with bass and sunfish. Gravel pits and quarries are usually on private land, but borrow pits are along public highways. They remain after fill was removed for road construction.

Phosphate pits, most common in Florida, are extremely fertile. Many offer great fishing for trophy largemouths and also produce redear sunfish and catfish.

Iron-ore pits, found mainly in the Iron Range of northern Minnesota, have extremely cold, clear water that makes excellent habitat for rainbow and brown trout. Some shallow pits support bass, sunfish and crappies.

Phosphate pits range in size from 50 to more than 1,000 acres. They have irregular shorelines and are shallow and fertile, so they produce large crops of gamefish.

Iron-ore pits range from only a few acres to nearly 300 acres in surface area. Some are more than 500 feet deep. Because the water is so infertile, the depths remain well-oxygenated year-round.

Strip pits may be more than a mile in length, with depths exceeding 50 feet. The sides are usually quite steep and weedy or woody cover is minimal, so they may require extensive improvements in order to provide good fishing.

Borrow pits are generally shallower than gravel pits or rock quarries. Most have a rectangular shape, with straight shorelines, so the fish habitat they provide is less than ideal.

WARMWATER RIVERS & STREAMS

A mainstem river is the largest waterway in a given drainage system. It is fed by dozens or, sometimes, hundreds of smaller rivers which, in turn, are fed by numerous smaller streams and creeks. Many of these rivers have a network of dams that control flooding and keep water levels high enough for safe navigation. Most mainstem rivers have diverse habitat, including a system of backwaters, and an equally diverse fish population.

Warmwater rivers and streams are freshwater fishing's last frontier. Despite the abundance of flowing water in North America, more than 3 million miles in the United States alone, the vast majority of our fishing is done in lakes.

Every kind of warm- and coolwater gamefish can be found in warmwater rivers and streams. Just what fish species live in what streams depends mainly on current speed which, in turn, depends on the gradient, or slope, of the streambed.

In a low-gradient stream, the current speed is not fast enough to keep silt in suspension, so it settles out in the streambed, making for a mucky bottom that is best suited for largemouth bass, panfish and catfish. In a medium- to high-gradient stream, the current sweeps most of the silt away. The cleaner bottom is better for fish like smallmouth bass and walleyes.

Another important consideration is water clarity. If a stream is continually muddy, sight-feeding gamefish have a hard time finding food. Such streams are better suited for scent feeders, like catfish.

An irregular, winding streamcourse makes much better fish habitat than a straight

Southern bass rivers have slow-moving water and are often connected to swampy, cypress-studded backwaters. In addition to largemouth, they usually support crappies, sunfish and catfish.

Midwestern small-mouth streams have moderate current and a clean, rocky bottom that produces plenty of aquatic insects and crayfish. Besides smallmouth, these streams may support pike and walleye.

one. In a winding stream, the current excavates holes and undercuts along outside beds and deposits sediment on inside bends, creating sandbars. Such streams usually have an assortment of pools, riffles and runs.

Many streams have been intentionally straightened, or channelized. This allows water to pass through more quickly for purposes of flood control. These streams produce few gamefish.

Warmwater rivers and streams defy classification. There have been numerous attempts to devise a logical classification system but, with the staggering variety of moving water that exists, no one has come up with a useful method.

What fishermen are really interested in, however, is the quality of the fishery. On these pages are the types of rivers and streams that offer the best freshwater fishing.

Tidewater rivers are so named because their water levels are influenced by tides. The lower reaches are salty; the middle, brackish; and the upper, fresh. Many tidewater rivers have excellent fishing for largemouth and striped bass, and some have good runs of American shad.

Canadian pike rivers have slow to moderate current with a lot of weed growth. Pike abound in weedy areas; walleyes, in faster water. These rivers offer superb fishing, but access may be difficult.

TROUT STREAMS

Limestone streams are fed by springs with a high level of calcium carbonate. The nutrient-rich water has abundant weed growth and produces a good crop of insects and crustaceans, so trout are plentiful.

The term, "trout stream," refers to any stream that remains cold enough to support trout (or salmon) year-round. Almost any stream could support trout for nine or ten months out of the year, but only streams fed by groundwater sources or snowmelt at high elevations stay cold enough for trout during the hottest part of summer.

Although trout streams vary greatly in size, good streams have several characteristics (besides cold water) in common:
• A clean gravel or rubble bottom that produces an abundance of insect life.
• An irregular streambed consisting of riffles, pools and runs.
• A narrow, deep channel rather than a wide, shallow one that would expose too much water to the warming rays of the sun.
• A sufficient year-round flow, even under drought conditions.

• Enough shade along the banks to keep the water cool in summer.
• Relatively clear water.
• A medium gradient (opposite).

Most trout streams vary greatly over their length. Many are fed by a distinct source of cold water, such as a large spring, so they start out very cold and have a minimal flow. This type of habitat is best suited to brook

trout, which thrive in the frigid water.

Farther downstream, tributaries flow in, increasing the flow and warming the water. The middle zone of the stream has the most insect life and often supports good numbers of brook, brown and rainbow trout.

As more and more tributaries enter the stream, its size increases even more and it gets warmer yet. The

Freestone streams are fed by runoff or infertile springs. Because of the low fertility, insect life is relatively scarce and plant growth, minimal. Unless there are fertile tributaries to add nutrients, trout populations are low to moderate.

streambed gradually flattens out and the bottom becomes siltier. Although the lower zone has the poorest habitat, it often yields the biggest trout. It's not unusual to catch a trophy brown in a big pool full of suckers and carp.

Many trout streams have been created by the construction of reservoirs. When water from the depths is discharged through a pipe at the base of the dam, the river below the dam may stay cold enough for trout for several miles.

Like warmwater rivers, trout streams are impossible to classify. But trout fishermen place them in two major categories, limestone and freestone, based on their fertility.

The Importance of Gradient

High-gradient streams have fast current with few pools or eddies to provide resting spots for trout. What fish there are will be found in stairstep-pools or behind boulders or log jams.

Low-gradient streams have a silty bottom that produces little insect life, and the water is usually too warm for trout. These streams may, however, produce a few large browns.

Medium-gradient streams have the riffle-run-pool habitat that trout prefer. The riffles make ideal feeding areas, and trout can rest in the deeper pools and runs. Medium-gradient streams also tend to meander, meaning that there are plenty of outside bends with deep holes and undercut banks.

FISHING EQUIPMENT

*T*he importance of equipment that suits your type of fishing cannot be overstated. This chapter will show you what you need for your style of fishing.

FISHING RODS & REELS

Shopping for a fishing outfit at a well-stocked tackle shop can be a confusing experience. You'll see rods and reels of all sizes, colors and prices, with no explanation as to which rod goes with which reel or what outfit is intended for what purpose. Unless you're lucky enough to find a savvy sales clerk, you'll have to figure things out for yourself.

Your selection depends on a combination of factors: the size of the fish you expect to catch, the size of the baits you'll be using and the type of cover in which you'll be fishing.

With a light spinning outfit and 6-pound line, you could land a 20-pound pike in unobstructed water. But you wouldn't be able to toss a heavy lure with such a light outfit and, in heavy weeds,

Baitcasting gear enables you to cast very accurately. By thumbing the spool, you can stop the lure right on your target. The relatively stiff rod and sturdy reel with a rotating spool easily handles heavy line, so you can cast heavy lures and extract good-sized fish from dense cover. The biggest drawback to baitcasting gear is the backlashing problem, but with a little practice, it won't be a major concern.

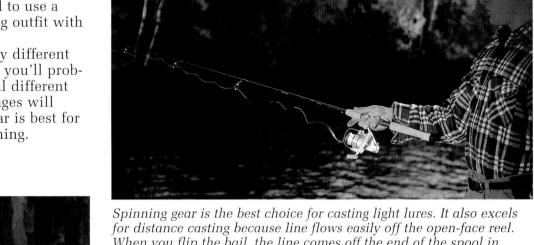

Spincasting gear is often the choice of beginning anglers because it's inexpensive and almost impossible to backlash. The enclosed spool prevents loops of line from falling off the reel and causing snarls. But spincasters don't cast as well as spinning gear because of the extra line friction, and they often have poor drag systems that can result in break-offs.

the fish would make short work of the light line. You'd be better advised to use a sturdy baitcasting outfit with 20-pound line.

If you do many different kinds of fishing, you'll probably need several different outfits. These pages will explain what gear is best for your style of fishing.

Spinning gear is the best choice for casting light lures. It also excels for distance casting because line flows easily off the open-face reel. When you flip the bail, the line comes off the end of the spool in loose coils, so the rod must have large guides to reduce line friction. Because there is no rotating spool, spinning gear cannot backlash, but twisted line can still cause nasty snarls.

Flycasting gear is needed to cast heavy fly line, which, in turn, propels the nearly weightless fly. Picking up and casting heavy line requires a long rod, usually from 8 to 9 feet in length. A long rod also helps in controlling the line and playing fish. Fly rods carry a weight designation, usually from 3- to 10-weight, that matches the weight of the line they're designed to cast.

Trolling outfits have the large-capacity reels needed for long-line trolling or downrigger fishing. The reels are not designed for casting. Trolling rods may be short and stiff for trolling heavy baits, or long and flexible for downrigger fishing. Although sensitivity is not an issue, many anglers prefer graphite trolling rods because they telegraph the action of the lure better than fiberglass.

Selecting Rods

You may be shocked at the price of today's top-shelf fishing rods, but you don't need to spend a fortune to get a rod that will catch just as many fish as the high-buck models.

When selecting a rod, here's what you really need to consider:

• **Length** - A long rod gives you better casting distance and accuracy, and allows you to cast lighter baits. It also gives you better line control and more powerful hooksets.

But a short rod enables you to set the hook more quickly and works better for casting in close quarters.

• **Action** - Slow-action rods work best for casting light baits. They're a good choice for live-bait fishing, because fish feel little resistance when they swim off with the bait. Slow-action rods also help in fighting fish, because the rod bends instead of the line breaking. Fast-action rods give you better sensitivity and a quicker hookset.

• **Power** - Just how much power you need in a rod depends on the weight of your lure or bait, the size of fish and the thickness of the cover. The difference between the terms, "power" and "action," is illustrated below.

• **Modulus** - The strength of the rod material is measured in modulus. In general, the higher the modulus, the lighter and more sensitive the rod, but the more brittle it will be.

Action vs. Power

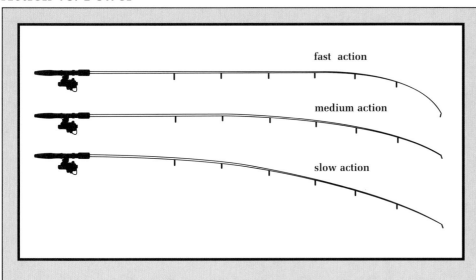

fast action

medium action

slow action

The term "action" is defined as where the rod flexes. A fast-action rod flexes mainly near the tip; a medium action starts flexing in the middle; a slow-action flexes over its entire length. The problem is, when sales clerks refer to a "medium-action" rod, they usually mean medium-power.

The term "power" refers to the rod's stiffness. It takes much more force to bend a heavy-power rod than it does a light-power. This illustration shows how much bend a given weight puts in heavy-, medium- and light-power spinning rods.

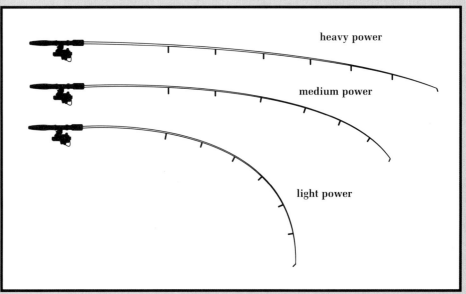

heavy power

medium power

light power

Selecting Reels

Too many anglers spend a lot of money on a fishing rod and then pair it with a cheap reel. That's not a wise decision.

On the surface, an inexpensive reel may look pretty much like a pricey one, but the differences will be apparent when you start fishing. Cheap reels have fewer ball bearings in the drive mechanism, so they aren't nearly as smooth. They are usually heavier, and they often have sticky drags. Some even have gears made of a low-grade metal that will stand little abuse.

In the case of fly fishing reels, however, quality is much less important, because the reel has no function in casting; it merely serves to store the fly line. But how fast you can take up line depends on whether you buy a single-action, whose spool turns one time for each turn of the reel handle, or a multiplier, whose spool turns more than once.

The reel you select must balance with the rod. If the

For better casting performance, select a spinning reel with a long, wide spool, rather than a short, narrow one. A long spool holds more line, so the line won't slap against the spool rim toward the end of the cast. A wide spool minimizes line kinking.

reel is too heavy, the rod will feel butt-heavy, making the tip seem less sensitive. If the reel is too light, the rod will feel tip-heavy, and keeping the tip up will tire your wrist. Before buying a rod and reel, hold it in your hand to make sure it is well balanced.

On this page are a few tips for selecting spinning, bait-casting and trolling reels.

A front drag on a spinning reel is generally smoother than a rear drag. A front drag has large washers that exert pressure on a flat surface. A rear drag pushes against the drive shaft, which has a much smaller surface area.

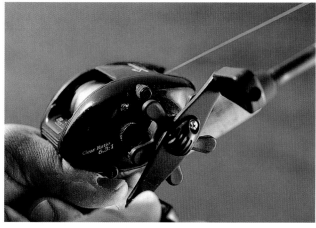

Use a high-speed reel (gear-ratio of at least 6:1) when you need a fast retrieve, or to pick up line in a hurry. A high-speed reel is a must for long-line trolling, where you may have to reel in 200 feet of line.

A trolling reel with a line counter makes it easy to reset your line at the same distance after catching a fish. Without a counter, you would have to count the passes of the level-wind bar or somehow mark the line.

FISHING LINE

When "superlines" were first introduced in the early 1990s, many folks assumed that they would soon dominate the fishing-line market. These super-thin lines, made of the same space-age materials used to make bullet-proof vests, had virtually no stretch, so they provided excellent sensitivity and powerful hooksets.

But superlines have not revolutionized the sport. They certainly have their place, but the vast majority of anglers still rely on monofilament for most of their fishing. The fact remains that mono is nearly invisible in water, which is a major advantage when dealing with finicky biters. And the stretch factor that everyone complained about turns out not to be so bad after all. It provides an extra cushion in fighting fish, and your rod won't snap on the hookset, as it sometimes does with superlines.

The information on these pages will help you select the right line for the type of fishing you do.

When selecting monofilament line, the main considerations are limpness, stretch and color. A very limp line, such as Trilene XL (extra limp), works well for casting, because the line doesn't form stiff coils that rub on the guides. A line with a harder finish, like Trilene XT (extra tough), is a better choice when fishing in weeds or rocks that could cause scuffing. Most experienced anglers use clear or green mono when fishing in clear water. Fluorescent line is easy to see and is a good choice in discolored water.

Superlines, usually made of Spectra, are about four times as strong as monofilament of the same diameter. They work exceptionally well for deep-water jigging or trolling. Mono has too much stretch for solid hooksets in deep water, and it is difficult to get down while trolling because its large diameter creates so much water resistance.

Lead-core line is used for deep trolling. It is color-coded, so when you start catching fish at a certain depth, you can easily return to that depth by letting the line out to the same color.

Weight-forward

Double-taper

Shooting-taper

Level

Fly lines come in a variety of tapers for different fishing purposes. Weight-forward (WF) lines have a thick belly behind the front taper, so they cast easily. Double-taper (DT) lines land delicately; they taper at both ends, so when one end wears out, you can reverse the line. Shooting-taper (ST) lines, also called shooting-head lines, give you maximum casting distance; they have a heavy front end and a long monofilament "running line". Level (L) lines have an equal diameter over their length. Though inexpensive, they are difficult to cast, so few anglers now use them. Be sure to match the weight of your fly line to your fly rod (p. 39).

Braided Dacron is used mainly on heavy baitcasting outfits, usually for pike or muskie fishing. It is also a popular choice for backing on a fly reel.

Wire line is often used for deep trolling and jigging. There are two types: braided and single-strand. The latter is thinner, but kinks much easier. Wire is losing popularity because of superlines.

Sinking

Floating

Sink-tip

Fly lines are designated as floating (F), used mainly for dry-fly fishing; floating/sinking (F/S), also called sink-tip, for moderately deep presentations; and sinking (S), for deep presentations.

TOOLS & ACCESSORIES

A well-equipped angler probably has two or three tackle boxes and a half-dozen rods in the boat, but may not remember some of the little things that are sometimes needed on a fishing trip.

Besides the items shown on these pages, here is a list of things that you'll probably want to keep in your boat:
• A tool kit, including extra boat fuses and wire connectors.
• A first-aid kit, for tending to fish cuts and other injuries.
• Matches, in case you need to start a fire for shore lunch or to warm up in chilly weather.
• A flashlight, in case you are stuck on the water after dark.
• A camera, for proving you caught what you claim to have released.
• A fire extinguisher, now a requirement in many states.
• Sunscreen.
• Life jackets and other required safety equipment.
• Rain gear.

A long-handled hook remover or a hemostat helps safely remove hooks from deep in a fish's mouth. If you try to use an ordinary pliers to remove hooks, you may injure the fish.

A marine-band radio is highly recommended if you fish big water. Not only does it have a weather band to inform you of approaching storms, you can use it to trade fishing information with friends.

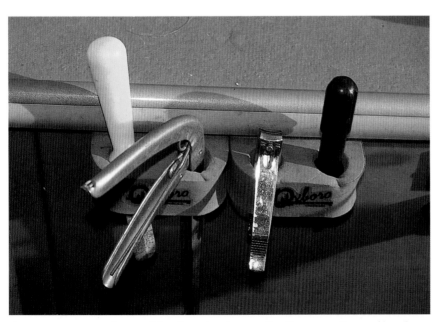

An accessory rack provides handy storage for items such as a hook remover, hook file, nail clippers and pliers. With an accessory rack, you'll always know where to find your tools.

Carry a long-handled landing net so you can reach fish that don't want to come close to the boat. Don't use a net with a loose weave; your hooks will constantly catch in the braid.

Carry an accurate scale so you can get the exact weight of fish you want to release.

A plug "knocker" comes in handy if you do a lot of fishing in snaggy areas. This model clips onto your line and slides down on a string to jar your bait loose.

Soft-packs make the ideal tackle-storage system, because they have pockets for gear of a variety of sizes. You can store different types of baits in individual plastic boxes, and take along only the boxes you need for a day's fishing.

An electric thermometer is a big help in locating the thermocline, finding spring holes or detecting other water temperature changes that could help you locate fish.

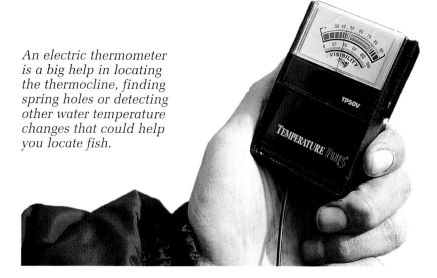

Marker buoys are a must for pinpointing precise spots on deep structure. This rack provides storage for three marker buoys.

MODERN TROLLING GEAR

Understanding Downriggers

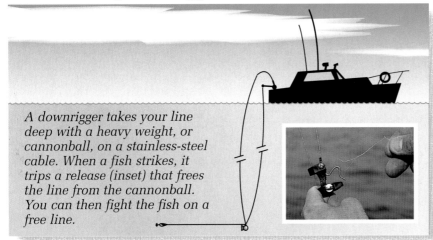

A downrigger takes your line deep with a heavy weight, or cannonball, on a stainless-steel cable. When a fish strikes, it trips a release (inset) that frees the line from the cannonball. You can then fight the fish on a free line.

Trolling is one of the oldest fishing methods, but new innovations in equipment have made the technique more effective than ever.

In the old days, there was a lot of guesswork involved in trolling. You were never sure how deep your lure was running or what depth the fish were at. All you could do was experiment until you found them.

Today, you can use sophisticated electronics to pinpoint the depth of fish, and then set downriggers to present your lures at precisely the right level.

If you really want to go high-tech, you can buy a unit that gives you water temperature and trolling speed at the downrigger, so you know you're trolling in the right temperature zone and moving at the right speed.

You can also buy bottom-tracking downriggers that have a built-in sonar to keep the cannonball at a pre-set distance off the bottom. When the water gets shallower, the cannonball automatically comes up; when it gets deeper, it goes down.

Downriggers enable you to cover water vertically but, to cover it horizontally, you'll need side planers. By fishing downriggers and side planers together, you could cover a swath of water more than 100 feet wide and 100 feet deep.

On these pages are the most important types of gear used by modern-day trollers.

Side planers attach to the line, pulling it to the side. They can be rigged two ways. When a fish strikes, the planer detaches from the line; you land the fish and go back to pick up the planer. Or the planer stays on the line and you reel it in with the fish.

Trolling boards are attached by a cord to an elevated mast. The fishing line is attached to a release (inset) which slides down the cord until you lock the reel to stop it. When a fish strikes, it trips the release, allowing you to fight the fish on a free line. With boards out both sides of the boat, you can cover a swath more than 100 feet wide.

A diving planer takes your line down and to the side. In order for the planer to dive, the bar (arrow) must be locked in the groove. When a fish strikes, the bar breaks free, causing the planer to flatten out so you can easily reel it in, along with the fish.

A speed indicator keeps your lures moving at precisely the right speed, despite wind or current. This model monitors current speed and water temperature, both at the surface and at downrigger level.

Rod holders pointing out to the side, as shown, help trollers cover more water. Some anglers use rods up to 9 feet long; this way, they can spread their lures about 25 feet without using planers.

Ice Fishing Gear

Modern technology has had a major impact on every aspect of freshwater fishing, and ice fishing is no exception. Changes in the sport over the past decade have been enormous.

No longer do savvy ice fishermen spend all day sitting in a shanty, watching their line in hopes that a fish will happen along.

Today, they find a productive spot, possibly using a handheld GPS to return to a waypoint that produced during the open-water season. Then, they drill a couple dozen holes with a super-sharp auger. Using a portable shelter, they fish each hole for a few minutes while looking for fish on their flasher. If nothing shows up, they're off to try another waypoint.

Mobility is the name of the game in modern ice fishing. You've got to keep moving to find the fish, just as you would in summer. The equipment on these pages makes mobility a lot easier.

Rig your flasher on a "blue box" for portability. A motorcycle or gel-cel battery provides enough power for two or three days of fishing. The transducer can be set on a rigid rod (above), or you can use a self-leveling transducer.

Things to Look For in an Ice Fishing Flasher

A self-leveling transducer enables you to move from hole to hole without stopping to level the transducer after each move.

A backlit screen is much easier to see at night. With a regular screen, you can see the signal, but not the numbers on the dial.

For fishing in water more than 50 feet deep, use a unit with at least 1,000 watts of peak-to-peak power.

Other Important Ice-Fishing Equipment

Tip-ups make it possible to spread out your lines and cover more water. They have an underwater reel and a flag that pops up when a fish bites.

Portable shelters make it easy to move from spot to spot. This model has a flip-up top and doubles as a sled that can tow your gear.

A flashlight-type depth finder lets you easily check the depth before drilling your holes. Just set it in a little water, and it will sound through the ice.

A graphite jigging rod gives you the sensitivity you need to detect subtle wintertime bites. Select one with the right power for your type of fishing.

Ice cleats attach to the bottom of your boots to give you traction on slippery ice. Cleats are usually not necessary when there is snow on the ice.

Specially designed sleds have a place to carry your auger, minnow bucket, depth finder, rods, tip-ups and other accessories, such as an ice scoop, lure box and chisel (for testing ice thickness).

Use a fast-cutting auger so you can drill plenty of holes. Most modern augers will cut through a foot of ice in five seconds or less.

FISHING BOATS

Bass boats are designed for speed and fishing ease. The low-profile fiberglass or aluminum hull enables anglers to fish shallow water, and the elevated bow and stern decks make casting easy. Bass boats range from 17 to 21 feet in length and are powered by 75- to 225-horsepower outboards. Some can reach speeds exceeding 70 miles per hour.

There is no single boat suited to all types of fishing. Many would argue that a well-equipped bass boat is the ultimate fishing machine, but you wouldn't be able to use it in waters that don't have a good boat ramp, and it wouldn't handle big water as well as a walleye boat. Don't buy a boat because of its

Aluminum semi-Vs are the perfect all-purpose fishing boats. They're very light, yet can handle fairly rough water. Most are 14 to 18 feet long and designed for tiller-operated outboards, usually 25 to 50 hp. Small semi-Vs usually have bench seats; larger ones, pedestal seats.

flashy looks; be sure it suits your style of fishing and the waters you fish.

One of the biggest decisions in buying a boat is choosing the hull material. Fiberglass hulls can be molded in such a way that they easily part the waves, making for a smooth ride. Many have beautiful metal-flake finishes. Aluminum hulls are lighter, more durable and less expensive.

Shown here are some of the most popular types of boats used in freshwater angling.

Walleye boats are designed for big water. They have a deep-V aluminum or fiberglass hull that can handle big waves. They come in tiller and console models from 16 to 19 feet in length and are powered by 50- to 225-horsepower motors.

Canoes are a good choice for fishing hard-to-reach waters. They're easy to portage and paddle, but are quite unstable. Some models have a square stern that accommodates a small outboard. Or, you can rig a regular canoe with a motor bracket.

Jon boats, because of their flat bottoms, are very stable and ideal for use in shallow water. Models with a square bow, however, are not a good choice in rough water. Some have a semi-V bow (shown), which helps split the waves.

OUTBOARD MOTORS

When selecting an outboard, remember that a little extra power often comes in handy. If your boat is rated for 60 horsepower, for example, you could probably get by with 50 horsepower, but it may be hard to get up on plane with a full load of anglers and gear. The extra power also helps control your boat in rough water and gets you in faster when a storm threatens. A bigger motor may even give you better fuel economy, because your boat is on plane rather than plowing water.

For many anglers, trolling speed is an important issue. Before buying a particular outboard, ask a fisherman who has one how it trolls.

Another important consideration is the type of propeller. You can get by with an aluminum prop, but a stainless-steel prop will improve performance and take a lot more abuse. Although stainless-steel props are considerably more expensive than aluminum, they will probably save you money in the long run.

Be sure your propeller has the right pitch for your boat. You'll normally find a number designating the pitch stamped somewhere on the propeller. A 13-pitch prop, for instance, pushes the boat forward 13 inches with each turn. You may have to try several different props to find the one that gives you the right combination of speed and power.

Until recently, practically all outboards were 2-cycle, meaning you had to mix oil with the gas. But when studies began to show that exhaust from 2-cycle motors was polluting the water, some manufacturers began making 4-cycle outboards.

Although 4-cycles are bigger and more expensive, they run quieter and smoother and burn much less gas. Many anglers who have made the switch say they'll never go back to a 2-cycle.

"Kicker" motors are small outboards used on large fishing boats for trolling or as an emergency backup should the main outboard fail. Kickers range in size from 2 to 15 horsepower.

Electric Trolling Motors

For precise boat control, an electric trolling motor is a must. Not only is an electric much quieter than an outboard, you don't have to spend the day inhaling gas fumes.

A bow-mount trolling motor with a foot control is the best choice for casting, because it leaves your hands free. But for trolling, many anglers prefer a transom-mount. By backtrolling (trolling in reverse), you can follow a specific contour much more closely, because the transom is not blown off course by the wind as much as the bow.

It pays to select a motor with more power than you think is necessary. Then, you can make quick course corrections to stay on fish.

Many boats are rigged with a pair of trolling motors. The bow-mount is used for casting and the transom-mount for backtrolling.

Handy Trolling Motor Features

A bow mount with a foot control frees your hands for casting. Some models have electronic foot controls, so there is no clumsy cable.

A Maximizer is an electronic device that makes your trolling motor more efficient. As this graph shows, your battery will last twice as long with a Maximizer at 50% speed; 4 times as long at 10%.

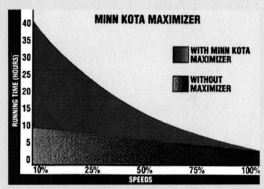

An extension handle makes steering easier. Instead of stretching your arm and contorting your body to reach the handle, you can steer comfortably from your seat.

A reversible head enables you to backtroll with much more power. By spinning the head 180 degrees on the shaft and reattaching it, you can backtroll in forward rather than reverse.

FISHING BOAT OPTIONS

Most of today's fishing boats come well-equipped, but it pays to do a little shopping to make sure you're getting the right options for the type of fishing you do.

One thing you can never have enough of is storage space, particularly dry storage. Look for a boat that has compartments with sealed lids, otherwise your gear will mildew.

With all the electronic gear found on modern fishing boats, you'll need enough space to store two, maybe three batteries. Besides a starting battery, you'll need one or two others to power your trolling motor. Don't attempt to use

An electronics compartment protects your depth finder, GPS, marine radio, etc., from rain and boat spray. The compartment should be lockable and large enough to house all your electronic gear.

Hydraulic seats smooth out the ride in rough water. A lever on the pedestal allows you to raise or lower the seat. Many anglers install extra bases, so the seats can be rearranged as needed.

the same battery for both purposes or you may wind up paddling home.

You certainly don't need a stereo system with a tape deck in order to catch fish, but a radio with a weather band serves an important safety function.

Here are some of the most important fishing boat options.

A rod locker should be at least 7 feet long and large enough to hold a half-dozen rods. If the locker is too short or too small, you'll damage your rods when removing them or putting them away.

An aerated livewell is a must for anyone who needs to keep their fish in good condition. Some livewells are equipped with a timer, so they run intermittently and save battery power.

Splash guards make it possible to backtroll in rough water without waves splashing over your head. The best splash guards are made of indestructible Lexan and attach with thumb screws.

A bilge pump enables you to easily drain water from a heavy rain or from trolling in big waves. Some bilge pumps are automatic, turning on whenever the water reaches a certain level.

An on-board charging system makes battery charging a snap. All you have to do is plug the charger into an extension cord, and it will charge all of the boat's batteries.

Storage compartments should be large enough to hold items like tackle boxes and tool kits. Dry storage is a must for rain gear, life preservers, extra jackets or anything that could mildew.

BOAT TRAILERS

When shopping for a fishing rig, most anglers put a great deal of thought into choosing the right boat and motor, but the trailer is of much less concern.

If you wind up with the wrong trailer, however, you'll have trouble launching and loading your boat, and your hull could suffer serious damage.

The most common mistake is selecting a trailer that is too light for your boat. Be sure the trailer you select is rated for several hundred pounds more than the combined weight of the boat, motor and gear you'll be carrying. Otherwise, the frame may buckle or the axle bend when you hit a bump.

If you choose a roller trailer, be sure there are enough rollers to distribute the boat's weight. With only a few rollers, a bumpy road could crack the hull.

On these pages are some tips for selecting the right trailer and outfitting it with the right equipment. We'll also show you how to "power-load" your boat.

Roller trailers work well with aluminum boats. The best trailers have a set of rollers in both the front and back. If the rollers are adjusted properly, the boat will center itself when you drive it on (opposite).

Bunk trailers are the best choice for fiberglass boats, because they give the hull full-length support. With rollers, too much pressure is exerted on a small area of the hull, sometimes causing cracks.

How to Power-Load with a Drive-On Trailer

1 Back the trailer in just far enough that the rear rollers or bunks are at water level. If you back in too far, the rollers or bunks will be too deep to center the boat.

2 Trim up your outboard at least one-third of the way to prevent the prop from hitting bottom when you drive on.

3 Line the boat up so it is centered in the rear roller and then run the boat forward until it just bumps the roller on the winch stand.

4 Hook up the winch rope and safety chain, tilt up your motor and drive the boat out. With a little practice, you can load in less than a minute.

Handy Boat Trailer Features

A tongue jack comes in handy for lifting the trailer to hook it up or unhook it from your vehicle.

Bearing Buddies have zerts that make it easy to add grease to your wheel bearings.

A spare-tire carrier bolts to your boat trailer, so you don't have to carry the spare in your vehicle.

DEPTH FINDERS

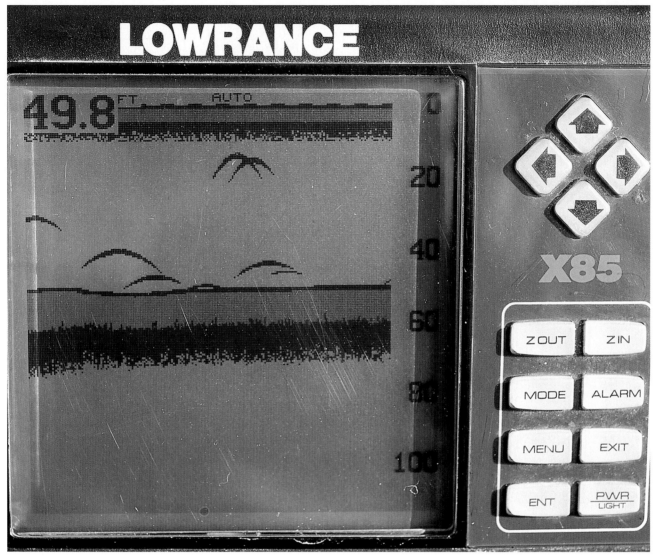

Liquid-crystal recorders (LCRs) are, by far, the most popular type of depth finder. They have a display consisting of tiny "pixels." The smaller the pixels, the better the resolution. A good unit generally has a vertical pixel count of at least 160, and the best units have more than 200. Liquid-crystals are not recommended at temperatures below 20°F, however, because the signal is slow to appear on the screen.

Ask a veteran angler to name his or her most important piece of equipment, and the answer will most likely be a depth finder. A good depth finder gives fishermen "underwater eyes," making it possible to find the right structure and even see the fish.

All depth finders operate the same way: a transducer sends a sonar signal to the bottom and picks up the returning echo. The time differential determines the depth. If the signal hits fish or weeds, their depth will be recorded as well.

The main difference between the various types of depth finders is in the way the reading is displayed. A flasher, for instance, gives you exactly the same information as a liquid-crystal, but the reading appears on a dial, rather than a screen.

One of the most important considerations in choosing a depth finder is the transducer's cone angle. The higher the transducer's frequency, the narrower the cone of sound that it emits. A narrow cone (20 degrees or less) is best for detecting fish lying close to the bottom. A wider cone is a better choice when you want to see more of the bottom or watch your lure, as you may wish to do while vertically jigging.

Although the types of depth finders shown on these pages make up the vast majority of the market, some anglers still prefer paper graphs, because they provide a permanent record. Should you turn away from the dial for a few seconds, you could miss seeing a fish on a liquid-crystal, but it will still be there on a paper graph.

Whatever type of depth finder you buy, you must learn to adjust it properly and interpret its signals. That information is presented on pages 74-75.

Other Popular Depth Finders

Liquid-crystal flashers display the signal on a round dial, rather than a rectangular screen. Compared to color flashers, these units are easier to read on a sunny day, and they have a backlit dial for night fishing.

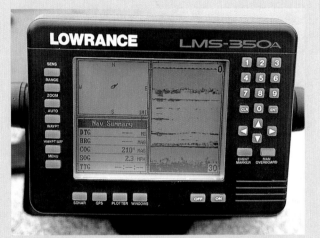

Combination units can be switched from an LCR to a GPS by pushing a button. If desired, you can split the screen to get sonar and navigation information at the same time.

Color flashers are very sensitive and display signals in different colors, depending on target size and position in the cone. But they are hard to read in direct sun and may not have enough power for use in very deep water.

Color videos provide the best resolution of any depth finder. The signal is displayed on a cathode-ray tube (CRT) like that of a TV set, with different size targets shown in different colors. On the downside, videos are bulky and hard to read in direct sun.

NAVIGATION DEVICES

Not long ago, fishermen were marveling at the magic of Loran (long-range navigation) devices. Finally, anglers on big lakes could return unerringly to a precise spot where they had caught fish in the past.

But the popularity of Loran has been limited by several factors: it depends on signals from Coast Guard towers, so it doesn't work everywhere, many anglers find it difficult to use and it can be affected by storms. It also requires a long whip antenna to pick up the signals and it processes them very slowly.

GPS (Global Positioning System) technology has greatly simplified the navigation process. It is the same technology the U.S. armed forces use to guide their "smart bombs."

But concerns that GPS technology could fall into the wrong hands have led the U.S. government to downgrade the GPS signal available to the public. With a clean signal, GPS could put you within a few feet of your spot; with the downgraded signal, 50 to 200 feet. There have been rumors that the government will soon be offering a clean signal, but at this printing, it is still being downgraded.

For specifics on how to use GPS navigators, turn to pages 76-77.

Handheld GPS units are rapidly gaining popularity because of their portability and low cost. But the small screen can be difficult to read, especially in plotter mode (opposite).

Important GPS Features

Be sure the GPS unit you buy has a parallel channel receiver. By processing signals from different satellites at the same time, rather than separately, the unit responds more quickly and has better accuracy.

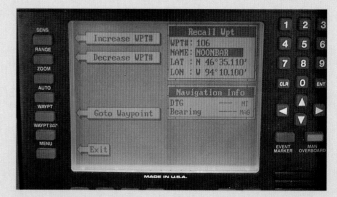

Select a unit that has enough memory to store all the waypoints (destinations) that you want to save. For most anglers, 200 waypoints is plenty, but those who fish many different waters may need a lot more.

GPS units are much more reliable than Loran units. They work anywhere in the world and are not affected by weather. They have a module that picks up signals from at least four satellites, and the data is processed in seconds, so you can navigate much more accurately.

Make sure the unit has a plotter screen with a minimum scale of no more than .1 miles. This way, you will be able to closely track the boat's path in relation to a waypoint. With a larger minimum scale, it would be difficult to tell.

A steering screen is a handy feature because it allows you to navigate to your waypoint simply by keeping the boat icon on the center line until it arrives at the waypoint.

FISHING SKILLS

*O*wning all the right equipment is one matter; learning to use it properly is another.
  In this chapter, we'll give you some pointers on skills like casting, tying knots, reading hydrographic maps, using electronics, and mastering one of the toughest skills of all: boat control.

CASTING

A beginning angler just learning to cast wants to throw the bait halfway across the county. An experienced angler practices tossing the bait into a coffee cup only a few feet away. You soon learn that accuracy is a lot more important than distance in most types of fishing. Nevertheless, you should know how to make a long cast when the situation requires it.

The biggest mistake of most novice casters is trying to throw the bait rather than cast it. They whip the rod as hard as they can, and the bait flies erratically, usually not too far. A veteran caster, on the other hand, lets the rod do the work. Snapping the rod back with a flick of the wrist lets the natural spring of the rod propel the bait.

For good casting performance, you need a rod that suits the weight of the bait you're using. If you try to cast a light lure with a stiff rod, it won't flex, or *load*, enough on the backcast, so there won't be enough forward spring. If you try to cast a heavy lure with a whippy rod, it will flex too much and won't have enough power to recover.

The rod's action (where it bends) is also important. A slow action works best for very light baits, because the entire rod flexes to generate more tip speed. Length is also important. A long rod is the best choice for distance casting, because it has more leverage. But a short rod is better for flicking the bait under a bush.

Casting with a Baitcasting Outfit

Adjust your spool tension so the weight of the lure slowly pulls line off the spool.

With the reel in free spool and about a foot of line hanging off the rod, firmly thumb the spool to prevent it from turning.

Briskly draw the rod into the backcast and stop it at about 2 o'clock. For accuracy, bring it straight back over your shoulder.

Cast with a smooth forward stroke, releasing your thumb from the spool when the rod is at about 10 o'clock.

Prevent backlashes by lightly thumbing the spool as necessary as the line flows out. Thumb the spool harder to stop the lure on a precise spot.

Be sure to choose a rod with closely spaced guides. Otherwise, the line will form a belly between the guides and slap against the rod, shortening your casts. The guides should be large enough that they don't restrict the flow of line off the reel (p. 67).

A spinning reel with a long, wide spool will cast farther than one with a short, narrow spool. A wide-spool baitcasting reel will also cast farther than one with a narrow spool, but the latter is not as likely to backlash.

The spool should be filled almost, but not quite, to the lip. If the line level is too low, the line will slap against the lip and your casts will fall short. If you overfill the spool, the line will spring off and cause tangles.

Strive for accuracy, not distance.

Casting with a Spinning Outfit

Fill the reel to within about 1/8 inch of the lip of the spool. If the line level is low, line will slap the edge of spool when you cast.

Open the bail and pick up the line with your index finger. Leave about a foot of line hanging off the end of the rod.

Briskly draw the rod into the backcast and stop it at about 2 o'clock. The lure's weight should put a sharp bend in the rod.

Cast with a smooth forward stroke, releasing the line from your index finger when the rod is at about 10 o'clock.

Control casting distance by brushing the line with your index finger as it flows off the spool.

1 Strip off line as much line as you think you'll need. Let it pile neatly at your feet or float downstream with the current. Then, point your rod in the direction you wish to cast, lift the rod and smoothly accelerate until all of the line is in the air.

2 Propel the line into the backcast with a short, fast "speed stroke." This causes the rod to bend and generates enough power to draw the line backward.

3 Stop the rod just past the vertical and allow a loop to form as the line shoots backward.

4 Wait until the backcast unrolls into a narrow, J-shaped loop.

5 Sharply stroke the rod forward and then stop it abruptly at the position shown. The line should shoot forward and settle gently to the water. Lower the rod tip to begin fishing.

Six Casting Tips

After making a long cast, place a piece of electrical tape on the spool of your baitcaster. Then, should you get a backlash, the tangle can't go any deeper than the tape.

Long-handled rods give you extra casting distance. Not only does the extra length provide more leverage, you can grip the handle with both hands to generate more power.

Use a baitcasting reel with a narrow spool for short-range casting. Because the spool is lighter than a wider spool, it has considerably less momentum, so it is less likely to backlash.

A short rod is the best choice for casting in tight spots. When you're fishing in a narrow, brushy stream, for example, you don't have enough room for a casting stroke with a long rod.

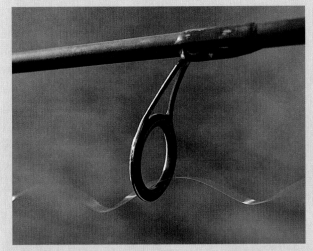

Use a spinning rod with guides that are large enough so the line coils don't rub on them when you cast. The friction will reduce casting distance.

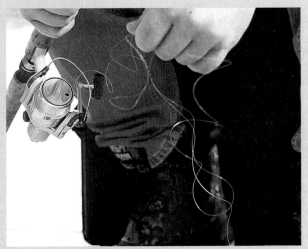

Discard any old, kinky monofilament. Not only is kinky line hard to cast, it is usually much weaker than fresh mono.

TYING KNOTS

Learning to tie good knots is one of the most important fishing skills. Even a strong, well-tied knot may be the weakest link between you and the fish, and a poorly tied knot practically guarantees losing any big fish that you hook.

The more kinds of fishing you do, the more knots you'll need to learn. Fly fishermen, for instance, use different knots than spin fishermen. Saltwater anglers use still different knots. And some of the knots that work well with mono are a poor choice with superlines.

Dozens of different knots have been devised for different fishing purposes. But some of them are so difficult to tie that you'd need an instruction manual in the boat. The best advice is to learn a few easy-to-tie knots and practice until you have them down pat.

Whatever knot you tie, it's a good practice to moisten it before snugging it up. This reduces abrasion that could weaken the line. After the knot is snugged up, test it by giving it a firm tug; better to break then than after you hook a fish.

Retie your knots periodically throughout the day. Repeated casting weakens knots, as does catching fish. When you retie, strip off a few feet of line ahead of the knot to get rid of any abraded spots.

Shown on these pages are some of the most useful fishing knots.

Attaching Line to Spool—Arbor Knot

The arbor knot is so named because it tightens firmly around the arbor, preventing the line from slipping when you reel.

(1) Pass the line around the spool, (2) wrap the free end around the standing line and make an overhand knot, (3) make an overhand knot in the free end, (4) snug up the knot by pulling on the standing line; the knot should tighten firmly around the arbor.

Attaching Hook or Lure—Trilene Knot

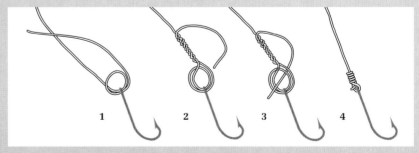

The Trilene knot has a double loop around the hook eye and is one of the strongest hook-attachment knots.

(1) Form a double loop by passing the free end through the hook eye twice, (2) wrap the free end around the standing line 4-5 times, (3) pass the free end through the double loop, (4) pull on the standing line and hook to snug up the knot.

Attaching Hook or Lure—Palomar Knot

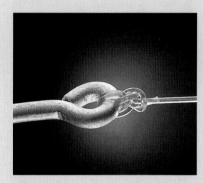

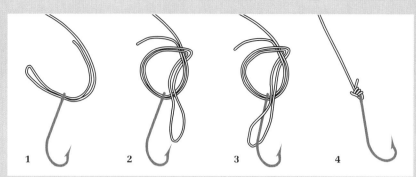

The Palomar knot, like the Trilene knot, has a double loop around the hook eye. But some anglers find it easier to tie.

(1) Form a double line then push it through the hook eye; *(2)* with the double line, make an overhand knot around the standing line and free end; *(3)* put the hook through the loop; *(4)* hold the hook while pulling on the standing line and free end to snug up the knot.

Attaching Hook or Lure—Loop Knot

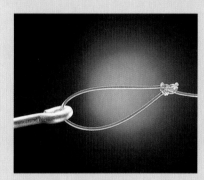

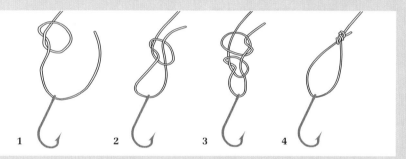

A loop knot allows your hook or lure to swing more freely, so it has better action than a hook or lure that is snubbed down tightly.

(1) Make an overhand knot several inches from the end of the line and put the free end through the hook eye; *(2)* pass the free end through the overhand knot; *(3)* with the free end, make an over-hand knot around the standing line (where you tie the second over-hand determines the size of the loop); *(4)* tighten the overhand knots and pull the standing line to snug up the knot.

Tying a Loop—Double Surgeon's Loop

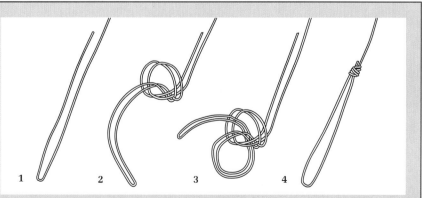

The double surgeon's loop is very easy to tie and makes a secure loop in the end of your line or leader.

(1) Form a double line, *(2)* tie an overhand knot in it, *(3)* pass the doubled line through the overhand knot again, *(4)* pull on the loop and standing line to snug up the knot.

Splicing Lines—Bloodknot

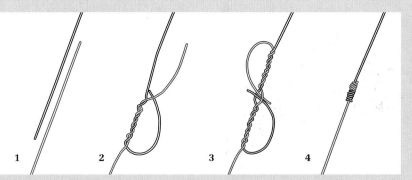

A blood knot looks complex, but is quite simple to tie. Don't try it with lines of greatly different diameters or different materials.

(1) Hold the lines alongside each other, with the ends facing opposite directions; (2) wrap one line around the other 4-5 times, and pass the free end between the two lines, as shown; (3) repeat step 2 with the other line; (4) pull on both lines to snug up the knot.

Splicing Lines—Double Uni-Knot

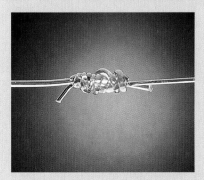

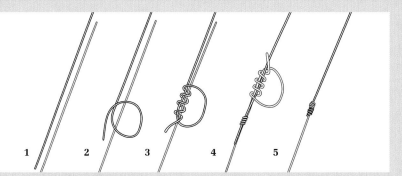

The double uni-knot is the best way to splice mono to superline. It works well for any lines of different material or diameter.

(1) Hold the lines alongside each other, with the ends facing opposite directions; (2) form a loop with one of the lines, as shown; (3) pass the free end through the loop and around the other line 4-5 times and then tighten; (4) repeat steps 2 and 3 with the other line; (5) pull on both lines to draw the two knots together and snug them up.

Tying a Bobber Stop—Sliding Stop

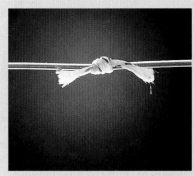

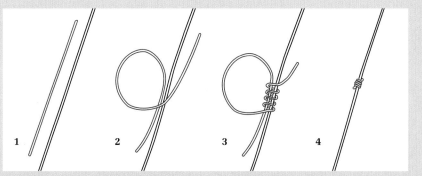

A sliding stop comes in handy for slip-bobber fishing and also has other uses, like marking your depth.

(1) Lay a foot-long piece of Nylon or Dacron line alongside your fishing line, (2) form a loop in the short line, as shown, (3) pass the free end of the short line through the loop and around the standing line 4-5 times, (4) pull on both ends of the short line to snug up the knot.

The Ultimate Guide To Freshwater Fishing

Attaching Mono to Wire—Albright Special

The Albright Special enables you to attach mono to wire or much heavier mono without a bulky barrel swivel.

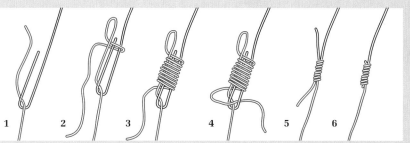

(1) Double the wire, then pass the free end of the mono through the loop; (2) hold the mono alongside the wire and wrap the free end around the wire; (3) make 8 wraps, moving toward the loop in the wire; (4) pass the free end of the mono through the loop; (5) alternate pulling on the free end and standing line to snug up the knot; (6) trim wire and mono.

Attaching Hook or Lure to Wire Leader —Haywire Twist

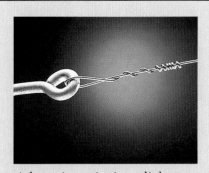

A haywire twist is a slick method for connecting a single-strand wire leader to a hook or lure. Don't try this with braided wire.

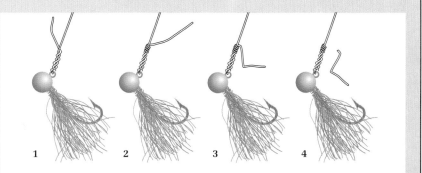

(1) Pass the wire through the eye of the lure or hook and make 3 loose twists; (2) make 5 tight wraps, winding the free end of the wire around the standing wire; (3) make a right-angle bend in the free end; (4) turn the "handle" until the excess wire breaks off.

Attaching Fly Line to Leader —Tube Knot

A tube knot makes a smooth connection between a fly line and leader.

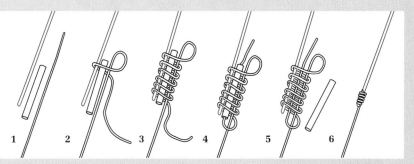

(1) Lay a small plastic drinking straw alongside the end of the fly line; (2) wrap the leader butt around the fly line, straw and standing portion of the leader; (3) make about 5 wraps, winding toward the end of the fly line; (4) push the butt of the leader back through the straw; (5) carefully remove the straw; (6) pull on both ends of the leader to snug up the knot.

READING MAPS

If you know how to read a hydrographic map, you can gather loads of fishing information before you ever put your boat in the water. State or Federal agencies have surveyed practically every important fishing lake in the country, and maps showing bottom contours and other features important to anglers are available at a reasonable price.

A hydrographic map won't show you exactly where to fish, but it will give you a good idea of spots to check out with your depth finder. It will pinpoint features like small humps, sharp inside turns on the breaklines, extended lips of points and other spots that could be found only by hours of exploring.

If you're planning on fishing an unfamiliar lake, and you have a friend that commonly fishes there, ask him to mark a lake map for you. This will save you even more time.

Fishing maps with GPS coordinates are now starting to appear and will undoubtedly be the wave of the future. These maps take all the guesswork out of finding a productive fishing spot.

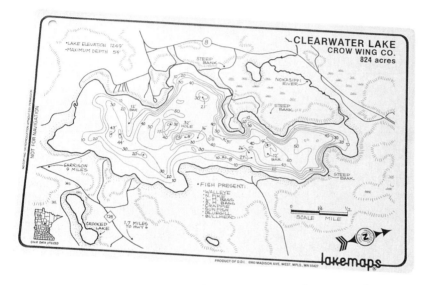

Hydrographic maps show the lake's structure with contour lines at regular depth intervals, usually 10 feet. Some maps also show bottom type, identifying rocky or weedy areas.

Reservoir maps not only show the bottom contour, they pinpoint the location of fish-attracting features such as old roadbeds, house foundations and stock ponds that existed before the lake filled.

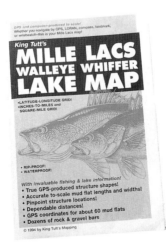

GPS maps provide the exact latitude and longitude of good fishing spots. All the angler has to do is enter the coordinates in a GPS unit and navigate to the precise location.

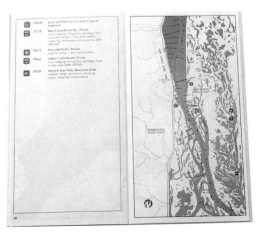

River charts show the location of features such as boat ramps, resorts, mileage markers, riprap banks, wing dams, side channels and dams. The Corps of Engineers publishes maps for most big rivers.

How to Read a Hydrographic Map

A gradually sloping break (A) appears as a series of widely spaced contour lines.

An inside bend (B) has contour lines opposite those of a point.

An underwater point (C) appears as a series of nearly parallel contour lines jutting out from shore.

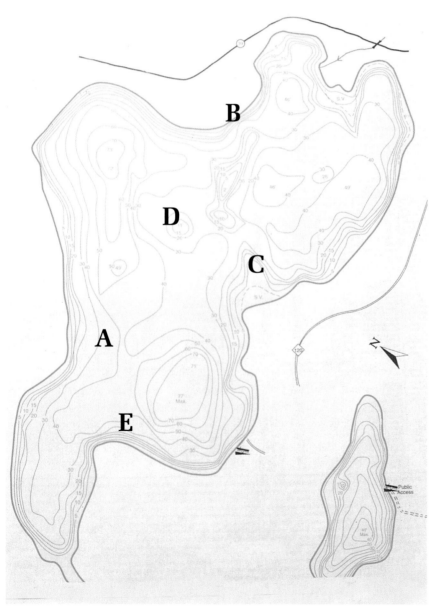

A hump (D) has a series of circular contour lines with the shallowest spot near the center.

A sharp-sloping break (E) appears as a series of closely spaced contour lines.

GETTING THE MOST FROM YOUR DEPTH FINDER

To get strong fish marks, your gain must be set properly. If it's set too low (left inset) the fish barely show up. If it's set too high, the screen will have too much "scatter" (right inset).

How to Get a Good High-Speed Reading

Place the transducer where there is a smooth flow of water under the boat. While the boat is running, look over the transom to find a slick spot (arrow); that's the best place for mounting your transducer.

Tilt the transducer back about 5 degrees so the water flow hits the transducer's face, which should be just slightly below the boat bottom. If the transducer's face is pointing straight down, there will be too much turbulence to get a good high-speed reading.

A good depth finder is the most valuable tool in your fishing boat but, to make the best use of it, you must set the transducer properly (opposite) and adjust the unit to suit the fishing situation.

Most liquid-crystals default to "automatic" to set your gain (power or sensitivity), depth range and chart speed. But automatic may not be best for your specific situation. That's why many experienced anglers prefer manual settings. In automatic, for example, the unit may give you a 0 to 40-foot depth scale in water 25 feet deep. But by manually setting the scale to 0 to 30 feet, or zooming in to 20 to 30 feet, you can better see what's happening below.

When sounding at high-speed, your chart speed should be set to maximum. Otherwise, any fish you graph will show up as tiny marks that may not even be noticeable.

At right are some tips for interpreting the signals your depth finder is sending you. Liquid-crystals are used in the examples, but the principles are the same for any kind of depth finder.

Interpreting Depth Finder Signals

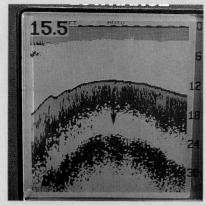

Hard bottom appears as a thick line with a sharp upper edge. If your gain is set high enough, you may also see a double echo at twice the depth (arrow).

Soft bottom (arrow) appears as a thin line with a fuzzy upper edge. Usually, there is no double echo.

Standing weeds, such as cabbage, appear as vertical columns coming up off the bottom.

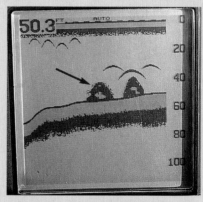

Baitfish schools (arrow) appear as clusters of tiny marks. If the school is tightly packed, it may just look like a solid clump.

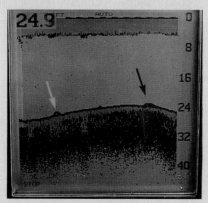

A fish lying on bottom may look like a hump (blue arrow) with some open space or "air" underneath it. A rock (red arrow) looks similar, but has no air beneath it.

A large fish shows as a thick, black mark (blue arrow); a small fish, a thin, light one (red arrow). The length of the mark has little to do with the size of the fish.

Getting the Most from your GPS

A GPS navigator does a lot more than just navigate. For example, you can use it as an "invisible marker," a trolling-speed indicator or a mapping device for plotting the shape of the structure you're fishing.

Some GPS units even have a "man overboard" feature that enables you to instantly mark the spot where you dropped a fishing rod – or a passenger – into the water.

Here are some basic GPS guidelines, along with some tips for using GPS to put a few extra fish into your boat.

Navigation Basics

Push the waypoint key and then punch in the latitude and longitude of a waypoint (spot) that you got from a map or from a fishing friend. When the numbers are entered, assign the waypoint a number and give it a name, so you will be able to recognize it on your waypoint log. You can also enter a waypoint you've just found by pressing "quick save".

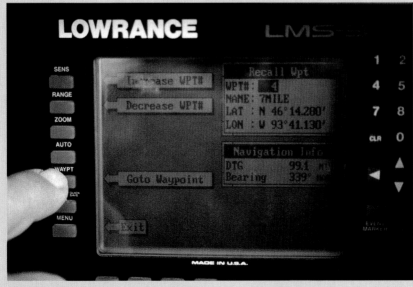

Recall the waypoint from your log and push "go to waypoint". The unit will give you the bearing and distance to the waypoint and, while you're moving, tell how far you are to the side of a straight line to the waypoint (XTE or cross-track error).

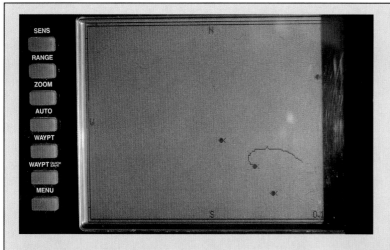

When you locate fish, put fish "icons" on the screen of your GPS; this way, you can keep your boat in the vicinity of the school.

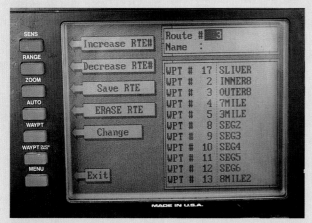

To navigate on waters where you can't travel in a straight line, such as an island-studded lake, make a route consisting of several waypoints. When you reach the first waypoint, the unit will automatically switch to the second and tell you how to get there.

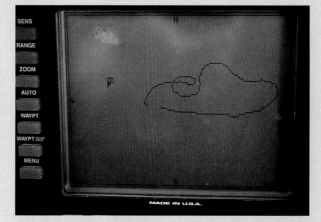

Map out the structure you're fishing by putting the unit in plotter mode. Set the plotter's range to match the size of the piece of structure. Just follow the edge of the structure with your depth finder and the plotter will map its shape.

Mapping modules are available for most of the United States and Canada. These modules make navigation easier, because you can see points, islands and other features in relation to the path of the boat. Some maps even show bottom contours.

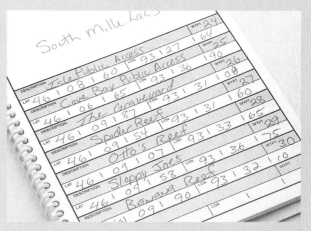

Keep a log book listing all of your important waypoints. This way, should your unit's way-point log get erased, your waypoints won't be lost forever. You can buy waypoint logs printed on heavy, waterproof paper.

BOAT CONTROL

Backtroll into the wind for precise boat control. Splash guards will prevent waves from lapping into your boat. The reason backtrolling allows such precision is that the wind doesn't affect your transom as much as your bow. And, with your depth finder's transducer mounted right next to your motor, it's easy to follow a contour.

Boat control has been referred to as "the little-known secret of big-time anglers." If you can't keep your boat on the fish, all the best equipment and hottest new lures won't matter.

Whether you're trolling, drifting or anchoring, boat control is an important issue.

If you have a deep-hulled boat, backtrolling (above) is your best option. If you try to troll forward, the wind will catch the bow and blow you

Controlling Your Drift

Use your trolling motor to control your drift path. If you're trying to follow a contour, and the wind is blowing you closer to shore, keep kicking the boat out with the motor to stay at the right depth.

Toss out a drift sock to slow your drift on a windy day. The bigger the sock you use, the more it will slow you down. To pull a drift sock in quickly and easily, attach a rope to the narrow end.

Anchoring Tips

Prevent your anchor from slipping by using a heavier anchor than you think you'll need and attaching about 6 feet of heavy chain to it. The chain lowers the angle of pull, so the flukes dig in.

Let out plenty of rope to further reduce the angle of pull. As a rule, the length of your anchor rope should be at least four times the water depth.

When anchoring on a windy day or in a current, turn the handle of your outboard to adjust the lateral position of the boat. Turning the handle to the left will push the boat to the right and vice versa.

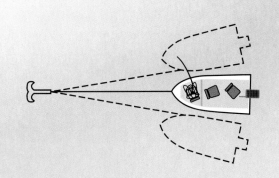

Changing your tie-off point will also adjust the lateral position of the boat. If you're tied off to the bow, for example, you can move the boat a few feet to the right by tying to the left-front cleat.

off course. If you own a low-profile bass boat, however, the bow is not affected as much by the wind, so forward trolling may work fine. Either way, always troll into the wind, straight or at an angle, for the best boat control.

A powerful electric trolling motor is the best investment a troller can make. By using a motor with half again as much thrust as is recommended for your boat, you can make course corrections much faster and spend more of your time fishing where the fish are.

A powerful trolling motor is also a big help in drifting. Seldom does the wind blow you in exactly the direction you want to go. With a hefty trolling motor, you can keep your boat on the desired drift path and control your drift speed.

Another handy tool for drifting is a sea anchor, or drift sock. Some anglers use two of them, one off the bow and one off the stern, to slow their drift in windy weather. A drift sock also helps control the boat while trolling; not only does it slow you

down, it keeps the bow from swinging in the wind.

Anchoring is a subject you hear very little about, but it's by far the best way to stay on a tight school of fish. If you repeatedly trolled or drifted over them, you'd probably spook them. But you must know how to anchor in exactly the right spot, with no chance of your anchor slipping and dragging right through the school of fish.

Take some time to study the boat-control tips on these pages. They're sure to make a big difference in your fishing.

FISHING TECHNIQUES

*T*his chapter will help you understand each species of freshwater gamefish and show you the spots where they're most likely to be found, and demonstrate the most popular techniques for catching them.

LARGEMOUTH BASS

Micropterus salmoides

The largemouth bass is America's favorite gamefish – and for good reason. It is found in all of the lower 48 states and its range extends from southern Canada to Mexico and Cuba.

But widespread distribution is not the only reason for its popularity. The largemouth is a willing biter, eagerly attacking practically any kind of artificial lure or live bait. And once you get one on the end of your line, you'll know what all the fuss is about. A hooked bass will jump, sizzle off line, try to wrap you around weeds and otherwise carry on like few other gamefish.

Largemouth Facts

Largemouth bass belong to the sunfish family and are classified as warmwater fish. Although they can survive near-freezing temperatures, they do very little feeding when the water dips below 50°F.

There are two subspecies of largemouth bass: the northern largemouth and the Florida largemouth. They look nearly identical, the only difference being that the scales are a little smaller on the Florida bass. The latter, which were originally found only in the Florida Peninsula, grow much faster and reach a considerably larger size than northern bass, with several 20-plus pounders on record. The giant bass currently being caught in California, Texas and Mexico are Florida largemouths.

You can find largemouth in weedy natural lakes, reservoirs with plenty of woody cover, sluggish streams and small ponds or pits that do not freeze out in winter. They can tolerate water clarity

Largemouth bass range.

Largemouth bass are greenish to tannish in color with a darker back, lighter belly and a dark horizontal band. The jaw is longer than that of the smallmouth, extending past the rear of the eye.

ranging from only a few inches to 20 feet or more. They are more salt-tolerant than most freshwater fish, which explains why they are found in tidewater rivers. The largemouth's preferred temperature range is 68 to 78°F.

Largemouth may well be the least-selective feeders of all freshwater fish. The bulk of their diet includes a variety of small fish, including their own young, crayfish and larval aquatic insects, but they also eat small mammals, salamanders, frogs, worms, leeches, snails, turtles and even small snakes.

When the water warms to the lower 60s in spring, male largemouths move into the shallows to begin building their nests. They normally nest in a bay or along a shoreline that is sheltered from the wind, usually around weedy or woody cover. Using his tail, the male fans away silt to reach a firm sandy or gravelly bottom, then the female moves in to deposit her eggs. By the time the water reaches the upper 60s, most spawning is completed. The male guards the nest and remains with the fry until they disperse.

Largemouth have been known to live as long as 16 years, but it is unusual for them to live for more than 10. Although the growth rate of Florida bass far exceeds that of northern bass, Floridas stocked in the North grow no faster than the native bass. An 8-year-old northern largemouth typically weighs about 5 pounds; a Florida of the same age, about 10 pounds.

Key Largemouth Locations...

In Natural Lakes
Early Spring:
- Shallow mud-bottomed bays, channels and harbors that warm earliest

Spawning Time:
- Protected bays and shorelines with a firm bottom

Summer and Early Fall:
- Weedlines, humps and points that have weedy or rocky cover and slope gradually into deep water
- Slop bays, where dense overhead vegetation keeps the water cooler

Slop bay

Late Fall and Winter:
- Points, humps and other structure that slopes rapidly into deep water
- Inside turns along breaklines
- Shallow flats on warm days

In Man-Made Lakes
Early Spring thru Spawning:
- Back ends of shallow, brushy creek arms

Brushy creek arm

Late Spring and Summer:
- Main lake points adjacent to the old river channel
- Bends and intersections in the old river channel or in deep creek channels
- Humps with standing timber or submerged weeds
- Timbered flats

Early Fall:
- Back ends of creek arms

Late Fall and Winter:
- Deep main-lake points
- Main river channels

In Rivers
Early Spring thru Spawning:
- Shallow, dead-end sloughs and other backwaters off the main river
- Shallow sandbars
- Stump fields

Late Spring to Early Fall:
- Sloughs with current
- Deep backwaters
- Side channels into backwaters

Side channel

- Wingdams
- Deep eddies and outside bends
- Undercut banks and ledges

Late Fall and Winter:
- Deep areas of main channels
- Deep holes in backwaters
- Near warmwater discharges

Largemouth Bass Techniques

Largemouth bite best when water temperatures are in the 60s and 70s. They're most active under dim-light conditions. On bright, sunny days, they usually tuck into dense cover, where it's difficult to get a lure to them. They do most of their feeding early and late in the day. On cloudy days, they roam farther from cover and feed throughout the day. An approaching storm often triggers a flurry of feeding, but the action slows dramatically following a cold front.

Good largemouth fishermen are versatile. There are times when the fish want topwaters and times when they want a spoon jigged in 50 feet of water. Perhaps the most important consideration in selecting lures is the type of cover. In heavy weeds, for instance, you need a spinnerbait, Texas-rigged worm, weedless jig or other bait that won't foul or hang up. On a clean bottom, you're better off with a bait that has open hooks. On the pages that follow, we'll

The plastic worm is the number-one bass producer.

acquaint you with the major largemouth techniques used across North America.

Fishing Soft Plastics

Soft plastics are a favorite of largemouth anglers nationwide. Not only do they look and feel like real food, they can be rigged Texas-style (with the hook point buried in the worm), so they can be fished in the densest cover.

When fishing soft plastics on a clean bottom, many anglers prefer to use a Carolina rig with an open hook. With a slip-sinker attached well up the line, the lure sinks more slowly and

has a more enticing action than a Texas-rigged bait. Some anglers use sinkers weighing up to 1 ounce, enabling them to make very long casts and cover more water. When a bass picks up the bait, the line slips through the sinker, so the fish feels no resistance.

Another popular option for fishing on a clean bottom or in sparse weeds is rigging the lure on a light jig head.

Soft plastics are normally fished quite slowly, so they work best when you have a pretty good idea of where the fish are located. They are not a good choice for exploring new water.

Recommended Tackle

The type of tackle you use for largemouth depends mainly on the type of cover you're fishing. When casting a curlytail grub on a clean bottom, you can get by with a light spinning outfit and 6-pound monofilament. But when working a jig-and-pig in a dense weedbed or tree top, you'll need a heavy flippin' stick spooled with mono or superline of at least 20-pound test.

Types of Soft Plastics

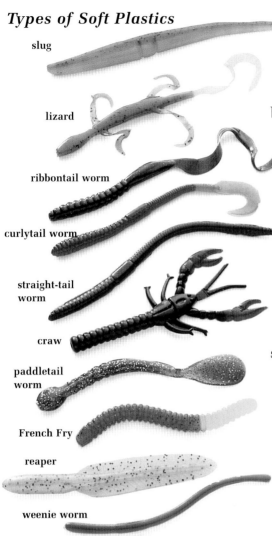

slug

lizard

ribbontail worm

curlytail worm

straight-tail worm

craw

paddletail worm

French Fry

reaper

weenie worm

Because they are retrieved so slowly, soft plastics are effective in cold water or at other times when bass are lethargic and unwilling to chase fast-moving baits. But they also work well in warm water.

You can retrieve a soft plastic with a slow, steady crawl, hop it along the bottom with a jigging motion, or even reel it rapidly on or just beneath the surface. The only way to determine what retrieve works best is to experiment.

When bass are finicky, it may take a super-slow presentation with a light spinning outfit and a small bait to draw a strike. Try rigging a 3- or 4-inch soft plastic on a plain hook with only a split-shot for weight and then inching the rig along the bottom. This technique is called "finesse fishing."

Always watch the line and rod tip closely. If you see a twitch, feel a "tick," notice the line moving off to the side or detect anything out of the ordinary, point the rod tip at the bait and reel up slack until you start to feel the weight of the fish. Then, set the hook with a strong upward sweep of the rod.

A bass will usually hold on to a soft plastic bait for several seconds before it lets go. Some anglers prefer to hesitate for a few seconds before setting the hook; others say you should set right away. If you're rigging Texas-style, it takes an extra-hard hookset to drive the hook though the plastic and into the bass' jaw.

Popular Rigging Methods

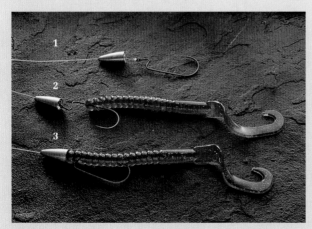

Make a Texas rig by *(1)* threading on a bullet sinker and then attaching an offset worm hook. *(2)* Push the hook into the bait about ³/₈ inch, then bring it out the side. *(3)* Twist the hook 180 degrees and then push the point back into the bait so it almost, but not quite, comes out the opposite side.

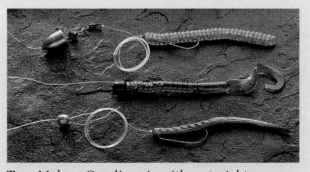

Top: *Make a Carolina rig with a straight worm hook, brass sinker and glass bead. The "brass and glass" creates a loud clicking noise that bass love.*
Center: *Rig a soft-plastic on a mushroom-head jig. Mushroom heads are a good choice because they butt up flush with the bait, leaving no gap to catch weeds.*
Bottom: *Rig a small grub or a "weenie" worm on a thin-wire hook with a single split-shot.*

Hang a weighted minnowbait, or "jerkbait," in a largemouth's face to tempt a strike. This technique works best during coldwater periods or whenever the fish are lethargic.

at the depth you want to fish.

Crankbaits were once considered warmwater lures because, in cold water, bass were too lethargic to chase them. But anglers have discovered that they work well in cold water when fished with a slow, stop-and-go retrieve.

Minnowbaits are long and slim, with a narrow lip that gives them more of a wiggle than a wobble. They generally run shallower than crankbaits, although some long-lipped models dive deep. Some of these lures are weighted to make them neutrally buoyant. This way, you can stop your retrieve and hang the bait in a fish's face (left) without it floating up.

Vibrating plugs don't have a lip; the attachment eye is on the back. These baits have a very tight wiggle and, because they sink, can be fished at any depth.

Fishing Subsurface Plugs

Subsurface plugs make it possible to cover a lot of water in a hurry, even when the bass are deep. And a largemouth finds the enticing wiggle hard to resist.

The three main types of subsurface plugs used in largemouth fishing are crankbaits, minnowbaits and vibrating plugs.

Crankbaits have a relatively short, deep body and a broad lip that gives them a wide wobble. Some dive to depths of 30 feet; others run only a few feet beneath the surface. You need to select a bait that runs

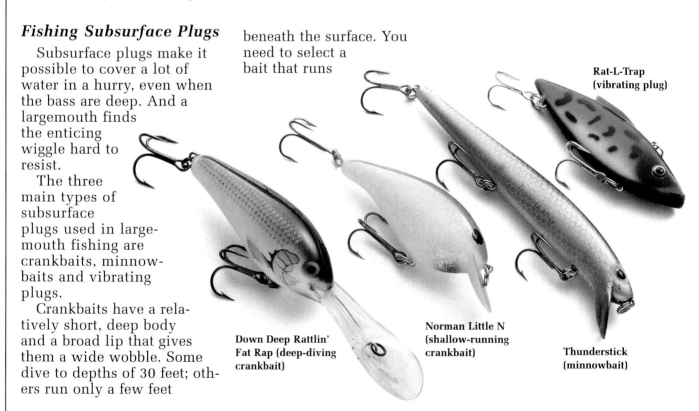

Rat-L-Trap (vibrating plug)

Down Deep Rattlin' Fat Rap (deep-diving crankbait)

Norman Little N (shallow-running crankbait)

Thunderstick (minnowbait)

Spinnerbait Fishing

A spinnerbait is a good choice for largemouths in heavy cover. You can toss it into weeds or brush and not worry about it hanging up or fouling, because the spinner shaft acts as a weedguard for the upturned single hook.

tandem-spin

single-spin

There are two basic types of spinner-baits. Single-spins, which have only one blade, are a good all-around choice and work well for helicoptering. The blade spins easily as the bait sinks.

Tandem-spins have a pair of blades that give the bait extra lift. They're the best choice for fishing over shallow weed tops or for other shallow-water presentations.

The performance of a spinnerbait is also affected by the type of blade(s). Colorado blades have the most water resistance, so they provide the most lift. The blade spins easily on a slow retrieve. Willow-leaf blades have less water resistance, so they can be fished faster and deeper.

Although spinnerbaits are generally considered shallow-water baits, heavy models (¾ ounce or more) work well in water as deep as 30 feet. If you need a little extra depth, add a pinch-on sinker to the bait's lower arm or hook shank.

For extra attraction, many anglers tip their spinnerbaits with a pork frog or a soft-plastic grub.

Popular Spinnerbait Retrieves

Slow-roll a spinnerbait by reeling slowly and allowing it to bump bottom or the top of weedy or brushy cover.

Reel your spinnerbait to the edge of vertical cover, like a tree or breakwall, and let it helicopter down to reach tight-holding bass.

Bulge a spinnerbait by keeping your rod tip high and reeling fast enough that the blades almost break the surface.

Jigging

Jigging for largemouth can be done with a variety of baits, primarily lead-head jigs and jigging spoons.

Lead-head jigs are available in many different head shapes, each serving a certain purpose. Jigs are tied with or tipped with various dressings, including hair, feathers, rubber skirts or soft-plastic trailers.

Technically, the term "jigging" means working your bait with a rapid up-and-down motion. But jigs are not necessarily fished that way. More often, they're just inched along the bottom.

Jigging spoons have a heavy body and sink rapidly, so they're ideal for jigging bass in deep water. Some anglers use them to fish in depths of 50 feet or more. With their long, thin shape, they look like an injured minnow.

If you get snagged in heavy cover, just let your line go slack. The weight of the spoon usually pulls the hook free.

A jig-and-pig is hard to beat when bass are tucked into heavy cover.

Popular Types of Jigs & Jigging Baits

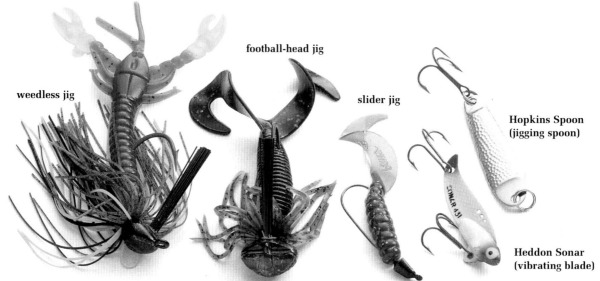

weedless jig

football-head jig

slider jig

Hopkins Spoon (jigging spoon)

Heddon Sonar (vibrating blade)

Use a weedless jig to avoid hang-ups in dense weeds or brush; a football jig for a crayfish-like, tip-up action on a rocky bottom; a slider jig for working the weed tops; and a vibrating blade or jigging spoon for vertically jigging in deep water.

Types of Topwaters

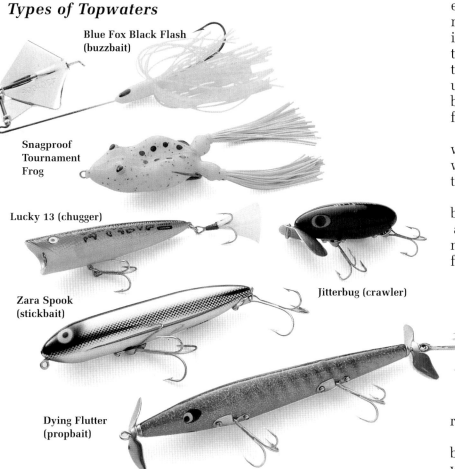

Blue Fox Black Flash (buzzbait)

Snagproof Tournament Frog

Lucky 13 (chugger)

Zara Spook (stickbait)

Jitterbug (crawler)

Dying Flutter (propbait)

Topwater Fishing

To many anglers, an explosive surface strike is the ultimate fishing thrill. And when conditions are right, largemouth bass are one of the most cooperative surface feeders.

Topwaters are most effective when the surface is calm and the water temperature exceeds 60°F. They work best early or late in the day or at night but, when the fish are in heavy cover, they'll hit topwaters in the middle of the day. Largemouth anglers use practically every kind of bait that floats for topwater fishing.

Stickbaits, long, thin plugs with no built-in action, are weighted in the tail to give them a side-to-side action.

Propbaits look like stickbaits, but they have propellers at one or both ends. They're normally fished with twitches followed by pauses.

Chuggers have a concave or flat face that throws water when you jerk. They're often retrieved with a series of rapid twitches.

Crawlers have a broad face plate or arms that make the bait wobble or crawl. A slow, steady retrieve usually works best.

Buzzbaits have a large blade that throws a lot of water. Retrieve them slowly and steadily; they'll sink if you stop reeling.

Frogs and rats are made of soft rubber or plastic and have a weedless design. They are the best choice for fishing heavily matted weeds.

Popular Topwater Retrieves

A twitch-and-pause retrieve can be used with most topwaters, but it works especially well with prop-baits and chuggers. The latter can also be fished using a rapid series of twitches, with no pauses.

Retrieve a stick-bait by holding your rod tip low and giving it a series of evenly-spaced jerks to make the head swing from one side to the other. This retrieve is called "walking the dog."

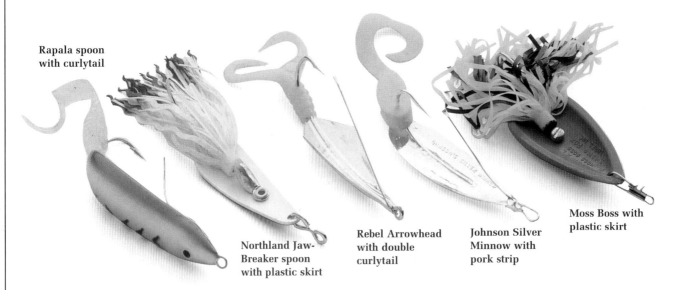

Rapala spoon with curlytail

Northland Jaw-Breaker spoon with plastic skirt

Rebel Arrowhead with double curlytail

Johnson Silver Minnow with pork strip

Moss Boss with plastic skirt

Fishing Weedless Spoons

A weedless spoon, with its wire or nylon bristle weed-guard, can slither its way through the densest weedbed. And, when tipped with a pork strip or plastic trailer, the bait has an incredibly lifelike swimming action.

Although weedless spoons are not as popular as they once were, they are still an important tool for anglers who do a lot of fishing in heavy vegetation or brushy cover.

Some weedless spoons are made of metal; others, hard plastic. Metal spoons, because they are heavier, work best for fan-casting large expanses of weedy cover. They sink rapidly and are fished beneath the surface.

Hard-plastic spoons are light enough to slide over matted weeds. Because they ride with the hook up, there is little chance of fouling.

One drawback to the weedless spoon is the tendency for fish to strike short. Many anglers make the mistake of setting the hook when they feel a bass nip at the trailer. Be sure to hesitate until you feel the weight of the fish before setting.

The Skitter-and-Drop Retrieve

1 *Make a long cast and start your retrieve before the lure can sink. Keep your rod tip high and reel just fast enough so the spoon skitters over the weeds or runs just beneath the surface.*

2 *Stop reeling when you come to a pocket in the weeds. Drop your rod tip to let the spoon sink into the pocket. That's when a bass that has been tracking the spoon will strike.*

Fly Fishing

Not only is fly fishing for largemouth a lot of fun, there are times when it is one of the most effective bass-catching methods.

When bass are in shallow water, the chugging action of a bass bug draws their attention from a considerable distance. And when they spot the hairy bug, they're almost sure to grab it.

Besides bass bugs, fly fishermen use poppers, big streamers, crayfish patterns and leech imitations to catch largemouth. If you'll be fishing in dense cover, you'll need a fly with a wire or mono weedguard.

Recommended tackle includes a 7- to 9-weight fly rod with a floating, weight-forward or bass-bug taper line, for punching the heavy flies into the wind. Use a 6- to 9-foot leader with a 0X to 4X tippet.

A mono weedguard prevents most hang-ups, yet is flexible enough that it doesn't interfere with your hookset.

Popular Bass Flies

Wiggle-Legs Frog

deer-hair popper

Dahlberg Diver

wool streamer

Blackhare Leech

SMALLMOUTH BASS

Micropterus dolomieui

If you ask a well-travelled angler to name the fightingest freshwater fish, the smallmouth bass will most likely get the nod.

Known for its aerial antics, a smallmouth almost always heads straight for the surface when it feels the hook. It explodes out of the water, fiercely shaking its head in an attempt to throw the bait. If it doesn't succeed on the first jump, it will try several more times. Some anglers have even had a smallmouth jump into their boat!

Smallmouth Facts

Like its close cousin, the largemouth, the smallmouth belongs to the sunfish family and is considered a warmwater fish. However, smallmouth lean slightly toward the coolwater category. They prefer water in the 67- to 71-degree range, although they're sometimes caught at temperatures in the low 80s. Feeding slows considerably when the water temperature drops below 50°F, and stops altogether at about 40.

There are two recognized subspecies of smallmouth bass. The northern smallmouth (*Micropterus dolomieui dolomieui*) is, by far, the most common. The Neosho smallmouth (*Micropterus dolomieui velox*) has been nearly wiped out by construction of dams on its native waters.

Smallmouths are found in most types of natural lakes and reservoirs as well as in rivers and streams with moderate current. They rarely inhabit small ponds, shallow lakes, sluggish streams or any muddy or badly polluted water. They prefer a hard bottom, usually rock or gravel, and are seldom found on a soft, mucky bottom.

Spawning takes place in spring, usually at water temperatures in the 60- to 65-degree range. The male selects a spawning site on a sand-gravel or rock bottom in a protected area, often next to a boulder or log. He fans the silt from the bottom with his tail, then the female moves in to deposit her eggs. After spawning is completed, the male stays on the nest to guard the eggs and, later, the fry.

Smallmouth are especially fond of crayfish, but they also eat a variety of other foods, including frogs, insect larvae, adult insects and many kinds of minnows and other small fish. As a rule, they prefer smaller food items than largemouth, explaining why anglers generally use smaller baits.

In the North, smallmouth bass may live as long as 18 years. They rarely live half that long in the South, but

Smallmouth have a jaw extending to the middle of the eye. They are greenish to bronze in color, accounting for their common name, bronzeback. They have dark vertical bars or diamond patterns on the side, but these marks are not always present and may come and go. The cheek also has dark bars. The eye is often reddish.

Smallmouth bass range.

they grow considerably faster. It takes about 8 years for a smallmouth in northern waters to reach 3 pounds, and only 4 years to achieve the same weight in the South.

Fishing Techniques

If you've ever reeled in a smallmouth and spotted several more following it, attempting to take away its meal, you know how aggressive these fish can be.

That type of behavior is most often seen on lightly fished waters. But where fishing pressure is heavy, the fish are a lot more selective.

There are times when smallmouth will grab big baits, but they generally prefer baits a little smaller than those normally used for largemouth. Many small-mouth lures, like jigs and crankbaits, are intended to mimic crayfish and are available in crayfish colors. But don't get too hung up on the crayfish connection. Smallmouth will hit many other kinds of lures, as well, including minnowbaits, in-line spinners, spinnerbaits and topwaters.

Although size and action of a bait is more important than color, most smallmouth anglers opt for dark or drab colors rather than bright or fluorescent hues.

Recommended Tackle

On clean structure, a medium-power spinning outfit with 6- to 8-pound mono is adequate for most presentations. In heavier cover, a medium- to medium-heavy-power baitcasting outfit with 10- to 14-pound mono is a better choice.

When fishing is tough, live bait is the best option. Crayfish, especially softshells, are hard to beat, but many anglers swear by hellgrammites (dobson-fly larvae). Other good baits include shiners, nightcrawlers and leeches. Present these baits on a slip-sinker or slip-bobber rig, just as you would for walleyes (pp. 132-134). Or simply fish them on a plain hook with only a split-shot for weight.

Although small-mouth are good to eat, we strongly urge you to release them. Because of their willingness to bite, they can easily be overfished. And their value on the end of a fishing line far outweighs their value on a dinner plate.

Key Locations for Smallmouth Bass...

In Natural Lakes

Early Spring through Spawning:
- Sheltered sand-gravel bays
- Bulrush beds adjacent to deep water
- Shallow points with scattered boulders for cover

Point with scattered boulders

Late Spring through Early Fall:
- Gradually tapering points with a sandy, gravelly or rocky bottom
- Mouths of major inlets, particularly in shield lakes

Tributary stream

- Rocky reefs in lakes with a sandy bottom
- Sandy, weedy humps in lakes with a rocky bottom
- Sandy bays in rocky lakes
- Flats adjacent to deep water with rocks, logs or scattered weeds for cover

Late Fall and Winter:
- Steep-sloping points
- Irregular breaklines that drop rapidly into deep water
- Deep gravel or rock humps

In Man-Made Lakes

Early Spring:
- Creek arms with flowing inlet streams
- Shallow secondary creek arms

Spring (spawning):
- Rocky shorelines in protected creek arms
- Shallow, rocky points in the main lake

Summer and Early Fall:
- Rocky reefs or sandy humps, especially those near the old river channel
- Timbered flats along the old river channel (nighttime feeding area)

Timbered flat

- Rock slides along steep canyon walls (canyon reservoirs)
- Long points extending into the old river channel

Extended point

- Man-made fish attractors

Late Fall and Winter:
- Deep main-lake points
- Deep inside turns along the old river channel
- Eddies in tailrace areas

In Rivers

Early Spring through Spawning:
- Tributaries with a rocky bottom draw smallmouth if there are few rock areas in the river itself
- Shallow gravel shoals
- Backwaters with some moving water
- Shallow, riprapped banks

Summer and Early Fall:
- Eddies below rocky points
- Deep pools below riffles
- Steep ledges along limestone banks
- Wingdams

Wingdam

- Deep riprap along shorelines and islands
- Eddies below boulders
- Side channels connecting the main channel and backwater areas
- Eddies alongside the swift water below a low-head dam

Late Fall and Winter:
- Deep holes in the main river channel that have very little or no current
- Warmwater discharges

Eddy below low-head dam

Jigging

The lead-head jig is arguably the deadliest of all smallmouth baits. You can inch it along a rocky bottom to mimic a crayfish or minnow and, because of the upturned hook, it's less likely to snag than most other baits.

Lead-head jigs are dressed with hair or feathers or tipped with a rubber skirt, soft-plastic grub or live bait (usually a leech, minnow or piece of nightcrawler). The fly n' rind (a hair jig with a pork trailer) is a popular smallmouth bait throughout much of the South.

Another effective smallmouth technique is vertical jigging using a variety of jigging lures, including jigging spoons, tailspinners and vibrating blades. You can also jig vertically with a lead-head jig. In deep, clear, southern reservoirs, anglers vertical jig for smallmouth in water more than 40 feet deep.

Vertical jigging is a simple technique, but there's a trick to it. Give your rod a quick snap to lift the bait, then follow the line back down with your rod tip, keeping the line slightly taut, but not tight. Nine times out of ten, the bass will grab the bait as it is sinking and, if your line is not taut, you won't feel a thing. When you feel a tap, bump or anything out of the ordinary, set the hook.

A jig tipped with a smoke grub is a top smallmouth producer.

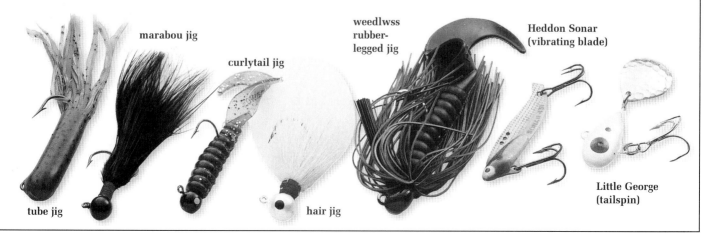

marabou jig

curlytail jig

weedlwss rubber-legged jig

Heddon Sonar (vibrating blade)

tube jig

hair jig

Little George (tailspin)

Subsurface Plugs

Serious smallmouth anglers carry a good supply of crankbaits, minnowbaits and vibrating plugs. With these baits, you can cover a lot of water quickly to locate active fish. Then, after the bite slows down, you can switch to a slower bait, like a jig, and work the area more thoroughly.

Plugs used for small-mouth are usually 2 to 3 inches long, a little smaller than those used for large-mouth. Although crayfish colors (browns and oranges) are most popular, shad and shiner colors are equally effective.

As a rule, minnowbaits, with their tighter wiggle, work better than crankbaits when the water is cool. They're also a good choice at spawning time. Fish them on the surface with a twitch-and-pause retrieve.

Crankbaits and vibrating plugs are excellent summer-time baits and are a better choice for fishing deep structure.

Vibrating plugs are proven smallmouth baits.

Rebel Deep Wee-R (crankbait)

Rattlin' Rap (vibrating plug)

Rebel Floating Minnow (minnowbait)

Spinnerbaits

Most anglers think of a spinnerbait as a dynamite shallow-water lure for largemouth, but few consider using it for smallmouth.

But that's a big mistake, especially when the fish are in weedy cover. Spinnerbaits also excel for night fishing in clear lakes. The thumping blades draw smallmouths up to the surface from deep water, often from depths of 20 or 30 feet.

Although 1/8- to 3/8-ounce spinnerbaits are the usual choice of smallmouth fishermen, some savvy anglers have found that heavy spinnerbaits (3/4- to 1-ounce models) work well for deepwater smallmouth. Just slow-roll the bait across a deep rock pile or other deep-water structure, or let it helicopter straight down a cliff wall or a steep channel break.

For extra attraction, try tipping your spinnerbait with a soft-plastic grub. The rapidly wiggling tail may double the number of strikes.

In-Line Spinners

These simple baits don't get much press, but when smallmouth are cruising a rocky shoreline or other shallow, clean-bottomed structure, an inline spinner works exceptionally well. Because of its open hooks, this bait is not a good choice in weeds or brush.

In-line spinners come with two different styles of blades. A standard blade is attached to a clevis, which spins around the shaft. A sonic blade spins directly on the shaft. The latter is concave at one end and spins at a lower retrieve speed. A size 2 or 3 blade usually works best for smallmouth.

There isn't much skill involved in fishing an in-line spinner; you just cast it out and reel it in. Retrieve just fast enough to keep the blade spinning.

One drawback to in-line spinners is that the whole bait tends to spin when you retrieve, badly twisting your line. You can solve the problem by attaching the bait with a snap swivel. Or, just bend the front of the shaft at about a 30-degree angle, creating a keel effect (right).

Haddock Single-Spin

Hart Sniper (tandem-spin)

A slight bend keeps the bait from spinning.

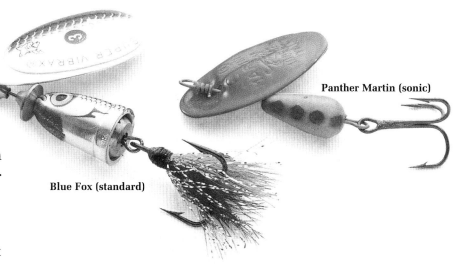

Panther Martin (sonic)

Blue Fox (standard)

Topwaters

One of the hottest new smallmouth techniques is using topwater baits to "call up" smallmouth from deep water. The technique works best in clear-water lakes, where anglers have been successful in calling the fish up from as deep as 30 feet. Some smallmouth experts have found this method to be even more effective at night.

Topwaters normally work best in spring, when smallmouth are cruising the shallows in preparation for spawning. They're feeding heavily and will take most any kind of topwater offering, including propbaits, chuggers, stickbaits and high-floating minnowbaits.

It may take a little experimentation to find the right retrieve. Sometimes twitches followed by long pauses work best; other times, the fish seem to like a series of rapid twitches with no pauses.

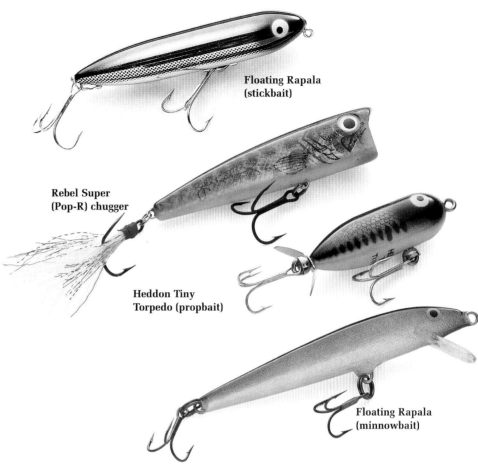

Floating Rapala
(stickbait)

Rebel Super
(Pop-R) chugger

Heddon Tiny
Torpedo (propbait)

Floating Rapala
(minnowbait)

Soft Plastics

You can buy soft-plastic baits that are near-perfect imitations of some of the smallmouth's favorite foods, such as crayfish, hellgrammites and lizards. The baits can be Texas-rigged for fishing in heavy cover, or Carolina-rigged for fishing on a clean bottom. Another good choice is a soft-plastic leech. These flattened baits have ripples molded into them so they undulate in leech-like fashion.

But exact imitations are seldom necessary to pique the interest of a smallmouth. You'll get plenty of strikes on plastic worms, as well. Most smallmouth anglers opt for worms from 4 to 6 inches long.

In recent years, tube baits have emerged as one of the top all-around smallmouth lures. Their slim profile and wiggling tentacles seem to be just what the fish want.

You can rig a tube bait on a jig head for fishing in deep water, or fish it weighted or unweighted on a weedless HP hook.

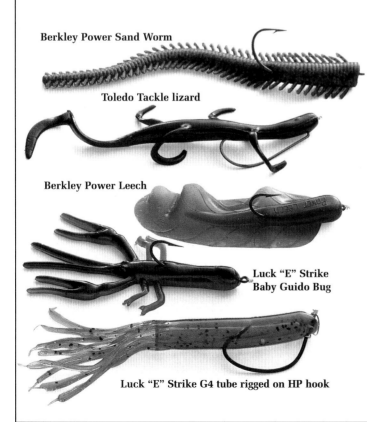

Berkley Power Sand Worm

Toledo Tackle lizard

Berkley Power Leech

Luck "E" Strike
Baby Guido Bug

Luck "E" Strike G4 tube rigged on HP hook

The Ultimate Guide To Freshwater Fishing

Fly Fishing

Smallmouth feed heavily on larval aquatic insects and, to a lesser extent, on adult forms, so it's not surprising that fly fishing is so effective. Many other fly patterns are intended to mimic hellgrammites, crayfish, leeches and shiner minnows – all smallmouth favorites.

While there is no denying the effectiveness of these realistic subsurface flies, many fishermen find "bugging" a lot more exciting.

The best bugs are made of clipped deer or elk hair. They float high on the surface, and when a smallmouth grabs one, it's not likely to let go, because the fly feels like real food. Perhaps the most popular of all bugs is the diver, which floats at rest but dives when you strip line (below).

A 6- to 8-weight fly rod with a matching weight-forward or bass-bug taper line is a good choice for smallmouth. Use a 6- to 9-foot, 2X to 5X leader and a size 1 to 6 fly.

Muddler Minnow

crayfish

Woolley Bugger

Hare Sculpin

cork popper

deer-hair swimming frog

Clauser Minnow

How to Fish a Diver

After making a cast, strip line rapidly to make the fly dive.

Hesitate after stripping line; the hair traps air and when the fly is pulled under, an air bubble floats to the surface.

The action and gurgling sound draw many strikes, but don't set the hook until you feel the weight of the fish.

CATFISH

If you've ever wondered why catfish are so popular, consider these facts:
• Catfish reach weights of 50 to 100 pounds.
• The table quality of catfish is excellent.
• Catfish are powerful fighters.
• Catfish are within easy reach of the vast majority of North American anglers.

Originally, no catfish were found west of the Rockies, but stocking programs have greatly expanded their range.

Channel, flathead and blue catfish are the species most commonly sought by anglers. But white catfish are also popular in certain areas along the east and west coasts. Whites are considerably smaller than the other species, seldom exceeding 5 pounds.

Catfish are easy to recognize because of their whiskers, or *barbels*; their smooth, scaleless skin; and the *adipose* fin on their backs.

Catfish Facts

Catfish are classified as warmwater gamefish, preferring water temperatures from the mid 70s to mid 80s. They're found naturally in large warmwater rivers, including large tributaries of those waters, and have been stocked in many lakes and ponds. Catfish can tolerate muddy water but, contrary to popular belief, cannot survive where pollution levels are high or dissolved oxygen levels, low. Blue cats prefer clearer, faster water than the other catfish species.

Catfish spawn in late spring or early summer, when the water temperature is in the low to mid 70s. One or both of the parents build a nest in the shade of a log or boulder or in other dark, secluded areas, such as holes in the bank or sunken barrels. The male guards the nest until the fry are ready to leave.

Many anglers believe that catfish feed mainly on dead or rotting food, explaining

The channel catfish (Ictalurus punctatus) has bluish gray to silvery sides, usually with dark spots on smaller individuals. The tail has a deep fork. The anal fin is shorter and more rounded than that of a blue cat.

Channel catfish range.

why "stinkbaits" are so popular. It is true that channels and, to a lesser extent, blues, consume foods of this type. But live foods, such as fish, clams, snails, crayfish and aquatic insect larvae, comprise most of their diet. In fact, flatheads rarely eat dead or rotting food.

Catfish do some feeding during the day, but they feed more heavily at night, especially in waters that are relatively clear.

Compared to most freshwater gamefish, catfish have poor eyesight. But their barbels have a good supply of taste buds, enabling them to find food in muddy water or after dark.

Channel cats have been known to live up to 40 years but, compared to blues and flatheads, they grow slowly. It takes 9 to 15 years for a channel cat to reach 5

pounds. Blues and flatheads, on the other hand, may reach weights of 20 to 30 pounds in only 10 years. It is not known how long blues and flatheads live, but their life span is surely in excess of 20 years.

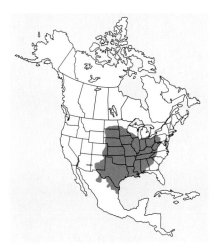

Flathead catfish range.

Blue catfish range.

The flathead catfish (Pylodictis olivaris) has a flattened forehead; very small eyes; mottled, brownish yellow sides; a squarish tail and a lower jaw that protrudes beyond the upper.

The blue catfish (Ictalurus furcatus) looks much like the channel cat. It has a deeply forked tail, but the sides have no spots and the anal fin is longer and straighter.

Key Locations for Catfish...

In Rivers

Early Spring through Spawning:
- Shallow backwaters where catfish can find undercuts and holes in the bank to serve as spawning sites
- Cavities in rocky bluffs
- Crevices in riprap banks

Summer through Mid-Fall:
- Running sloughs that are fed by water from the main channel
- Riprap banks with a slow current
- Tailwaters below dams, where catfish collect because of the concentration of forage fish

Slack-water areas of tailwaters

- Outside bends, where the current has carved a deep hole, hold cats most of the year
- Deep pools and the riffles just above them (smaller rivers)
- Deep holes downstream of tributaries
- Deep holes below wingdams

Late Fall and Winter:
- Certain deep holes in the river channel are traditional wintering sites, drawing thousands of catfish each year

Washout hole below wingdam

In Man-Made Lakes

Early Spring through Spawning:
- Timbered flats leading into shallow creek arms (pre-spawn)
- Shallow creek arms, especially those that are brushy or have cavities of some type in the bank to serve as nesting sites
- Wooded, brushy humps in creek arms

Summer through Mid-Fall:
- Main-lake points, particularly those that have standing timber and are near the mouths of spawning creeks
- Flooded stock ponds or old lake basins
- The old river channel and deeper creek channels
- Suspended in open water
- Flooded roadbeds
- Submerged humps, particularly those near the old river channel
- Saddles between submerged humps or between a hump and a shoreline point
- Timbered flats, especially those near deep water

Timbered flats along the old river channel

Late Fall and Winter:
- Deep holes and outside bends in the old river channel and in major creek channels
- Deep flooded lake basins

Fishing for Catfish

Serious catfish anglers rely almost exclusively on natural or prepared baits including but not limited to the following: congealed chicken blood, chicken livers, chunks of soap, animal entrails, clam meat (fresh or rotten), frogs, catalpa worms, nightcrawlers, mice, crayfish, Limburger cheese, doughballs, stinkbait, and live or dead fish. For large cats, anglers commonly use baitfish weighing 1 to 2 pounds.

Flatheads are most likely to take live baitfish; channels, dead or prepared baits. Blues will take either and so (at times) will channels and flatheads.

Because catfish commonly hang around logs and other obstructions, you need heavy tackle to pull them away from the cover before they can hang you up. Heavy tackle is also needed to cast the big sinkers and baits.

Although catfishing is best at night, you can often catch cats during the day, especially in low-clarity waters. Rising water also seems to trigger a daytime bite.

As a rule, cats bite best in summer, when the water temperature is 70°F or higher. But anglers seeking trophy blues are finding that they bite well in winter and spring as well.

Recommended Tackle

For channel cats on an unobstructed bottom, you can get by with medium-heavy-power spinning gear with 10- to 14-pound mono. For blues or flatheads in heavy cover, use a heavy baitcasting outfit with 30- to 50-pound superline.

Still-Fishing

Most catfish anglers take advantage of the fish's strong sense of smell by still-fishing with natural or prepared baits and letting the scent draw cats.

The most common still-fishing technique is slip-sinker fishing. With a slip-sinker rig, a catfish can move off with your bait without feeling resistance.

Most anglers use a slip-sinker rig with an 18- to 24-inch leader; a barrel swivel connects the leader to the line and serves as a sinker stop.

When you're fishing in snaggy cover, however, you may want to eliminate the swivel and let the sinker slide all the way down to your hook. This way, you can keep the bait snubbed closely to the hook so it can't swim around and tangle in the cover.

A slip-sinker rig may not be necessary when you're fishing for big cats. A little resistance doesn't bother them, so you can affix the sinker to the line.

When catfish are suspended, try a slip-float rig (below). If you can see the fish on your depth finder, set the float to keep the bait at precisely the same depth. A slip-float rig is also a good choice when catfish are scattered over a large flat with a consistent depth. Simply cast the rig upwind and let it drift across the flat.

When still-fishing for channel cats, you can greatly boost your odds by chumming. Before fishing your spot, spread fermented corn, wheat or milo over the area, then come back at least an hour later and fish right in the area you chummed.

Make a slip-sinker rig by sliding a ½- to 3-ounce egg sinker onto your line and then attaching a barrel swivel, leader and hook suited to your bait.

Popular Catfish Baits

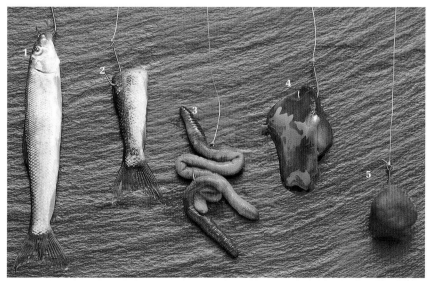

(1) Live baitfish, such as a sucker or sunfish hooked through the lips or the back; (2) cut sucker, shad or herring: (3) gob of crawlers; (4) chicken liver; (5) ball of stinkbait.

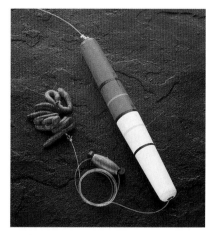

Make a slip-float rig by tying a bobber stop onto the line and then sliding on a bead and a cylinder float. Tie on a barrel swivel and add a leader, sinker and hook.

Drift-Fishing

Drift-fishing with several rods is even more effective than slip-float fishing when catfish are scattered over large flats. It also works well for cats around boulders, logs or other obstructions in rivers.

Rig each rod with a 1- to 2-ounce sinker and a live baitfish or a piece of cut bait on a size 3/0 to 6/0 hook, and set the rod so the bait is just off bottom.

To drift-fish a large flat, motor to the upwind side and let the wind push you over it. Make parallel drifts until the entire flat has been covered. If necessary, use a sea anchor to slow your drift.

The same basic technique works well for drift-fishing in a river. Catfish often hold in eddies downstream of boulders and other large obstructions, and drifting your bait through these areas can be highly effective. Holding the rod in your hand, lower the bait to the bottom and keep your line as vertical as possible as you drift. Keep adjusting your depth as the bottom changes.

Should you find an eddy or hole that is holding good numbers of catfish, anchor just upstream of the spot and try still-fishing.

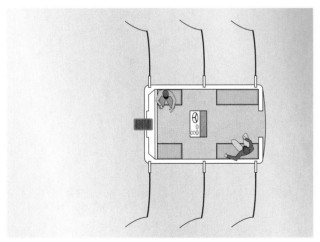

Outfit your boat with several rod holders along each gunwale and place an 8- to 9-foot rod in each. With the rods perpendicular to the gunwales, you can cover a 20- to 25-foot swath of water.

Drift-fish an eddy below a boulder or a deep slot by lowering your bait to the bottom and then reeling it up a few inches. Use a trolling motor to adjust your drift speed.

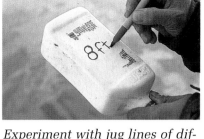

Experiment with jug lines of different lengths; mark the length of the line on each jug. Then, it will be easy to determine the most productive depths when you retrieve the jugs.

Jug Fishing

Jug fishing is one of the most effective ways to catch cats. Not only does it enable you to cover a wide expanse of water, it works well for cats that are suspended.

Simply attach a line to a sealed jug, add a pinch-on or twist-on sinker, tie on a hook and add your favorite bait. Then let the rig drift through a likely catfish spot.

Some fishermen use a dozen jugs or more.

When you're using small baits and there is little chance of catching big cats, one-quart jugs are adequate. But when you're using big baitfish or fishing for giant cats, use two-quart to one-gallon jugs. A big catfish can submerge a one-quart jug and snag up your line. For maximum visibility, your jugs should be white or fluorescent orange.

You can drift along with the jugs and keep an eye on them, or you can release them on the upwind side of a lake and pick them up later on the downwind side.

When you see a jug bobbing, dipping under or moving against the wind, a cat has taken the bait. There is no need to set the hook; the fish hooks itself when it tries to pull the jug under.

Make a jug-fishing rig by tying the line to the handle or neck. Then add a 1- to 3-ounce sinker and tie on a size 1/0 to 6/0 hook. If desired, use several hooks attached by short leaders to loops in the line.

SUNFISH

Catching sunfish is not much of a challenge; they abound in practically any body of water well-suited to largemouth bass. But catching big sunfish is another matter. In most waters, a 1-pound-plus sunfish is as hard to come by as a trophy bass, walleye or pike.

There are more than a dozen species of sunfish in North America, with the largest (and most popular) being the bluegill (*Lepomis macrochirus*) and the redear sunfish (*Lepomis microlophus*), also known as the shellcracker. Many anglers, particularly those in the South, don't even attempt to distinguish the different species, lumping them all together as bream, or brim.

A great deal of hybridization occurs among the sunfish species. In some waters, cross-breeding is so common that it's difficult to know what you are catching.

Sunfish Facts

Sunfish spawn in spring, when the water temperature is in the upper 60s. The male selects a spawning site, usually at a depth of 3 feet or less on a sandy or gravelly bottom protected from the wind. He sweeps away the silt with his tail, making a light-colored depression. After the female deposits her eggs, the male aggressively guards the nest until the fry disperse.

The reproductive potential of sunfish is extremely high, with a single female sometimes depositing more than 200,000 eggs. Spawning may occur at monthly intervals over the summer, usually around the full moon. Unless there is

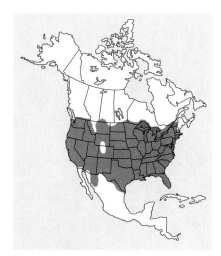

Bluegill range.

Bluegills have a light blue edge on the gill cover. The "ear" is pure black and there is a black blotch at the rear of the dorsal fin. The sides are brownish-gold with a purple sheen. The male's breast is copper colored; the female's, yellowish.

enough predation to thin the sunfish crop, stunting is likely. As a result, waters with low sunfish populations generally produce the largest fish.

Sunfish feed mainly on small crustaceans and mollusks, fish fry and aquatic insects. They eat more larval insects than adults, although there are times when bluegills take large numbers of adult insects off the surface. Redears seldom feed on the surface; they commonly pick up invertebrates, particularly snails, off the bottom, explaining why they're called shellcrackers.

Practically any warm, shallow, weedy waters will support sunfish. They abound in small, shallow lakes, in protected bays of larger lakes and in slow-moving reaches or backwater areas of rivers and streams. They prefer water temperatures in the mid to upper 70s.

Redear sunfish range.

Redear sunfish get their name from the reddish margin around the otherwise black ear. The sides are light greenish or goldish with scattered reddish flecks.

Of all the freshwater gamefish, sunfish are the most willing biters. And when you hook one on light tackle, it gives you a good tussle for its size. But there is another important reason for the tremendous popularity of sunfish – they're tops

on the dinner table. They have firm, white, flaky, sweet-tasting meat.

Sunfish may live up to 10 years, but their usual life span is 5 years or less. Their growth rate is highly variable, depending mainly on population density.

Key Sunfish Locations...

In Natural Lakes
Early Spring through Spawning:
- Shallow, mud-bottomed bays and channels that warm earlier than the main lake (pre-spawn)
- Shallow bays and harbors with a sandy or gravelly bottom (spawning)
- Sheltered sandy or gravelly shorelines (spawning)
- Gradually sloping points with emergent weeds (spawning)

Summer through Mid-Fall:
- Points along weedlines
- Underwater lips of shoreline points
- Weedy humps
- Around deep-water docks
- In deep weed beds

Late Fall and Winter:
- Shallow bays (early winter)
- Deep holes in shallow bays or shallow parts of the main lake
- Inside turns along weedlines

In Man-Made Lakes
Early Spring through Spawning:
- Back ends of creek arms
- Marinas
- Slow-tapering points in creek arms
- Shallow, brushy flats along creek channels
- Main-lake coves with woody cover

Summer through Mid-Fall:
- Main-lake humps
- Extended lips off points in main lake and deep creek arms
- Along the edges of creek channels and the old river channel
- Around intersections of creek channels and the old river channel
- Edges of old roadbeds

Late Fall and Winter:
- In old stock ponds or lake basins
- Deep holes at mouths of creek arms
- Deep sections of creek channels and old river channel

In Rivers
Early Spring through Spawning:
- Shallow, weedy backwaters
- In stands of emergent vegetation along shorelines with practically no current

Summer through Mid-Fall:
- In weedy or woody cover along the edge of the main channel (smaller rivers)
- Deep backwaters with weedy or woody cover
- Along riprap banks with slow-moving water
- Around piers and breakwaters
- Around weedy wingdams with slow current

Late Fall and Winter:
- Deep, slack-water holes in main channel (smaller rivers)
- Shallow backwaters (early and late winter)
- Deep holes in backwaters (midwinter)

Use an extra-long-shank hook, about size 8, when fishing with live bait. The long shank makes it easy to unhook the fish should it swallow the bait.

Recommended Tackle

A light spinning rod and a small reel spooled with 4-pound mono make a good all-around sunfish outfit. Don't use a long, whippy ultralight rod, however, because you'll have trouble getting solid hooksets.

For dabbling in heavy cover, use a 10- to 14-foot extension pole or cane pole with 8- to 12-pound mono.

Fishing for Sunfish

The key to catching sunfish is location. You can find the small ones in harbors, around docks and in most any kind of shallow, weedy cover. But once spawning is completed, the big ones head for deeper water. It's not unusual to catch them by accident on deep structure while fishing for bass or walleyes. A good depth finder makes the job of locating them a lot easier.

Once you find the fish, catching them shouldn't be much of a problem. A worm on a plain hook is usually all that's needed, but anglers use a variety of small baits and lures (right).

Live bait is normally fished beneath a small float weighted with enough split shot to keep it just above water. If you're fishing in water more than 8 feet deep, use a slip-bobber rig or just a plain hook and a split shot.

Remember that sunfish are not always on the bottom. Fish in 25 feet of water, for instance, may suspend as much as 10 feet off the bottom, so you'll have to set your float accordingly.

When sunfish are in shallow water, they're easy to catch on a fly rod. All sunfish species will hit small nymphs and wet flies, and bluegills don't hesitate to take tiny poppers and sponge bugs.

An extension pole enables you to place your bait in a small pocket in dense cover. You would have little chance of hitting the pocket by casting and, even if you did, the splash would spook the fish.

Sunfish Baits & Lures

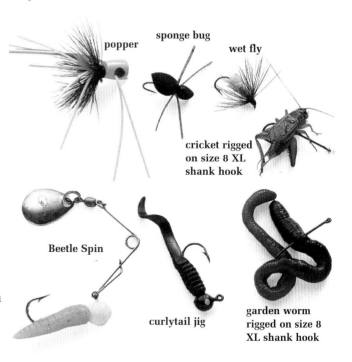

popper

sponge bug

wet fly

cricket rigged on size 8 XL shank hook

Beetle Spin

curlytail jig

garden worm rigged on size 8 XL shank hook

Ice-Fishing baits

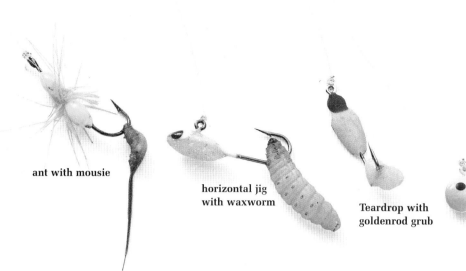

ant with mousie

horizontal jig
with waxworm

Teardrop with
goldenrod grub

Fat Boy with
Eurolarvae

*Look for goldenrod grubs
in the pods of goldenrod
plants.*

Ice Fishing

On many northern waters, more sunfish are taken through the ice than during the open-water season.

By far the most effective ice-fishing method is jigging with a small teardrop or ice fly tipped with a grub, such as a waxworm or maggot. Use a graphite rod with an extremely light tip (right) and spool up with 2- to 4-pound mono. You'll be able to detect the lightest sunfish nibble.

Sunfish bite best just after freeze up. Look for them in the same shallow bays where you found them in spring. They move to deeper water in midwinter and don't bite as well. They return to the shallows in late winter and fishing picks up again.

Select an ice-fishing rod with an extremely flexible tip (top). An ordinary rod won't flex enough to signal a bite, so you'll have to add a spring bobber (bottom).

Jigging your bait rapidly and then letting it rest is a deadly sunfish method – in winter and summer.

CRAPPIES

outdoor press is now devoting more space to crappie fishing and tournament crappie fishing is on the increase.

Crappie Facts

Black crappies *(Pomoxis nigromaculatus)* and white crappies *(Pomoxis annularis)* are often found in the same lakes and streams, but whites can tolerate murkier water. Blacks are most numerous in the North; whites, in the South. Both species prefer a water temperature in the 70- to 75°F range, although they

Black crappie range.

Black crappies have 7 or 8 spines on the dorsal fin and are deeper-bodied than whites. Black speckles on the silvery green sides explain why crappies (black and white) are often called "specks."

The phrase "here today, gone tomorrow," must have been coined by a crappie fisherman. Crappies are known for their nomadic habits, and finding a consistent locational pattern is nearly impossible, especially in summer. This explains why most crappie fishing is done in spring, when the fish move into the shallows to feed and, later, spawn. You can generally find them in the same springtime locations year after year.

Despite the difficulty of staying on the fish, the popularity of crappie fishing has exploded in recent years. The

can survive at temperatures in the upper 80s.

Compared to most other gamefish, crappies can tolerate lower levels of dissolved oxygen. Consequently, they are usually one of the most common gamefish in lakes that periodically freeze out.

Crappies spawn in spring, usually at water temperatures in the low 60s. They nest on a sandy or gravelly bottom, usually with brush or emergent vegetation for cover. In the North, stands of dead bulrushes from the previous year are key spawning sites. The nests are not as apparent as those of sunfish, because the bottom is not swept as clean. After spawning has been completed, the male remains to guard the eggs and newly hatched fry.

At spawning time, male crappies turn considerably darker than the females and are sometimes nearly black. The males are much more

White crappie range.

White crappies have 5 or 6 spines on the dorsal fin and the forehead has a deeper depression than that of the black crappie. The sides normally have 7 to 9 vertical bars.

aggressive and easier to catch than the females.

The main reason crappies are so difficult to locate is that they spend a good deal of their time feeding on suspended plankton in open water. Other important foods include small fish and aquatic insect larvae.

Crappies are willing biters but, compared to sunfish, are

not strong fighters. They have white meat with a mild flavor, but it is softer than that of sunfish.

Black crappies have a longer life span than whites, with some individuals surviving to an age of 10. But the usual life span for both species is 5 or 6. In the North, a 1-pound crappie is usually 7 or 8 years old; in the South, only about 5.

Key Locations for Crappies...

In Natural Lakes

Early Spring:
- Shallow mud-bottom bays, dead-end channels and harbors
- Channels between lakes

Spring (spawning):
- Sheltered bays and shorelines with a firm bottom and emergent weeds
- Shallow humps with emergent weeds

Summer and Early Fall:
- Deep rock piles
- Edges of weedy humps
- Irregular weedlines
- Gradually tapering points

Late Fall and Winter:
- Inside turns along deep weedlines
- Deep holes in a shallow basin
- Deep water off ends of points
- Deep flats

In Man-Made Lakes

Early Spring:
- Secondary creek arms
- Marinas
- Shallow coves on main lake
- Breakline near spawning cover
- Standing timber
- Fallen trees and brush piles

Spring (spawning):
- Brushy back ends of creek arms
- Feeder creeks with woody cover
- Marinas

Summer and Early Fall:
- Edges of main river channel
- Edges of creek channels
- Main-lake points

Late Fall and Winter:
- Main river channel
- Deep creek channels
- Deep main-lake coves

In Rivers

Early Spring through Spawning:
- Shallow, dead-end sloughs and other backwaters off the main river
- Fallen trees and brush piles
- Shallow sandbars
- Stump fields
- Boat harbors

Late Spring to Early Fall
- Sloughs with current
- Deep holes in backwaters
- Side channels leading into backwaters
- Deep eddies
- Deep outside bends
- Undercut banks and ledges

Late Fall and Winter:
- Deep holes in backwaters
- Deep eddies in main channel

Fishing for Crappies

Whether you're fishing a shallow bay in early spring, a brush pile at spawning time or a deep hump in mid-summer, you can catch crappies on a small minnow dangling beneath a float. This simple technique accounts for more crappies than all other methods combined.

In spring, when the fish are shallow, you can use a float that clips onto or is pegged to your line. In summer, when the fish may be at depths of 20 feet or more, a slip-bobber works much better.

You can also catch crappies on a variety of small, minnow-imitating lures, the most common being a lead-head jig with a soft-plastic or chenille-and-marabou dressing.

Regardless of what lure or bait you use, depth control is of utmost importance in crappie fishing, because of the fish's habit of suspending in a specific depth zone. Experienced anglers rely heavily on their depth finders, spotting the fish and adjusting their depths accordingly.

Recommended Tackle

A light spinning outfit with 4- to 6-pound mono is ideal for fishing crappies in open water. However, when they're buried in brush or other woody cover, you'll need a heavier spinning outfit with 10-pound mono. This, way, you'll be able to straighten a light-wire hook, should it hang up on a branch.

Small jigs are hard to beat for springtime crappies.

Popular Crappie Baits

minnow on size 4
long-shank, light-wire
hook

chenille jig

curlytail jig

Norman Baby-N
(crankbait)

Blue Fox Big
Crappie Spinnerbait

Jigs aren't just for open water; you can use them through the ice as well.

When using a small jig or other slow-sinking bait, try the countdown technique. Make a cast, count while the bait sinks, then begin your retrieve. Keep trying different counts until you get a strike, then repeat the same count on subsequent casts.

Fly fishing with small, light-colored streamers and wet flies can be quite effective, but don't bother trying poppers. Crappies are not nearly as surface-oriented as bluegills.

Ice fishermen also depend on their depth finders to locate crappies. After spotting some fish, drop down a minnow on a size 4 hook or a small jigging bait and fish right above the level of the fish.

Crappies move about just as much in winter as they do in summer, so it's important for ice fishermen to be mobile. If you don't catch anything in a few minutes, try another hole.

Ice-Fishing Baits

Jigging Rapala

teardrop tipped with
Eurolarvae

Purist (icefly)

Vingla (jigging spoon)

Swedish Pimple
tipped with waxworm

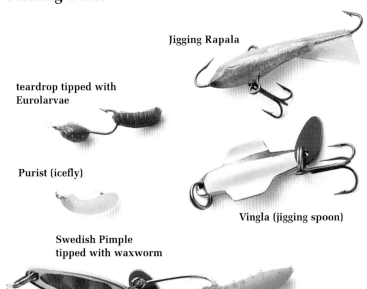

Spider-Rigging for Crappies

In the South, where most states allow anglers to use multiple lines, crappie fishermen spider-rig vast expanses of open water to locate schools of suspended crappies.

Although there are times when spider-riggers troll at random, following no distinct structure, they more often follow a breakline. It might be the edge of a creek channel leading into a spawning cove, or it could be a drop-off along a main-lake point.

Start by selecting lures that run at different depths; most anglers use curlytail jigs, hair jigs, jig-spinner combinations or small spinnerbaits (right). Any of these baits can be tipped with small minnows, but it may not be necessary.

For maximum coverage, use the longest rods you have. Ten- to twelve-foot rods are ideal, although some anglers use 16-footers. Be sure the rods have a fast tip; otherwise, the fish won't hook themselves when they strike.

Trolling speed is critical. Crappies seldom strike a fast-moving bait, so it's important to move as slowly as possible, keeping your lines near vertical.

Keep a close eye on your sonar unit to determine if you're on fish. With a wide-angle transducer, you may even be able to see if your lines are tracking at the right depth.

Lures for Spider-Rigging

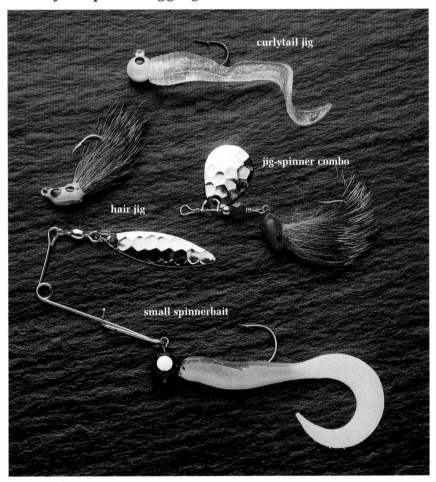

curlytail jig

jig-spinner combo

hair jig

small spinnerbait

Sight-fish for crappies on clear waters during the spawning period. They're easy to see if you wear polarized sunglasses. Use an extension pole; this way, you can dangle a jig in their faces from a distance without spooking them.

Look for male crappies, which are considerably darker than the females at spawning time. Males are far more aggressive than females during the spawning period.

Use a floating "crappie light" when night fishing. The light is directed downward to attract minnows, which, in turn, draw crappies.

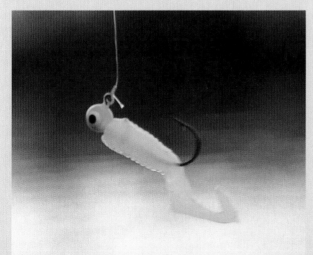

Position your knot so the jig hangs horizontally. If your knot slides to the front of the eye, the jig will hang vertically and will not look natural.

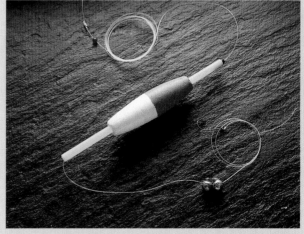

Make a slip-bobber rig by tying a slip-bobber knot on your line and threading on a small bead and a float. Then add a split shot and a hook. Adjust the stop to fish at the desired depth.

YELLOW PERCH

Perca flavescens

When the yellow perch are biting, word travels fast. And if you've ever dined on a plate of fresh perch fillets, you know why. Many fish connoisseurs rate them ahead of walleyes on the table-quality scale.

Yellow perch are close relatives of walleyes and inhabit many of the same waters. They abound in large, clear northern lakes with clean, sandy bottoms and have been stocked extensively throughout the country.

Perch, like walleyes, are considered coolwater fish. Their preferred temperature range is 65 to 72°F, but they continue to feed aggressively at much lower water temperatures and are very popular among ice anglers.

Spawning takes place in early spring at water temperatures in the mid-40s. Gelatinous strands of eggs are deposited on sticks, rocks, weeds and other debris and, when conditions are right for a successful hatch, the shallows are soon teeming with huge numbers of young perch.

Yellow perch eat small fish, fish eggs, larval aquatic insects, snails and crustaceans, especially crayfish and scuds. Perch do most of their feeding near the

Yellow perch have yellowish sides with 6 to 9 dark, vertical bars. The lower fins often have an orange tinge, particularly in spawning males.

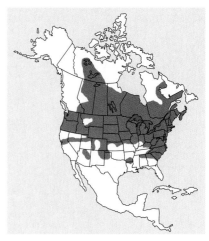

Yellow perch range.

A plain jig or a jig and minnow probably account for more perch than any other bait. Simply bounce it slowly along the bottom and set the hook whenever you feel a tap or the bait suddenly feels lighter.

Popular Perch Baits

small minnow on size 4 hook

in-line spinner

marabou jig

piece of nightcrawler on size 4 hook

Most yellow perch fishermen rely on live bait fished on either a split-shot or slip-sinker rig with a size 4 to 6 hook, or tipped on a jig or spinner. It's possible, however, to take perch on small artificials, such as marabou jigs and in-line spinners.

Interest in ice fishing for yellow perch has exploded in recent years. Anglers use their electronics to pinpoint schools of perch on mid-lake structure and then jig for them using a 2½- to 3-foot graphite jigging rod, 4-pound mono and a small spoon or lead-head jig tipped with live bait. The fastest action is usually in late winter, when meltwater starts running down the holes.

bottom and commonly root in the mud for the larvae of mayflies and other insects.

In many small lakes, perch never reach a size large enough to interest fishermen. Your best bets for "jumbo" perch (those weighing ¾ pound or more) are large, shallow, sandy natural lakes with minimal weed growth.

A light spinning outfit with 4- to 6-pound mono is ideal for yellow perch. The fish are not powerful fighters, and the light outfit makes it easy to cast lightweight baits.

Ice-Fishing Baits

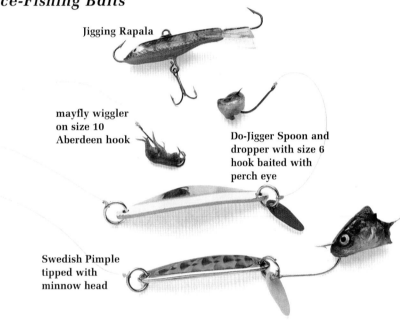

Jigging Rapala

mayfly wiggler on size 10 Aberdeen hook

Do-Jigger Spoon and dropper with size 6 hook baited with perch eye

Swedish Pimple tipped with minnow head

Tips for Catching Perch

A tandem-hook rig allows you to catch perch two at a time. Tie a pair of double-surgeon's loops (p. 69) in your line, attach leaders and hooks and add a bell sinker.

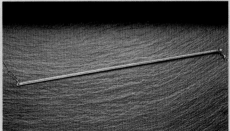

Use a "hanger rig," consisting of a steel rod with a hook at the end, to get down quickly and stir up the bottom. The disturbance attracts perch.

Modify a jigging spoon by adding a mono dropper and size 6 hook. Bait up with a minnow head, perch eye or waxworm. The spoon gets the bait down fast and adds attraction.

Northern Pike & Muskellunge

Esox lucius & Esox masquinongy

When you catch a glimpse of a huge pike or muskie inches behind your lure, your knees are bound to get a little shaky. And when the fish grabs your bait and makes a screeching run toward the weeds, you'd better hope you spooled on heavy enough line and tied good knots.

Besides the northern pike and muskie, the pike family also includes the chain pickerel, which seldom exceeds 5 pounds, and the grass and redfin pickerel, which rarely reach 1 pound.

Northern pike range.

Pike & Muskie Facts

Although pike and muskies are both found in weedy portions of natural lakes and in slow-moving, weedy rivers, muskies seldom thrive in waters with an abundance of pike. The pike hatch earlier in the season and, because they are larger, prey upon the newly hatched muskies.

Both species are classified as coolwater fish, preferring water in the mid-60s to low 70s. But once pike reach a length of about 30 inches, they favor water that is considerably cooler, about 50 to 55°F.

Pike spawn in early spring, usually when the water reaches the low to mid 40s. Spawning sites include tributary streams, connecting marshes and shallow, weedy bays. Muskies spawn several weeks later, as water temperatures reach the upper 40s to upper 50s. They scatter their eggs in weedy bays, but may also spawn on weedy flats in the main lake. Neither species make any attempt to guard the eggs or young.

Because of the great difference in spawning time, hybridization between pike and muskies rarely takes place in nature. But hybrids, called tiger muskies, are commonly raised in hatcheries and have been stocked in many parts of the country. Tiger muskies are more aggressive than purebred muskies, so they're easier to catch, but they don't grow quite as large.

The genetic makeup of muskies is quite variable. There are three distinct

Muskie range.

Northern pike have dark greenish sides with rows of oval-shaped, cream-colored spots. The tail has large dark spots and the lobes are rounded.

Muskies have dark spots or bars on light greenish to silvery sides. Or they may be unspotted. The tail has smaller spots, or no spots, and sharper lobes.

Muskies lurk in heavy cover, waiting for unsuspecting baitfish.

attacking quickly. Pike are primarily daytime feeders; muskies, especially those in clear lakes, also feed at night.

All members of the pike family have long, sharp teeth with a razor-like edge (below) that can easily cut your line. Contrary to popular belief, they do not lose their teeth in summer. Rather, their teeth are continually being broken off and replaced by new ones.

In warmwater lakes and streams, pike seldom live longer than 6 years, but muskies may live up to 12. Both species have a much longer life span in colder waters, with pike living as long as 25 years; muskies, 30. Muskies grow much faster than pike. A 20-pound pike is likely to be more than 20 years old; a muskie of the same size, only 10.

color phases: barred, spotted and clear. But these varieties are not considered true subspecies. Because of widespread muskie stocking, any of these color phases may be found throughout the muskie's range.

Fish make up most of the diet of both species, but they also eat frogs, mice, ducklings and even muskrats. Pike, however, are more aggressive feeders, striking most anything that comes into view. Muskies size up their prey more carefully, lying dormant until the moment is right, then

Tiger muskies have light sides with dark, narrow, vertical bars, which are often broken into spots. The lobes of the tail are rounder than a muskie's.

Pike and muskies have large teeth with very sharp edges (inset).

Key Locations for Pike and Muskie...

In Shallow Natural Lakes

Early Spring through Spawning:
- Marshes connected to the main lake

Spawning bay

- Shallow, weedy bays

Late Spring through Early Summer:
- Weedlines and weedy humps and points, particularly those near spawning bays
- Shallow gravel or rock bars

Mid-Summer through Early Fall:
- Beds of lily pads or other floating-leaved vegetation that keeps the water slightly cooler
- Bars, points and flats with a healthy growth of submerged weeds, particularly cabbage

Cabbage bed

- Edges of deep bulrush beds
- Weedy saddles connecting two islands or a point and an island
- Inflowing springs (pike)

Late Fall and Winter:
- Deep, rocky humps
- Deep holes surrounded by shallow water (in lakes that do not have low oxygen levels)

In Deep Natural Lakes

Early Spring through Spawning:
- Shallow, mud-bottomed bays attract pike soon after ice out, and muskies a few weeks later

Late Spring through Early Summer:
- Shallow flats just outside of spawning bays, particularly those

Rocky flat outside of spawning bay

with weedy or rocky cover
- Channels leading from the spawning bay to the main lake

Mid-Summer through Early Fall:
- Mouths of good-sized inlet streams (these areas hold pike and muskies from late spring through fall)
- Rocky reefs below the thermocline (pike)
- Shallow rocky reefs (muskie)
- Deep narrows that have moving water on windy days
- Clusters of islands that have extended lips with submerged weed beds
- Weedy or rocky points that slope gradually into deep water

Late Fall:
- Gravelly shoals and points that serve as spawning areas for ciscoes (when the water temperature drops to the mid-40s)
- Rocky points and humps that slope sharply into deep water

Winter:
- Shallow bays

In Rivers

Early Spring through Spawning:
- Shallow backwater lakes (big rivers)
- Seasonally flooded sloughs (smaller rivers)

Late Spring through Early Summer:
- Tailwaters of dams
- Deep, weedy backwaters and side channels

Mid-Summer through Mid-Fall:
- Good-sized eddies that form below islands, points or sand bars
- Current breaks, where there is a distinct line between fast and slow water
- Spring holes (pike)
- Mouths of coldwater streams (pike)

Cold tributary flowing into river

Late Fall and Winter:
- Shallow backwater areas (through early winter)
- Deep holes in backwaters (late winter)
- Impoundments above low-head dams (smaller rivers)

Year-Round Locations (smaller rivers):
- Deep pools with light current
- Deep oxbow lakes off main river

Oxbow lake

Fishing Techniques

Pike and muskies consume a wide variety of foods, so it's not surprising that they'll strike most any kind of bait. As a rule, size and action of the bait are a lot more important than color.

Experienced pike and muskie anglers know that big baits catch big fish, so they do not hesitate to use lures measuring nearly a foot long. Of course, you'll need stout tackle to cast baits this size and to drive the hooks into the fishes' bony mouths.

Muskies, especially those in heavily fished waters, are notorious followers. They will pursue the bait right up to the boat and then turn away at the last instant. But you can often make them strike by reeling the bait to within a foot of the rod tip, then pushing the tip as far into the water as you can and making large figure-eights. This tactic is seldom necessary with pike.

To preserve quality pike and muskie fishing, anglers must learn to practice catch-and-release. Otherwise, the big fish are quickly removed. Always carry jaw spreaders and heavy longnose pliers. If possible, remove the hooks while the fish is still in the water.

Recommended Tackle

A medium-heavy-power bait-casting outfit with 12- to 20-pound mono or superline is adequate for the majority of pike and muskie fishing. For trophy-caliber fish, however, you'll need a heavy-power outfit with 25- to 50-pound line. Always use a steel leader for pike and muskie fishing.

Spinnerbaits work well in heavy cover. Because of the safety-pin design, the hook is protected.

Fishing with Spinnerbaits & Bucktails

When pike or muskies are in weedy cover, a spinnerbait is hard to beat. You can retrieve it over a weedy flat, keeping it just above the weed tops or allowing the blade to slightly "bulge" the surface. You can also let it helicopter into any holes in the weeds, or fish it on the bottom with a jigging motion. When the fish are suspended, try counting a spinnerbait down to their level.

Spinnerbaits come in single- and tandem-blade models. Singles are best for helicoptering, but tandems give off more vibration, an advantage for fishing in murky water or at night.

Bucktails are large in-line spinners with dressings of natural or synthetic hair. They can be fished in sparse weeds but, because they have open hooks, are not a good choice in dense vegetation. The combination of the billowing hair, thumping blade and good hooking performance makes bucktails a favorite of many veteran pike and muskie anglers.

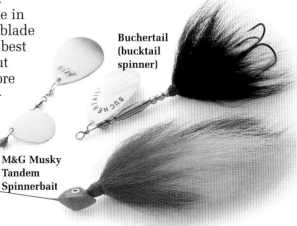

Buchertail (bucktail spinner)

M&G Musky Tandem Spinnerbait

Topwaters

If you've ever seen a pike or muskie attack a duckling, frog or mouse, you know they're accustomed to grabbing food on the surface. Yet, for some reason, topwater fishing never enters the minds of many pike and muskie anglers.

There are times, however, when topwaters work even better than the standard subsurface fare. When the fish are buried in dense weeds, for instance, you can often draw them out with a topwater. And the bait won't foul as much as a subsurface offering.

Muskie fanatics know that topwaters are deadly for night fishing. The more noise and splash the lure produces, the better.

Topwaters are not a good choice in cool water. When the water temperature is below 60°F, choose a subsurface bait.

The topwaters used for pike and muskie fishing are similar to those used for bass fishing, but are considerably larger.

Propbaits have a propeller on the front or back end, or both. On some baits, the whole head or tail serves as a propeller. A slow, steady retrieve usually works best.

Buzzbaits come in safety-pin and in-line models. You can retrieve them rapidly, so they're a good choice when you're trying to locate fish.

Crawlers, with their cupped face or "arms," swim with a wide wobble and make a loud gurgling sound. They're most effective with a slow, straight retrieve.

Stickbaits are weighted in the tail, so they have a highly erratic, side-to-side motion when retrieved with a series of sharp downward jerks. Although their action is attractive to pike and muskies, the fish may have a hard time zeroing in on the darting bait.

Work a stickbait with sharp downward jerks.

Poe's Giant Jackpot (stickbait)

Gooch's Tallywacker (propbait)

Creeper (crawler)

Buchertail Super Buzz

Fishing with Subsurface Plugs

With fish being such an important food for pike and muskies, the effectiveness of subsurface plugs should come as no surprise.

Because of their open hooks, these baits are used mainly in sparse cover or open water. If you're fishing in weeds, select a bait that runs just above the weed tops. In open water, the bait should periodically contact the bottom.

Pike and muskie anglers rely mainly on three kinds of subsurface plugs. Minnowbaits, with their narrow lip and slim body, have a tight, natural-looking wobble. Crankbaits have a broader lip or flattened head that produces a wider wobble. Vibrating plugs, with the attachment eye on the flattened back, have the fastest, tightest wiggle.

The best plugs have hooks anchored to an internal wire, rather than attached with screw eyes that a big fish could pull out.

Any of these plugs can be fished by casting or trolling. Although you can catch fish with a steady retrieve, a stop-and-go presentation usually draws more strikes.

Use a thin, braided-wire leader with a round-nosed snap for attaching subsurface plugs. A heavy wire leader would restrict the plug's side-to-side action.

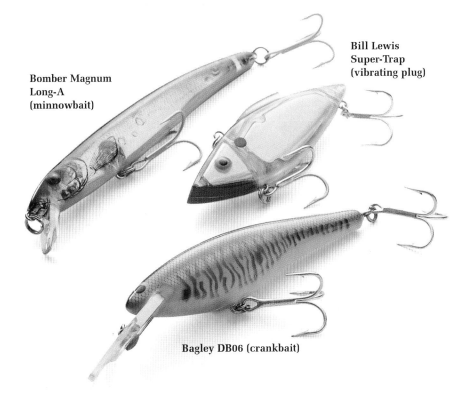

Bomber Magnum Long-A (minnowbait)

Bill Lewis Super-Trap (vibrating plug)

Bagley DB06 (crankbait)

Jerkbait Fishing

The erratic, struggling-baitfish action of these big wooden plugs has a special appeal to pike and muskies.

The term, "jerkbait," is somewhat of a misnomer, because the baits are retrieved with a series of smooth, downward strokes, rather than sharp jerks. Jerkbaits have no action other than that which the angler provides.

Use a short, stiff rod for jerkbait fishing. If you use a long rod, the tip will hit the water on the downward stroke. Attach the bait with a stiff wire leader.

There are dozens of different styles of jerkbaits, but they fall into two categories:

Divers dart downward when you jerk; *gliders* dart from side to side. Divers generally run deeper than gliders, but both types of baits can be doctored for extra depth by adding lead weights (internal or external) or wrapping solder around the hooks.

Spoon Fishing

Spoons are great for beginners because it's nearly impossible to fish them the wrong way. You can use a fast, slow or stop-and-go retrieve, jig them in deep water and even skitter them across the surface.

But spoons aren't just for amateurs; you'll find a good selection in the tackle box of practically every serious pike and muskie angler.

Thick-metal spoons are best for casting, but thinner ones have a wider wobble and are ideal for trolling. In heavy cover, use a weedless spoon. Attach your spoon to a braided-wire leader.

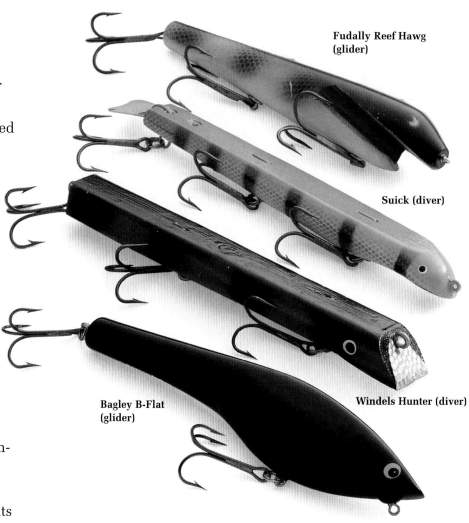

Fudally Reef Hawg (glider)

Suick (diver)

Windels Hunter (diver)

Bagley B-Flat (glider)

Eppinger Dardevle

Johnson Silver Minnow with curlytail

Jig Fishing

Jig fishing does not enjoy widespread popularity in pike-muskie circles, but when fishing gets tough, it often outshines any other method.

Jigs are a good choice, for instance, when cold water slows pike and muskie activity to the point where they won't chase a bait with a fast or erratic action. They may, however, inhale a jig dropped in front of their nose.

A round-head jig works well in sparse cover or open water but, for fishing in weeds, you'll need a bullet-head with the eye at the front. For fishing over weed tops, try a swimmer-head.

Most pike-muskie jigs come with a soft-plastic dressing, such as a large shad, reaper, creature or curlytail. Some anglers prefer a plain jig head tipped with a big minnow.

Use the lightest jig that you can keep on the bottom. Pike-muskie jigs range from 3/8 to 3/4 ounce. Attach your jig to a braided-wire leader.

bullet-head jig with reaper

swimmer-head jig with curlytail

round-head jig with shad tail

Dahlberg Mega Diver

Barr's Bouface

streamer

Fly Fishing

You don't hear much about fly fishing for pike and muskies, but the sport is growing in popularity. And those who go about it the right way know just how effective it can be.

Fly fishing works well any time the fish are in shallow water. Then, they'll take divers, poppers, streamers and frog imitations in sizes 1 to 4/0. Be sure to select a fly with a weedguard if you'll be fishing in heavy cover.

Pike and muskie anglers generally use a 7- to 10-weight fly rod with a floating, weight-forward or bass-bug-taper line. Make sure your leader has a braided-wire shock tippet.

anglers. Oily fish, like smelt and ciscoes, seem to have the most appeal.

Live or dead baitfish can be fished beneath a float or still-fished on the bottom. Live baitfish can also be retrieved slowly on a jig head or slip-sinker rig.

Always rig baitfish on a braided-wire leader with a size 2/0 to 6/0 single hook or a quick-strike rig consisting of a pair of double or treble hooks.

chub

golden shiner

sucker

smelt

Live-Bait Fishing

When pike and muskies are finicky, nothing triggers more strikes than real food.

Although the fish will strike a variety of live baits, including frogs, waterdogs, leeches and nightcrawlers, most anglers opt for large baitfish, such as suckers, chubs and golden shiners.

If you're after good-sized pike or muskies, the problem may be finding baitfish that are large enough. For fish over 10 pounds, you should have lively baitfish at least 8 inches long, and many anglers prefer 10 to 12 inchers.

Dead bait is growing in popularity among pike

Rig a baitfish on a single hook by pushing it in the mouth and out the top of the snout. For float fishing, you can also hook the bait through the back.

Rig a baitfish on a strip-on spinner by pushing the wire through the bait's mouth and out the vent. Then, put the double hook on the wire with the points up.

Rig a baitfish on a quick-strike rig by pushing one hook into the body near the pectoral fin and the other near the dorsal. When a fish strikes, set the hook immediately.

Ice Fishing

Because of their coldwater habits, pike remain active all winter and are a favorite of ice anglers. Muskies, on the other hand, are seldom taken through the ice.

Live or dead baitfish on tip-ups account for the majority of winter pike.

Popular Rigs for Tip-Up Fishing

Add a small Colorado spinner blade just above a size 2 to 1/0 treble hook, then push one prong of the treble through the back of a lively baitfish. As the baitfish swims about, the blade flashes, drawing extra strikes.

Rig a dead smelt or cisco on a size 3 or 4 Swedish hook. Push the hook into the vent up to the bend, turn the shank up, then push the point of the hook out just behind the head. The bait should ride in a level position.

Spool your tip-ups with 25- to 40-pound-test braided Dacron or superline and tie on a braided-wire leader with a size 2/0 to 6/0 single hook, a spinner rig or a quick-strike rig (opposite).

Add enough weight to keep the bait at the desired depth, which may be almost anywhere in the water column. When oxygen levels are low in late winter, it's not uncommon to find pike swimming just under the ice.

Tip-ups enable you to cover a large piece of structure, such as a weed flat or deep hump, much more efficiently than you could with any other method. Scatter your tip-ups at first, then concentrate them after you find the fish.

WALLEYE & SAUGER

Stizostedion vitreum & Stizostedion canadense

Widespread stocking has put walleyes within easy reach of the majority of North American anglers. Saugers are much less common but, where they exist, rival walleyes in popularity.

Walleyes and saugers belong to the perch family. Although walleyes are often called "walleyed pike" and saugers, "sand pike," they are not related to pike or muskies. To further confuse the matter, walleyes in parts of Canada are called "pickerel."

Their firm, white meat, with no fishy taste, explains why walleyes and saugers are among the most popular table fish.

Walleye & Sauger Facts

The eyes of walleyes and saugers differ from those of other freshwater gamefish in that they have a layer of light-reflective pigment, called the *Tapetum lucidum*, in the retina. This layer gives the fish excellent night vision and also causes them to avoid bright sunlight. Saugers have a larger tapetum than walleyes.

It's not unusual for anglers to catch a mixture of walleyes and saugers in the same spot. But saugers, because of their larger tapetum, are usually found in slightly deeper water and are more tolerant of high turbidity.

Considered coolwater fish, walleyes and saugers prefer water temperatures in the 60s to low 70s. Walleyes are most numerous in large, windswept natural lakes of moderate clarity; saugers, in big rivers or reservoirs of low to moderate clarity.

Saugers (left) and walleyes (right) are commonly caught in the same water.

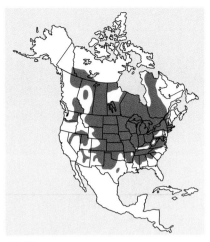

Walleye range.

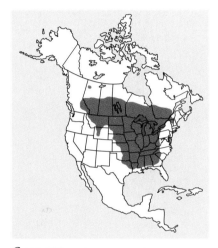

Sauger range.

Walleyes have golden sides and a white belly. The spiny dorsal fin is not spotted, but has a black blotch at the rear base. The lower lobe of the tail has a large, white tip.

Saugers are grayish to brownish with dark blotches. The dorsal fin has rows of distinct black spots, and the pectoral fins have a dark spot at the base. The lower lobe of the tail may have a thin, white streak.

Walleyes spawn in spring, generally at water temperatures in the upper 40s. Saugers spawn several days later than walleyes. Both species are random spawners, depositing their eggs on clean gravelly or rocky bottoms. Saugers usually spawn a little deeper than walleyes.

The two species sometimes hybridize to produce the *saugeye,* which is intermediate in looks and behavior between the parents.

There are two subspecies of walleyes: the yellow walleye *(Stizostedion vitreum vitreum)* and the blue walleye *(Stizostedion vitreum glaucum).* But the latter, once common in lakes Erie and Ontario, is now believed to be extinct.

Small fish make up most of their diet, but walleyes and saugers also feed on leeches, crayfish, snails, larval aquatic insects and larval salamanders. They feed most heavily in dim-light periods, when their excellent night vision gives them a predatory advantage over most baitfish. Research has shown that rapidly decreasing light levels trigger walleye feeding.

Walleyes and saugers are not flashy fighters; they do not jump or make speedy runs. Instead, they wage a strong, determined battle, staying deep and stubbornly shaking their heads until they tire.

Walleyes reach a considerably larger size than saugers, mainly because of their longer life span. Walleyes have been known to reach a documented age of 26 years, although they seldom live longer than 10. Saugers may live up to 13 years, but an age of more than 7 is rare.

In the North, walleyes and saugers normally reach a weight of 2 pounds in about 7 years; in the South, they grow to that size in 3 to 4 years. The biggest walleyes come from southern waters, but the largest saugers are found in the North. In the same waters, walleyes usually grow a little faster than saugers.

Saugeyes have a spotted or mottled dorsal fin, but the spots are not as distinct as those of a sauger.

Key Locations for Walleye*...

In Natural Lakes

Early Spring through Spawning:
- Gravel or rubble shorelines that are exposed to the wind
- Inlet streams with rocky or gravelly bottoms
- Shallow, rocky reefs close to shore

Late Spring:
- Gradually tapering points near spawning areas
- Large, shallow flats connected to points

Shallow flat extending off point

- Shallow bays barely connected to the main lake (shield lakes)
- Gravel patches on shallow mud flats
- Shallow, slow-tapering reefs

Summer to Mid-Fall:
- Gradually sloping reefs
- Irregular breaklines with a gradual taper
- Outer tips of long, gradually tapering points
- Mouths of good-sized inlets, particularly in shield lakes
- Breaklines around island clusters
- Sandy, weedy humps in rocky lakes
- Suspended over deep water, particularly in lakes with cisco forage base
- Weedy flats in shallow, fertile lakes

Late Fall and Winter:
- Deep, sharp-sloping reefs
- Irregular breaklines that slope sharply into deep water
- Fringes of bulrush beds on shallow points

In Man-Made Lakes

Early Spring through Spawning:
- Deep pools in tributary streams concentrate the fish before spawning
- The upper end of the old river channel is a pre-spawn staging area (shallow reservoirs)
- Riffles in tributary streams are prime spawning sites
- Gravelly shorelines in the upper end of the reservoir
- Riprap shorelines, such as those along causeways and dam faces

Riprap bank

Late Spring:
- Timbered flats along edges of creek channels
- Shallow, sand-gravel points in creek arms
- Mud flats at upper end of the reservoir

Summer to Mid-Fall:
- Brushy main-lake points near deep water
- Wooded humps near the old river channel
- Timbered flats along the old river channel
- Steep eroded banks with rock slides
- Rocky main-lake points with shallow food shelves

Late Fall and Winter:
- Steep, timbered points and inside turns along the old river channel
- Old ponds and lake basins (shallow reservoirs)
- Deep holes above the dam (mainly in shallow reservoirs)

In Rivers

Early Spring through Spawning:
- Eddies in the vicinity of tailraces hold walleyes prior to and after spawning
- Pools downstream from spawning riffles are pre-spawn staging areas (smaller rivers)
- Riffle areas and rocky shorelines downstream of riffles are prime spawning areas (smaller rivers)
- Flooded willows along the fringes of the main channel draw spawners
- Flooded marshes adjacent to the river draw spawners in high-water years
- Riprap shorelines with small rocks make excellent spawning areas

Late Spring:
- Current-brushed points downstream of spawning areas
- Deep cuts connecting main channel and backwaters
- Deep backwaters
- Deep pools and eddies downstream of spawning areas

Current-brushed point

Summer to Mid-Fall:
- Rocky banks brushed by light current
- Rocky points extending into the river and the eddies formed by them
- Wingdams
- Deep banks with fallen trees
- Upper ends of deep pools (smaller rivers)

Late Fall and Winter:
- Deep holes along outside bends
- Deep eddies and slow-moving slots in tailrace areas

---

* Note: Sauger inhabit many of the same areas as walleye, but are slightly deeper.

A jig tipped with live bait is one of the most consistent walleye and sauger producers.

vertically jig it on the bottom as you drift or slowly troll. How much action you impart to the jig depends on the water temperature and the mood of the fish. When the water is below 50°F, or the fish are not aggressive, work the jig with short hops or just drag it along the bottom. When the water is warmer and fish are active, retrieve with bigger hops. Be sure to keep your line taut when the jig is sinking; that's when the fish normally strike. Whenever you feel a light tap or anything out of the ordinary, set the hook.

Walleye & Sauger Techniques

The challenge of catching these finicky biters is exactly what appeals to so many anglers. For consistent success, you must be proficient with a variety of live-bait and artificial-lure presentations.

The techniques used for walleyes and saugers are much the same, with the main difference being that saugers are usually caught in slightly deeper water.

Both species are schooling fish, so once you locate a few, you can bet there are more nearby. Serious walleye and sauger anglers rely heavily on their electronics to find fish and lock in the location of the spot, so they can return at a later time.

Jig Fishing

A lead-head jig is the simplest walleye-sauger bait, yet it is arguably the most consistently effective. It's also one of the least expensive.

Most walleye-sauger jigs weigh from $1/16$ to $1/2$ ounce and have hair, feather or soft-plastic dressings. Jigs can also be tipped with a minnow, leech or piece of nightcrawler.

You can cast a jig and retrieve it along the bottom, or

Fireball Jig with clip-on stinger hook

bullet-head bucktail jig

Fuzz-E-Grub

curlytail jig

jig tipped with Sassy Shad

Slip-Sinker Fishing

Slip-sinker fishing gives you the most natural live-bait presentation possible. And when a fish takes the bait, it feels no resistance; as it swims away, the sinker stays put.

To fish a slip-sinker rig, simply lower it to the bottom, let out just enough line so you can maintain bottom contact, and then slowly troll or drift over good walleye structure. Keep your bail open and hold the line with your finger. This way, you can release the line immediately when you feel a pick-up.

Feed line until the fish stops running, point your rod at the fish, reel rapidly until you feel some weight and then set the hook with a sharp, upward snap of the wrists.

Don't make the mistake of slowly tightening up to see if the fish is still there; that's when it usually drops the bait.

It's important to choose the right type and size of weight. For fishing on a clean bottom, use an egg sinker or walking sinker; in weedy cover, a bullet sinker. You'll need about $1/8$ to $3/16$ ounce of weight for every 10 feet of depth. It takes a little extra weight to maintain bottom contact in windy weather.

Most anglers rig their bait on a plain hook, but some prefer to add a small float to keep the bait off bottom and provide a little color. You can also add a small spinner blade or a colored bead.

Another important issue is leader length. When the fish are hugging bottom, a 3-foot leader is adequate. But when they're suspended, you'll want a much longer leader and some type of float. Some anglers use leaders more than 10 feet long.

A $6^{1}/_{2}$- to $7^{1}/_{2}$-foot spinning rod with a soft tip and a stiff butt is the best choice for slip-sinker fishing. Then, should you fail to release the line when a fish bites, it won't feel too much resistance and drop the bait. Yet, you'll be able to get a firm hookset.

Be sure to keep your reel filled to within about $1/8$ inch of the rim. If the reel is not full, the line will catch on the lip when a fish runs, causing it to feel resistance and drop the bait. A nick on the lip of the spool can cause the same problem.

A slip-sinker rig allows a walleye to take the bait and swim away without feeling resistance.

Making & Fishing a Slip-Sinker Rig

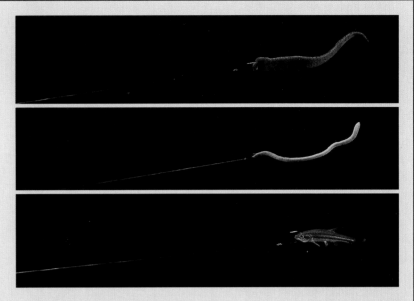

1 Tie a slip-sinker rig by threading a weight onto 6- to 8-pound mono and then tying on a small barrel swivel. Add a 3- to 5-foot leader of 4- to 6-pound mono and attach a size 4 to 6 short-shank hook.

2 Hook a leech (top) just in front of the sucker using a size 6 hook; a nightcrawler (middle), through the head with a size 6 hook; a minnow (bottom), through the lips with a size 4 hook.

1 After dropping the rig to the bottom, keep your bail open and hold the line on your finger.

2 Release the line immediately when you detect a bite. Sometimes, all you feel is a little extra resistance.

3 When the fish stops running, quickly reel up the slack until you feel some weight, then set the hook.

Optional Slip-Sinker Rigs

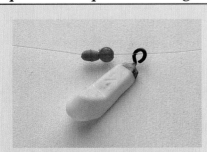

A rig with a rubber stop and bead enables you to change leader length easily. You can buy pre-tied rigs or make your own using a slip-bobber knot (p. 70).

Keep your bait off bottom with **(1)** a floating jig head or **(3)** slip-on float. For extra attraction, add a **(2)** colored bead.

Use a **(1)** bullet sinker for fishing in weeds; a **(2)** walking sinker or **(4)** egg sinker on a clean bottom; and a **(3)** clip-on sinker for changing weights quickly.

Slip-Bobber Fishing

When walleyes are suspended or not feeding aggressively, you can often tease them into biting by using a slip-bobber rig to put the bait right in their faces.

The beauty of a slip-bobber rig is that it can be set to fish at any depth, yet will still allow you to reel the bait right up to the rod tip. Otherwise, you would not be able to cast the rig.

A long spinning rod, at least 6½ feet, is recommended for slip-bobber fishing. A long rod helps you get a strong hookset, which may be difficult because the bobber causes your line to form a right angle between you and the fish. When the bobber goes down, be sure to reel in line until you feel weight before setting.

Most slip-bobber fishing is done with leeches, crawlers or minnows, either on a plain hook or a ¹/₁₆- to ¹/₃₂-ounce jig head. For night fishing, use a lighted slip-bobber.

Tie a slip-bobber knot (p. 70) on your line, thread on a small bead and the slip-bobber, then tie on a size 4 to 6 hook or a small jig head. Add enough split shot to balance the bobber.

How a Slip-Bobber Works

Cast a slip-bobber rig, then feed line as the bait sinks. The knot moves toward the bobber, which is resting on its side.

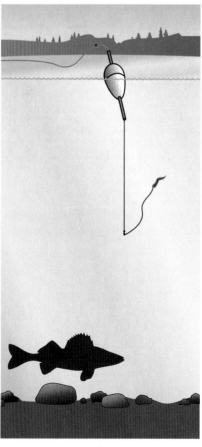

Continue feeding line as the knot approaches the bobber. If you stop feeding line, the rig will pull back toward you.

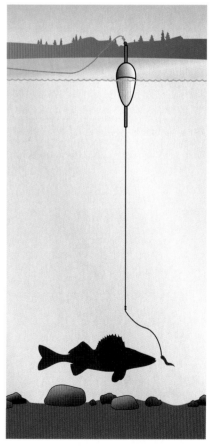

When the knot reaches the bobber, the weight will stand it upright and the bait will be at the desired depth.

Spinner Fishing

It's easy to understand why trolling or drifting with a spinner and live bait is a time-proven method for walleyes and saugers. The vibration and flash from the spinner blade draw attention to the bait.

Spinner rigs are most effective in low-clarity water, where the fish may not spot plain live bait. But many anglers believe that a spinner blade is an asset in any kind of water.

Most spinner rigs are made with a Colorado blade, usually size 2 to 4, because it spins easily even at very slow trolling speeds. In low-clarity waters, use a fluorescent orange, green or chartreuse blade; in clear to moderately clear waters, a silver, gold or brass blade.

A single-hook spinner rig works best for minnows or leeches; a tandem- or triple-hook rig, for nightcrawlers.

A tandem- or triple-hook harness reduces the number of short strikes when you're fishing with a spinner and crawler.

Other Popular Spinner Rigs

floating spinner rig with bottom bouncer

single hook spinner rig with egg sinker

How much weight you use depends on the water depth and how fast you're trolling or drifting. If you're fishing in 10 feet of water and moving slowly, you need only a ⅜- to ½-ounce sinker. But if you're trolling fast ("power trolling") in 20 feet of water, you may need a 3-ounce weight.

Many spinner addicts prefer bottom-bouncers to ordinary weights, because they keep the bait off bottom and are relatively snagless.

Plug Fishing

Anglers on the pro-walleye circuit will attest to the effectiveness of plug fishing. Trolling with crankbaits, minnowbaits and vibrating plugs is one of the hottest tournament techniques, especially on big water.

Plugs enable you to cover a lot of water in a hurry, a big advantage when you're working highly mobile schools of fish suspended in open water.

To increase their horizontal and vertical coverage, anglers often troll with side planers and weight their lines differently. Some even use lead-core line, downriggers and 3-way swivel rigs.

But plugs are also effective for casting, especially when the fish move into the shallows in the evening. When the water is cool, a neutrally-buoyant minnowbait works especially well, because you can stop reeling and "hang" it right in their faces.

Big walleyes love minnowbaits!

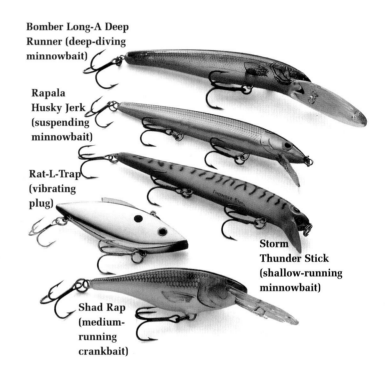

Bomber Long-A Deep Runner (deep-diving minnowbait)

Rapala Husky Jerk (suspending minnowbait)

Rat-L-Trap (vibrating plug)

Storm Thunder Stick (shallow-running minnowbait)

Shad Rap (medium-running crankbait)

Plug-Fishing Tips

Side planers make it possible to cover a lot of water and, because your lines are far to the side of the boat, you're not as likely to spook the fish.

Cast a minnowbait over rocky shoals starting at sunset. The fish move in to feed on minnows and are often caught in water less than 5 feet deep.

The Ultimate Guide To Freshwater Fishing

Ice Fishing

Like most coolwater fish, walleyes and saugers continue to feed at near-freezing temperatures, so they're a prime target for ice fishermen. Although you can catch them throughout the winter, the fastest action tends to be early and late in the ice-cover season.

As a rule, the spots that produced fish in summer and fall will continue to produce after freeze up. If you have a hand-held GPS unit, you can easily return to a waypoint entered during the open-water season.

A minnow dangled beneath a tip-up or bobber accounts for plenty of walleyes and saugers, but jigging is even more productive. Not only does the jigging action attract more fish, you can move about more easily because you don't have to reset your depth every time you switch holes.

One of the best ways to locate walleyes and saugers is to drill at least a dozen holes, all at different depths, then set out tip-ups in some of the holes and jig in the others. If you start catching fish in a certain area or at a certain depth, move the rest of your lines accordingly.

If the fish don't bite in an hour or so, try another spot; it normally doesn't pay to wait them out.

Whatever technique you use, be sure to arrive at your ice-fishing spot well before you expect the fish to start biting. If they normally bite at dusk, for instance, start drilling your holes in late afternoon. If you wait until the fish are feeding to start drilling holes, the sound of the auger may put an end to the action.

A good flasher not only tells you what depth the fish are at, it shows you how they react to different jigging actions.

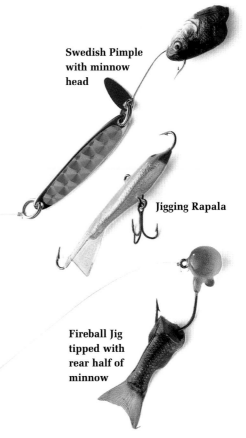

Swedish Pimple with minnow head

Jigging Rapala

Fireball Jig tipped with rear half of minnow

A good jigging outfit includes a fast-action graphite rod about 30 inches long with at least 3 guides and a fly-rod-style tip, a small spinning reel that balances with the rod, and limp 6-pound-test mono.

WHITE & STRIPED BASS

Morone chrysops & Morone saxatilis

These super-aggressive feeders offer some of the fastest freshwater fishing – if you can find them. Both species are known for their pelagic habits, spending a good deal of their time chasing baitfish in open water.

White and striped bass belong to the temperate bass family and are not related to the largemouth or other black bass. Other members of the family include white perch and yellow bass.

Hybrids can be produced by crossing male white bass and female striped bass. Called wipers, these popular fish are stocked in many southern waters.

White bass are also known as "sand bass" or "silver bass," and striped bass are often called "rock-fish." The name "striper" often leads to confusion, because it may be applied to both species.

White & Striped Bass Facts

Although white and striped bass are closely relat-ed, white bass spend their entire lives in fresh water, while striped bass are anadromous, spending most of their lives at sea and entering freshwater streams to spawn. But striped bass are capable of living solely in fresh water and have been widely stocked, mainly in southern reservoirs.

White and striped bass are warmwater gamefish, prefer-ring water temperatures from the mid 60s to the mid 70s. White bass thrive in big-river systems, including

White bass range.

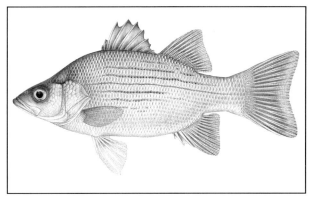

White bass have silvery sides with black horizontal stripes that are usually unbroken above the lateral line but broken below.

Striped bass range.

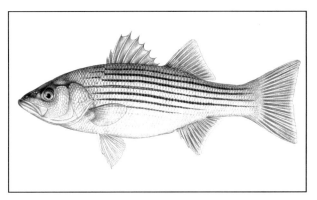

Striped bass have silvery sides with 7 or 8 horizontal stripes that are unbroken. The body is more elongated than that of a white bass.

action is usually short-lived, especially when boats get too close. The pack sounds, but may soon reappear in a different location.

Striped bass grow much faster and live much longer than white bass. In 5 years, a white bass normally grows to about $1\frac{1}{2}$ pounds; a striper, about 10 pounds. White bass seldom live longer than 6 years, while stripers may reach an age of 20 or more.

Striped bass grow to a larger size in salt water than in fresh water. Commercial fishermen off the Atlantic coast once netted a striped bass that weighed 125 pounds.

connecting lakes. Striped bass are well suited to large reservoirs with an ample supply of open-water forage, usually shad.

Both white and striped bass spawn in spring, generally at water temperatures in the mid 50s to low 60s. They swim up tributary streams, usually until their progress is blocked by a dam, and then deposit their eggs in light current. They make no attempt to guard the eggs.

Fish make up most of the diet, but both species also eat crustaceans and a variety of aquatic insects. They are known for their pack-feeding behavior. When a hun-

gry pack surrounds a school of baitfish, you'll witness a feeding frenzy more explosive than anything else you'll ever see in fresh water. They herd the baitfish to the surface, slashing at them from below, while gulls and terns dive down to grab those that get injured in the melee. Anglers lucky enough to encounter a feeding pack often catch a fish on every cast. But the

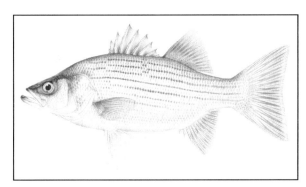

Wipers have stripes that are broken above and sometimes below the lateral line. The body is deeper than that of a striper but not as deep as a white bass.

Key Locations for White and Striped Bass...

In Man-Made Lakes

Early Spring through Spawning:
- Tailwaters of upstream dams
- Creek arms at the upper end of the lake, particularly those with a significant flow

Tailwaters

Late Spring through Mid-Fall:
- Edges of shallow flats
- Mouths of major creek arms
- Suspended over the old river channel and creek channels or in the submerged timber along the edges
- Edges of shallow main-lake points
- Narrows between main-lake basins

Late Fall and Winter:
- Coves between main-lake points
- Junction of creek channel and old river channel
- Deep holes in the old river channel at the lower end of the lake (late fall to early winter)
- Deep holes in the old river channel at the upper end of the lake (late winter)
- Deep main lake points, especially those at the upper end of the lake

Deep point extending into river channel

In Rivers

Early Spring through Spawning:
- Large backwaters that warm earlier than the main river
- Tailwaters of upstream dams
- Mouths of large tributaries

Tributaries carry warmer water that draws spawners

Late Spring through Mid-Fall:
- Sandy flats around mouths of tributaries
- Pools with rocky feeding riffle just upstream
- Deep riprap banks along outside bends
- Slots and washouts below boulders and other large objects that break the current
- Eddies created by sharp turns in the river
- Eddies created by points projecting into the river

Deep pool below rocky riffle

Late Fall and Winter:
- Deepest pools in the river
- Holes along outside bends
- Deep washouts in the tailwaters of upstream dams

Fishing for Temperate Bass

The secret to catching temperate bass is finding them. White bass, striped bass and wipers are constantly on the move, and the spot that held a huge school yesterday may not produce a single fish today.

Finding the fish is easiest in spring, when they congregate below dams to spawn. But once they complete spawning and move back downstream or into a lake, locating them can be a challenge. That's when most anglers rely on trolling so they can cover lots of water.

The fish begin their pack-feeding behavior in late summer or early fall. Then, circling gulls will help you pinpoint feeding schools.

As a rule, temperate bass bite best early and late in the day but, during the spawning period, time of day is not much of a consideration. The action slows considerably when the water temperature drops below 50°F, although white bass are often caught by ice fishermen.

You can use similar techniques to catch white and striped bass, but the latter require bigger lures and heavier tackle. Live bait, however, is seldom necessary for white bass.

Recommended Tackle

A light- to medium-power spinning outfit with 4- to 8-pound mono is adequate for most types of white bass fishing. A medium-heavy- to heavy-power baitcasting outfit with 14- to 25-pound mono is a good choice for striped bass.

Trolling

Trolling for temperate bass can be as simple as tossing a jig or crankbait behind the boat or as complicated as rigging 6 or 8 lines on planer boards and downriggers to cover a wider, deeper swath of water.

Live shad are the favorite trolling bait of many striped bass anglers. Hook them through the nostrils and use an electric trolling motor to move them along very slowly. Watch your depth finder for signs of fish or baitfish schools, and set your lines to fish just above them.

Jigs and plugs can be trolled much faster, so they're a better choice when you're searching for fish.

Should you find a good-sized school of fish, stop the boat and try casting or vertical jigging. Not only will you cover the area more thoroughly, you'll be much less likely to spook the fish.

For Stripers

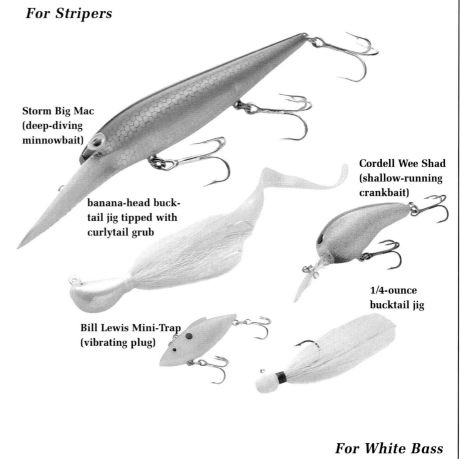

Storm Big Mac (deep-diving minnowbait)

banana-head bucktail jig tipped with curlytail grub

Cordell Wee Shad (shallow-running crankbait)

1/4-ounce bucktail jig

Bill Lewis Mini-Trap (vibrating plug)

For White Bass

Circling gulls lead you to feeding white bass and stripers.

Jump-Fishing

In late summer, when young-of-the-year shad have grown large enough to make a decent meal, white bass and stripers begin pack-feeding. If you watch closely for circling and diving gulls, they'll lead you to the fish.

To some, the term "jump-fishing" means anglers jumping from school to school; to others, it means fish jumping bait. Either way, jump-fishing provides incredible action. Just toss out any bait that looks even remotely like a shad and there's a good chance you'll hook up immediately.

Veteran jump-fishermen rely mainly on jigs, because they can unhook the fish and get back into the water in a hurry. That's important, because the action may not last long, especially if you get your boat too close to the school. Some white bass anglers use a tandem-jig set-up (right), so they can catch two fish at a time.

But there are times when crankbaits, tail-spinners or topwaters work better than jigs. Striped bass anglers know that a big, noisy popper, one that throws water a foot into the air, often draws strikes when nothing else is working.

For Stripers

Cordell Redfin (shallow-running minnowbait)

Creek Chub Striper Strike (chugger)

Roadrunner Jig tipped with paddletail worm

Pop-R Plus (chugger)

Little George (tailspinner)

Tandem jig setup

For White Bass

A lively shad can easily tow a high-floating balloon.

Balloon Fishing

Big striped bass have a penchant for heavy cover; they often hole up in flooded timber or other cover where it's virtually impossible to throw a lure. But southern striper guides have devised an innovative method for drawing them out of the tangle. They hook on a live, 12- to 15-inch shad and let it swim enticingly over the cover, using a balloon as a float.

A balloon works much better than a bobber. Because it floats considerably higher, it has less water resistance, so a lively shad can tow it around more easily and cover more water.

If the balloon breaks or starts bobbing violently, a striper has taken the bait. Reel up slack until you feel the weight of the fish and set the hook hard. Keep maximum pressure on the fish to keep it from diving.

The major challenge in balloon fishing is collecting the shad. You can't buy them at a bait shop, so you'll have to net your own. Serious striper fishermen catch their bait with a cast net and keep it alive in an aerated, insulated bait tank.

When you're fishing stripers in timber or other dense cover, heavy tackle is a must. When you hook a big fish, it invariably makes a power run for the thickest cover and, if you're not able to turn it immediately, you have little chance of landing it. Many anglers use a light saltwater rod and a heavy baitcasting reel spooled with 50-pound-test mono or superline.

Inflate a small balloon to a diameter of 4 or 5 inches, stretch out the neck and tie a single overhand knot around your line. Set the balloon to the desired depth.

Push a size 3/0 to 6/0 hook through shad's lips or nostrils, or hook it just in front of the dorsal fin. Don't attach a sinker; it will restrict the shad's movement.

STREAM TROUT

The term "stream trout" refers to species of trout that require moving water for successful spawning. Stream trout are also found in lakes, if there is a suitable tributary stream available for spawning. If not, they must be stocked.

The major stream-trout species include brown, rainbow, cutthroat and brook trout. The latter is actually a char and is more closely related to the lake trout than to the other stream trout. Char are easy to distinguish from trout because they have light spots on a dark background; trout have dark spots on a light background.

Stream Trout Facts

Stream trout are coldwater fish. Whether they inhabit streams or lakes, they require water that stays cold and well-oxygenated throughout the year.

Brook trout, like other chars, need very cold water; they prefer a water temperature of about 54°F. Brown trout can tolerate relatively warm water. They favor a water temperature of about 65°F, but can endure temperatures in the upper 70s. Rainbow and cutthroat have intermediate temperature preferences.

All of these stream trout species develop *anadromous,* or seagoing, varieties. The best known of these is the steelhead, a variety of rainbow trout that spends most of its life at sea and then enters coastal streams to spawn. Anadromous forms are usually sleeker and more silvery than their landlocked counterparts.

Steelhead and other anadromous stream trout have been stocked in large inland lakes, particularly the Great Lakes. There, the fish spend most of their lives in the open waters of the lakes, and run up tributary streams to spawn.

Rainbows and cutthroats are spring spawners, while browns and brooks spawn in fall. All stream trout build *redds,* depressions in the streambed gravel into which the eggs are deposited. The eggs are then covered with gravel and allowed to incubate. Water must flow through the gravel to keep the eggs aerated, explaining why stream trout cannot spawn successfully in lakes. The parents do not protect the redd or guard the young.

Aquatic insects, including both larval and adult forms, are an important food source for all stream trout. But as the trout grow older, small fish make up

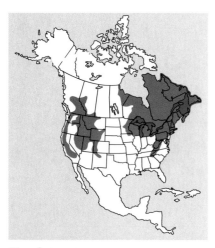

Brook trout range.

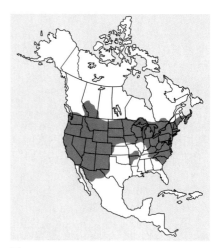

Brown trout range.

Brook trout (Salvelinus fontinalis), also called speckled trout, have brownish to greenish sides with light spots and a few red spots with blue halos. The back has light wormlike markings and the leading edges of the lower fins are white.

Brown trout (Salmo trutta) have light brownish or yellowish sides with black spots along with a few red or orange spots. The spots sometimes have lighter halos. The tail is usually unspotted, but it may have a few spots.

a larger portion of their diet. Fish are especially important in the diet of large brown trout. Other stream trout foods include crustaceans, worms, frogs, plankton and fish eggs.

Stream trout are known for their selective feeding habits, explaining why fly fishermen take great pains to "match the hatch." But selectivity varies greatly among species, with browns being by far the most choosy. Rainbows are less selective, while brook trout and cutthroat will take most anything you throw at them.

Stream trout are not particularly long-lived. The maximum life span is 8 to 10 years, although brook trout have been known to live 15 years. Growth is extremely variable. As a rule, lake-dwelling and anadromous forms grow much faster and reach a considerably larger size than stream-dwelling forms. Male stream trout generally grow faster than females.

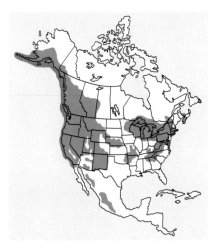

Rainbow trout range.

Cutthroat trout range.

Rainbow trout (Oncorhynchus mykiss) have a bluish or greenish back and silvery sides with a pinkish horizontal band that extends over the gill cover. The back, sides and tail are heavily spotted.

Cutthroat trout (Oncorhynchus clarki) get their name from the orange or red slash marks on the throat. The sides usually have a yellowish tinge, with black spots. The tail is heavily spotted.

Fishing for Stream Trout

Hundreds of books have been written about techniques for outwitting stream trout. But regardless of what method you use, there are several common threads:

- Don't let the fish see or hear you. That means keeping a low profile, wearing drab clothing and keeping movement to a minimum. If you're wading, move slowly and silently. If you're in a boat, don't drop anything on the bottom or run the motor anywhere near the fish. If you're walking along the bank, use streamside vegetation to conceal your approach, and step lightly to minimize vibrations. And never allow your shadow to fall over a potential lie. Once the fish detect you, no amount of coaxing will convince them to bite.
- Use a delicate presentation. If your lure or line splashes down near the fish, they'll head for cover.
- Use a light, low-visibility leader or tippet, because trout are extremely line-shy. Never use fluorescent mono.
- When a major insect hatch is in progress, small- to medium-size trout feed almost exclusively on the hatching insect, and the only effective way to catch them is fishing with a fly of the same size, shape and color. But the biggest trout are usually more interested in baitfish than insects, so they're susceptible to lures such as spinners, spoons, minnowbaits and streamers.

Key Locations for Stream Trout...

In Streams
- Gravelly tributaries or gravelly tails of pools serve as spawning sites for rainbows and cutthroats
- Riffles (shallow, turbulent water) hold feeding trout in morning and evening
- Runs (deep channels excavated by the current), hold trout most anytime
- Pools (deep, flat water) are ideal resting areas. They often hold the stream's biggest trout
- Undercut banks offer shade and overhead cover
- Spring holes in the headwaters (brook trout)
- Spring areas draw trout during the hottest part of the summer (marginal trout streams)
- Plunge pools that form at the base of a waterfall are prime spots for big trout
- "Pocket water" (scattered boulders on shallow flats with pockets of deep water behind them) holds a surprising number of trout
- Gravelly reaches near the headwaters and gravelly tributaries draw spawning brook and brown trout in fall

Undercuts often form along outside bends

In Lakes
- Shallow bays warm earlier than the main body of a lake, so they attract trout in early spring
- Shorelines with a gradual taper are prime spots in deep, cold lakes
- Rocky points with a slow taper make good morning and evening feeding sites
- Inlet streams carry an abundance of food and draw good numbers of trout

Look for trout around weedy or brushy cover

- Cool water in the thermocline may hold practically all the trout in mid-summer, when the surface water is too warm for trout and the depths have too little oxygen
- Weedy or woody cover is a must for trout in shallow water; otherwise, the fish would be vulnerable to kingfishers, herons and other predators

Recommended Tackle

A light- to medium power spinning outfit with 4- to 8-pound mono is adequate for fishing with spoons, spinners and other "hardware".

A 3- to 5-weight fly rod, a double-taper or weight-forward line and a 9-foot tapered leader with a 5X to 6X tippet is suitable for the majority of stream-trout fishing. But if you're casting big flies or fishing for good-sized trout in fast water or heavy cover, you'll need a 7- to 9-weight fly rod and a 0X to 4X tippet.

to stand downstream of a riffle where you suspect trout are feeding, cast upstream of the riffle and crank the lure rapidly through it.

Medium- to deep-diving crankbaits are a good choice for fishing deep pools or trolling for suspended trout in lakes.

Lake fishermen often use side planers to spread their lines and catch trout that spook from the boat. They also use downriggers and diving planers to take their lures to the desired depth (pp. 46-47).

When stream-fishing, quarter your casts upstream far enough that you don't have to retrieve against the current (red line). If you cast too far downstream, the current will catch your line, forming a belly, speeding up the lure and causing you to retrieve upstream (yellow line).

Fishing with Hardware

The vast majority of trophy-class stream trout are taken on "hardware," primarily spinners, spoons, and plugs. That should come as no surprise, because these lures imitate baitfish, the favorite food of big trout.

Spinners are popular among both stream and lake fishermen, because they produce a lot of flash and vibration, even on a very slow retrieve. You can reel them rapidly through a fast riffle or slow them way down to fish a deep pool.

Heavy spoons are ideal for distance casting on big water, and they have enough weight to get down in fast current. But thinner spoons have more action and work better for trolling.

Minnowbaits are more difficult to cast, but their lifelike appearance appeals to selective trout. One of the best ways to fish a minnowbait is

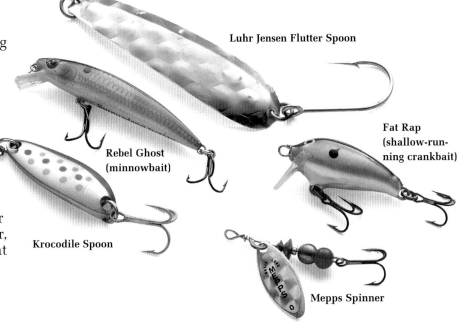

Luhr Jensen Flutter Spoon

Rebel Ghost (minnowbait)

Fat Rap (shallow-running crankbait)

Krocodile Spoon

Mepps Spinner

Fly Fishing

Fly fishing for trout is the passion of millions of anglers. For some, learning to make perfect casts with a fly line is the source of fascination; for others, it's tying flies that match natural insect hatches. Many consider fly fishing an art form, but it's also an extremely effective way to catch trout.

Flies can be tied to match most anything that a trout eats, but the majority of flies imitate larval or adult forms of aquatic insects.

Dry flies mimic newly-hatched adult insects. Many have upright hair or feather wings. A collar of feather fibers, or *hackle*, along with a hair or feather tail, gives the fly buoyancy, but it must be periodically dipped in floatant to keep it from sinking. Dry flies are fished on a dead drift.

Wet flies imitate many different trout foods, including larval aquatic insects, drowned terrestrial insects, minnows and crustaceans. Most wet flies have swept-back wings and are intended to sink. Wet flies can be fished on a dead drift or twitched to resemble a darting minnow or insect.

Nymphs usually simulate the nymphal, larval or pupal stages of aquatic insects, but some patterns imitate scuds, shrimp and other crustaceans. They are tied on heavy hooks and fished beneath the surface on a dead drift. Some are weighted so they can be fished on the bottom.

Streamers are tied on extra-long hooks and have long hair or feather wings to make them resemble minnows. They are fished beneath the surface with long strips to mimic a darting baitfish.

Popular Trout Flies

Adams (dry)

Royal Coachman (wet)

Hare's Ear (nymph)

Matuka (streamer)

Fishing Dry Flies

Cast the fly upstream, either straight or at an angle. Let it float naturally downstream.

Strip in slack line as the fly drifts toward you, but do not disturb the natural drift.

If a belly develops, mend the line by flipping it upstream. Otherwise, the current causes drag on the fly.

Fishing Streamers & Wet Flies

Hold the fly line under a finger of your rod hand while stripping line with your other hand. Let excess fly line fall to the water. Experiment with different strip lengths to find the right action. Wet flies are usually fished with shorter strips than are streamers.

Fishing Nymphs

Angle your cast upstream and strip in slack to keep the line tight as the fly drifts. Otherwise, you won't feel the strike. If desired, use a strike indicator (inset).

If necessary, add a small split shot to keep your nymph on the bottom. Don't use too much weight, however, or the fly will hang up.

Bait Fishing

With their highly developed sense of smell, trout can easily detect natural bait, even in water too murky for flies or hardware.

Natural bait is also a good choice in early spring, when the water is cold and very few insects are hatching.

Garden worms, nightcrawlers and salmon eggs are the most popular natural baits but, in some areas, anglers rely heavily on minnows, cut bait, leeches, crayfish, grasshoppers, crickets and aquatic insects, both larval and adult.

"Grocery baits," such as corn and marshmallows, prepared baits that mold onto the hook and soft plastics impregnated with scent also work well, particularly for freshly stocked trout.

You can fish natural bait beneath a small float, attach a sinker and still-fish it on the bottom or weight it lightly so it tumbles along the bottom at the same speed as the current. The latter presentation is most realistic and enables you to cover the greatest amount of water.

Popular Baits for Stream Trout

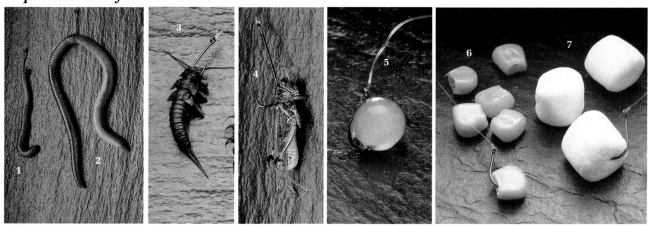

(1) Garden worm, *(2)* nightcrawler, *(3)* mayfly nymph, *(4)* grasshopper, *(5)* single salmon egg, *(6)* kernel of corn, *(7)* marshmallow.

It takes a sturdy jigging rod to land trout like this.

Jigging Rapala

Little Cleo Spoon

icefly tipped
with waxworm

Fat Boy jig tipped
with Eurolarvae

Ice Fishing

Ice fishing for stream trout is much like ice fishing for sunfish and crappies. You can use the same kinds of lures, but you may need a little heavier tackle, because trout fight especially hard in the frigid water.

Mobility is the key to success with most types of ice fishing, and it's no different with stream trout. Anglers drill lots of holes and use jigging techniques that enable them to move about easily. A depth finder is a must, because trout frequently suspend well off the bottom.

Popular jigging baits include swimming minnows and teardrops or small jigging spoons tipped with waxworms, Eurolarvae, scuds or pieces of red worm.

A medium-power graphite jigging rod, about 30 inches long, is ideal for jigging stream trout. Pair it with a small spinning reel that has a smooth drag, and spool up with 4- to 6-pound-test clear monofilament.

LAKE TROUT

Salvelinus namaycush

Lake trout are truly "denizens of the deep." "Lakers," also called gray trout and mackinaw, require very cold water, so they are commonly found in depths of 50 to 100 feet and may be considerably deeper. Their preferred temperature range is 48 to 52°F, lower than that of any other freshwater gamefish.

But lakers are not always found in deep water. In very large lakes, such as Lake Superior, they're commonly caught on the surface, even in summer, because the water temperature is within their comfort zone.

Lake trout may be crossed with brook trout to produce a hybrid called the *splake.* These fish are sometimes stocked in infertile northern lakes.

Lake Trout Facts

Lake trout are found primarily in deep, infertile lakes. Shallow lakes, unless they are located in the Arctic, do not have cold enough water. And fertile lakes, even if they are deep, do not have adequate dissolved oxygen in the depths.

Lakers spawn in the fall, usually at water temperatures in the upper 40s or low 50s. They deposit their eggs on rocky reefs from a few feet to more than 30 feet deep. The eggs fall into crevices in the rocks, where they can incubate safe from predators until they hatch in spring. Lake trout spawn on the same reefs each year.

In most waters, the lake trout's diet consists mainly of fish. They commonly eat cold-water species, such as ciscoes, whitefish, smelt and burbot, but they will take whatever is available. In lakes where forage fish are scarce, lakers feed on plankton, crustaceans and insects. But, in this situation, they rarely grow larger than two or three pounds.

The feeding habits of lake trout are unusual in that they can move up and down considerable distances in the water to find food. A laker in 80 feet of water, for instance, can easily swim up 50 feet to take ciscoes suspended in the thermocline. They compensate for water pressure changes by burping up air through a duct connecting their swim bladder to their esophagus.

Lake trout grow very slowly, but may live as long as 40 years. Typically, it takes about 11 years for a lake trout to reach 5 pounds and, in the Far North, where

Lake trout range.

Key Locations for Lake Trout...

Early Spring:
- Off slow-tapering shorelines and islands
- Ends of gradually sloping rocky points
- Narrows between two basins of the main lake

Narrows make a natural funnel

Summer and Early Fall:
- Sharp-breaking lips of islands and points
- Deep humps
- Deep slots and holes in an otherwise shallow part of the lake

Trout like the steep breaks that cliff walls provide

- Off steep cliff walls

Mid-Fall through Spawning:
- Shallow, flat-topped reefs
- Shallow, rocky points with long extended lips
- Shallow, rocky shelves along shorelines and islands

Winter:
- Same structure that held trout in summer, although the fish may be shallower

the growing season is extremely short, it may take twice that long.

Nevertheless, lake trout reach astonishing sizes. In northern Canada and a few large lakes in the western states, 30- to 40-pound lakers are fairly common and anglers take an occasional giant exceeding 50 pounds. The

biggest lake trout on record was netted in Saskatchewan's Lake Athabasca. It weighed 102 pounds.

The extremely slow growth of the lake trout means that fishing regulations must be quite restrictive to prevent overharvest. Bag limits are generally low and open seasons, relatively short.

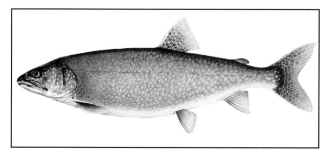

Lake trout have light spots on a greenish to grayish background, and a deeply forked tail. The lower fins have white leading edges.

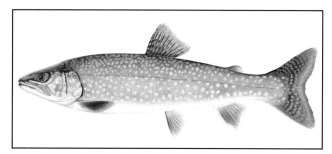

Splake resemble lake trout, but they have the brook trout's worm-like markings on the back, and the tail is not as deeply forked.

Fishing for Lake Trout

Anglers use a wide array of techniques to catch lake trout, depending mainly on depth of the water.

When the fish go deep in summer, you can reach them with downriggers, by deep-trolling with 3-way rigs or by vertical jigging.

When they're shallow, try casting or long-line trolling with spoons or plugs, or still-fishing with dead bait, such as a smelt, cisco or chunk of sucker meat.

Lake trout are usually taken in water that is relatively snag-free, so there is no need for extremely heavy tackle. Lakers, like stream trout, are quite line-shy, and heavy line will reduce the number of strikes you get.

Downriggers give you precise depth control. When you see the fish on your graph, lower the cannonball to keep your bait tracking just above them.

Popular Vertical Jigging & Trolling Baits

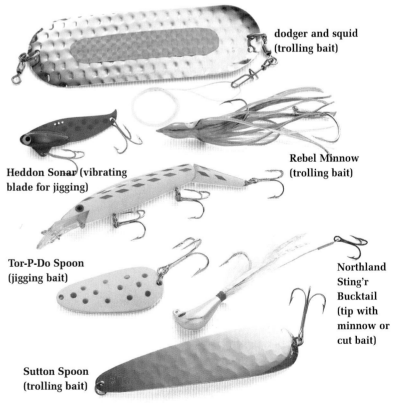

dodger and squid (trolling bait)

Rebel Minnow (trolling bait)

Heddon Sonar (vibrating blade for jigging)

Northland Sting'r Bucktail (tip with minnow or cut bait)

Tor-P-Do Spoon (jigging bait)

Sutton Spoon (trolling bait)

Other Lake Trout Techniques

Vertical jigging with a 1- to 2-ounce lead-head jig or jigging spoon enables you to work deep lake trout schools that you've located with your graph. Lift the lure with long sweeps of the rod, keeping the line taut as the lure sinks.

Trolling with a 3-way-rig (inset) is an excellent big-trout method. The larger the trout, the less susceptible they are to vertical jigging. They would rather lie close to the bottom and grab a lure trolled at their level.

A 3-foot, medium-heavy-power jigging rod and a baitcasting reel spooled with 20-pound-test superline make an ideal outfit for jigging lake trout through the ice.

Ice Fishing

Because of their preference for frigid water, lake trout stay active all winter and are relatively easy to catch by ice fishing. And they're found in pretty much the same areas you would find them in summer.

The two main methods used by ice anglers are jigging and tip-up fishing. Where multiple lines are legal, set out one or more tip-ups baited with live or dead baitfish, and jig with another line. When the fish are active, they'll hit the jig; when they're not, tip-ups usually work better.

Popular Ice-Jigging Lures

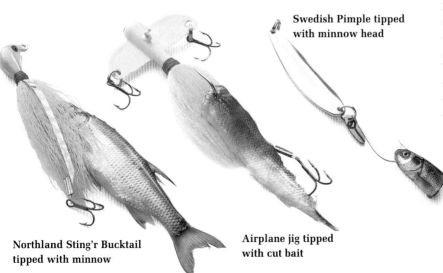

Swedish Pimple tipped with minnow head

Northland Sting'r Bucktail tipped with minnow

Airplane jig tipped with cut bait

SALMON

Thanks to massive stockings of Pacific salmon in the Great Lakes and the prairie reservoirs of the Dakotas, you no longer have to travel to Alaska or the Pacific Northwest to tangle with these world-class fighters.

Because salmon are anadromous fish, they can survive in fresh as well as salt water. When stocked in fresh water, salmon spend most of their lives roaming the vast expanses of inland lakes, just as they as they would roam about at sea. And just as saltwater salmon spawn in coastal streams, freshwater salmon spawn (or attempt to) in streams flowing into the big lakes.

Of the five species of Pacific salmon (chinook, coho, pink, sockeye and chum), the chinook and coho have been stocked most widely in fresh water. Chinooks are also called king salmon and cohos, silver salmon.

Sea-run Atlantic salmon, considered one of the world's premier gamefish, enter streams along the North Atlantic Coast, mainly in Canada. Landlocked Atlantic salmon have been widely stocked, primarily in the New England states.

Salmon Facts.

All salmon are coldwater fish, preferring water temperatures in the low to upper 50s. They go wherever they must to find temperatures in this range, swimming across miles of open water or drastically changing depths as temperatures change because of wind or current.

Small fish make up most of the diet of chinooks and cohos. In the Great Lakes, they feed mainly on alewives; in the Dakota reservoirs, smelt. Atlantics and land-locks feed primarily on insects and crustaceans, although they may eat small fish as well.

All species of salmon spawn in the fall. They ascend tributary streams, often jumping high falls and wiggling their way through shallow riffles until they find a gravelly spawning shoal that suits them. They deposit their eggs in redds in the same manner as stream trout. Spawning in tributaries of

Chinook salmon range.

Coho salmon range.

Chinook salmon (Oncorhynchus tshawytscha) have silvery sides with dark spots on the back. Both lobes of the tail are spotted. The anal fin is considerably longer than it is deep. The teeth are set in black gums.

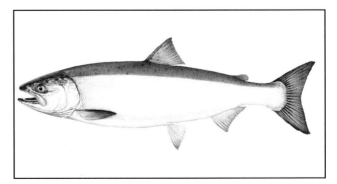

Coho salmon (Oncorhynchus kisutch) have silvery sides with dark spots on the back, but only the upper lobe of the tail is spotted. The anal fin is about as long as it is deep, and the teeth are set in whitish gums.

fixed life cycle, so they continue to feed during their spawning run. They may live as long as 10 years.

The chinook is the largest salmon species. In Alaska, sea-run chinook commonly reach weights of 50 to 60 pounds in 4 years. In the Great Lakes, chinooks over 30 pounds are unusual. Sea-run cohos grow only slightly faster than cohos in the Great lakes. In fact, the world-record coho was taken in a Lake Ontario tributary. Sea-run Atlantic salmon grow much faster than landlocks. A typical sea-run Atlantic reaches a weight of 25 pounds in 6 years; a landlock grows to only 5 pounds in that time.

Atlantic salmon range.

inland lakes is not often successful, although reproduction of chinooks and cohos has been documented in the Great Lakes.

Pacific salmon have a fixed life cycle, meaning that they live a certain number of years, then spawn and die. Chinooks generally spawn at age 4; cohos, age 3. Prior to spawning, the fish change color, usually turning pink, red or olive, and their flesh begins to deteriorate. They do not feed once they begin their spawning run, although they may strike lures out of aggression.

Atlantic salmon do not have a

Sea-run Atlantic salmon (salmo salar) have silvery to yellowish-brown sides with irregular X- or Y-shaped black marks. They often resemble brown trout, but the tail is slightly forked and the adipose fin is unspotted.

Fishing for Salmon

Despite the fact that Pacific salmon are highly aggressive feeders, triggering them to strike may be a challenge, especially as spawning time approaches. By the time they begin to congregate around the mouths of spawning streams, their digestive tract has already started to deteriorate and they are striking mainly out of aggression.

Even before feeding slows, the fish can be highly selective. They're known for their tendency to pick out a particular bait in a certain color, to the exclusion of everything else. Then, a day or two later, they want something completely different.

Salmon are sensitive to sunlight, explaining why they do their heaviest feeding early and late in the day. Most anglers agree that early morning is best; in fact; you'll often catch more fish during the first hour of daylight than you will the rest of the day.

Salmon often feed in shallow water close to shore in the morning but, as the sun rises higher, they usually move to deeper water, sometimes several miles away from shore.

Because salmon are so sensitive to changes in water temperature, open-water anglers pay close attention to the wind. When an offshore wind blows the warm surface water away from shore, and cold water from the depths wells up to replace it, salmon move closer to shore and are often caught by anglers casting from piers and breakwaters. But when the wind blows in, warm water piles up along shore and the salmon move out.

Trolling is, by far, the most productive method for catching Pacific or landlocked-salmon in open water. You can use downriggers and planer boards to spread your lines vertically and horizontally, greatly increasing your area of coverage.

Once fish enter the streams, you can cast for them with spoons and spinners or drift-fish with yarn flies or fresh spawn.

Key Locations for Salmon...

Large numbers of salmon gather around stream mouths prior to spawning

In Lakes
- Edges of deep shoreline shelves
- Deep humps
- Deep edges of long, gradually tapering points
- Stream mouths
- Off steep cliff faces

- Suspended wherever the water temperature is in the mid 50s
- Along surface temperature breaks between warm and cold water
- Around baitfish schools

Great Lakes salmon often congregate in deep water off steep cliffs in summer

In Rivers
- Deep pools
- Deep slots along outside bends
- Shallow riffles (spawning)
- Tails of pools (spawning)

Tails of pools are popular fishing spots

Salmon Fishing Tips

Adjust your transducer by tipping it back slightly (inset) so your graph picks up your cannonballs. Then, you can easily keep your lures tracking just above the fish.

Set downrigger rods with enough tension so they bend into a deep arc. Then, when a fish strikes and the line releases, the rod will stand up straight to signal a strike before the fish removes all the slack.

Downrigger Fishing

Downriggers greatly improve your trolling efficiency. Not only do they enable you to precisely control your depth, they make it possible to spread lines at various levels.

But, most importantly, they allow you to fish in deep water without a heavy weight on your line to take away from the enjoyment of fighting the fish. An 8- to 12-pound cannonball attached to a steel cable takes your line to the desired depth. When a fish strikes, your line releases from the cable and you can fight the fish with no weight to interfere.

To run lines at different levels, simply use several downriggers, or rig a single downrigger with *stackers,* release devices that attach to the downrigger cable. Stackers enable you to run as many as three lines off the same downrigger but, if the release holding your bottom line trips, you'll have to reset all the lines.

A good graph is a big help in downrigger fishing. It will show you how deep the fish are running, so you can set your lines accordingly. And, if the transducer is aimed properly, you can see your cannonballs, so you're sure they're in the fish zone.

Popular Downrigger Baits

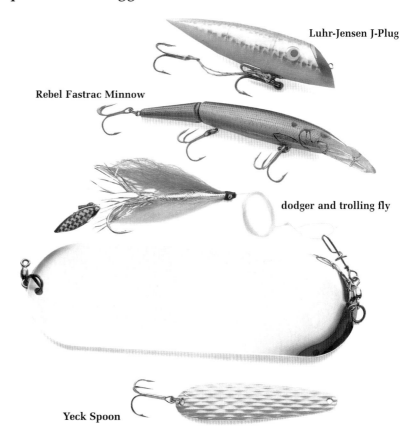

Luhr-Jensen J-Plug

Rebel Fastrac Minnow

dodger and trolling fly

Yeck Spoon

Trolling boards allow you to run your baits far to the side of the boat's wake. Some anglers use two or even three lines spaced along the cord going to each board, so you can thoroughly cover a wide swath of water.

Fishing with "Boards"

When salmon are in shallow water or holding close to the surface, they're likely to spook from the boat when you troll over them. But you can solve the problem by using trolling boards or side planers to spread your lines. Use the same lures as you would in downrigger fishing.

Trolling boards plane up to 75 feet to the side of the boat, meaning that lines can be spread more than 150 feet apart. Your lines attach to the cord with releases much like those used for downrigger fishing. When a fish strikes, you can fight it on a free line.

Side planers (p. 47) do not pull as far to the side as trolling boards. Because they stay on your line while you're landing the fish, they not only detract from the fight, they drag in the water

and increase the chances that you'll lose the fish.

In rough water, trolling boards work better than side planers, because they're less likely to tip over or skip in the waves. Double boards are even more stable than single ones.

How to Use Trolling Boards

After letting out the board, let your fishing line out the desired distance. Clip the line to a release and let it slide down the cord to within a foot or so of the board. Engage the reel to keep the line from sliding farther, and place the rod in a rod holder.

Let out another line and clip it to a release. Let the second release slide halfway down the cord and then stop it by engaging the reel. Set the rod in a rod holder. Repeat the procedure to set a pair of lines on the opposite side of the boat.

Stream Fishing

The sheer numbers of salmon jammed into a stream during the spawning run explain why stream fishing can be outstanding, even when the fish are not feeding.

Nobody really knows why spawning Pacific salmon bite when their digestive tract is deteriorating. Some suspect it's a reflex action; others say they're protecting their territory. Whatever the reason, they'll hit flashy baits, such as spoons and spinners, as well as spawn bags and yarn flies.

Casting with spoons and spinners works best when salmon are scattered over large areas of the stream. Be sure to quarter your casts upstream far enough that the lure gets down to the bottom, because that's where most of the fish are.

When salmon are holding in specific runs or near redds, try drift-fishing with yarn flies or spawn bags. Be sure to use a long rod, at least 8½ feet, so you can keep most of the line out of the water and control the bait in the current. With a rod this long, there is no need to cast; simply work the spot by repeatedly picking up the bait and flicking it back upstream.

Pixie Spoon

Vibrax spinner

spawn bag

yarn fly

Luhr-Jensen Hotshot

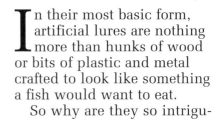

PART II

ARTIFICIAL LURES

INTRODUCTION

In their most basic form, artificial lures are nothing more than hunks of wood or bits of plastic and metal crafted to look like something a fish would want to eat.

So why are they so intriguing?

Artificial Lures explores the major classes of artificial lures available to today's anglers. It highlights the situations where each class or bait performs best.

Expert anglers will appreciate the dozens of tips for making their artificial lures more effective, while beginners will learn where, when and how to use them.

Artificial Lures also helps you select the proper tackle for the baits you use. After all, the right rod can mean the difference between success and failure, as can something as simple as the knot you choose.

Artificial Lures is your personal guide to the many baits gracing your tacklebox.

SUBSURFACE PLUGS

*S*ubsurface
plugs are
among the oldest
of gamefish lures,
and they are just
as effective now
as ever.

SUBSURFACE PLUGS

Webster's Dictionary defines a plug as "an artificial angling lure used primarily for casting and made with one or more sets of gang hooks." Some plugs are designed for surface fishing; others, to run beneath the surface. This chapter deals with the latter.

To be a little more specific, subsurface plugs usually have a wooden or plastic body shaped like a baitfish. But a few models are designed to mimic crayfish, waterdogs or other aquatic fare.

Following are the most popular types of subsurface plugs:
- **Crankbaits** - A crankbait has a plastic or metal lip at the front that gives the lure a side-to-side wiggling or wobbling action and causes it to dive.
- **Minnowbaits** - Similar to a crankbait, a minnowbait also has a front lip, but the body is slimmer for its length.
- **Vibrating Plugs** -These plugs have a thin body with the attachment eye on the back, giving them a tight wiggling action.
- **Trolling Plugs** - These plugs vary greatly in shape, but most have a broad, flat forehead which makes them quite wind-resistant and difficult to cast. Normally fished by trolling, they have an intense wobble.
- **Jerkbaits** - Used primarily for large pike and muskies, these giant plugs have no built-in action. They dart erratically from side to side when retrieved with downward sweeps of the rod.
- **Magnum Bass Plugs** - These huge plugs, usually made of wood, have an extremely wide wobble. Although they were originally designed for giant Florida bass, anglers have found them to be effective for many other kinds of large gamefish.

Plug-Selection Guide

Fish Species	Plug Length
Crappie	1-2 inches
Small trout	1-3 inches
White bass	1$^{1}/_{2}$-3 inches
Smallmouth and spotted bass	2-3 inches
Northern largemouth bass	2-6 inches
Walleye	3-6 inches
Large trout and salmon	3-7 inches
Northern pike, muskie, striper and Florida largemouth bass	4-12 inches

Jerkbait

Magnum bass plug

Vibrating plug

Trolling plug

Crankbait

Minnowbait

CRANKBAITS

The tempting wobble of a crankbait often triggers fish to bite, even when they're not actively feeding. Although crankbaits work best at water temperatures above 55°F, they can be retrieved very slowly to catch fish at much lower temperatures.

Crankbaits are most often used for casting, but they can also be trolled. Because crankbaits are usually retrieved at a relatively fast speed, they're ideal for covering a lot of water in a hurry.

Any kind of gamefish that feeds on baitfish can be caught on a crankbait. Anglers use crankbaits only an inch or two long for species such as crappies, white bass and trout, while 8- to 12-inchers are commonly used for pike, muskies, stripers and big largemouth.

Crankbaits are effective in water of most any clarity. Even in very muddy water, fish can detect a crankbait's wobble using their lateral-line system. Most anglers agree that a crankbait with a tight wiggle works better in low-clarity water than one with a loose wobble. Internal rattles also make it easier for fish to locate the bait.

Because crankbaits have exposed hooks, they are not the best choice for fishing in dense weeds or other heavy cover. But they are not as prone to snagging or fouling as many anglers believe. The lip runs interference for the hooks, deflecting off rocks and logs. And, in some types of weeds, a rapid retrieve will shatter the leaves, so they don't foul the hooks.

You can also minimize snagging or fouling by selecting a crankbait that runs at the proper depth. If the weeds top out at 10 feet, for instance, choose a crankbait that runs at that depth. This way, the bait will occasionally tick the weedtops, but won't dive way into the weeds. A crankbait with a straight lip is less prone to snagging because it runs nose-down, minimizing the chances that the hooks will contact the cover.

In selecting a crankbait, the most important considerations are running depth and action. The way a crankbait performs depends on the following:

• **Lip Design** - The running depth of a crankbait depends primarily on the size, shape and angle of the lip. In general, the larger the lip and the straighter its angle in relation to the plug's

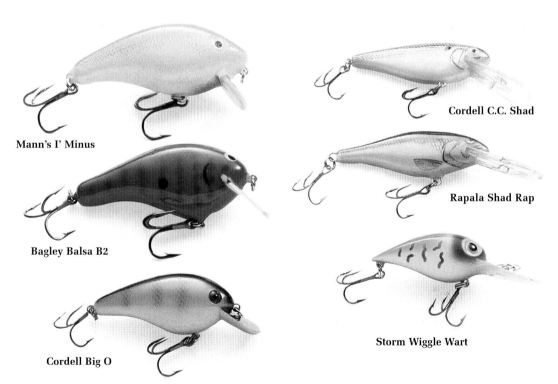

Shallow Runners

Mann's I' Minus

Bagley Balsa B2

Cordell Big O

Medium Runners

Cordell C.C. Shad

Rapala Shad Rap

Storm Wiggle Wart

Shallow runners track at depths of 1 to 7 feet; medium runners, 8 to 15 feet and deep runners, more than 15 feet. Running depth depends mainly on the size and angle of the lip (opposite).

How the Lip Affects Running Depth

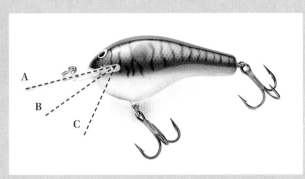

A deep-running crankbait has a lip at an angle of no more than (a) 10 degrees to the plug's horizontal axis; a medium-running crankbait, no more than (b) 30 degrees and a shallow-running crankbait, no less than (c) 60 degrees.

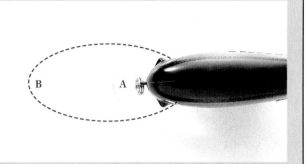

A shallow-running crankbait normally has (a) a shorter, narrower lip than (b) a deep-runner. The lip of a medium runner is intermediate in shape.

horizontal axis, the deeper the plug will dive.

The shape and angle of the lip also affects a crankbait's action. The wider the lip, the more side-to-side wobble. The greater the angle of the lip, the more roll.

Deep Runners

Mann's 20+

Rapala Down Deep Rattlin' Fat Rap

Storm Lightnin' Shad

The position of the plug's attachment eye also affects its action. A plug with an eye close to the nose or on the nose will roll more than one with the eye farther down the lip.

• **Body Material** - The majority of crankbaits have hollow plastic, foamed plastic or wooden bodies, so they float at rest. Hard-plastic crankbaits are the most durable and the best choice for casting. But foamed plastic or wooden ones are lighter and more responsive, so they have more action on a slow retrieve. Balsa crankbaits, though relatively expensive, are the lightest and most responsive of all.

Although most crankbaits float, some have internal lead

weights to make them sink or suspend. A bait that sinks can be counted down to reach fish at any depth; one that suspends can be fished very slowly, yet will not float up like a normal crankbait.

• **Body Shape** - The shape of a crankbait's body affects its action and stability. As a rule, the thinner the body, the tighter and faster the wobble. But a thin-bodied bait does not run as true as one with a fatter body; it is more likely to tip to the side and lose depth as you increase the retrieve speed. It is also harder to keep a thin-bodied bait in tune (p. 171).

Roll (left) vs. wobble (right)

How to Fish Crankbaits

Crankin' has emerged as one of the top tournament fishing methods, and for good reason. No other technique enables you to cover so much water in such a short period of time.

An angler who is not familiar with a body of water can use crankbaits to search out prime fishing areas. When he starts catching fish, he may then switch over to a slower method that allows him to strain the water more thoroughly.

Fishermen also use crankbaits to fish a "milk run" consisting of several key pieces of structure or cover. They make a few casts in one spot, hoping to tempt the active feeders, and then quickly move on to the next. This technique is usually more effective than camping on a good spot, waiting for the fish to turn on.

The main consideration in crankbait fishing is selecting a lure that runs at the right depth. If you're fishing a rock pile that tops off at 15 feet, for instance, you want a crankbait capable of reaching that depth or even a little deeper. That means you may snag up once in a while, but that's better than selecting a lure than runs only 12 feet deep and never gets snagged.

You can determine a crankbait's running depth by referring to a depth chart (opposite), but the surest method is testing it yourself. Experiment by making casts in different water depths until you determine the depth at which the lure just "ticks" bottom.

A crankbait's running depth varies somewhat depending on line diameter, line length and retrieve speed.

The thinner your line, the deeper the lure will run, because there is less water resistance against your line. Some crankbait anglers are switching to superlines, because they have a thinner diameter for their strength.

Crankbait trollers know that they can reach greater depths by letting out more line – up to a point. After that, it makes no difference how much line you let out, the lure will only run so deep. This explains why long casts are so important in crankbait fishing. You must cast well past your target so the lure has time to reach its maximum running depth before it gets to the fish zone.

Many anglers share the mistaken belief that the faster they retrieve, the deeper their crankbait will run. But, in fact, every crankbait has an optimum retrieve speed. If you retrieve slower or faster, the lure will not run as deep. The only way to determine the perfect speed is to experiment.

For a crankbait to reach its maximum depth, it must be properly tuned, meaning that it tracks perfectly straight. If the attachment eye is bent even the slightest bit to one side or the other, the lure will veer to the side and lose depth. You can tune your crankbait by bending the eye as shown on the opposite page.

Veteran crankbait anglers know that an erratic retrieve triggers more strikes than a steady one. They make every effort to retrieve the lure so it periodically bumps the bottom or some type of cover, interrupting its action. When fishing in woody cover, for instance, they intentionally aim their casts so the bait will bump a stump or log as they reel in.

If there is no cover to alter the lure's action, try a stop-and-go retrieve. Reel rapidly, pause for a second and let the bait float up slightly, then reel rapidly again. Strikes often come on the pause.

How fast you retrieve depends not only on the particular lure you're using, but also on water temperature. As a rule, the cooler the water, the slower your retrieve. But you may also want to slow down your retrieve when fish are in a negative mood.

When fish strike a fast-moving crankbait, they normally hook themselves. But if a fish grabs the lure from behind, you may just feel the line go slack or notice a slight change in its action. Whenever you feel anything out of the ordinary, set the hook.

Recommended Tackle

For heavy cover, where lines up to 25-pound test are required, most anglers opt for baitcasting gear. Because lengthy casts are important in crankbait fishing, it pays to use a long rod, $6^1/_2$ to $7^1/_2$ feet, for extra casting leverage. Many anglers prefer a rod with a soft tip, which allows the fish to take the bait farther into its mouth before you set the hook. The reel should have a high gear ratio, at least 5:1, which enables a rapid retrieve.

A spinning outfit with 6- to 12-pound mono is adequate for fishing crankbaits in open water or light cover.

Tips for Fishing Crankbaits

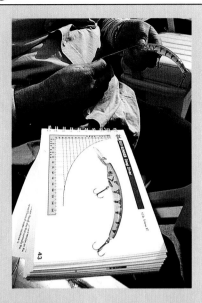

Refer to a depth chart to determine how deep a certain crankbait will run with various amounts of line. Such charts require a correction factor for use with different line diameters.

Bump your crankbait off of rocks, logs or other obstructions; the sudden change of action often triggers a strike.

If the attachment eye has a split ring, tie your line directly to it. Extra hardware adds weight and inhibits the lure's action.

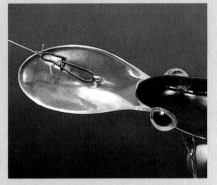

If the lure has a plain wire eye, attach your line with a round-nosed snap. Don't use a sharp-nosed snap or a bulky snap-swivel.

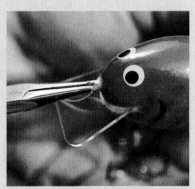

Tune a crankbait by bending the attachment eye in the direction opposite to that in which the lure is tracking. If it's tracking to the left, for example, bend the eye to the right and then test the action.

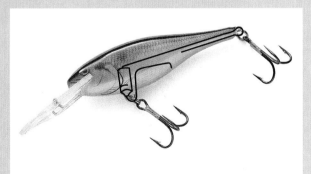

For large, strong-fighting gamefish, select a crankbait with hooks attached to an internal wire. Screw eyes may pull out.

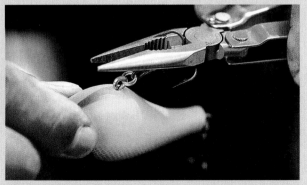

Clip off the leading points on a crankbait's treble hooks when fishing in weedy cover. The remaining points are turned up and much less likely to foul in the vegetation.

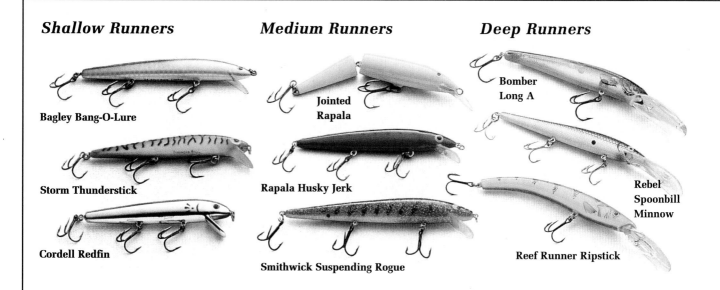

Shallow Runners

Bagley Bang-O-Lure

Storm Thunderstick

Cordell Redfin

Medium Runners

Jointed Rapala

Rapala Husky Jerk

Smithwick Suspending Rogue

Deep Runners

Bomber Long A

Rebel Spoonbill Minnow

Reef Runner Ripstick

MINNOWBAITS

Minnowbaits bear many similarities to crankbaits, but there are some significant differences:

• The body of a minnowbait is longer and slimmer, so it more closely resembles the shape of slim-bodied baitfish, such as shiners.

• The lip is smaller and usually narrower, so the lure has a tight rocking action rather than a wide, side-to-side wobble. This type of action more closely resembles that of a swimming baitfish, but produces much less vibration.

• Because of its smaller lip, a minnowbait generally runs shallower than a crankbait.

• The slimmer body of a minnowbait has less stability, meaning that slower retrieve speeds are normally required.

• Minnowbaits are comparatively light, so they're more difficult to cast than crankbaits.

Like crankbaits, minnowbaits come in shallow-, medium- and deep-running models, although the maximum depths for each of these categories is considerably shallower.

Extra-Deep Runners

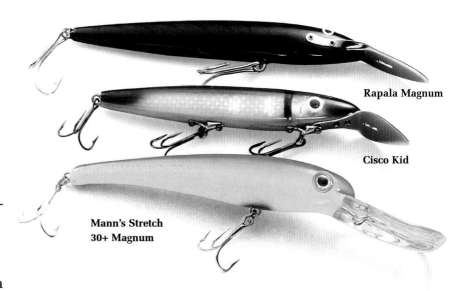

Rapala Magnum

Cisco Kid

Mann's Stretch 30+ Magnum

The first minnowbaits were made of balsa wood, and many still are. But plastic baits are gaining in popularity. Plastic baits are more durable and slightly heavier, so they are somewhat easier to cast. But balsa baits are more responsive and have more action at a slow retrieve speed.

Some "big-game" minnowbaits have thick plastic bodies and metal lips. They can be retrieved faster than ordinary minnowbaits and will stand up to toothy freshwater and saltwater gamefish.

Most minnowbaits float at rest, but some are weighted to sink. Sinking models can be counted down to the desired depth, but they have less rocking action than floaters.

Neutrally-buoyant minnowbaits are rapidly gaining popularity, because you can stop them during the retrieve without them floating up. Negative gamefish that refuse

moving baits may strike these baits on the pause.

The effectiveness of minnowbaits is due, in part, to their realistic look and action. But there's another even more important reason: most predator fish, given a choice, prefer slim-bodied baitfish to those with deep bodies. Slim-bodied forage is easier to swallow and less likely to wedge in the fish's throat.

This explains why many anglers prefer minnowbaits to crankbaits in clear water, where the fish can get a good look at the bait. Minnowbaits are not as effective as crankbaits in discolored water, however, because they produce considerably less vibration.

Minnowbaits are an excellent choice in cool water, because they can be retrieved more slowly and still retain their action. But they do not work as well in weedy or snaggy cover; the smaller lip provides less protection for the hooks.

Shallow-running minnowbaits are one of the top lures for night fishing. They have enough buoyancy to be fished over shallow shoals or weedbeds without fouling, and fish can easily make out the plug's silhouette against the surface.

How to Fish Minnowbaits

Today, floating minnowbaits enjoy tremendous popularity, due mainly to their ultra-realistic action. No other bait so closely mimics a swimming minnow.

But floating minnowbaits can be difficult to cast, particularly when you're bucking the wind. That explains why most anglers use light spinning tackle and try to keep the wind at their back.

Floating minnowbaits are usually fished with a steady, slow- to moderate-speed retrieve. Or you can alternately speed them up and slow them down. But their high buoyancy makes them difficult to fish with a true stop-and-go retrieve, because they float up too far and too fast on the pause.

Another popular method for using a floating minnowbait is long-line trolling in shallow water. Simply let out a lot of line (as much as 200 feet), and pull the lure directly behind the boat. Because of the great distance between the boat and the lure, spooking is not much of a problem. If your lure is not running deep enough, add a split shot or two several feet up the line.

When bass are in the shallows, you can use a floating minnowbait as a topwater. Retrieve it with a twitch-and-pause motion, making it dive a few inches and then hesitating while it floats back to the surface.

For years, savvy fishermen recognized the need for a minnowbait that didn't float up on the pause, so they added lead weights to floating minnowbaits to make them neutrally buoyant. The small cadre of anglers who were familiar with this "secret

> **"At first I couldn't get the tackle industry to take the Rapala seriously. A store owner would pick one up and hand it right back, grumbling that it was too light to cast."**
>
> *Ron Weber, President of Normark Corporation, recalling his early attempts to sell minnowbaits imported from Finland in the late 1950s and early '60s.*

method" made astounding catches of bass, walleye and other gamefish, even under the worst fishing conditions.

But as the secret began to leak out, pre-weighted minnowbaits began to appear on the market. These baits, sometimes referred to as "jerkbaits," should not be confused with the large (sometimes giant) jerkbaits used for pike and muskie (p. 182).

Jerkbaits, as their name suggests, are fished with a jerky, stop-and-go retrieve. But when you stop, the bait hangs in the face of a following gamefish rather than floating up, greatly boosting the odds that the fish will strike.

Sinking minnowbaits are weighted even more heavily than jerkbaits, so they are easy to cast. To fish the lure near the bottom, allow it to sink until the line goes slack, reel it a short distance, and then allow it to sink again. To reach suspended fish, try counting it down to different depths before starting your retrieve. When you get a strike or hook a fish, repeat the same count on the next cast.

Although you can reach fish in deep water with sinking minnowbaits or deep-diving floaters, many experienced anglers prefer to use shallow-running floaters fished with a variety of deep-trolling gear, such as downriggers, Snap-Weights (opposite), lead-core line or three-way rigs. Not only does this gear make it easier to control your depth, shallow-running floaters have an action superior to that of sinkers or deep-divers.

Sinking minnowbaits, because they are heavily weighted, do not have as much of the realistic rocking action of a typical narrow-lipped minnowbait. And deep-diving minnowbaits have an entirely different action; their long, broad lip gives them the wide wobble of a crankbait.

Recommended Tackle

For casting lightweight, shallow-running minnowbaits, use a medium-power spinning rod with a tip soft enough to flex from the lure's weight on the backcast. If your rod is too stiff, you'll have to throw the bait, because the tip won't do the work. Use a long-spool spinning reel filled nearly to the brim with 6- to 8-pound mono; go a little heavier when the fish are in cover.

You can also use spinning gear for casting weighted minnowbaits, but many anglers prefer medium- to medium-heavy-power baitcasting gear with 8- to 12-pound mono. The same baitcasting gear can also be used for trolling, but many fishermen prefer 10- to 20-pound-test superline because it has less water resistance and allows the lures to run deeper.

Tips for Fishing with Minnowbaits

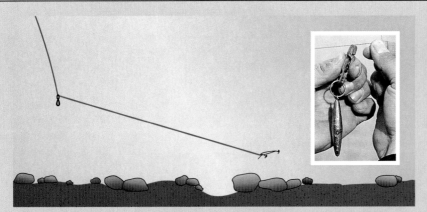

Let out 100 to 150 feet of line, and then attach a Snap-Weight (inset). Continue letting out line until you feel the lure bump bottom, then reel up a few turns. When you hook a fish, reel down to the Snap-Weight and remove it before landing the fish.

Use a floating minnowbait as a surface lure by twitching it sharply, pausing to let it float back up and then twitching it again.

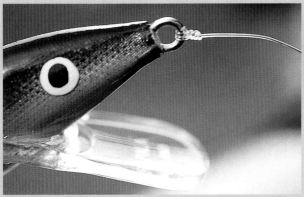

Increase the rolling action of a minnowbait by attaching it with a secure clinch knot, preferably one with a double line around the eye (left), and then pulling the knot slightly below the horizontal axis. Or, you can accomplish the same thing by bending the eye slightly downward (right).

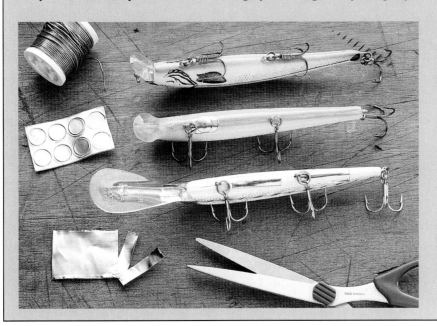

Add weight to a floating minnowbait to make it neutrally buoyant by wrapping the hooks with thin-diameter solder (top) or adding strips of golfer's tape to the lure's belly. The buoyancy of a pre-weighted jerkbait increases in cold water, but you can add enough weight to offset the additional flotation by adding small, adhesive-backed lead weights, such as Storm's SuspenDots (middle) or SuspenStrips (bottom).

VIBRATING PLUGS

Often called "lipless crankbaits," these thin-bodied plugs have a tighter wiggle than ordinary crankbaits and produce higher-frequency vibrations. Gamefish can easily detect these vibrations with their lateral-line systems, even in extremely murky water.

Like crankbaits, vibrating plugs appeal to practically any gamefish that feed on minnows or other baitfish. But because of their deep, thin body shape, they work especially well for species that feed on shad, sunfish or other deep-bodied forage. Vibrating plugs weighing as little as 1/8 ounce are used for crappies and white bass, while models weighing up to 1 1/2 ounces are popular for striped bass, big largemouths and pike.

Because they do not have a lip to make them dive, the majority of vibrating plugs are designed to sink. Some have solid plastic bodies; others, hollow-plastic bodies filled with shot. The shot not only makes the lure sink, it produces a rattling sound.

Vibrating plugs are heavy for their size, so they cast easily. You can count them down to any depth (opposite), and you can even use them as a deep-water jigging bait, allowing them to sink to the bottom then jigging them vertically in the same manner as you would a jigging spoon (p. 264).

Because it has no lip to run interference for the hooks, a vibrating plug is more prone to snagging than a crankbait. But depth control is much easier, so you can avoid snagging or fouling by keeping the lure just above or along the edge of the cover.

For maximum wiggle, always attach a vibrating plug with a loop knot, split-

Recommended Tackle

A light- to medium-power spinning outfit with 6- to 8-pound mono is adequate for vibrating plugs of 1/8 to 1/4 ounce, but for larger ones, you'll need a medium-heavy-power baitcasting outfit, preferably one about 6 1/2 or 7 feet long with a fairly light tip. This way, you can make long casts, yet the light tip prevents you from pulling the lure away too soon when a fish strikes. A high-speed baitcasting reel (gear-ratio of at least 6:1) gives you a wide range of retrieve speeds. It should be spooled with 10- to 17-pound test mono.

ring or small, round-nosed snap, not a heavy snap-swivel.

Vibrating Plugs

Cordell Super Spot

Rapala Rattlin' Rap

Mann's Manniac

Bill Lewis Rat-L-Trap

The Countdown Technique

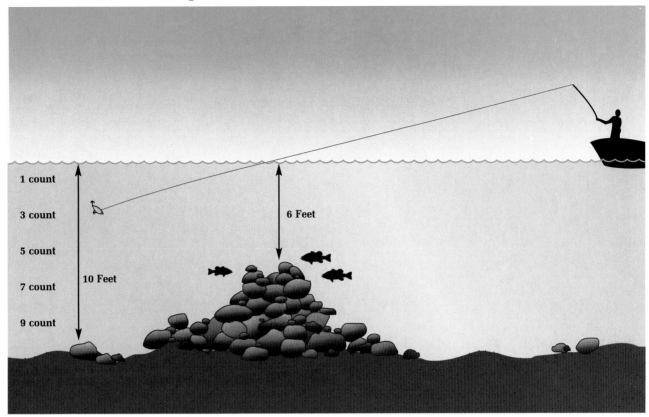

Make a long cast and then count the seconds as the lure sinks on a slack line; if it takes 5 seconds to reach bottom in 10 feet of water, the sink rate is 2 feet per second. You can then use this rate to calculate the depth of subsequent retrieves. To reach these fish on a 6-foot-deep rock pile, for example, let the plug sink for 3 seconds before starting to reel. Retrieve at a moderate speed to keep the lure at the desired depth as long as possible. Too fast, and the lure will run too shallow; too slow, and it will run too deep.

Bill Lewis Super Trap

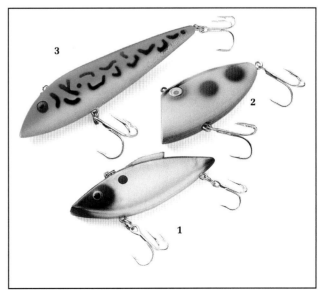

Vibrating plugs have the attachment eye on the back, creating an extremely tight wiggle rather than a loose wobble. Although most models have *(1)* a shad-shaped body, some have a *(2)* sharply sloping forehead or *(3)* a sleeker body.

TROLLING PLUGS

Although you can troll with most any kind of subsurface plug, trolling plugs are intended mainly for that purpose. Most of these lures have a broad forehead, a long snout or a flattened or scooped-out face that gives them a very wide wobble or an erratic action.

Most trolling plugs are made of hollow plastic, so they float. The majority of these lures run at depths of only 5 to 15 feet, but can be trolled much deeper by adding sinkers or using downriggers, diving planers, lead-core line (opposite) or three-way-swivel rigs.

While you can fish these lures by casting, they tend to be wind-resistant or prone to tangling. And many of them are too heavy to cast, unless you use heavy gear.

Trolling plugs work well for fishing expanses of open water or large flats. They're most often used for open-water species such as striped bass, trout and salmon, but they're also effective for walleyes, pike, muskies and bass when they're suspended or holding along a weedline.

For maximum water coverage, many trollers rely on side planers or trolling boards (pp. 180-181). These devices move the lure away from the

(pp. 180-181)

Recommended Tackle

An ordinary medium-heavy power baitcasting outfit with 10- to 20-pound test superline works well for most plug-trolling situations.

For downrigger trolling, use a 7 1/2- to 8 1/2-foot, soft-tipped trolling rod and a high-capacity level-wind reel spooled with 12- to 20-pound test mono.

For lead-line trolling, select a heavy-power trolling rod and a high-capacity trolling reel spooled with 18- to 40-pound-test metered lead-core.

For speed-trolling, use a stiff trolling rod no more than 5 1/2 feet long. A lighter rod would bend too much from the strain of high-speed trolling.

Common Types of Trolling Plugs

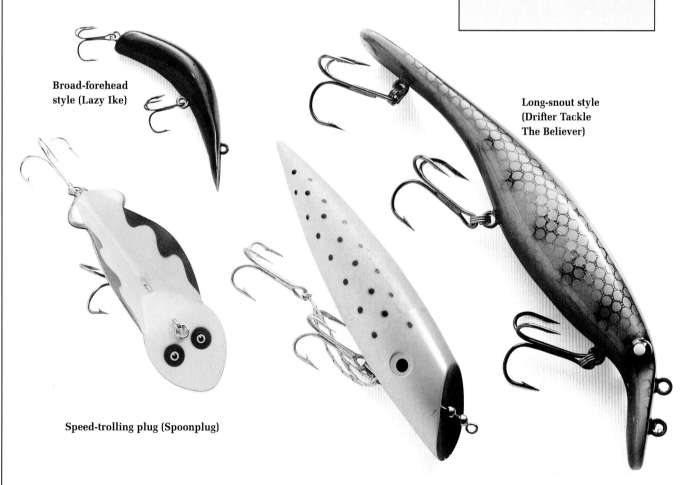

Broad-forehead style (Lazy Ike)

Long-snout style (Drifter Tackle The Believer)

Speed-trolling plug (Spoonplug)

Scooped-out-face style (Luhr Jensen J-Plug)

How to Troll with Lead-Core Line

Tie a barrel swivel to the end of the lead-core, and then attach a 6- to 10-foot, 12- to 20-pound-test mono leader with a round-nosed clip at the end for attaching the plug.

Let out line until you feel the lure bumping bottom, and then reel up a few turns so the lure bumps only occasionally. Let out more line when the water gets deeper; reel in when it gets shallower.

Most lead-core line changes color every 10 yards. When fishing for suspended fish, pay close attention to line color. Then, should you hook a fish, you can easily return to the same color.

Cover more water by placing long (8-foot-plus) trolling rods in horizontal rod holders placed at a right angle to the transom. Other rods can be fished directly out the back.

boat's wake, reducing the spooking factor.

Depending on their design, different trolling plugs run best at different speeds. Some attain good action at speeds of less than 2 mph, while some speed-trolling plugs develop their best action at speeds of 5 to 7 mph. Because plug trollers usually fish with multiple lines, it's important to select lures that are compatible, meaning that they run well at the same speed.

With multiple lines, you can frequently change lures to determine the most productive color, size, action and depth. Then, you can change your lure spread accordingly.

Plug trollers rely heavily on their electronics to help them locate and stay with fish.

Besides a good depth finder, many use water-temperature and trolling-speed indicators. And once they find a school of fish in open water, they punch a waypoint into their GPS unit so they can easily find it again on the next trolling pass.

Let out cord until the board has planed out the desired distance, usually about 50 feet. The elevated mast prevents the cord from dragging in the water; otherwise the board would not plane properly.

Let the plug out the desired distance (at least 100 feet in clear water) and then attach your line to a sliding release.

Continue to let out line until the release is within a foot or so of the board, then engage your reel to hold it there. Place your rod in a rod holder.

Let out a second line and attach it to a sliding release. Let it slide about halfway down the cord, then engage the reel and place the rod in a rod holder.

Let out the board on the opposite side of the boat and repeat the procedure. With boards out both sides of the boat, you can cover a swath of water more than 100 feet wide. When a fish strikes, it trips the release, so you can fight the fish on a free line.

Fishing with Side Planers

Let your plug out the desired distance (10 to 100 feet, depending on the depth you want to fish and water clarity), and then attach your line to a side planer.

Feed line as the planer takes your lure to the side of the boat's wake. Engage your reel when you feel the planer is far enough out and place the rod in a rod holder.

Let out additional planers on both sides of the boat to cover the desired amount of water.

When a fish strikes, reel in line until a partner can detach the planer; then you can land the fish on a free line.

Tips for Fishing with Trolling Plugs

Rig your planer board to release automatically and slide down your line when a fish strikes by threading your line through a snap, as shown. Be sure to add a large barrel swivel to keep it from sliding all the way to the lure.

Use a line-counter reel when fishing with trolling plugs. This way, you can easily monitor the amount of line that is out and, should you hook a fish, easily return to the same depth. With an ordinary level-wind, count the number of passes of the level-wind guide to keep track of line length.

JERKBAITS

Large predator fish are constantly on the lookout for an easy meal, so they're quick to home in on a smaller fish that is swimming erratically. Jerkbaits take advantage of this behavior, mimicking an injured fish by diving beneath the surface and then floating up or darting wildly from side to side.

These large, wooden plugs fall into two categories: divers and gliders. Divers swoop downward when pulled forward; gliders veer to the side. Jerkbaits have no action of their own; the way they move in the water depends on how the angler works them.

Although jerkbaits are used mainly for big pike and muskies, it's not unusual for a good-sized walleye or bass to grab the bait. You can catch fish on jerkbaits throughout the open water season but, when the water temperature dips below 60°F, a glider is a better choice than a diver. Retrieve it more slowly than you would in warm water.

Because jerkbaits move so much water, they produce sounds and vibrations that are easy for gamefish to detect, even in low-clarity water or under low-light conditions. With their open hooks, they are not a good choice for fishing in dense weeds, but they can be worked over weed tops or threaded through slots in the vegetation. A diver works better than a glider for fishing slots, because it has very little lateral movement.

Jerkbaits are not a good choice in water more than 10 feet deep. Few jerkbaits run deeper than 8 feet and, if you add heavy sinkers, they won't have the proper action. Some anglers, however, add internal weights for a little extra depth or to make the bait neutrally buoyant (p. 185).

The Ultimate Guide To Freshwater Fishing

Popular Divers

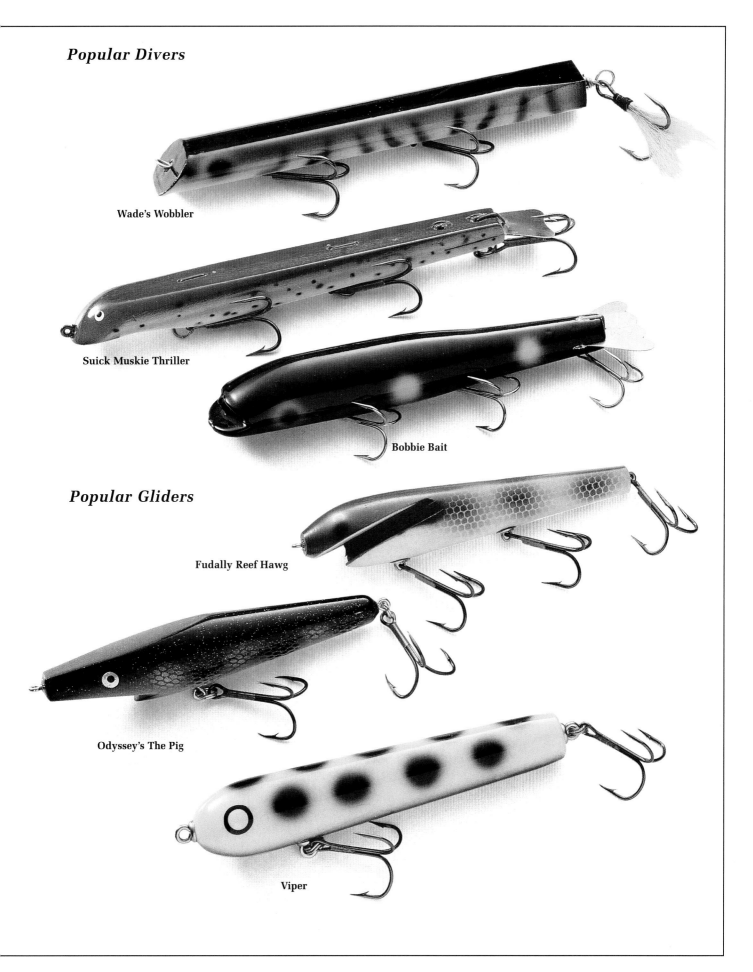

Wade's Wobbler

Suick Muskie Thriller

Bobbie Bait

Popular Gliders

Fudally Reef Hawg

Odyssey's The Pig

Viper

Jerkbait Fishing

Serious pike and muskie anglers rank jerkbaits near the top of their list of favorite lures. The injured-minnow action draws strikes even when the fish are not actively feeding.

Jerkbaits are almost always fished by casting and retrieving with downward sweeps of the rod. Divers are normally retrieved with longer sweeps of the rod than gliders (below), but it pays to experiment with different sweep lengths and durations between sweeps until you discover what the fish want on a particular day.

But trolling with jerkbaits also works well. Motor slowly along a distinct weed edge or over a weedy flat while making a series of sideways sweeps of the rod.

Because the majority of jerkbaits run very shallow, normally at depths of 2 to 4 feet, many experienced anglers add weight to make them run deeper. Weighting is most commonly done with divers; not only does it increase their running depth, it makes them float up more slowly. This way, you can reduce the length of your sweeps and the duration between them without losing depth.

To weight a jerkbait, wrap solder around the hooks, add golfer's tape to the belly or implant lead sinkers into the wood and seal them in with epoxy.

One of the biggest problems in jerkbait fishing is setting the hook. Fish may have trouble zeroing in on the erratically moving bait and,

How to Retrieve Jerkbaits

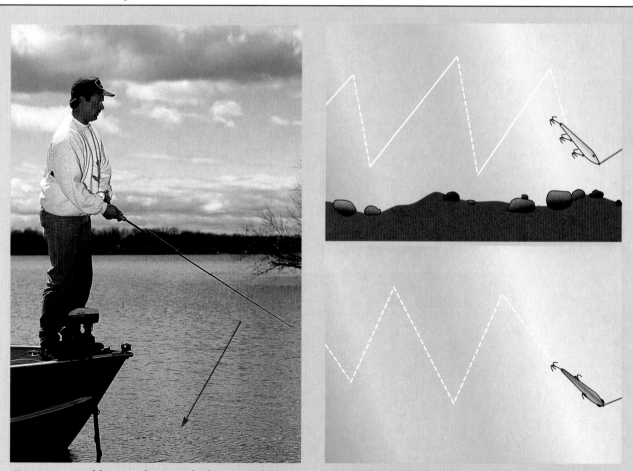

Retrieve a jerkbait with smooth downward sweeps of the rod. To fish a diver, start by pointing your rod at the bait and make a long sweep, stopping the rod at 5 or 6 o'clock. Reel up slack and return the rod to its original position as the bait floats up and then give it another downward sweep. This imparts an erratic up-and-down motion to the lure (upper right). To fish a glider, start by pointing your rod at the bait and make a shorter sweep, stopping the rod at about 4 o'clock. Reel up slack before the lure finishes its glide and then make another downward sweep to make the lure change direction. This gives the lure an enticing side-to-side motion (lower right).

even when they do hit, there could be slack in your line if you're between sweeps.

Adding to the difficulty is the fact that a big pike or muskie often sinks its teeth into the wood when it grabs a jerkbait, so you can't move the lure enough to sink the hooks.

Because jerkbaiting requires a stiff, powerful rod, you must play the fish carefully. If you attempt to horse it in, there's a good chance that you'll tear out the hooks. Keep your drag tight on the hookset, but loosen it a little for playing the fish.

Most jerkbaits have three large trebles, so it's not uncommon for a fish to become so entangled in the hooks that it can't be released in good condition. This explains why many anglers carry a pair of sidecutters. Then, should a fish become badly hooked, they can simply cut off the barbs and release the fish unharmed.

Recommended Tackle

Casting and retrieving these heavy lures requires a stiff, powerful baitcasting rod no more than 6 1/2 feet long. A longer rod would slap the water on the downward sweep. A rod with an extra-long handle gives you more leverage for casting these big baits and making powerful hooksets. Use a sturdy baitcasting reel with a smooth drag and spool up with 30- to 50-pound test Dacron or superline. For pike or muskie fishing, be sure to add a heavy solid-wire or braided-wire leader.

Jerkbaiting Tips

Weight a diver so it floats level, with its back just breaking the surface. A bait weighted this way will run several feet deeper than it otherwise would.

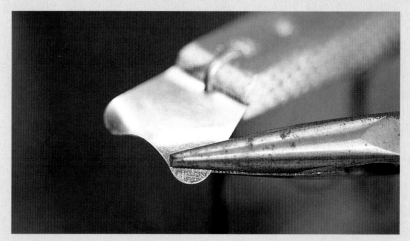

Some divers have metal tails that can be bent slightly downward to make them dive deeper.

A wire leader inhibits the action of a glider, but you can improve the side-to-side movement by adding a split ring between the clip and the attachment eye.

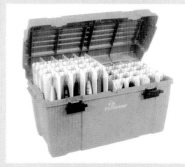

Carry your jerkbaits in a specially designed tackle box, such as a Flambeau Maximizer, that protects the hooks. Some anglers use a styrofoam cooler, but this leaves the hooks exposed.

MAGNUM BASS PLUGS

These lures defy classification, but they all have one thing in common: they're big. Most measure at least 10 inches in length and some are as long as 15.

Many of these lures were designed by California anglers who were trying to find lures big enough to tempt giant Florida bass, which are known to be fond of stocked rainbow trout. But the lures have found many applications for other large gamefish species, including striped bass, muskies and lake trout.

The majority of these lures are made of wood. Some have a flexible rubber tail, which gives them a realistic swimming action. Not surprisingly, the most popular color is rainbow trout, although they come in other colors as well.

One reason these baits attract big fish is that their wide wobble results in a low-frequency vibration, which replicates that produced by a good-sized baitfish. This means that gamefish can easily identify the bait as a desirable food item from a distance, even in water where it's not possible to see it.

Magnum bass plugs can be fished by casting or trolling. Because of their large size, it takes a fairly rapid retrieve to generate the best action, although some anglers fish them slowly on the surface.

Like crankbaits, these lures work best when allowed to periodically bump logs, rocks or other cover, or tick the bottom to interrupt the action.

Although magnum bass plugs are proven big-fish baits, don't plan on finding a large selection at your local tackle shop. Many of these

lures are produced by hand by local anglers and sell for more than $50 each. Some major manufacturers, however, have started to mass-produce baits of this type.

Recommended Tackle

Magnum bass plugs may weigh more than a quarter-pound, so it takes a long, stiff rod to cast them. Many anglers prefer a 7 1/2-foot, heavy-power, fast-action flippin' stick, but some favor a 7-foot muskie rod or a light surfcasting rod. Because these lures pull so hard, they're easiest to fish with a baitcasting reel that has a gear ratio no greater than 5:1. It should be spooled with 20- to 30-pound-test mono.

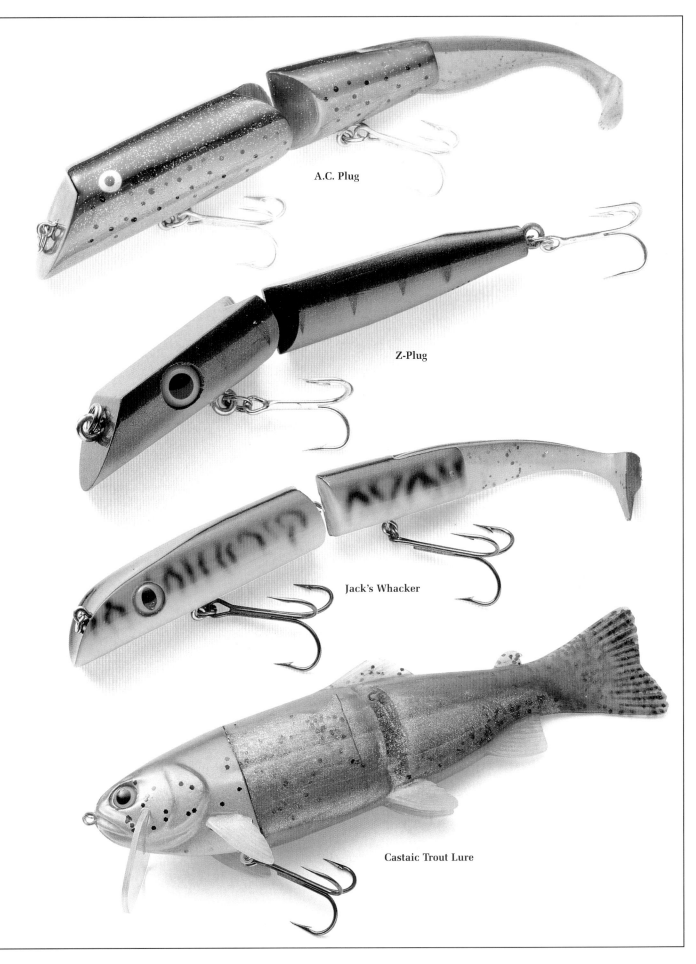

A.C. Plug

Z-Plug

Jack's Whacker

Castaic Trout Lure

TOPWATER LURES

*N*othing in freshwater fishing matches the thrill of a topwater strike. But there's another reason for the popularity of topwater lures: They catch lots of fish.

189

TOPWATER LURES

It's easy to understand why so many anglers get hooked on topwater fishing. No other form of angling is as visual — you actually see the fish take the lure.

Some topwater lures imitate injured minnows; others, frogs, rats, mice or even large insects. But what the lure looks like is much less important to the fish than its action and the sound it produces. Most topwaters make a gurgling, spluttering, chugging or popping sound, but some barely disturb the surface, making no sound at all.

Although surface feeding fish will take most any kind of lure that floats, the following types of lures are intended solely for topwater fishing:

The Ultimate Guide To Freshwater Fishing

- **Stickbaits** - These long, thin plugs are weighted in the tail, so they "walk" from side to side when retrieved with a series of twitches.
- **Propbaits** - These plugs resemble stickbaits, but they have propellers at one or both ends and are not weighted in the tail. They have a sputtering action when fished with a twitch-and-pause retrieve.
- **Chuggers** - With their flattened or dished face, these plugs make a popping sound and throw water when given a sharp twitch.
- **Crawlers** - A wide face plate or arms give these plugs a crawling action that produces a gurgling sound.
- **Frogs & Rats** - Made of soft rubber or plastic, these lures usually have weedless hooks, so they work well in heavy vegetation. Some have legs that produce a kicking action while others barely make a ripple.
- **Buzzbaits** - A large blade throws water when the lure is reeled steadily across the surface. If you stop reeling, the lure sinks.

Topwater Selection Guide

Fish Species	Lure Length
Smallmouth and spotted bass	2-4 inches
Northern largemouth bass	2-6 inches
Florida largemouth bass	4 -8 inches
Northern pike, muskie and striper	6-12 inches

Frog

Buzzbait

Rat

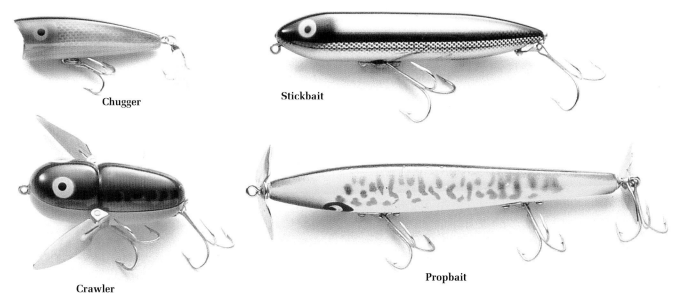

Chugger

Stickbait

Crawler

Propbait

BUZZBAITS

A buzzbait is an excellent "locator" lure; you can cast it a long way and retrieve it rapidly to draw strikes that reveal the whereabouts of gamefish. Once you've located the fish, you can switch to a slower presentation to put more of them in the boat.

Buzzbaits will catch most any surface-feeding gamefish, but they're most popular with largemouth bass anglers. And giant buzzbaits have recently started to gain favor among pike and muskie addicts.

With its large, double- or triple-winged *buzzblade*, a buzzbait creates more surface disturbance than most other topwaters. The blade turns on a straight-wire or safety-pin shaft, producing an intense gurgling action that attracts fish even in murky water. Some buzzbaits have a pair of counter-rotating blades that create even more commotion.

A buzzbait with a safety-pin shaft is the best choice for fishing in weedy or brushy cover. The shaft, like that of a spinnerbait, runs interference for the upturned hook, preventing it from fouling or hanging up.

Some in-line buzzers have a treble hook instead of a single. They work well in snag-free cover, because they give you a better hooking percentage.

Like other topwaters, buzzbaits should be tied directly to your line, unless you're fishing pike or muskies. A heavy leader or clip will

Recommended Tackle

A fast-action, 7 1/2-foot flippin' stick is a good choice for buzzbait fishing, because it enables you to make long casts and keep your rod tip high at the start of the retrieve. You'll need a high-speed baitcasting reel (gear ratio of at least 6:1) for rapid retrieves. Spool up with 17- to 20-pound-test mono.

sink the nose, preventing the blade from spinning.

In-Line Buzzers

Safety-Pin Buzzers

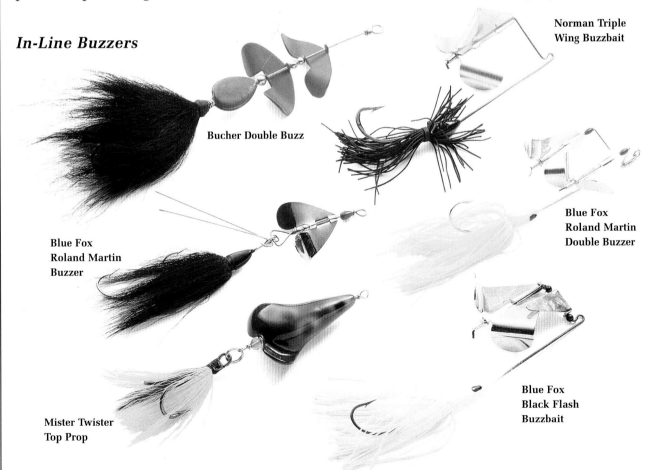

Norman Triple Wing Buzzbait

Bucher Double Buzz

Blue Fox Roland Martin Buzzer

Blue Fox Roland Martin Double Buzzer

Mister Twister Top Prop

Blue Fox Black Flash Buzzbait

How to Retrieve a Buzzbait

Make a long cast and start your retrieve with your rod tip high. This keeps the bait riding high in the water so the blade can spin freely.

Gradually lower the rod tip as the bait approaches the boat. Keeping the rod tip high would pull the bait out of the water so the blade wouldn't spin.

Four Buzzbaiting Tips

Add a "clacker" blade for extra attraction. Remove the buzzblade, slide some beads and a clevis with a small Colorado blade onto the upper arm and then replace the buzzblade. When the buzzblade turns, it will clack against the Colorado blade.

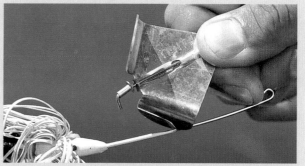

Bend the shaft slightly so the blade barely ticks the arm as it spins. The extra noise often makes a big difference.

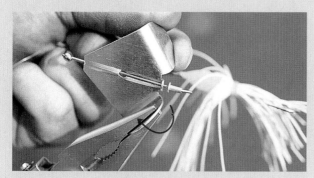

Buzzbaits do not work well when retrieved slowly, because the blade won't spin. But you can solve the problem by cupping the blades, as shown, to make them catch more water. The more you cup the blades, the slower you can retrieve.

Drill several holes in each wing of a buzzblade, causing it to leave a trail of bubbles when you retrieve. The bubbles make it easier for fish to track the bait.

CRAWLERS

Of all the topwaters, crawlers are the easiest to fish because all you have to do is cast them out and reel them in. And, because they can be retrieved quite rapidly, crawlers are excellent "locator" lures.

Crawlers produce an enticing gurgle that draws the attention of any surface feeding gamefish. This sound, along with the predictable action, explains why crawlers are so effective for night fishing. While fish may have trouble zeroing in on a lure moving erratically, they have no trouble tracking one with a steady action.

Some of these lures get their crawling action from a broad, cupped face plate; others, from arms at the sides of the body. Models with arms usually have a more-intense action than those with face plates.

Because of their open hooks, crawlers are not a good choice for fishing in weedy cover. Face-plate models work well in sparse weeds, but models with arms tend to collect sprigs of vegetation.

The only variable in fishing a crawler is the speed of the retrieve. Every model has a certain speed at which it works best. If your retrieve is too fast, the lure will skitter across the water with practically no action. If it's too slow, the lure won't wobble enough or produce the gurgling sound.

Although a steady retrieve will normally draw the most strikes, there are times when the fish prefer a stop-and-go or twitch-and-pause retrieve.

Tie a crawler directly to your line or attach it with a small clip. A crawler's balance is not as critical as that of most other topwaters, but try to avoid weighting down the nose with a heavy leader or snap-swivel.

Recommended Tackle

Long casts are important in crawler fishing, so you'll want a fairly long rod. A 7- to 7 1/2-foot, medium-heavy-power baitcaster with an extra-long handle for two-handed casting is ideal. Pair this with a high-speed baitcasting reel spooled with 12- to 17-pound-test monofilament.

How to use a Crawler as a "Locator" Lure

Fancast a large, weedy flat using a crawler (left). Retrieve at a fairly rapid rate and note the exact location of any boils or short strikes (right). Try another cast or two with the crawler and then, if the fish doesn't strike, switch to a "slower" subsurface lure, such as a jig or plastic worm, and thoroughly work the area where you saw the boil. The slower presentation will often trigger a strike.

Popular Crawlers

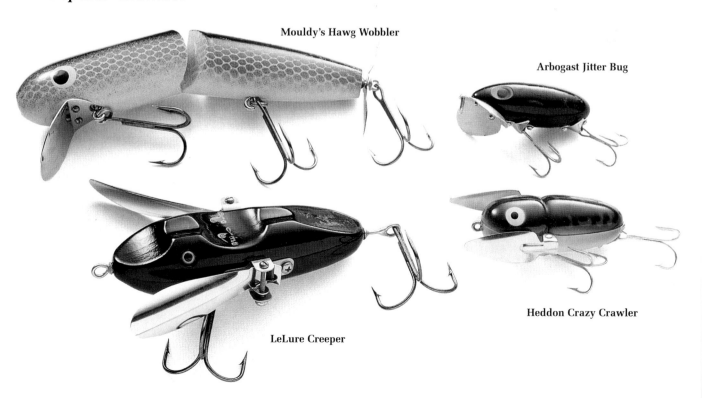

Mouldy's Hawg Wobbler

Arbogast Jitter Bug

LeLure Creeper

Heddon Crazy Crawler

STICKBAITS

When retrieved properly, a stickbait has an erratic, side-to-side action that gamefish evidently mistake for a crippled minnow. In clear water, it's not uncommon for a stickbait to "call up" fish from depths of 20 feet.

Stickbaits are known as big-fish lures. For decades, they have been popular for largemouth, smallmouth and spotted bass, but anglers are now discovering that larger models work equally well for northern pike, muskies and striped bass.

Most stickbaits are made of hollow plastic and have an internal lead weight near the tail, so they float with their head up. This allows for the free lateral head

movement necessary for the side-to-side retrieve called "walking the dog" (below).

The key to getting the right action from a stickbait is learning to throw slack into the line after each downward stroke of the rod. If you keep the line taut, the lure will not scoot to the side as far as it should and you will not get a sharp enough twitch on the next stroke.

Stickbaits don't throw a lot of water and their action is less intense than that of most other topwaters, so they work best in water that is relatively clear and calm. They're ideal for calling fish up out of submerged weed beds, but they're not a good choice for fishing in emergent vegetation, because

their lateral action causes them to hang up on the stems.

Recommended Tackle

Use a fast-action baitcasting rod no more than 6 1/2 feet long for walking the dog. A longer rod will slap the water on the downward stroke, and a rod with a soft tip will not give you the sharp twitches necessary to make the lure change direction. Ten- to 14-pound mono is adequate for most stickbait fishing but, for pike, muskies and stripers, use 17- to 20-pound mono.

Walking the Dog

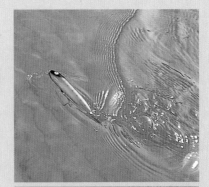
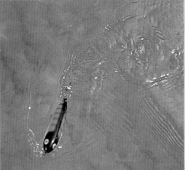

Retrieve a stickbait by pointing your rod directly at the lure, giving it a sharp downward stroke and then stopping it at 5 or 6 o'clock (left). Immediately after completing the downward stroke, lift your rod to throw slack into the line. This way, the lure will dart sharply to the side (upper right). After the lure completes its sideways glide, give it another sharp jerk and throw slack into the line to make it dart the opposite way (lower right).

Popular Stickbaits

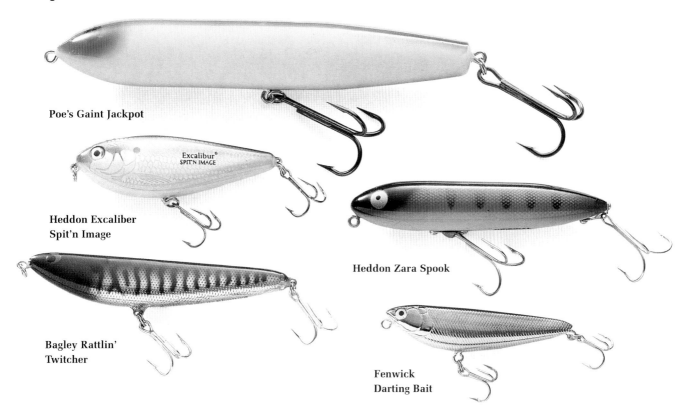

Poe's Gaint Jackpot

Heddon Excaliber Spit'n Image

Bagley Rattlin' Twitcher

Heddon Zara Spook

Fenwick Darting Bait

The lateral action also makes it difficult for fish to home in on the bait, so you'll experience a fair number of missed strikes. But you can improve your hooking percentage by pausing until you feel the weight of the fish before setting the hook.

Unless you're fishing for pike or muskies, tie your stickbait directly to your line. Heavy snaps or leaders inhibit the side-to-side action.

Tips for Fishing with Stickbaits

If your stickbait has "old-style" hook hangers (left), replace them with screw eyes and split rings (right). This way, the hooks can move more freely, making it more difficult for fish to throw the lure.

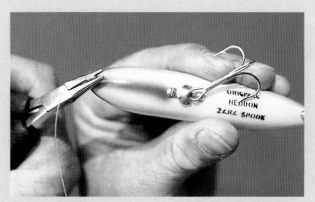

To make your lure veer to one side, bend the attachment eye to the opposite side. This makes it possible to work the bait under a dock or other overhead cover.

PROPBAITS

Gamefish can't help but notice the sputtering action of a propbait, even in choppy or discolored water. While some propbaits have small blades that throw only a little water, others have huge blades that churn the water violently.

The majority of propbaits have propellers at both ends, but some have blades at one end or the other. In a number of large propbaits, the blade is affixed to the head or tail, so that entire part of the body spins. This creates more surface disturbance than a propeller alone.

Propbaits resemble stickbaits and are used for the same species of gamefish, but they are retrieved somewhat differently. Because most propbaits have no tail weight, they do not work well for a walk-the-dog retrieve. Instead, they are normally fished with a straight twitch-and-pause retrieve. Vary the length of your twitches and the duration of your pauses until you find the combination that works best for the conditions.

Accomplished propbait fishermen know how to work the lure very slowly so the blades throw water without the lure moving ahead too much. The secret is twitching it sharply on a slack line.

There are times, however, when a steady retrieve may work better. When the fish are active, they may grab a steadily moving bait to prevent it from getting away.

Like stickbaits, propbaits should be tied directly to the line. A heavy leader or snap weights down the nose, preventing the front propeller from throwing water. For pike or muskie fishing, attach a short wire leader to prevent bite-offs.

Twin-Blade Propbaits

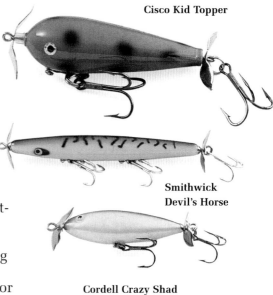

Cisco Kid Topper

Smithwick Devil's Horse

Cordell Crazy Shad

Recommended Tackle

A medium-heavy power, fast-action baitcasting rod from 6 1/2 to 7 feet in length is ideal for propbait fishing. For pike or muskie fishing, or for propbaits with a front propeller, use 17- to 20-pound mono; lighter line is too limp and may catch on the blade. Twelve- to 14-pound mono is usually adequate for lures with only a rear propeller.

Tips for Using Propbaits

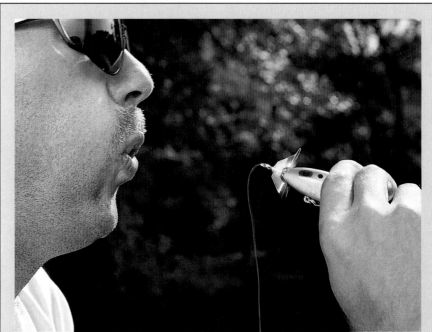

Blow on the propellers to make sure they spin easily. If they do not, try bending the blades backward or forward or twisting them to change their pitch.

Single-Blade Propbaits

Head- or Tail-Spinning Propbaits

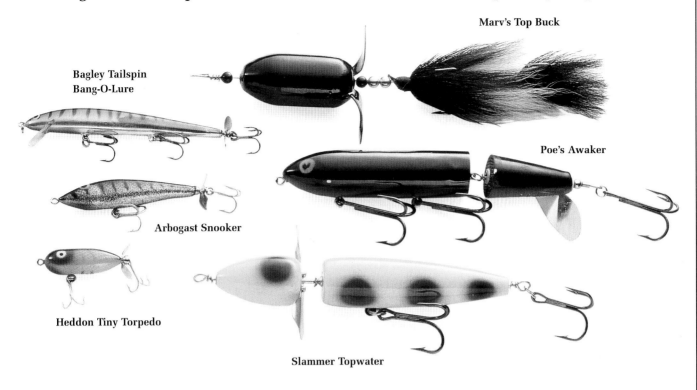

Marv's Top Buck

Bagley Tailspin
Bang-O-Lure

Poe's Awaker

Arbogast Snooker

Heddon Tiny Torpedo

Slammer Topwater

Bend the propeller blades forward, as shown, to catch finicky gamefish. Bending the blades this way reduces the distance the bait moves forward when you twitch it.

Be alert for a bulge just behind your propbait; it's the back of a fish that is following the lure. Resist the tendency to slow down. Instead, reel faster to entice the fish to strike.

FROGS & RATS

Topwater frogs are among the earliest of artificial lures. And the fact that they've survived so long is no accident; they're one of the most effective baits for drawing bass out of dense, weedy cover.

Topwater rats resemble frogs, but they do not have legs. Although they are not as popular as frogs, they are no less effective.

These lures are hard to beat for working large expanses of matted weeds, such as beds of lily pads with a mixture of other weeds and moss. They also work well in matted-out hydrilla or milfoil. Most other surface lures would foul in this type of cover, but a frog or rat will slide right over the top.

Frogs and rats are made of foam rubber or hollow plastic. Some are extremely lifelike; others bear only a vague resemblance to the real

thing. Many frogs come with pliable legs that have a kicking action when retrieved with a twitching motion.

Practically all topwater frogs and rats have upturned hooks or some type of weed-guard, so they can be worked through the heaviest surface vegetation. Some have no built-in hooks and are designed to be Texas-rigged on an ordinary worm hook.

Popular Frogs & Rats

Snag Proof Moss Mouse

Mann's Skirted Frog

Snag Proof Tournament Frog

Recommended Tackle

Because they are normally fished in heavy cover, frogs and rats require heavy tackle. A 7 1/2-foot flippin' stick and a baitcasting reel spooled with 20- to 30-pound abrasion-resistant mono or superline makes an ideal setup. The fish are usually buried in dense weeds, so they don't notice the heavy line.

How to Retrieve Frogs & Rats

Make a long cast over a bed of matted vegetation and keep your rod tip high while drawing the frog into an open pocket.

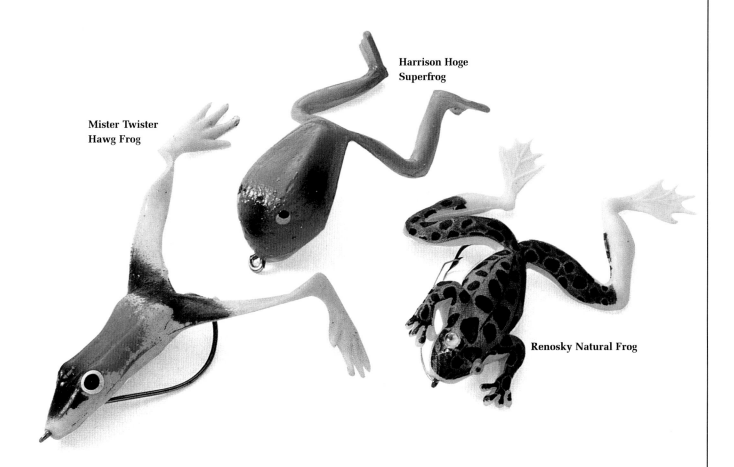

Mister Twister Hawg Frog

Harrison Hoge Superfrog

Renosky Natural Frog

Because of their pliable bodies, frogs and rats feel like real food. So when a bass grabs the lure, it's not likely to let go. This gives the angler a little longer to set the hook than if he were using a hard bait.

Frogs and rats are primarily hot-weather baits, because that's when bass seek out matted surface weeds, which keep the water below a few degrees cooler than the surrounding water.

When the bait reaches an open pocket, hesitate for a few seconds until all the ripples subside. Then, continue reeling until it reaches another pocket.

Cut a slit in a frog or rat and insert a rattle for extra casting weight.

Topwater Lures

CHUGGERS

Also called poppers, these lures have a concave, grooved or flattened face that makes a popping or chugging sound and throws water when the lure is given a sharp twitch.

Chuggers most closely imitate a kicking frog, so it's not surprising that they work so well for largemouth, small-mouth and spotted bass. Noisy chuggers up to a foot long are highly effective for stripers tearing into schools of shad on the surface, and small chuggers are proven white bass producers. Although a chugger will occasionally take a pike or muskie, it usually doesn't work as well as a stickbait or propbait.

A chugger can be retrieved with a series of nonstop twitches, with twitches followed by short pauses or with twitches followed by pauses long enough to allow all the ripples to subside.

Nonstop twitches enable you to cover a lot of water in a short time and are most appealing to active fish. Long

How to Retrieve a Chugger

To retrieve a chugger with a series of nonstop twitches, make a cast and then start twitching your rod while holding it at a 45-degree angle to prevent the line from sinking. As the lure approaches the boat, keep twitching while gradually lowering the rod. If you kept the rod high, you'd lift the face of the bait too much so it wouldn't throw water.

To fish a pocket in the weeds, twitch the lure and then wait for the ripples to die before twitching it again. Some anglers pause for up to a minute after the twitch.

Give the lure an explosive twitch when fishing for pack-feeding stripers or white bass. These fish are extremely aggressive feeders and the intense action gets their attention.

The Ultimate Guide To Freshwater Fishing

pauses are ideal for working pockets in the cover. When the lure reaches a likely-looking opening, give it a sharp twitch and wait several seconds for the ripples to die; that's when the fish usually strike.

Let the fish dictate how hard you twitch your popper. Sometimes they prefer subtle twitches that barely disturb the water; other times, they favor sharper jerks. Only rarely will you catch fish by jerking so hard that the lure makes a loud splash; that

much commotion usually spooks the fish.

Always attach a chugger by tying it directly to your line; if you weight down the nose

with a heavy snap or clip, the face of the lure will catch too much water when you twitch, ruining the action.

Popular Chuggers

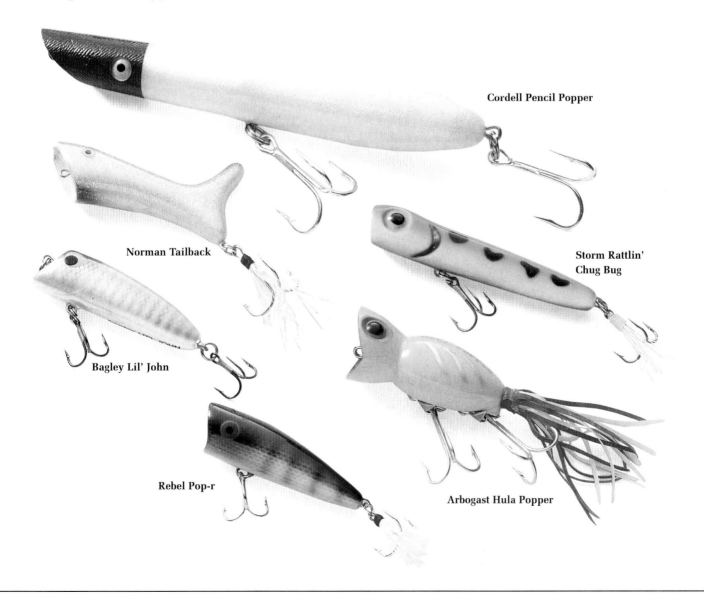

Cordell Pencil Popper

Norman Tailback

Storm Rattlin' Chug Bug

Bagley Lil' John

Rebel Pop-r

Arbogast Hula Popper

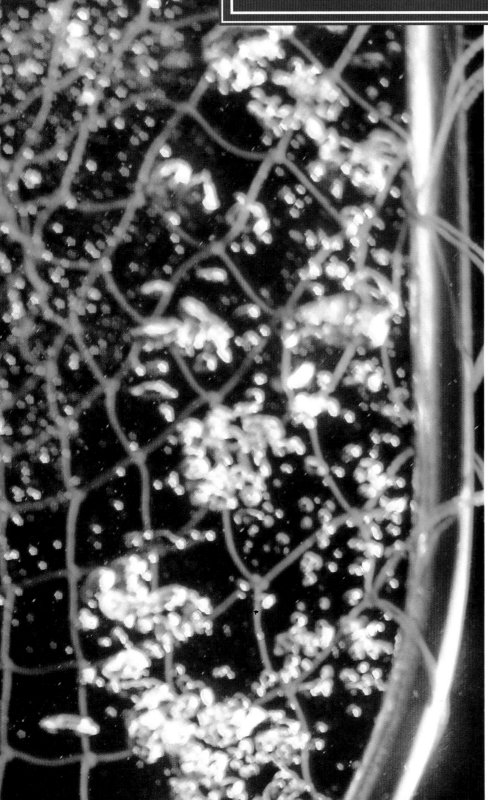

SPINNERS & SPINNERBAITS

Spinners and spinnerbaits offer a combination of flash and vibration that appeals to practically every type of gamefish that swims in fresh water.

SPINNERS & SPINNERBAITS

Spinners are one of the few lures that enjoy *worldwide* popularity, and it's easy to understand why. The spinning blade produces intense vibrations that are easily detected by a fish's lateral-line system, and the vivid flash adds a visual stimulus.

As a result, spinners work well in clear or discolored water.

Practically any kind of freshwater gamefish will strike a spinner. And the lures are equally effective in warm or cool water. The spinning blades provide plen-

ty of lift, so you can retrieve very slowly when frigid water slows fish activity.

Another reason for the popularity of spinners: they're very easy to use. They work well with a straight retrieve and, when a fish strikes, it usually hooks itself.

There are two basic types of spinners: in-line spinners and spinnerbaits. The blade of an in-line spinner rotates around a straight-wire shaft with a hook at the rear. A spinnerbait has a safety-pin-style shaft with the spinner blade(s) attached to the upper arm and a weighted head and single hook on the lower arm.

One of the main considerations in selecting a spinner is the blade shape. Colorado, Indiana and willow-leaf blades make up the majority of the market, although there are many other types with slightly different shapes. Each of these blade types varies in the amount of lift it generates and the amount of vibration it produces.

Anglers should also pay close attention to blade size. Blades come in sizes 00 (the smallest) to 7 (the largest). Small blades rotate faster, so they produce high-frequency vibrations that gamefish identify as the rapid tail movement of a small baitfish. Larger blades have a lower frequency and simulate the slower movement of a larger baitfish.

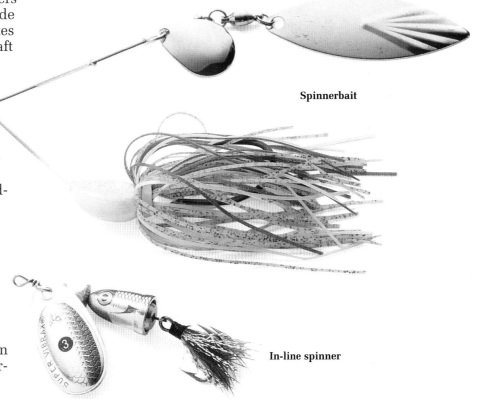

Spinnerbait

In-line spinner

Blade-Size Guide

Fish Species	Blade Size
Crappie, sunfish, perch, small trout	00 to 1
White bass	0 to 2
Smallmouth and spotted bass	1 to 3
Northern largemouth bass, walleye	2 to 4
Large trout and salmon	3 to 6
Northern pike, muskie, striper and Florida largemouth bass	4 to 7

Blade Styles & Sizes

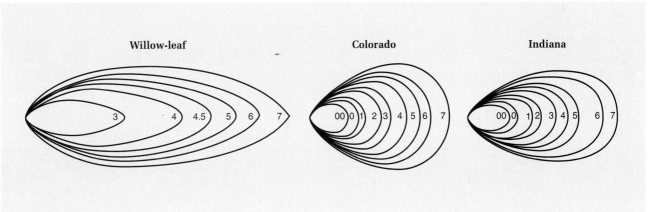

Willow-leaf   Colorado   Indiana

In-Line Spinners

Ask a seasoned trout angler to name the best "hardware" for stream trout and he's likely to say the in-line spinner. Ask a veteran muskie fisherman to divulge his favorite artificial and you'll probably get the same answer. Not only are in-line spinners effective on a wide variety of gamefish, they rank among the top-rated lures for many of them.

Here are the main types of in-line spinners:
- "French" spinners, which are small to medium in size and usually have a sparse hook dressing or no dressing at all.
- Bucktails, which are large spinners used mainly for pike and muskies. They have bushy deer-hair or synthetic-fiber tails that give the bait an attractive billowing action.
- Weight-forward spinners, which are the only type that has the weight in front of the blade.
- Sonic spinners, which have a blade that is concave on one end and convex on the other, so the blade turns very easily and will spin at a very slow retrieve speed.

In the other types of in-line spinners, the blade rotates around the shaft on a clevis, which is a small metal or plastic attachment device. But in sonic spinners, the shaft fits through a hole in the blade; there is no clevis.

In-line spinners are used mainly in water that is relatively free of obstructions. They are not a good choice in heavy cover. If you try retrieving them through dense vegetation, weed fragments will foul the open hooks and stop the blade from turning.

If tied directly to your line, in-line spinners will cause excessive line twist. Be sure to attach these lures with a snap-swivel, preferably the ball-bearing type.

On the pages that follow, we'll explain how to use each type of in-line spinner and offer some tips for making these lures more effective.

Types of In-Line Spinners

Bucktail (Blue Fox Musky Buck)

Weight-forward (Erie Dearie)

French (Mepps Aglia)

Sonic (Panther Martin)

French & Sonic Spinners

These spinners are a natural for stream fishing, because even slowly moving water causes the small blade to spin. This means that you can "hang" the lure in the current, letting it flutter in the face of fish holding behind a boulder or other cover. And by changing your rod position, you can present the bait to various fish lies without having to cast.

In lakes, these lures can be fished over rocky points, gravelly shoals, weed tops or other shallow cover. Or they can be counted down to fish weed edges, humps or other deeper structure.

French and sonic spinners are normally fished with a slow, steady retrieve. The trick is reeling just fast enough to make the blades turn. But some anglers prefer to fish these baits with a lift-and-drop retrieve, much like you would fish a jig.

When you're fishing in discolored water, a French spinner is usually a better choice than a sonic spinner, because the blade vibrations are more intense. These strong vibra-tions also mean that fish can detect a French spinner from a greater distance.

A sonic spinner is a top stream-trout lure.

Popular French & Sonic Spinners

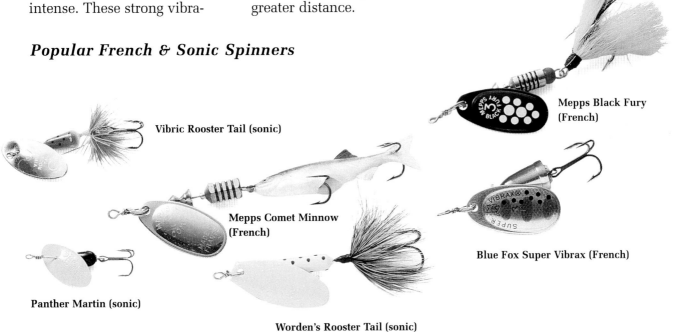

Vibric Rooster Tail (sonic)

Mepps Black Fury (French)

Mepps Comet Minnow (French)

Blue Fox Super Vibrax (French)

Panther Martin (sonic)

Worden's Rooster Tail (sonic)

Weight-Forward Spinners

Weight-forward spinners differ from other types of in-line spinners in that the positioning of the weight causes the blade to turn while the lure is sinking headfirst. As a result, these lures are ideal for catching suspended fish using the "countdown technique."

The method is simple. Just make a long cast and count while the lure is sinking. Start your retrieve on different counts until you determine the best depth, and then continue counting down to that level.

Most weight-forward spinners are weighted quite heavily, so they can be cast long distances. This explains their popularity with big-water anglers who need to cover a lot of water to find the fish. Weight-forward spinners are also a good choice for fishing in fast current because they hold their depth so well.

Weight-forward spinners are usually tipped with a

Big walleyes find it hard to resist a weight-forward spinner and a crawler.

Popular Weight-Forward Spinners

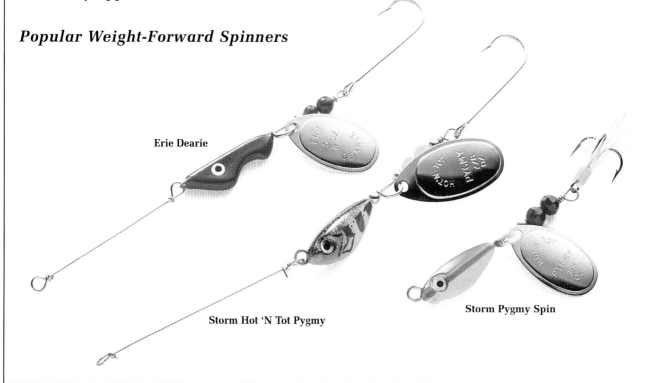

Erie Dearie

Storm Hot 'N Tot Pygmy

Storm Pygmy Spin

nightcrawler, minnow or some other type of live bait. They can also be tipped with pork rind or a soft-plastic grub. Most models come with a single hook that rides with the point up to minimize snagging and fouling.

Unlike other types of in-line spinners, weight-forward spinners aren't likely to twist your line. In most models, the weight acts as a keel, preventing the lure from spinning. Consequently, there is no need to use a snap-swivel; just tie your line directly to the lure.

Recommended Tackle

A medium- to medium-heavy-power, long-handled baitcasting rod from 6¹/₂ to 7 feet in length works well for distance casting with weight-forward spinners. For maximum casting distance, use a wide-spool baitcasting reel spooled with 8- to 12-pound-test monofilament.

How to Fish a Weight-Forward Spinner

Tip a weight-forward spinner by hooking a crawler several times, so only about an inch of the tail is trailing. Hook a minnow by pushing the hook through the mouth, out the gill and into the back.

Lob cast with a sidearm motion to avoid tearing off the bait and to prevent the hook from catching the line. Because the lure sails headfirst, the hook tangles easily, especially if you snap-cast.

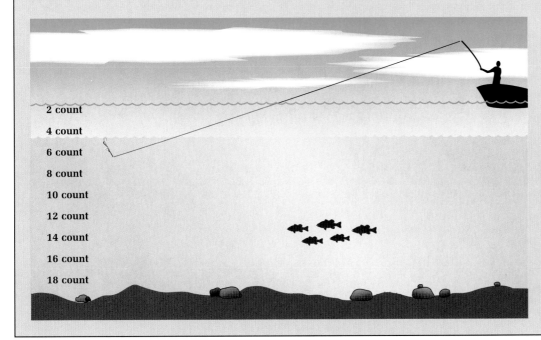

2 count
4 count
6 count
8 count
10 count
12 count
14 count
16 count
18 count

Count the lure down to different depths to locate the fish, and then stick with that count. Here, the angler failed to catch fish on counts of 6, 8 and 10. He began catching them on a count of 12 and found the most fish at a count of 14.

Bucktails

Big pike and muskies find it hard to resist the "breathing" action of a bucktail spinner. As the bait tracks through the water, the rippling hair creates an ultrarealistic look.

At water temperatures of 60°F or below, try a 4- or 5-inch bucktail; above 60, use a 6- to 12-incher. Small bucktails usually come with a single dressed treble hook, but larger ones usually have two in-line trebles.

Bucktails can be used in sparse weeds but, because of their open hooks, do not work well in heavy vegetation. There, a spinnerbait (p. 214) would be much better choice.

How deep a bucktail runs depends on the amount of dressing, the bait's weight and the type of blade. For maximum depth, select a heavily weighted, sparsely dressed bait with a willow-leaf blade.

Recommended Tackle

A typical "bucktail" rod is about 7 1/2 feet long with a fast action and a long handle for extra casting leverage. The long rod not only makes casting easier, it helps you guide the lure through slots in the weeds and "bulge" it on the surface. The rod should be paired with a sturdy baitcasting reel spooled with 30- to 50-pound-test Dacron or superline. Bucktails are usually fished on a solid-wire leader.

Popular Bucktail Spinners

Blue Fox Musky Buck

Buchertail

Mepps Giant Killer

Windel's Harasser

Bend the shaft of an in-line spinner, as shown, to eliminate line twist.

Angle your casts upstream when fishing a spinner in current. If you cast cross-stream or downstream, the current will create too much water resistance and cause the lure to break water.

Trim the hair on a bucktail to reduce the bait's buoyancy. This way, the bait will stay deep, even when you're "burning" it (reeling rapidly) to draw strikes.

Hang a spinner in the current and move your rod tip to fish boulders, logs and other visible cover without moving your feet.

Figure-eight a bucktail when you see a muskie or pike following it. With a foot of line out, plunge your rod tip as deep as you can and pull the bait in a large, slow figure-eight pattern. Make sure your reel is in free-spool and your thumb is on the spool. That way, you can easily feed line should a fish strike.

SPINNERBAITS

The spinnerbait is arguably the most versatile of all artificial lures. You can run it through dense weeds, bulge it on the surface, slow-roll it over brushy cover, helicopter it down a steep break or jig it along the bottom. No other lure lends itself to so many retrieves and such a variety of cover types.

Although spinnerbaits are known mainly as bass lures, they're also used for catching pike, muskies, pickerel, crappies, sunfish and even walleyes.

The design of a spinnerbait is nothing less than ingenious. The safety-pin shaft runs interference for the blade and upturned hook, and the weighted, bullet-shaped head provides stability, so the lure won't tip or twist.

Hundreds of models are available, but there are just three basic styles: the single-spin, the tandem-spin and the twin-spin (right).

Besides the blade configuration, here are some other considerations in selecting spinnerbaits:

- **Length of Upper Arm** - Most spinnerbaits are designed so the blade rides directly above the hook point. That way, when a fish strikes at the blade, it usually gets hooked. But a spinnerbait with a shorter-than-normal upper arm works better for helicopter-ing and, because it produces intense vibrations, is a good choice for fishing at night or in muddy water. However, the arm should not be so short that it doesn't protect the hook.

- **Shaft Thickness** - For the best action, your spinnerbait should have a thin-wire shaft that transmits the blade vibrations to the skirt, giving it a shimmering, lifelike appearance. And a thin-wire shaft bends inward when a fish strikes, upping your hooking percentage. But the constant bending fatigues most thin-wire shafts, causing them to weaken and eventually break. Titanium shafts solve the problem. They transmit vibrations extremely well, and can be bent repeatedly without weakening.

- **Type of Skirt** - Most spinnerbait skirts are made of live-rubber or silicone. Silicone skirts are a good choice in clear water; the clear or translucent material has a lifelike look. Rubber

A titanium shaft is virtually unbreakable.

skirts work better in murky water, because they produce more vibration.

You can also buy spinnerbaits with hair, feather, vinyl, tinsel or mylar skirts. Some skirts are made of a combination of these materials.

Some spinnerbaits, called spin-rigs, have no skirt at all. They're intended to be tipped with live bait or a pork trailer.

- **Blade style** - Like other types of spinners, spinnerbaits are made with Colorado, willow-leaf and

Popular Trailers

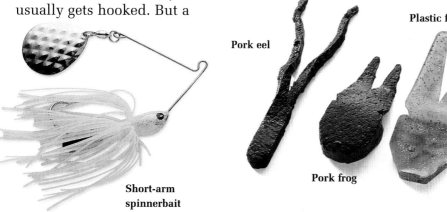
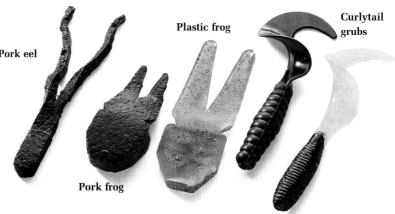

Pork eel

Pork frog

Plastic frog

Curlytail grubs

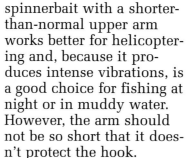

Short-arm spinnerbait

Indiana blades, with the first two being the most common. Colorado blades provide the most lift and vibration and are best for helicoptering. Willow-leaf blades have much less lift and vibration, but produce a lot of flash. Many tandem-spins have a large willow-leaf blade and a small Colorado.

For extra attraction, many anglers tip their spinner-baits with some type of trailer. A bulky trailer also gives the lure more buoyancy, so you can easily keep it above the weed tops.

The single-spin has a single spinner blade attached to the upper arm. Single spins produce a strong beat and work well for helicoptering (p. 218).

The twin-spin has a pair of upper arms, each with a single blade. The twin arms give the hook extra protection, so these lures are a good choice in heavy cover.

The tandem-spin has two blades on the upper arm that provide extra "lift." All other things being equal, a tandem-spin will run shallower than a single spin at the same retrieve speed.

Popular Tandem-Spins

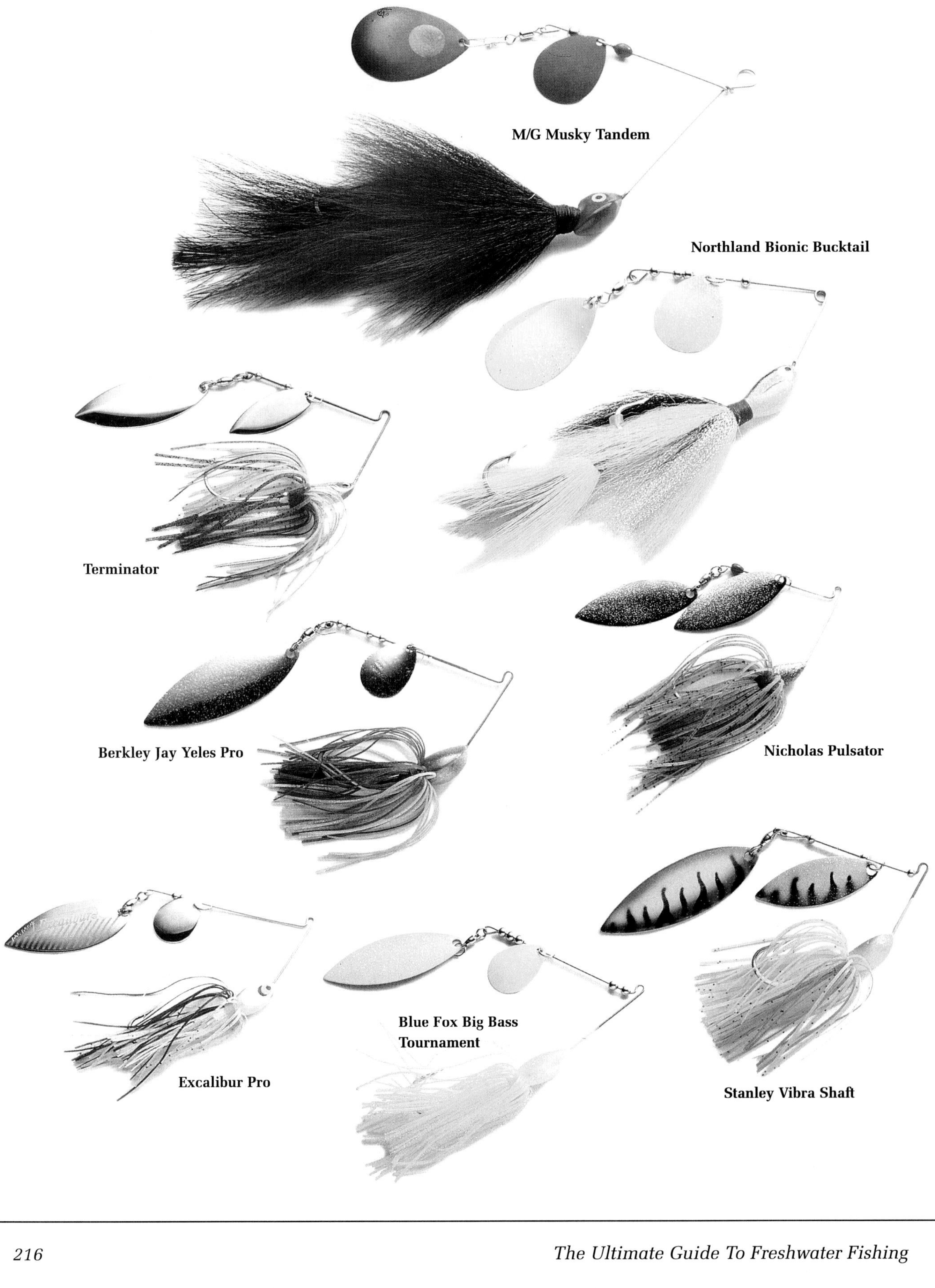

M/G Musky Tandem

Northland Bionic Bucktail

Terminator

Berkley Jay Yeles Pro

Nicholas Pulsator

Excalibur Pro

Blue Fox Big Bass
Tournament

Stanley Vibra Shaft

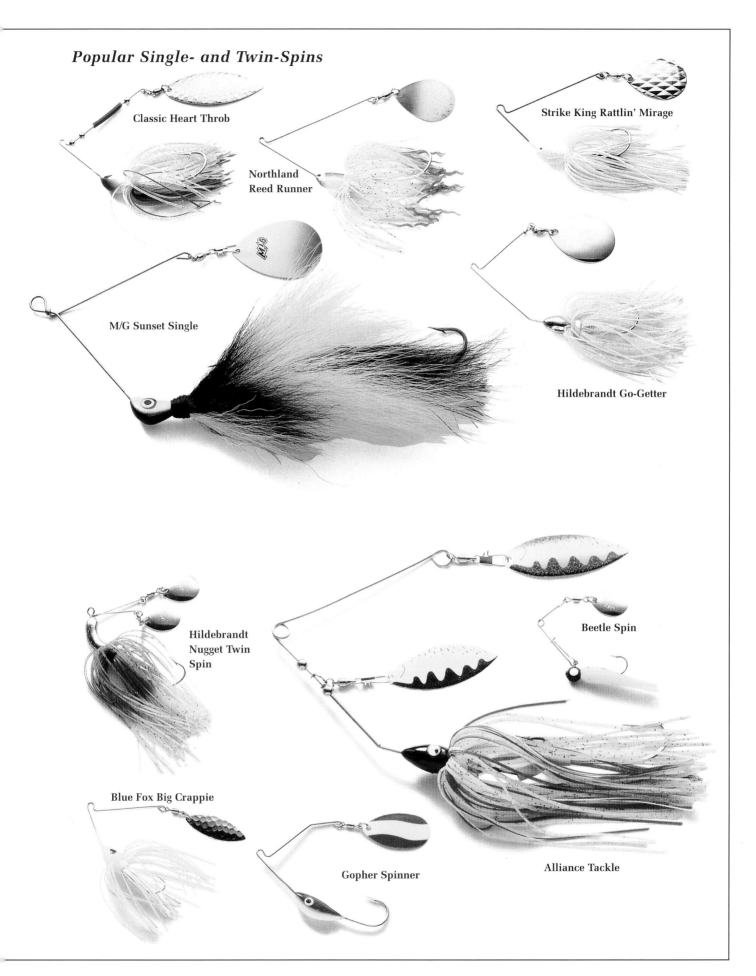

Popular Single- and Twin-Spins

Classic Heart Throb

Northland Reed Runner

Strike King Rattlin' Mirage

M/G Sunset Single

Hildebrandt Go-Getter

Hildebrandt Nugget Twin Spin

Beetle Spin

Blue Fox Big Crappie

Gopher Spinner

Alliance Tackle

How to Fish Spinnerbaits

All you have to do to catch fish on a spinnerbait is toss it out and reel it in. But spinnerbait specialists know that fine-tuning your presentation to suit the conditions will produce a lot more fish.

The first step is selecting a spinnerbait of the proper size. For crappies and sunfish, you'll want a $\frac{1}{32}$- to $\frac{1}{8}$-ounce spinnerbait; for smallmouth and spotted bass, $\frac{1}{8}$ to $\frac{3}{8}$ ounce; for largemouth bass and small to medium northern pike, $\frac{1}{4}$ to 1 ounce; for walleye, $\frac{1}{8}$ to $\frac{1}{2}$ ounce (spin-rig) and for large northern pike and muskies, up to 3 ounces.

The retrieves shown on these pages will catch fish in the majority of situations, but there will be times when you'll have to improvise by combining several retrieves. After letting your lure helicopter down a flooded tree, for instance, you may want to slow-roll it over an adjacent brush pile. Or, you may want to bulge the bait across a weed flat, bump it against an isolated stump on the flat and then helicopter it down a break at the edge of the weeds.

The speed of your retrieve can make a big difference. In most cases, you'll want to reel just fast enough to keep the blades turning, but there will be times when "burning" the bait works much better.

Sometimes spinnerbait strikes are aggressive, but other times, all you'll feel is a slight hesitation in the beat of the blade. Whenever you feel anything out of the ordinary, set the hook.

Always tie your spinnerbait directly to your line, unless you're fishing for pike or muskies. Then, you'll need a braided-wire leader. Many spinnerbaits have an open eye that will not accommodate a snap or swivel. Even if they would, the extra hardware increases the chances of the lure fouling when you cast.

Helicopter a spinnerbait by casting it to vertical cover, such as a rock cliff, flooded tree or breakwall, and then feeding line as the lure slowly sinks with the blade spinning. Keep enough tension on your line so you can feel a pick-up, but not so much that you pull the lure away from the cover.

Recommended Tackle

A 6- to 6$\frac{1}{2}$-foot medium-power baitcasting outfit is adequate for the majority of spinnerbait fishing. The reel should be spooled with 14- to 20-pound-test mono. For big pike or muskies, use a 7$\frac{1}{2}$-foot bucktail rod (p. 52) and a sturdy baitcaster filled with 30- to 50-pound-test Dacron or superline. For crappies and sunfish, use a light- to medium-power spinning outfit with 4- to 6-pound-test mono.

Popular Spinnerbait Retrieves

Slow-roll a spinnerbait over brushy cover, reeling just fast enough to make the blades turn. Allow the blades to bump the brush. Slow-rolling also works well for fishing distinct structure such as a rocky hump, or for crawling over a flat bottom.

A stop-and-go retrieve will usually draw more strikes than a steady retrieve. When you stop reeling, the blade beat changes and the lure flutters downward like an injured baitfish. Some days, long pauses work best; other days, the fish prefer just a short hesitation. You'll have to experiment to find the right tempo.

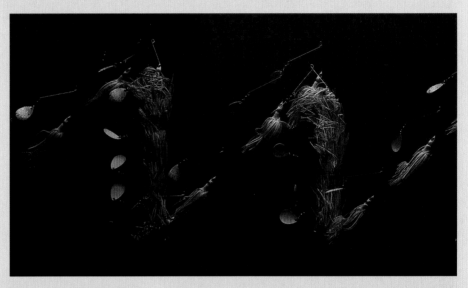

Bulge the surface with a spinnerbait in the same manner as you would a bucktail. With a spinnerbait, however, you may want to reel fast enough to make the blades break the surface.

Try reeling a little faster so the blades break the surface. At times, the fish prefer this to a bulging retrieve (left).

Bump your spinnerbait into a stump, stick-up or other type of cover to interrupt the blade's beat and make the lure hesitate. This erratic presentation will draw far more strikes than a steady retrieve.

Tune a spinnerbait by bending the upper shaft so it is perfectly aligned with the lower. If the shaft is canted, the lure will tip to one side.

Add a "stinger hook" to a soft-plastic trailer by threading a long-shank hook into a grub, as shown. Then, push the main hook through the grub and the eye of the stinger.

Shorten the upper arm of a spinnerbait to make it helicopter better. First, cut off a portion of the arm (left) so the blade, when reattached, will ride in front of the hook point. Then, reattach the blade by using needlenose pliers to make a new loop at the end of the arm, as shown (right).

To make a spinnerbait helicopter more slowly, replace the Colorado blade with one a size or two larger. Or, if the lure has an Indiana or willow-leaf blade, replace it with a Colorado.

Tip a spinnerbait with a piece of crawler or other live bait for extra attraction. Use a sidearm lobcast to prevent the bait from tearing off.

Add weight to the hook of your spinnerbait to make the lure run deeper. You can wrap thin-diameter solder around the hook (top) or pinch a sinker onto the hook (bottom).

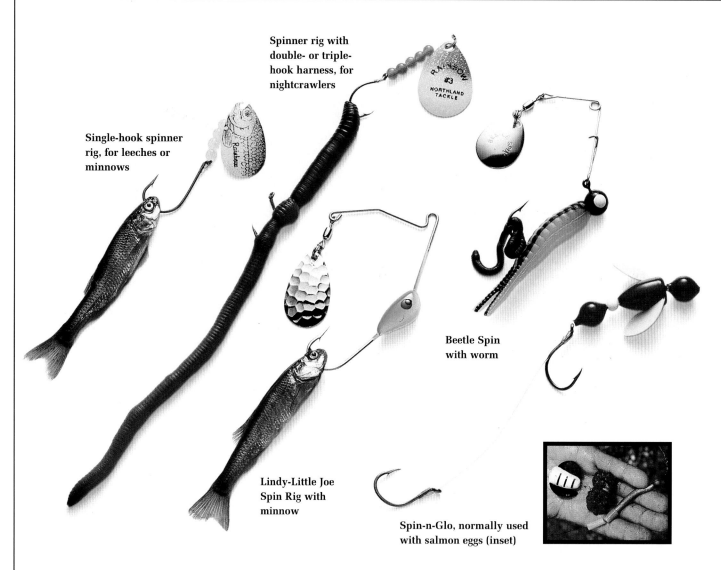

Single-hook spinner rig, for leeches or minnows

Spinner rig with double- or triple-hook harness, for nightcrawlers

Lindy-Little Joe Spin Rig with minnow

Beetle Spin with worm

Spin-n-Glo, normally used with salmon eggs (inset)

SPINNER/ LIVE-BAIT RIGS

Experienced anglers know there are times when a spinner/live-bait combination is far more effective than a spinner or live bait alone.

In discolored water, for example, the vibration of a spinner gets the fishes' attention, drawing them close enough to spot the bait.

A flashing spinner blade also seems to help when fish are "turned off" because of a cold front or some other unfavorable weather condition.

Yet another good time for a spinner/live-bait combo is during a baitfish glut. When food is super-abundant, gamefish may feed for only a few minutes a day and then rest in cover the remainder of the time. They'll often ignore live bait dangled right in their faces, but the flash of a spinner blade may trigger a reaction strike.

Live bait is sometimes fished on a spin-rig or a jig with a safety-pin spinner to work weedy cover. Without the spinner arm to protect the hook, fouling would be a constant problem.

You can buy a variety of spinner rigs designed to be tipped with live bait, but many anglers opt to make their own simply by threading a spinner, clevis and a few beads onto their line in front of the hook. Or, they just tip a weight-forward spinner or a spinnerbait with live bait

Spinner/live-bait combos are commonly used for walleyes, smallmouth bass, northern pike, muskies, crappies, sunfish, trout and salmon. Of course, the type of tackle used with spinner/live-bait rigs depends on the size of the fish and the type of cover you're fishing.

For working deep water, spinner/live-bait combos are usually rigged on a bottom-bouncer or a 3-way-swivel rig.

Spinner Rigs for Heavy Cover

Hook your bait on a jig head and then clip on a safety pin spinner to protect the hook.

Hook your bait on a spin-rig, which is a small, skirtless spinnerbait.

Spinner/Live-Bait Tips

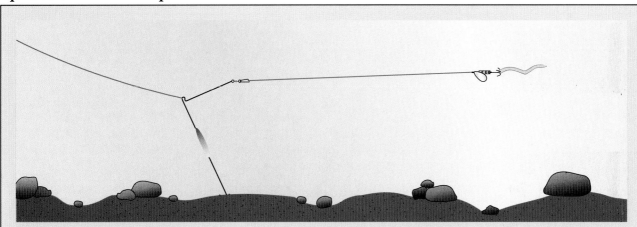

Fish a spinner/live-bait combo on a bottom-bouncer rig. A bottom-bouncer is relatively snag-free and it keeps your spinner riding above snaggy cover.

Use a spinner rig with a quick-change plastic clevis; this way you can switch to a different blade without tying on a whole new rig.

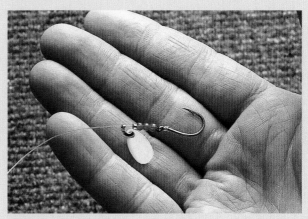

Add a "flicker" blade to your live-bait rig for extra attraction. Just thread on a clevis with a size 0 or 1 Colorado blade (convex side forward), thread on some beads and tie on a bait hook.

SOFT PLASTICS

*M*anufacturers just keep coming up with improvements on these incredibly lifelike baits.

SOFT PLASTICS

Soft-plastic lures have a big advantage over other types of artificials: not only do they look like real food, they feel like real food.

Rubber baits have been around since the 1860s, but soft plastics (made of polyvinyl chloride resin) are a fairly recent phenomenon. Although the first soft plastics were introduced in 1949, the lures didn't gain widespread popularity until the 1960s.

The first soft-plastic baits available were shaped like a worm, and worms still dominate the soft-plastics market. But today, soft plastics are available in shapes that mimic nearly every conceivable item in a fish's diet.

Many soft-plastic lures are amazingly realistic. They have antennae, fins, legs with realistic toes and other features that give them a natural look. Some soft plastics, such as "French-fry baits," bear no resemblance to any food item, but are no less effective.

Soft plastics come in a wide range of hardnesses. Some have an extremely soft, almost jellylike texture, which gives them a lively action in the water. But these lures won't last long; after catching a fish or two, they'll be ripped to shreds. Cheap soft plastics are often made of a firm material that has practically no action. The best advice is to buy lures of intermediate hardness.

One big advantage to soft-plastic lures is that they can be rigged "Texas-style," with the hook point buried in the plastic. This way, the lure can be drawn through the heaviest cover without hanging up. A firm hookset will force the point through the plastic and into the fish's jaw.

Another advantage: the soft-plastic material absorbs scent, so any fish attractant that you apply will last a long time. Some soft plastics are impregnated with scent which, according to many experts, makes the fish hold onto the bait a little longer and increases your hooking percentage.

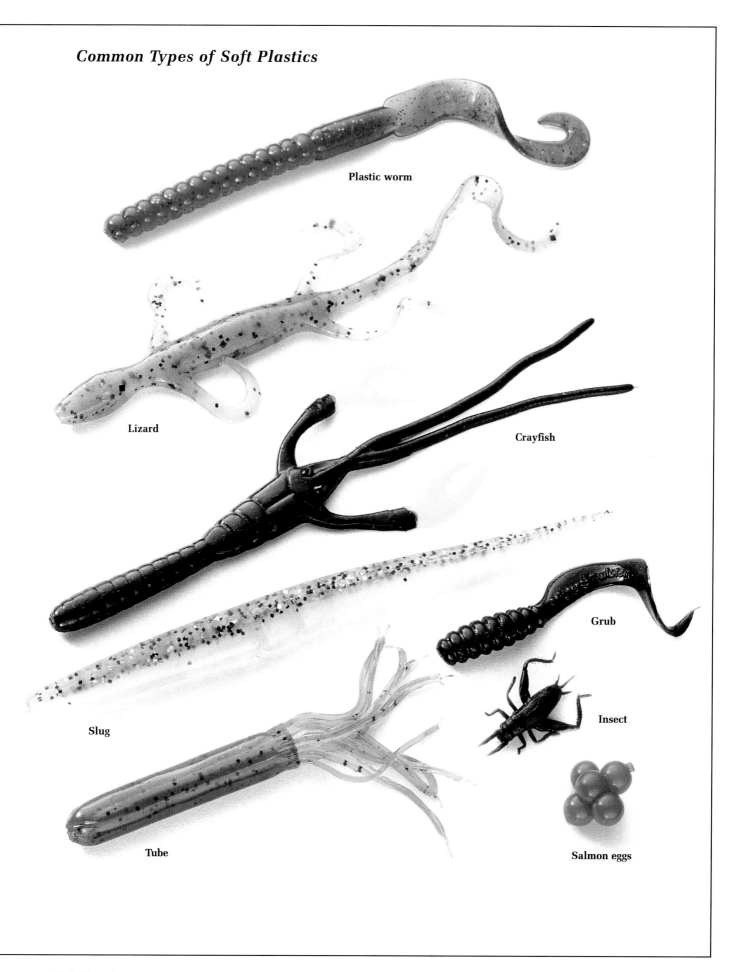

Plastic worm

Lizard

Crayfish

Grub

Slug

Insect

Tube

Salmon eggs

PLASTIC WORMS

Ask a professional bass angler to name his favorite lure, and there's a good chance he'll pick the plastic worm. But worms are not just bass baits; they're used for everything from sunfish to salmon.

Worms used for panfish measure only 2 to 3 inches in length, while those used for Florida largemouths may exceed 14 inches. The majority of largemouth anglers use worms in the 6- to 8-inch range.

Although some worms come pre-rigged, most come without hooks so you'll have to rig them yourself. There are many styles of hooks (opposite) and many different rigging methods (p. 232); versatile anglers are familiar with all of these methods and know when to use each of them.

A Texas-rigged plastic worm is probably the most weedless of all artificial

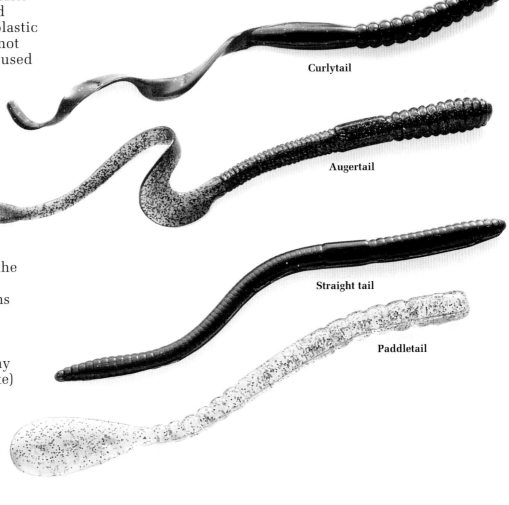

Curlytail

Augertail

Straight tail

Paddletail

Recommended Tackle

For most worm fishing, you'll need a medium-heavy-power, fast-action baitcasting outfit from 6- to 6 1/2 feet long with 12- to 20-pound mono. A fairly stiff rod is a must for driving the hook through the plastic. A 6-foot, medium-power spinning outfit with 6- to 8-pound-test mono is adequate for fishing small worms (up to 4 inches in length).

lures. You can toss a worm into the densest weed bed and snake it through the cover without picking up a sprig of vegetation. About the only thing that can foul the bait are strands of moss.

The main drawback to a Texas-rigged worm is that the weight carries it to the bottom where weeds or other cover may prevent fish from seeing it. In this situation, try a Carolina rig. Because the bait is separated from the weight, it floats up high enough for fish to get a good look at it.

Plastic worms are known as top baits for weedy cover, but

they also work well on a clean bottom. You can work them along the outside of a weed-line or over a rock pile or other distinct structure. They are not a good choice for exploring new water, because they must be retrieved slowly.

Many anglers locate fish with a "fast" lure, like a crankbait or spinnerbait, then switch to a worm for more thorough coverage.

Because plastic worms are retrieved so slowly, they're effective in cool water as well as warm. But at water temperatures below 50°F, you may have to downsize your lure. Smaller worms are also a good choice in very clear water. Where the water is muddy, bigger worms, especially those with some type of curly tail, work better.

The main consideration in choosing worms is the type of tail (opposite). Many worms come with some type of curly tail or paddle tail to provide more action, although straight-tail worms are still big sellers.

The worm's hardness is also important. A soft-bodied worm is a good choice for Texas rigging, because the hook point can easily penetrate the plastic on the hook-set. And a soft-bodied worm has a lot more tail movement. But a harder body is preferable on pre-rigged worms; otherwise, the hooks would tear out too easily.

Buoyancy makes a difference, as well. Most worms are somewhat buoyant; this way, they ride a little off the bottom where fish can see them. But if a worm is not buoyant enough, it will sink rapidly when you add a worm hook. For surface presentations, you'll need a highly buoyant worm with air bubbles impregnated into the material.

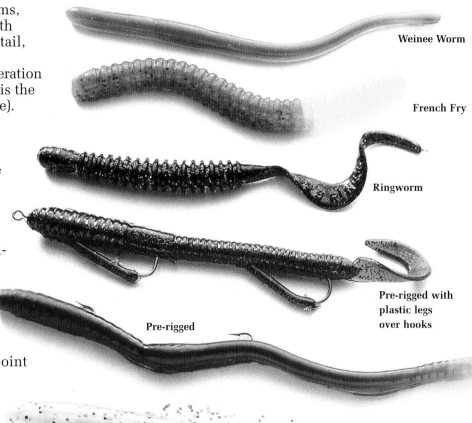

Specialty Worms

Weinee Worm

French Fry

Ringworm

Pre-rigged with plastic legs over hooks

Pre-rigged

Reaper

Worm Hooks

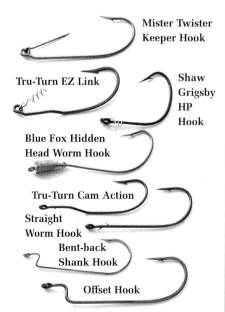

Mister Twister Keeper Hook

Tru-Turn EZ Link

Shaw Grigsby HP Hook

Blue Fox Hidden Head Worm Hook

Tru-Turn Cam Action

Straight Worm Hook

Bent-back Shank Hook

Offset Hook

Worm Hook Tips

Once you've selected a hook style, consider hook size. For a 4-inch worm, use a #1 or 1/0 hook; a 6-inch worm, a 2/0 or 3/0 hook; an 8-inch worm, a 4/0 or 5/0 hook; a 10-inch worm, a 5/0 or 6/0 hook. If your hook doesn't sport barbs or keepers and the worm slides down the shaft, push the worm's head over the hook's eye and anchor it in place with a toothpick (trim off the ends) through the worm and the eye. And keep a file on hand to keep your worm hooks sharp; this will improve your hook-up percentage.

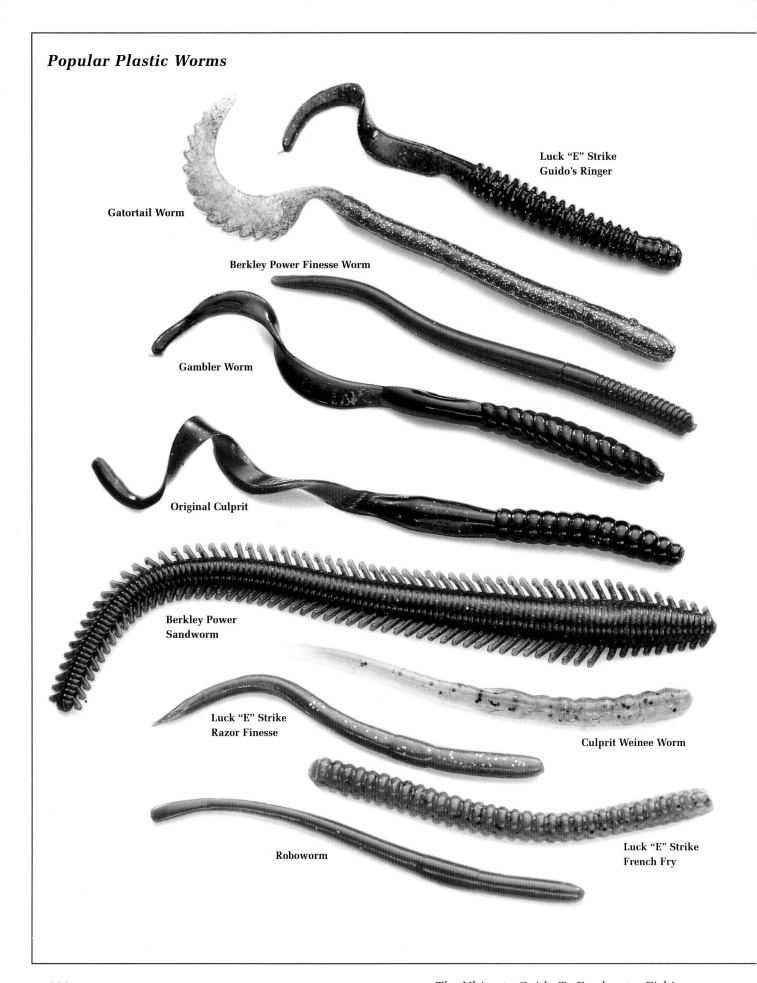

Gatortail Worm

Luck "E" Strike
Guido's Ringer

Berkley Power Finesse Worm

Gambler Worm

Original Culprit

Berkley Power
Sandworm

Luck "E" Strike
Razor Finesse

Culprit Weinee Worm

Roboworm

Luck "E" Strike
French Fry

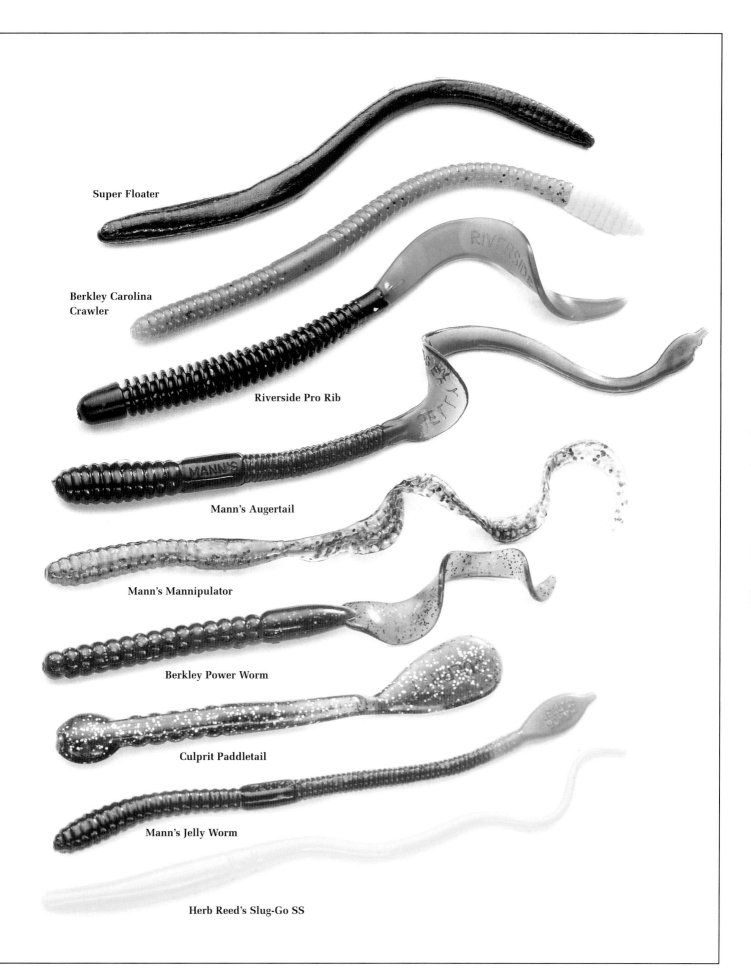

Super Floater

Berkley Carolina Crawler

Riverside Pro Rib

Mann's Augertail

Mann's Mannipulator

Berkley Power Worm

Culprit Paddletail

Mann's Jelly Worm

Herb Reed's Slug-Go SS

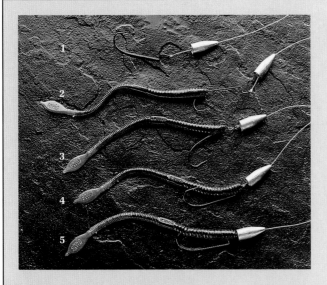

Texas-Rig. *(1) Thread a bullet sinker onto your line and tie on a worm hook. (2) Insert the point of the hook into the head, push it in about ¹/₂ inch and bring it out the side. (3) Push the hook all the way through the worm so only the hook eye protrudes at the head. (4) Rotate the hook 180 degrees. (5) Push the hook into the worm; the hook point should almost come out the other side and the worm should hang straight.*

Carolina Rig. *Thread a ¹/₄- to 1-ounce bullet sinker and a glass or plastic bead onto your line and attach a barrel swivel. Tie on an 18- to 36-inch leader of lighter mono and attach a worm hook. Push the hook into a buoyant worm and out the side, leaving the point exposed.*

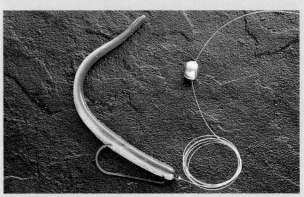

Split-Shot Rig. *Tie a size 1 or 2 worm hook onto 6- or 8-pound mono, add a split shot 12 to 18 inches up the line and Texas-rig a 4-inch worm. This rig is ideal for "finesse" fishing, retrieving very slowly with light line to tempt finicky biters.*

Florida Rig. *Thread a screw-in weight (inset) onto your line and attach a worm hook. Then screw the sinker into the head of the worm. This way, the weight won't separate from the worm when you hang up on a branch or other obstacle.*

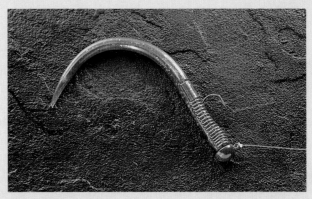

Jig Worm. *Attach a mushroom jig to your line and thread on the worm, leaving the hook point exposed. Be sure the worm is snugged up against the flattened head, so there is no gap to catch weeds or debris.*

1 *Make a cast and then hold the rod tip at 1 or 2 o'clock as the bait starts to sink. Keep your line slightly taut, but not tight. The fish often grab the worm when it's sinking and if your line is not taut, you won't feel the take.*

2 *Gradually lower your rod tip, keeping your line slightly taut as the bait continues to sink. By the time the bait hits bottom, your rod tip should be at the 3 o'clock position. If you kept your rod tip high, it would be hard to set the hook.*

3 *Continue retrieving with a lift-and-drop motion. When you feel a take or your line starts moving off to the side, drop your rod tip to reduce the tension. If the fish feels too much resistance, it will drop the lure.*

4 *Set the hook with a powerful upward snap of your wrists and forearms. A strong hookset is necessary to drive the hook through the worm and into the fish's jaw.*

Fishing a Carolina-Rigged Worm

Using a long-handled baitcasting rod, make a sidearm lob-cast. If you try tossing a Carolina rig with an overhand snap-cast, it will probably tangle.

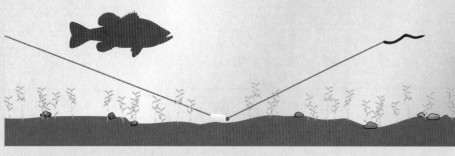

After the sinker hits bottom, begin a slow, steady retrieve. A rapid retrieve will pull the lure down so far that the fish may not see it.

Give the rig a periodic jerk to change the action. The worm will dip down and then slowly float back up, and the sinker will kick up a cloud of silt. The sudden change often draws a fish's attention and triggers a strike.

Other Worm Retrieves

Cast a jig worm along a weedline or into sparse weeds and retrieve slowly. When the open hook hangs up in the vegetation, free it with a sharp jerk of your rod; the bait will jet upward and then flutter back down, drawing a fish's attention.

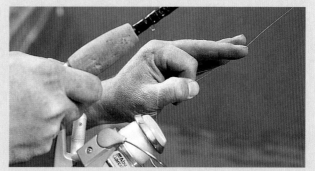

Retrieve a split-shot rig very slowly through cover that you suspect holds fish. A slow retrieve, using your fingers to "stitch" in line, is essential to keep the bait off the bottom. Split-shotting is not a good way to cover lots of water.

Four Tips for Using Plastic Worms

Thread on a brass sinker and a glass bead before tying on your worm hook. The sound of glass clinking against brass makes a sharp sound that the fish can easily detect.

Skip a thick-bodied worm under a dock or other overhead cover by making a sidearm cast with a spinning outfit. Slim-bodied worms do not have enough surface area to skip well.

Peg the bullet sinker onto the line so it won't separate from the worm in heavy cover. Just wedge a toothpick into the hole in the sinker and then break off the end.

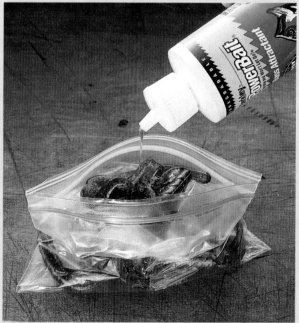

Place your plastic worms in a resealable plastic bag and then add a few drops of worm oil. The oil keeps the worms soft and pliable. Do not mix colors or they will bleed together.

LIZARDS & CRAWS

Some bass anglers swear that a soft-plastic lizard is the most effective bait during the spawning period, because bass will instinctively grab it to prevent it from robbing the nest.

In truth, bass never encounter a live lizard in the water, but they are exposed to salamanders, such as waterdogs and mudpuppies, which look much like soft-plastic lizards.

Numerous food-habit studies have shown that crayfish are a favorite food of smallmouth, largemouth and spotted bass, so it's not surprising that soft-plastic craws work so well for these species.

Craws and lizards can be used interchangeably with plastic worms, but savvy anglers know that there are times when lizards and craws work better. The reason for their effectiveness has less to do with their natural look than the fact that their wiggling arms and pincers make them sink more slowly and

Four Tips for Fishing with Craws & Lizards

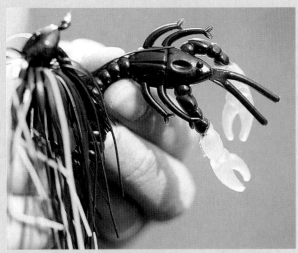

Tip a rubber-legged jig with a soft-plastic craw by threading it onto the hook, as shown. If desired, you can shorten the craw by biting a little off the end before threading it on.

When Texas-rigging a craw or lizard, skin hook the bait by inserting the hook point in the edge rather than the center. Then, when you set the hook, it does not have to penetrate the thick plastic.

Make a "firetail" lizard by dipping the tail in a dye intended for soft plastics. Popular tail colors include chartreuse, hot orange and blue.

Repair a damaged leg, tail or pincer by melting the plastic with a lighter and pressing the sections together. You can also use this method to splice on a different color tail.

wiggle more enticingly than a worm.

Lizards and craws are most commonly fished on Texas or Carolina rigs (p. 232). Be sure to hook a craw through the narrow end; this way, it will scoot backwards when you retrieve, just like a real crawfish.

You can retrieve lizards and craws in much the same way as you would retrieve a worm, and fish them with the same kind of tackle (p. 228).

Craws, and occasionally small lizards, can also be used as trailers for tipping jigs. Many anglers prefer them over a pork trailer.

Popular Lizards & Craws

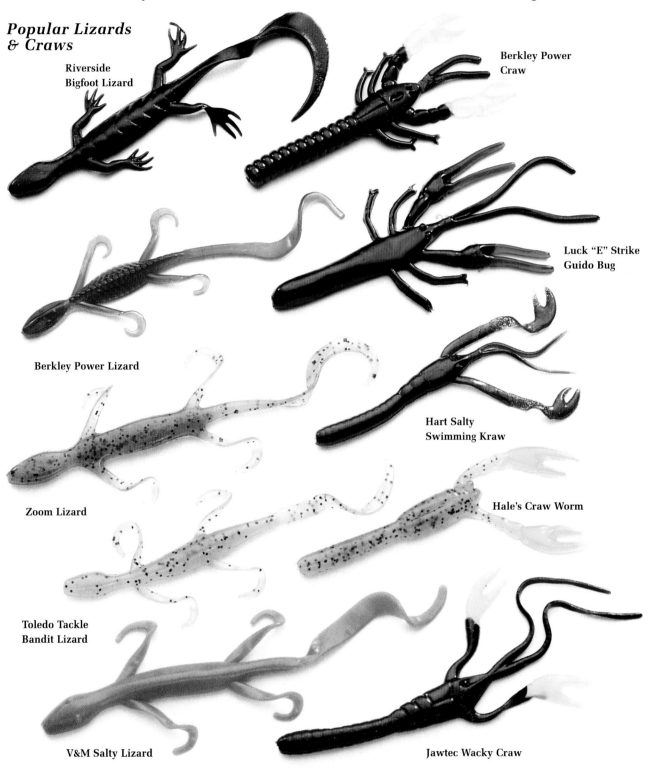

Riverside Bigfoot Lizard

Berkley Power Craw

Luck "E" Strike Guido Bug

Berkley Power Lizard

Zoom Lizard

Hart Salty Swimming Kraw

Hale's Craw Worm

Toledo Tackle Bandit Lizard

V&M Salty Lizard

Jawtec Wacky Craw

GRUBS & TUBEBAITS

The wiggling tail of a soft-plastic grub or the quivering tentacles of a tubebait appeal to all types of gamefish. Grubs and tubebaits from 1 to 2 inches long are deadly for sunfish, crappies, perch, white bass and stream trout; 3- to 5-inchers for bass, walleyes and lake trout; and 6- to 10-inchers for stripers, northern pike and muskies.

Soft-plastic grubs and tubebaits are commonly used as dressings for jigs or trailers for spinnerbaits and other lures, but some types can be fished on their own, much like a plastic worm.

By far the most popular type of grub is the curlytail (sometimes called the twister-tail or screw-tail). The flexible

Basic Types of Grubs & Tubes

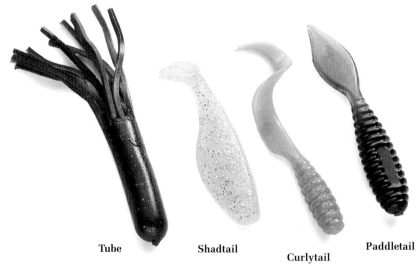

Tube   Shadtail   Curlytail   Paddletail

tail has a built-in curl that creates an irresistible rippling action. Curlytails can be fished on a jig, Texas rig, Carolina rig or split-shot rig.

The second most popular style, the shad-tail, has an expanded end that catches water and gives the tail a lifelike wiggle. It is most commonly fished on a jig.

Both curly-tails and shad-tails work well in dingy water, because the tail creates so much vibration. And they're ideal for fishing in current, because the moving water gives the tail action even when the bait is at rest.

Paddle-tails (also called spear-tails) have a flattened tail that results in a more subtle swimming action. Paddle-tails, which are an excellent choice for rapid retrieves, are usually fished on a jig. They are most popular in saltwater fishing although they are often used in fresh water, as well.

Tubebaits have a hollow body with 20 to 40 tentacles at the rear end. They work best in clear water and rank among the top "sight-fishing" baits. They can be fished on a jig head or rigged on a specially-designed clip-on hook.

Popular Grubs & Tubebaits

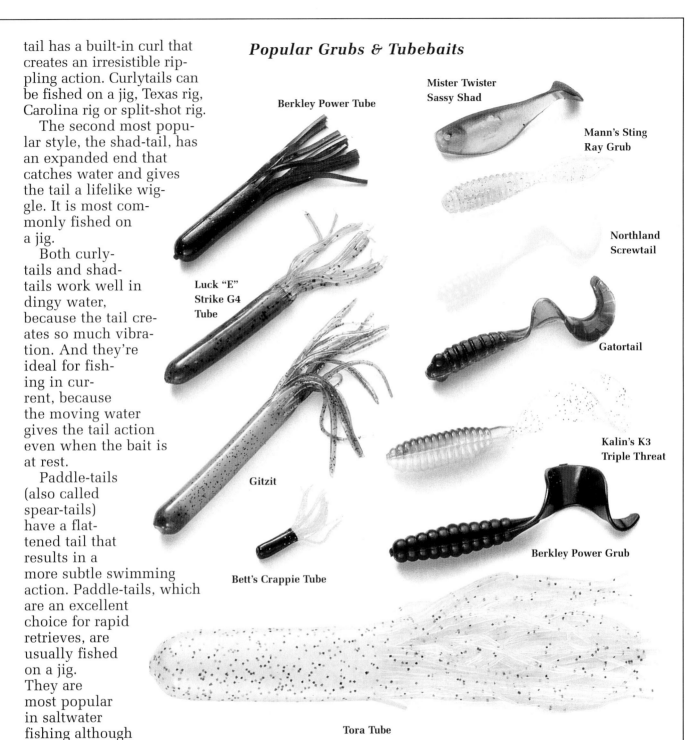

Berkley Power Tube

Mister Twister
Sassy Shad

Mann's Sting
Ray Grub

Luck "E"
Strike G4
Tube

Northland
Screwtail

Gatortail

Gitzit

Kalin's K3
Triple Threat

Bett's Crappie Tube

Berkley Power Grub

Tora Tube

Recommended Tackle

When using small- to medium-size grubs and tubes in snag-free water, you can get by with a medium-power spinning outfit and 4- to 8-pound mono. But when using magnum grubs or tubes, or fishing in snaggy cover, use a flippin' stick and mono of at least 15-pound test.

How to Rig Grubs

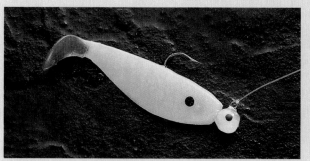

To rig a shad-tail on a jig head, push the hook through the body and out the back, as shown. Make sure the hook comes out the middle of the back.

Rig a curlytail grub **(1)** Texas-style with an ordinary bullet sinker, **(2)** Texas-style with "brass 'n' glass," **(3)** Carolina-style with an open hook, **(4)** on a split-shot rig or **(5)** on a jig head by pushing the hook through the body and out the side so the tail rides straight down or straight up.

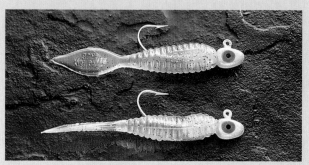

For the majority of fishing, rig a paddle-tail grub so the tail rides straight up (top). But to slow the sink rate or make the lure skip better, rig the tail so it rides horizontally (bottom).

Two Tips for Fishing with Grubs

Thread on a grub so your hook penetrates the top part of the plastic. This widens your hook gap and improves your hooking percentage.

Make a cavity in a grub body using a razor blade or specially designed tool called a "Grub-Gutter." Then, you can easily insert a float or rattle.

Three Ways to Rig Tubebaits

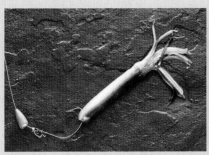

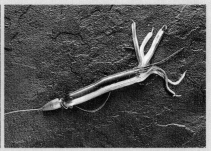

Thread on a bullet sinker and tie on an Eagle Claw HP hook. Push the hook through the nose of the bait and out the side (left). Push the hook through the tube so the point just barely starts to penetrate the opposite side (middle). Give the hook a half turn, push it through until only the eye protrudes, and then attach the wire clip to the shank (right).

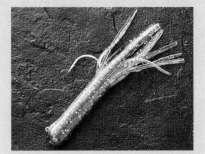

To rig a tube with an internal weight instead of a bullet sinker, drop a specially designed weight down the inside of the tube so the ring rests at the head of the bait (left). Next, push the hook point into the head of the bait and through the ring (right). Then, continue rigging as in the sequence above.

Rig a tube on a jig head by inserting the head into the tube and then pushing on the plastic until the attachment eye pokes through.

Two Tips for Fishing Tubebaits

When jigging for lake trout, poke a strip of cut bait into a tube to add scent. A strip from an oily fish, like a smelt or herring, works best. Or, push some cotton into the tube and soak it with bottled scent.

Jiggle a tubebait in front of an inactive bass to tempt a strike. Try to make the tentacles dance enticingly without moving the bait away from the fish.

SOFT JERKBAITS

Soft jerkbaits are one of the few really "new" lure innovations in recent years. When fished with an erratic twitch-and-pause retrieve, these slow-sinking baits will draw strikes from the fussiest bass.

Bass anglers rely mainly on the 6-inch baits, but when fishing gets especially tough,

dropping down to the 3-inch size may draw strikes.

But soft jerkbaits, also called jerkworms, soft stick-baits or slugs, are not just bass lures. Larger jerkbaits (up to 10 inches in length) work well for stripers, muskies and pike, and anglers in the northern Canada have found them to be a great bait for giant lakers.

What makes soft jerkbaits different than other soft plastics is their slow sink rate, which gives them a unique, wounded-baitfish action. They dart upward a little and then slowly settle back down.

A soft jerkbait looks a lot like a plastic worm, but it is designed to ride horizontally in the water, not sink nose-down, like a worm. You can fish a soft jerkbait on the surface in walk-the-dog fashion (p. 196), or let it sink a foot or two before starting your retrieve.

Soft jerkbaits are at their best in spring, when bass are in a negative mood following spawning. But the lures will work any time the fish are in shallow water. They are not particularly good deep-water baits; weighting them to sink

defeats the purpose, although they can be fished on a Carolina rig. They produce little vibration, so they do not work well in muddy water.

Soft jerkbaits are hard to fish in windy weather, because the wind puts a bow in your line and pulls the bait along too fast.

Recommended Tackle

A 6- to 6½-foot, medium-heavy-power baitcasting rod works well for distance casting and has enough power to drive the hook through the plastic and into a fish's jaw. A wide-spool baitcasting reel spooled with 14- to 20-pound test mono helps you make the long casts that are often necessary with these lures.

Popular Soft Jerkbaits

Berkley Power Slug

Luck "E" Strike Scatter Shad

Culprit Jerk Worm

Banjo Minnow

6" Slug-Go

10" Lunker City Fin-S-Fish

3" Slug-Go

Mister Twister Slimy Slug

How to Rig a Soft Jerkbait

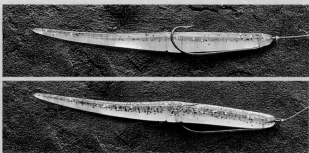

Push an offset worm hook into a soft jerkbait as far as the offset (left), then bring the hook out the bottom, turn it 180 degrees (top right) and push it through the body so the point rests in the depression on the back (bottom right).

How to Fish a Soft Jerkbait

1 Cast with the wind to reduce backlashing and prevent the wind from putting a bow in your line and pulling the bait too fast.

2 With your rod tip angled downward, give the lure a gentle pull, not a sharp jerk.

3 Pause while the bait glides upward and to the side and slowly sinks back down, then give the bait another gentle pull. It should glide to the other side.

4 When you feel a fish grab the bait and start swimming away with it, set the hook with a sideways sweep of the rod.

Four Tips for Fishing with Jerkbaits

To make the bait run deeper, push a lead insert or finishing nail into the plastic just ahead of the hook bend. An insert will also give you longer casts and keep the wind from blowing the bait too fast.

Don't attempt to fish with a soft jerkbait that is warped from being stored with a bend. It will not have the desired side-to-side action. Boil the bait later to remove the bend (see below).

Boil a warped bait to remove the bend. Check the bait after about 30 seconds; boiling it too long will soften it too much. Then, lay the bait on its back, making sure it is perfectly straight.

Add a stinger hook to improve your hooking percentage in snag-free cover. Just slip a size 4 treble over the worm hook before pushing it into the bait.

Soft-Plastic Specialty Baits

If you flip through the pages of your favorite fishing-tackle catalog, you'll see an astonishing variety of soft-plastic baits ranging in size from tiny imitation salmon eggs to "snakes" a foot and a half long.

Most soft-plastic specialty baits look like real food, but some bear no resemblance to a natural food item. Instead, they rely on impregnated scent to attract fish.

Although soft plastics can't duplicate the natural wiggle of live bait squirming on the hook, they have some major advantages over the real thing: they're a lot more durable, and you don't have to drive miles out of your way to find a bait shop.

Plastic salmon eggs are a godsend to trout and salmon anglers. Fresh eggs are available only seasonally, and even when you can get them, it's difficult to keep them fresh and make them stay on the hook. Some imitation eggs have an extremely soft texture, like that of a real egg, so when fish grab them, they don't let go. Many fake eggs have egg scent molded into them.

You can buy soft-plastic imitations of a variety of adult insects, including grasshoppers, crickets, spiders, ants and even flies. Larval-insect imitations, such as hellgrammites and mayfly wigglers, are also available. Insect baits are most commonly used for panfish and stream trout.

Although many anglers rely on the soft-plastic craws mentioned earlier in the chapter, these bait are not

very realistic. Some manufacturers, however, offer imitation crayfish that are made using molds of the real thing. You can also buy ultra-realistic replicas of many other common crustaceans, such as shrimp and scuds. Lifelike crustacean imitations are a favorite of anglers seeking bass and large stream trout.

Giant soft-plastic baits are made to mimic trout, eels, waterdogs, snakes and other large food items. Used mainly for stripers and large Florida bass, these baits are also catching on among pike, muskie and lake trout anglers.

Many of these giant baits are made by local "basement" operators, so they may

be difficult to find. But the market for these baits is growing, and more established manufacturers are adding them to their lines.

Most soft-plastic specialty baits come without hooks, so you'll have to rig them yourself using the techniques shown earlier. But many of the smaller baits, including a number of insect baits, come with hooks molded in.

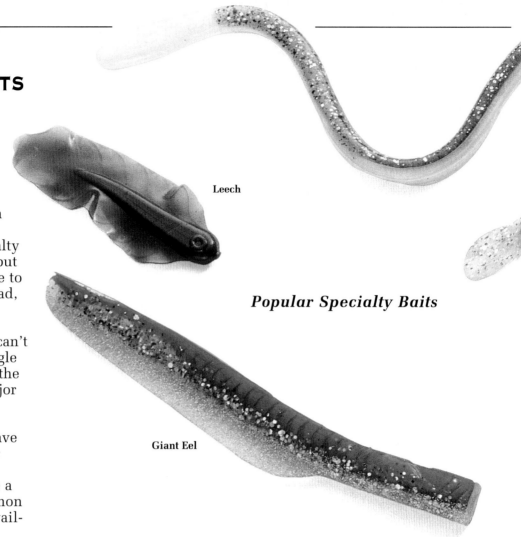

Leech

Popular Specialty Baits

Giant Eel

Opposite: Specialty baits can draw bites when nothing else will work.

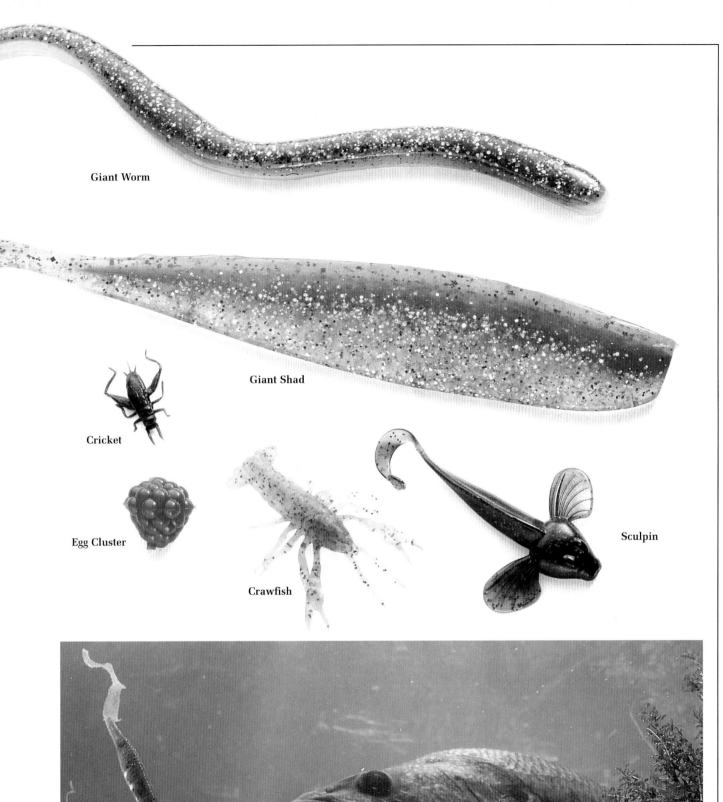

Giant Worm

Giant Shad

Cricket

Egg Cluster

Crawfish

Sculpin

How to Rig a Soft-Plastic Salmon Egg

Using a short-shank egg hook, (1) skin hook the egg, then (2) turn the hook 180 degrees and (3) insert the point into the opposite side of the egg.

How to Rig Other Specialty Baits

Rig an egg cluster onto a small treble hook, pushing two of the hooks into the plastic and leaving the third hook exposed.

Thread a worm hook into a soft-plastic crayfish by starting just above the tail and pushing it through until it comes out the snout, point up.

Rig an insect bait by threading it head-first onto a long-shank Aberdeen hook. The hook point should come out the abdomen.

Rig a giant soft-plastic Texas-style or Carolina-style on a size 3/0 to 6/0 worm hook. When Texas-rigging, the point of the hook should penetrate the plastic.

Fish a larval-insect imitation behind a plastic casting bubble. The bubble not only provides casting weight, it keeps the bait floating above weedy, brushy or rocky cover.

When Texas-rigging a giant soft-plastic, use a razor blade to cut a groove in the back. This way the hook point can rest in the groove for easier hooking, just as it does on a soft jerkbait (p. 244).

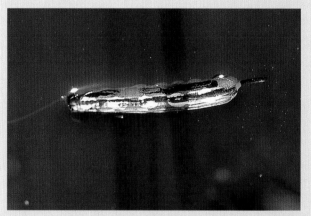

Fish an adult insect imitation, such a dragonfly, on the surface with no weight. This technique works well for bass and sunfish when bugs are hatching on a warm summer evening.

Tip a teardrop or other tiny jig with a soft-plastic grub to catch catch crappies, sunfish, perch and even trout. This rig works well in open water or through the ice.

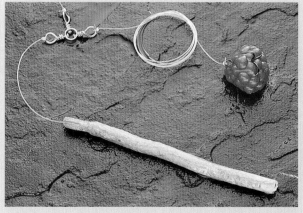

When river fishing with a single egg imitation or an egg cluster, use a drift-fishing rig. Splice a three-way swivel into your line, tie on a dropper and pinch on a drift sinker. Should the sinker snag, it will easily pull off the line and you can pinch on another.

JIGGING LURES

When it comes to tempting bites from stubborn gamefish, nothing is as effective as the tantalizing action of a jigging lure.

JIGGING LURES

Anglers equipped with a good selection of jigging lures can catch practically any kind of freshwater gamefish. The major types of jigging lures include:

- **Lead-head jig** – This is nothing more than a chunk of lead with a hook molded into it. Normally, the hook is covered with a hair, feather, tinsel or soft-plastic dressing.
- **Jigging spoon** – A thick metal spoon that sinks rapidly and has an erratic, tumbling action.
- **Vibrating blade** – With its thin metal body and lead head, this lure vibrates rapidly when pulled upward.
- **Tailspinner** – A heavy lead head makes it possible to cast this lure a long distance. The spinner on the tail turns when the lure is jigged upward and helicopters as it sinks back down.

In addition, anglers can choose from a selection of jigging lures designed primarily for ice fishing. Some of these lures, such as tear drops and swimming minnows (p. 270), are now becoming popular for open-water fishing, as well.

Because jigging lures are relatively heavy for their size, they work better than most other lures in deep water or current.

The fact that fish often strike a jigging lure as it is sinking has some important implications for anglers. For instance, it pays to choose the lightest lure that will still reach the desired depth; this way, the lure has a slow sink rate, and fish have more time to react to it.

When the lure is sinking, you must keep your line tight enough that you can feel the strike, but not so tight that the lure doesn't sink freely. If you have too much slack in your line, you won't feel the strike at all.

Each type of jigging lure is fished a little differently, as is explained on the pages that follow.

Types of Jigs & Jigging Lures

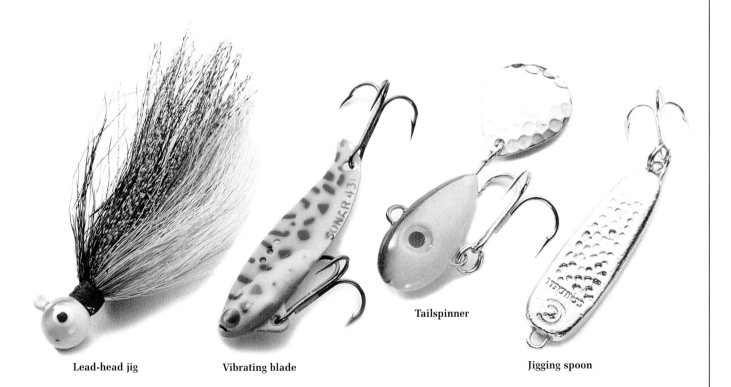

Lead-head jig

Vibrating blade

Tailspinner

Jigging spoon

A jig and curlytail grub will catch everything from sunfish to walleyes to stripers.

LEAD-HEAD JIGS

Although a jig is among the simplest of fishing lures, jig selection is not so simple. Here are the things you need to consider when buying jig heads and dressings:

Jig Heads

The jig head determines how fast the jig will sink and how well it will hook the fish that strike. It also affects the jig's action. Here are the main things to remember when selecting jig heads:

- **Head Shape** – Standard round jig heads work well for most jig fishing. Because of the way the hook eye is positioned in the head, the jig is well balanced, meaning that it hangs horizontally when tied to the line, so it resembles a swimming minnow. Plus, round-head jigs sink quickly, which is what is needed most of the time.

But there are times when other types of heads work better. In strong current, for instance, a bullet-head jig is hard to beat because it slips easily through the current and stays down better than any other type of head.

A slider-head jig, one with a horizontally flattened body, is the best choice for swimming over weed tops or any shallow-water obstructions. It sinks very slowly and has an attractive gliding action. Some have an upturned nose for even more lift.

Fishing in weeds is a problem with most jig heads, because they have a hook eye that protrudes from the top and catches bits of vegetation. A cone-shaped head with the hook eye right at the front tip slips through the weeds more easily.

A football-head jig has a unique rocking action. When the head wedges against a rock, a pull on the line causes the body to tip up in what has been described as a crayfish taking a defensive posture.

On a stand-up jig, the bottom of the head is flattened, so the jig rests with the hook pointing up. This design is relatively snag-free, and the upright position makes the jig more visible.

Mushroom-head jigs are an excellent choice for rigging with soft plastics, because the trailer abuts snugly with the flattened head, and the double barbs on the collar prevent it from sliding back, even when the bait is ripped through weeds.

Banana-head jigs work well for vertical jigging, because the attachment eye at the front gives the bait an exaggerated kicking action.

Keel jigs work well in deep water or fast current. The head has a vertically flattened shape that slices through the water easily and sinks rapidly.

Common Head Styles

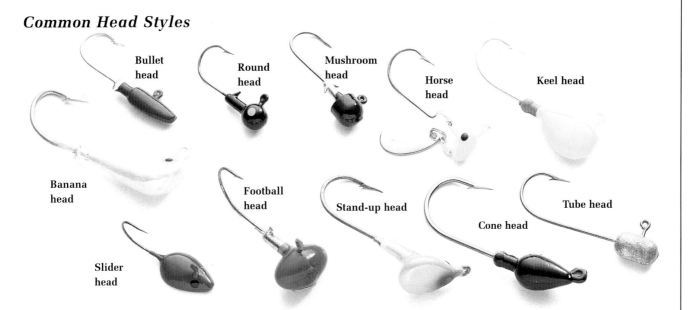

Bullet head

Round head

Mushroom head

Horse head

Keel head

Banana head

Slider head

Football head

Stand-up head

Cone head

Tube head

Horsehead jigs, also called pony jigs, have a horselike snout to which is attached a spinner blade. They are often used for casting or trolling in open water.

Tube heads are designed to fit inside of hollow, soft-plastic tubebaits. Insert the entire head inside the tube and push the attachment eye through the plastic. Rigged this way, the tube is firmly secured to the jig head.

- **Head Weight** – The general rule in choosing a jig head is to use just enough weight so the lure can reach bottom. The lighter the head, the slower the sink rate, so the fish get a better look at it.

   Remember that you'll always need a little more weight to get down when fishing in wind or current. And a bulky trailer will also slow your sink rate, meaning that you'll need more weight.
- **Shank Length** – The best shank length depends on whether or not you're tipping with live bait. A short-shank jig is the best choice for tipping; with the jig head closer to the bait, you get fewer short strikes.

A long-shank hook is a better choice for any kind of jig with a tail. The farther the hook extends back in the tail, the greater your hooking percentage.
- **Shank Diameter** – A thin-wire hook is best when tipping with live bait, because it does less damage to the bait than would a thick hook. And should you get snagged on a log, a strong, steady pull on the line will usually straighten the hook enough to free the jig. The obvious drawback to a thin-wire hook is that you risk losing a big fish. If you're using heavy tackle for big fish, use a hook with a shank thick enough so it won't straighten.
- **Hook Size** – If you're tipping your jig with a minnow, a soft-plastic grub or a pork chunk, you need a hook with enough gap to make the hook protrude well above the dressing. If the gap is too narrow, the point will rest right on the dressing and won't penetrate the fish's mouth.

- **Weedguards** – If you'll be fishing in weedy or woody cover, your hook should have some kind of weedguard or brushguard. Bristle-type weedguards are the most popular, although some anglers prefer the wire or plastic types. The weedguard should be stiff enough to protect the hook, but not so stiff that it significantly lowers your hooking percentage.

Types of Weedguards

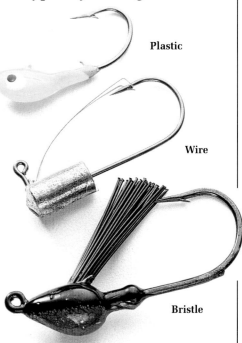

Plastic

Wire

Bristle

Jig Dressings

Some jigs come dressed with hair, feathers or synthetic material, but others must be dressed with a soft-plastic grub, a plastic worm, a pork "product" or live bait.

Types of Jig Dressings

Live rubber

Bucktail

Tinsel

Marabou

Chicken feather

Soft plastic

The dressing gives the jig its action, adds color and helps control the sink rate. A bulky plastic tail, for example, is much more buoyant than a sparse hair or feather tail, making a jig of the same weight sink more slowly.

Soft-plastic dressings have great action, look and feel like real food, and are inexpensive. The best ones are very soft and pliable, and the material is very thin, so the tail wiggles enticingly, even on a very slow retrieve or when held motionless in slow current.

Jigs can be tipped with practically any of the soft plastics shown on pages 227-247. In addition, jigs are commonly dressed with a soft-plastic body with a marabou insert.

Bucktail is one of the oldest jig dressings, but is just as effective today as ever. Because deer hair is hollow, the fibers are highly buoyant. They tend to flare out and have more of a "breathing" action than do synthetic fibers. Bucktail jigs must be well-tied, with a heavy wrapping of thread coated with a layer of epoxy. Otherwise, fibers will start to fall out after a few casts, the wraps will loosen and all the hair will fall off the bait.

Feather jigs, including marabou and chicken-feather models, may be hard to find because they're difficult to tie. But many anglers swear by them; they have a breathing action that is even more intense than that of a bucktail.

If you're tipping your jig with live bait, a tail may not even be necessary; in fact, it may detract from the bait's natural attraction. But if you do use a tail, it should be short and sparse so it doesn't cover up too much of the bait. Good choices include a small tube-bait, a sparsely tied feather jig or a soft-plastic/marabou body.

How to Tip Jigs with Live Bait

Minnow through lips

Minnow through mouth and out top of head

Half a crawler

Leech above sucker

Popular Lead-Head Jigs

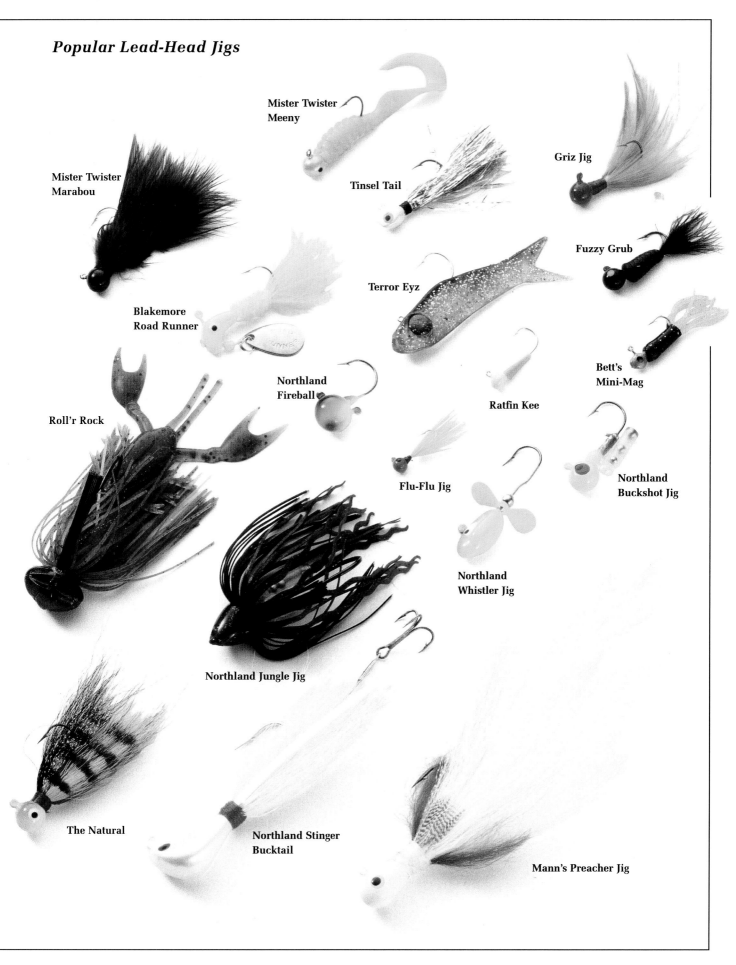

Mister Twister Meeny

Mister Twister Marabou

Tinsel Tail

Griz Jig

Fuzzy Grub

Blakemore Road Runner

Terror Eyz

Bett's Mini-Mag

Roll'r Rock

Northland Fireball

Ratfin Kee

Flu-Flu Jig

Northland Buckshot Jig

Northland Whistler Jig

Northland Jungle Jig

The Natural

Northland Stinger Bucktail

Mann's Preacher Jig

Jig-Fishing Techniques

Ask a dozen anglers to describe the best way to fish a jig and you'll get a dozen different answers. And under the right set of circumstances, all of them could be right.

Among the factors that influence how you fish a jig are: water clarity, water temperature, depth, current speed, weather conditions, time of day and mood of the fish. It's not always possible to predict in advance what type of retrieve will work best; you just have to experiment.

The most popular methods of fishing a jig are described below and on the following pages, but regardless of what technique you use, certain principles always apply:

- Fish tend to hit a jig on the drop, so you should keep a little tension on your line as the jig is sinking; otherwise, you won't feel the take. Don't keep your line too tight, however, or the jig won't have the right action.
- Becoming a proficient jig fisherman requires a delicate "feel" and fast reflexes, so it's important to concentrate. Fish often hit a jig with a solid thump or tap, but that's not always the case. Any twitch, hesitation or sideways movement of the line may signal a take. Or, sometimes the jig just doesn't sink because a fish has grabbed it.
- At the first hint of a strike, set the hook. When a fish takes a jig, it flares its gills and sucks in a volume of water that includes the jig; if you hesitate and the fish feels anything out of the ordinary, it will expel the jig as fast as it sucked it in.

The majority of jig fishermen use one of the following retrieves, or some variation of it:

- **Dragging** – Slowly retrieving the jig with very little, if any, vertical action, works well when the fish are lethargic because of cold water or when they're in a negative feeding mood. Although the jig is usually dragged along bottom or over the weedtops, you can also swim it slowly in midwater to catch suspended fish.
- **Lift-and-Drop** – This common retrieve involves giving the jig a short twitch (usually no more than a few inches long), keeping your line taut as it sinks back to the bottom, and then twitching it again. Experiment with the length of the twitches and the duration of the pauses until you find the tempo that works best on a given day. The twitch-and-pause retrieve can also be used to catch fish suspended far off the bottom.
- **Rip-Jigging** – This technique gives your jig an erratic action that may trigger strikes when other jigging methods fail. Before your jig sinks all the way to the bottom, give it a hard jerk, throw slack into the line on the drop, and then jerk again before the jig touches bottom. Fish usually grab the jig as it is sinking and, when you jerk the next time, the fish is hooked. This retrieve keeps the jig dancing above the fish's head and darting erratically, like an injured baitfish.

Any of these basic retrieves can be used whether you're casting, trolling or vertically jigging (opposite).

Always attach your jig directly to the line; it will not cause line twist (unless you're jigging vertically), so there is no need for a snap-swivel. Nor is there any need for a leader, except when fishing for pike or muskies. Then, a short wire "striker" (p. 260) will suffice.

When tipping jigs with live bait, you're often faced with the decision as to whether or not to use a "stinger" hook (p. 261). A stinger may be a big help when fish are striking short, but it usually reduces the number of strikes you'll get and increases fouling problems. The best strategy is to let the fish tell you when a stinger is needed. If you're missing more fish than you're hooking, add a stinger hook.

Recommended Tackle

The length and power of the rod and the weight of the line depend on what species of fish you're after and what kind of cover you're working.

No matter what type of jig fishing you're doing, sensitivity is a major issue, so you'll want a high-modulus graphite rod with a fast tip. The fast tip not only makes it easier to detect strikes, it gives you a quicker hookset. A slow-action rod takes a fraction of a second longer to transfer the power of the hookset to the jig, giving fish more time to eject it.

Most jig fishermen prefer monofilament line, because its stretch allows fish to easily suck in the jig. Missed strikes are common when jigging with superline, because the lack of stretch prevents fish from taking the jig as deeply.

Popular Jigging Methods

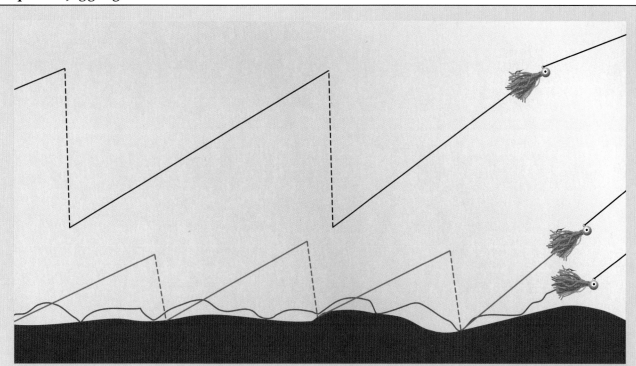

Basic jig retrieves include dragging (blue line), lift-and-drop (green line) and rip-jigging (red line).

Vertical jigging involves lowering your jig to the bottom and hopping it vertically as your boat drifts with the wind or current. For the best feel, use your trolling motor to hold the boat directly over your jig so your line stays as vertical as possible.

Jig trolling is not much different than trolling a crankbait, but you must move slowly enough that your jig can touch bottom. Most anglers backtroll for good boat control while working the jig with the lift-and-drop method.

Tip a jig with a bulky pork or plastic trailer to slow its sink rate and give fish a longer look at the bait. When the fish are fussy, this can make a big difference.

If your bristle weedguard is so stiff that you're missing fish, remove some of the bristles to make it more flexible.

Make a wire striker for pike or muskie fishing by twisting a length of single-strand stainless-steel wire to your jig and a barrel swivel. The striker should be only 4 to 6 inches long.

Splice a small barrel swivel into your line, about 18 inches from your jig, when vertically jigging. Otherwise, your line will twist badly and continually throw loops around your rod tip.

Flatten a ball-head jig to convert it to a slider head. Then, you can work it slowly over weed tops or other obstructions without it constantly snagging.

Attach a small float above your jig when fishing over woody or weedy cover. Give the float a twitch and then hesitate as the jig swings back to vertical; that's when the fish usually strike.

Outfit your jig with a stinger hook by (1) clipping a commercially made stinger onto a jig that has a bottom eye, (2) pushing a commercially made stinger with a latex-filled loop over the bend of your jig hook or (3) making your own stinger by tying a length of stiff mono to the bend of your jig hook and then adding a treble hook.

Do not insert the stinger into the tail of a minnow; it will impede its swimming action and reduce the number of strikes. Instead, let the stinger trail near the minnow's tail.

FLOATERS

This lure category includes floating jigs and floats that are threaded onto your line. These lures are normally used in combination with live bait.

Floaters add a splash of color and lift your bait above weeds and other cover, where fish can see it more easily. They also work well for keeping your bait from constantly fouling on a bottom covered with moss.

Floaters are most popular for walleyes, smallmouth bass, trout and salmon, but can be used for most any gamefish.

Floating jigs resemble ordinary jigs but the head, instead of being made of lead, is made of styrofoam, cork or some other highly buoyant material. Floating jigs are sometimes tipped with a soft-plastic grub instead of live bait.

Floats that thread onto your line come in a variety of shapes, the most common being a simple round ball, or corkie. Some floats have wings that make them spin when retrieved, adding vibration as well as visual appeal. Others are intended to look like a gob of salmon eggs.

You can peg a float with a toothpick to keep it away from the hook, but most anglers just let it slide on the line; the buoyancy keeps it pushed against the hook eye.

Floaters used for trout and salmon are usually fished on a split-shot rig; those used for walleyes and smallmouth bass, on a slip-sinker rig (opposite).

When used with an extremely long leader, floating jigs and other floaters can help you reach suspended fish. But there is a com-mon misconception as to how far they will lift the bait off bottom. Some anglers use leaders as much as 15 feet long under the mistaken assumption that they'll be able to float their bait up to reach fish 10 or more feet off the bottom. But, unless you're using a very large floater or moving extremely slowly, you'll be lucky to raise it more than two or three feet. It's just a matter of physics; there is simply not enough buoyancy to over-come the water resistance.

A light leader is a must when using any type of floater. If your leader is too heavy, the extra water resis-tance will keep the floater down.

Popular Floaters

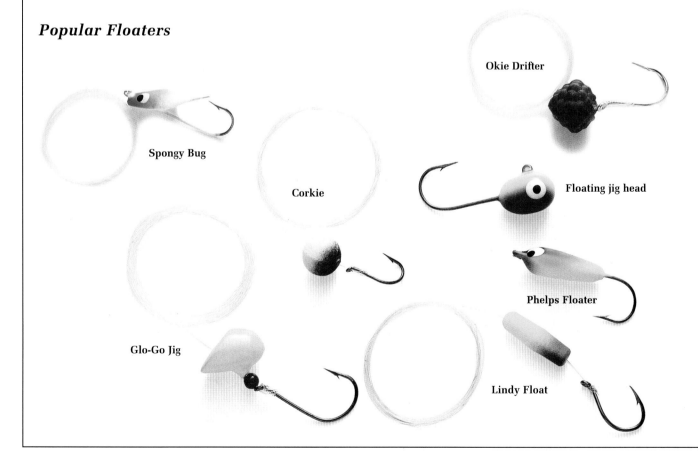

Okie Drifter

Spongy Bug

Corkie

Floating jig head

Phelps Floater

Glo-Go Jig

Lindy Float

Tips for Rigging and Fishing Floaters

Make an adjustable floating rig by threading a slip-sinker onto your line, adding a neoprene stop and then tying on a floater. When you want the bait to float higher, slide the stop farther from the hook.

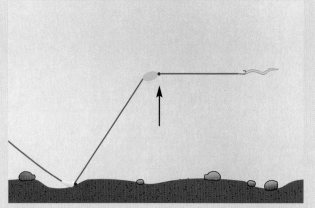

Add a second neoprene stop between the float and the hook; this way you can keep the float away from the hook so the bait looks more natural.

Make a drift-fishing rig for trout and salmon by tying on a floater, such as an Okie Drifter (left) tipped with fresh or soft-plastic salmon eggs, and pinching on just enough split shot to keep the rig bumping bottom as it drifts. Angle a short cast upstream and, with your rod tip high, let the rig float through a run.

For fishing in low-growing weeds, use a slip-sinker rig made with a bullet sinker and a floater. The sinker slides through the weeds easily and the floater keep the bait riding above the weed tops.

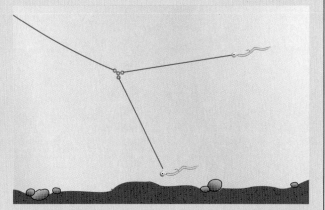

Fish a floating jig tipped with live bait on a 3-way swivel rig, using a lead-head jig for weight. This rig improves your odds, because a fish has the choice of taking the floater or the lead-head.

Jigging Spoons

Until recently, the jigging spoon was considered a deep-water bass bait, but anglers are discovering that these simple lures also work well for other gamefish such as lake trout, walleyes and even yellow perch.

A jigging spoon consists of a piece of lead, brass or stainless steel with a hook on the end of it. Most jigging spoons weigh from $1/2$ to more than 2 ounces, although some panfish models weigh only $1/8$- to $1/4$-ounce.

Long, thin spoons sink rapidly and are intended primarily for vertical jigging. Short, wide models (called slab spoons) are designed for distance casting. They make good shad imitations and are ideal for "jump fishing" for white bass and stripers.

To vertically jig a spoon, let it sink to the bottom, lift it from 6 to 18 inches, and then follow it back down with your rod tip until you feel it touch bottom. It's important to maintain contact with the spoon as it is sinking; if you allow the line to go slack, you won't feel the strike.

As in any kind of jig fishing, you must experiment to find the right jigging action. Some days, a big lift followed by a long pause works best; other days, a fast, short jigging stroke is more effective.

A good depth finder is a big help in vertical jigging, because it enables you to see fish that are suspended off the bottom and adjust your presentation accordingly. Reel the lure up and jig it just above the fish.

Because of the open hooks, hang-ups are common when vertically jigging in timber or other heavy cover. But if you get snagged, simply pull the line tight and then let the spoon drop; its heavy weight usually frees the hook.

Recommended Tackle

It's not uncommon to vertically jig in depths of 50 feet or more, so you'll need a long rod to get a solid hookset. Expert spoon jiggers prefer a $6 1/2$- to 7-foot, medium-heavy-power graphite baitcasting rod with a long handle and a sturdy baitcasting reel spooled with 20-pound mono. Lighter line would result in too many break-offs.

Spoon Jigging Tips

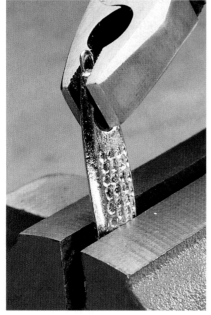

Bend a jigging spoon slightly to change its action. A bent spoon will flutter more erratically as it sinks than a straight one.

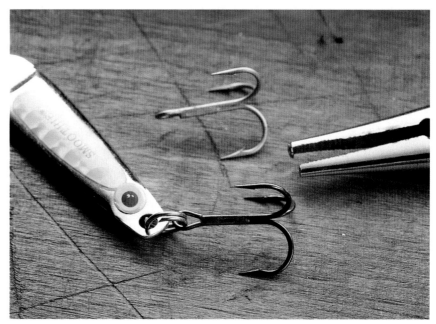

Replace cheap nickel hooks with quality bronze hooks that are sharper and straighten more easily when you get snagged. If the lure does not have a split-ring on the attachment eye, add one to improve the action and prevent damaging your line.

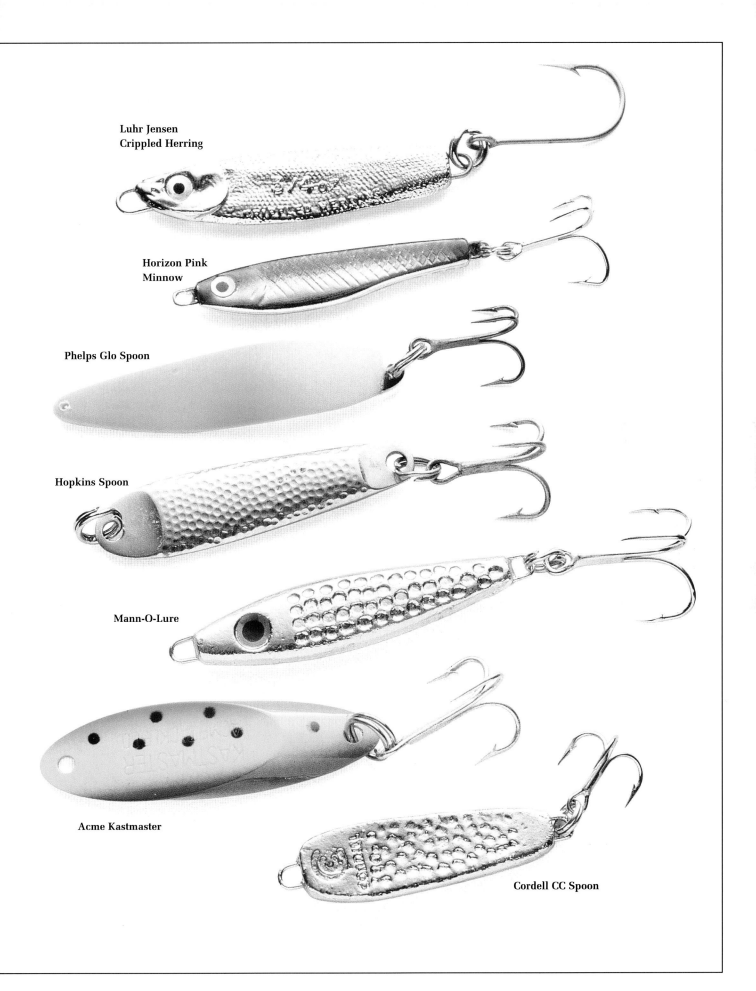

Luhr Jensen
Crippled Herring

Horizon Pink
Minnow

Phelps Glo Spoon

Hopkins Spoon

Mann-O-Lure

Acme Kastmaster

Cordell CC Spoon

Jigging Lures

VIBRATING BLADES

As their name suggests, vibrating blades have an intense wiggle that attracts gamefish, even in waters where the visibility is only a few inches. Fish detect the strong vibrations using their lateral lines.

A vibrating blade, also called a bladebait, consists of a thin, fish-shaped metal body with lead molded onto the head. The attachment eye is on the back, so the bait vibrates rapidly when pulled upward.

Some bladebaits come with more than one attachment hole along the back. By clipping your snap into different holes, you can change the bait's action. With the snap attached to the front hole, the bait has a very tight wiggle; to the rear hole, a looser wobble.

Small bladebaits, weighing as little as 1/8 ounce, are commonly used for panfish; medium-size baits (1/4 to 1/2 ounce) for walleyes and black bass; and large baits (up to 1 ounce) for stripers and lake trout.

Although bladebaits are used mainly for vertical jigging, they can also be reeled steadily, like a crankbait, or fished with a twitch-and-pause retrieve, like a lead-head jig.

Vertical jigging with a bladebait is not much different than vertical jigging with a lead-head jig. But blades are often fished with a much longer vertical sweep, sometimes more than 10 feet. At times, however, a sweep of a foot or less works better; you just have to experiment. As in fishing a lead-head, you must keep the line fairly taut on the drop in order to feel a take.

Bladebaits sink rapidly, so they're a good choice for fishing in very deep water. Using a 1/2-ounce bait, you can easily jig in water up to 60 feet deep, and a 1-ounce bait will get you considerably deeper.

Lake trout anglers, for example, often rely on bladebaits for catching summertime lakers at depths of 60 to 100 feet. With a bladebait, you can catch the fish on relatively light tackle, rather than relying on the traditional wire-line or heavy three-way rigs.

Popular Bladebaits

Recommended Tackle

For bladebaits weighing less than 1/2 ounce, use a medium-power, fast-action spinning outfit about 6 feet in length with 6- to 8-pound-test mono. For 1/2- to 1-ounce baits, use a 6 1/2- to 7-foot, medium-heavy-power, fast-action baitcasting outfit spooled with 10- to 14-pound-test mono. If you'll be fishing in water deeper than 50 feet, consider using 20- to 30-pound-test superline for stronger hooksets.

Bullet Blade

Cicada

Cordell Gay Blade

Heddon Sonar

Silver Buddy

Attach a bladebait with a locking-type snap rather than a snap-swivel. When you're vertically jigging, the hooks of a bladebait tend to foul on the line, and a long snap-swivel compounds the problem.

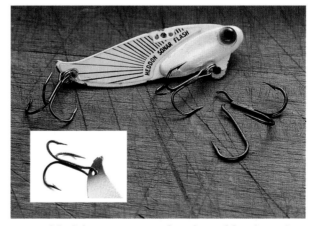

Many bladebaits come with split trebles (inset). But when these hooks get damaged, replacements are hard to find. To replace a hook, simply add a split ring and a standard treble hook.

The helicoptering action of a tailspin slows the sink rate, giving fish extra time to strike.

TAILSPINS

A tailspin is really a hybrid between a jigging lure and a spinner. It consists of a heavy lead body with a treble hook on the bottom and a spinner at the rear.

You can fish a tailspin like a spinner, making long casts and reeling steadily to cover a lot of water. Or you can fish it by vertically jigging or using a twitch-and-pause retrieve, as you would with a lead-head jig.

For crappies and white bass, use tailspins weighing $1/4$ to $1/2$ ounce; for walleyes and black bass, $1/2$ to $3/4$ ounce; and for stripers and lake trout, $3/4$ to 1 ounce.

Tailspins have some advantages over other types of jigging lures. Because the blade turns while the lure is sinking, as well as when it's pulled upward, the lure emits constant flash. And the spinning blade slows the rate of descent, meaning that

fish have more time to strike.

The lift provided by the blade also makes the tailspin a good choice when fish are suspended. Just make a long cast, count the lure down to the desired level and make a slow retrieve. With other types of jigging lures, you'd have to reel rapidly to keep the lure at the right depth.

Tailspins are a popular lure for jump fishing white bass and stripers. A surface-feeding "pack" will spook if you get your boat too close to them but, with a tailspin, you can keep your distance and still reach the fish. Anglers in southern reservoirs often keep an extra rod rigged with a tailspin just in case they spot a school of white bass or stripers breaking water.

Popular Tailspins

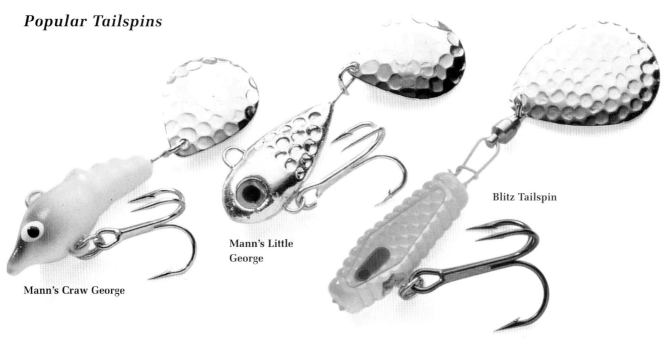

Mann's Craw George

Mann's Little George

Blitz Tailspin

Tips for Fishing Tailspins

Tie a tailspin directly to your line, rather than using a snap or snap-swivel. The lure will not cause line twist.

Replace the blade on a tailspin with a bigger one to give the lure more lift and make it helicopter more slowly. Straighten the tail wire just enough to remove the clevis, add the larger blade, put the clevis back on and reform the wire.

JIGGING LURES FOR ICE FISHING

Jigging lures enjoy tremendous popularity among ice anglers, and for good reason. Most gamefish are not as active in the icy water as they are in summer; the jigging action seems to arouse their curiosity and draw more strikes than a less vigorous presentation.

Another reason for the burgeoning popularity of jigging lures: they're ideal for the mobile style of today's ice anglers. With a jigging lure, you can easily hop from hole to hole. With a bobber rig, you would have to stop and adjust the depth of the bobber after each move.

Jigging lures are used for all species of fish caught by ice fishermen. The lures fall into the following categories:

- **Swimming Minnows** - These baits have a single, upturned hook at each end, a tail that causes them to swim and an attachment eye at the center of the back. Some have a treble hook on the belly. When you pull the bait upward, it darts ahead.

  Swimming minnows are usually attached with a tiny clip or tied directly to the line.

Popular Jigging Lures for Ice Fishing

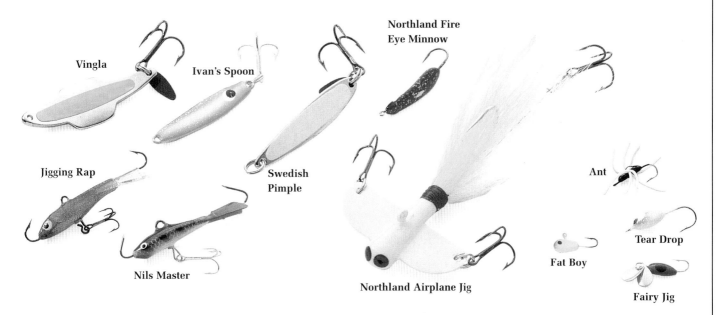

Vingla

Ivan's Spoon

Northland Fire Eye Minnow

Ant

Jigging Rap

Swedish Pimple

Tear Drop

Nils Master

Fat Boy

Northland Airplane Jig

Fairy Jig

- **Jigging Spoons** - The jigging spoons used for ice fishing are not much different than those used in open water, but most of them are smaller. Jigging spoons used by ice anglers normally weigh $1/2$ ounce or less and some weigh only $1/8$ ounce. With no wind or current to contend with, there is no need for a heavy spoon; lighter ones drop more slowly and have more action. When dropped on a slack line, a jigging spoon flutters to the side.

   If your jigging spoon does not have a split-ring on the attachment eye, add one. Then, tie your line to the split-ring or attach it with a small clip. If you tie directly to the eye, the sharp metal could cut your line.
- **Airplane Jigs** - An airplane jig is nothing more than a lead-head jig with metal wings. Most models have a trailer hook and some have treble hooks on each wing. When pulled upward, an airplane jig swims in a wide circle.

   Airplane jigs should be tied directly to the line or attached with a small clip.
- **Tear Drops** - Used primarily for panfish, these tiny lures get their name from the shape of their lead bodies. The size 8 to 12 fine-wire hook is usually tipped with a real or soft-plastic grub worm. Most tear drops have no action of their own; the angler imparts a rapid jiggling motion.
- **Ice Flies** - These tiny panfish lures have a lead body dressed with hair, feathers or live-rubber to give them a lifelike appearance and add action. Like tear drops, they are generally tipped with grubs and fished with a jiggling motion.

   Tear drops and ice flies should be tied directly to very light monofilament. Some anglers prefer to attach them with a loop knot; this way, the lure dances more erratically than if it were tied on with a clinch knot. Some anglers prefer to attach them with a loop knot; this way, the lure dances more erratically than if it were tied on with a clinch knot.

Recommended Tackle

Swimming minnows and jigging spoons are normally fished with a $2\frac{1}{2}$- to 3-foot graphite jigging rod and a small spinning reel spooled with 4- to 8-pound mono. An airplane jig requires long sweeps, so most anglers use a full-length spinning or baitcasting outfit with 8- to 12-pound mono. Tear drops and ice flies require a very sensitive tip; use an ultralight jigging rod or a stiffer jigging rod equipped with a spring bobber and 2- to 4-pound mono.

How to Fish a Swimming Minnow

Twitch the bait sharply to make it dart forward, then pause as it settles to rest. The fish normally strike when the bait stops moving.

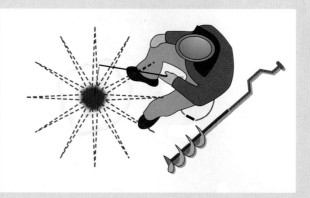

On each twitch, the bait darts out at a slightly different angle, so you can cover a large area surrounding the hole.

How to Fish a Jigging Spoon

Lift the bait one to three feet and then lower your rod tip rapidly to throw slack into the line. The bait will flutter to the side as it sinks and then settle to rest. That's when the fish usually strike.

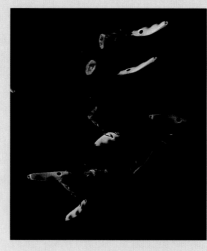

Shake the bait violently if nothing is biting. The action may draw the fish's attention. Then hold the rod tip motionless, wait for a fish to nudge the bait and set the hook.

How to Fish an Airplane Jig

Using a full-length rod, give the bait a long upward sweep to make it swim in a circle, then pause as it settles. After it stops moving, make another sweep. Fish normally strike on the pause.

How to Fish a Tear Drop or Ice Fly

Jiggle the bait rapidly, pause a few seconds, then lift the bait a few inches and repeat. Continue jiggling and lifting to entice the fish to strike the bait. After lifting it a few feet, drop to the bottom and start over.

How to Tip Jigging Lures with Natural Bait

Tip a jigging spoon with a minnow head for extra attraction. Hook the minnow through the head and then cut or pinch off the rest of its body.

Tip an airplane jig with a strip of cut bait. Push the wide end of the strip over the main hook and push one prong of the trailing treble hook through the narrow end.

Hook a perch eye (where legal), minnow head or grub worms on the middle treble hook of a swimming minnow.

Thread a waxworm or other type of grub worm onto the hook of a tear drop or ice fly. Make sure the bait hangs straight rather than sticking out to the side.

Two Tips for Ice Fishing with Jigging Lures

Use a rod equipped with a spring bobber when fishing with a tear drop or ice fly. A spring bobber is much more sensitive than a float and will signal the lightest bite.

Use a sensitive flasher so you can see how the fish are responding to your jigging motion. This screen shows the lure (green line) with a fish right below it (red line).

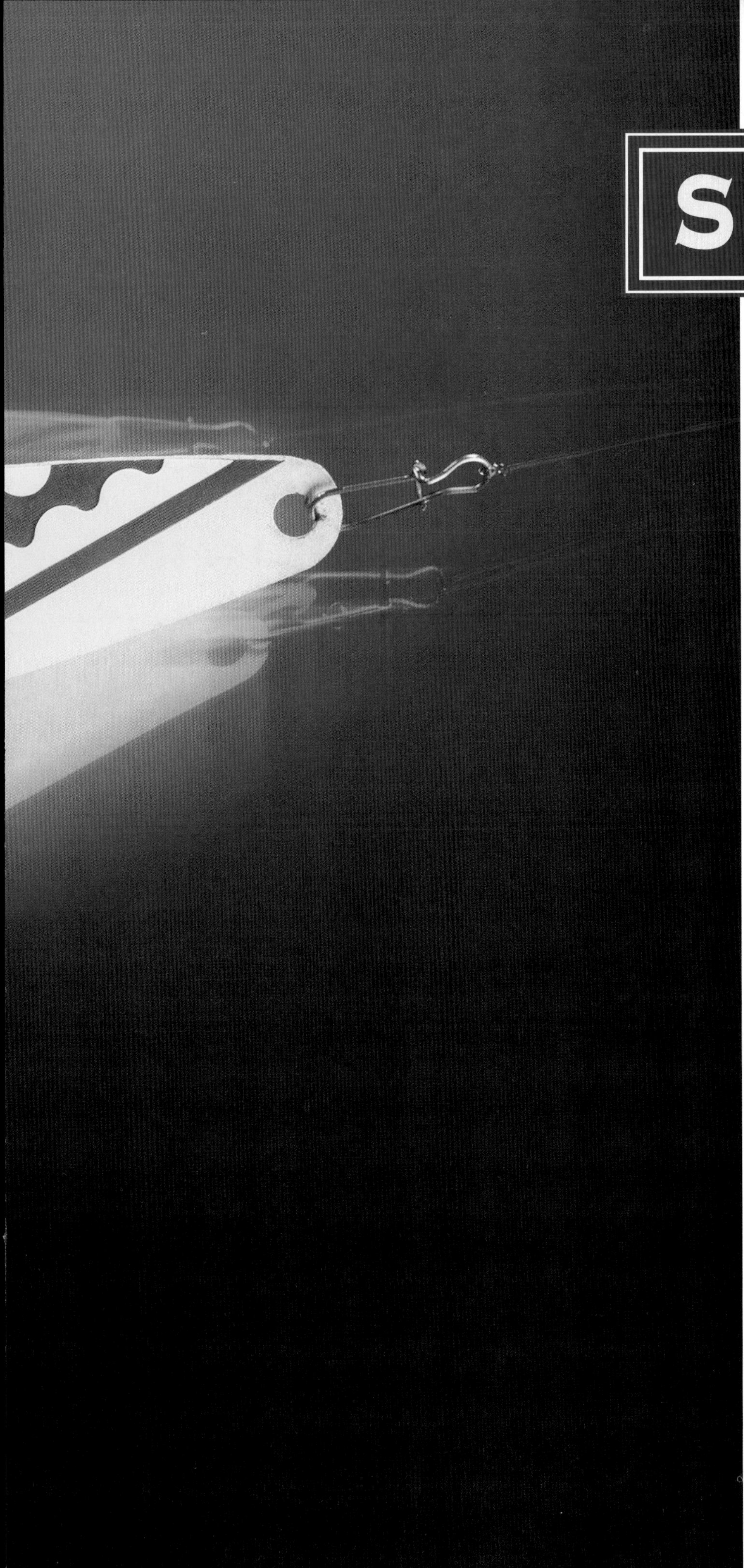

SPOONS

Spoons are among the simplest of artificial lures, but their unique combination of wobble and flash explains their near-universal fish appeal.

SPOONS

Although spoons have been around for centuries, they are as effective today as ever. Among the easiest lures to use, spoons appeal to most kinds of gamefish.

The vast majority of spoons are made of metal, usually steel or brass, although a few hard-plastic models are available. Most spoons have a treble hook at the rear, but some come with a single hook.

Spoons fall into three main categories: casting spoons, trolling spoons and weedless spoons. Casting spoons have thicker metal than trolling spoons, so you can toss them much farther, but they have considerably less wobble. Weedless spoons have some type of weedguard protecting the fixed single hook.

Most spoons are convex on one side and concave on the other, so they have an enticing wobble. The deeper a spoon is dished, the more water it catches on the retrieve and the greater the wobble.

Another factor affecting a spoon's wobble is its body shape. The longer and thinner the body, the wider the wobble tends to be.

In most spoons, at least one side is left unpainted, so they produce plenty of flash. Some spoons come with a hammered finish that reflects light in all directions. When flash is an important consideration, as it normally is in clear water, choose a spoon with a plated finish. A silver-plated spoon, for example, is many times more reflective than an unplated steel spoon.

The size and shape of your spoon is just as important as its action. Select a spoon of approximately the same dimensions as the baitfish your target species is eating.

With any spoon, it's important to find the right retrieve speed. If your retrieve is too fast, the spoon will spin; too slow, and it will barely wobble. Whether you're casting or trolling, keep adjusting your speed until the wobble is just right.

Types of Spoons

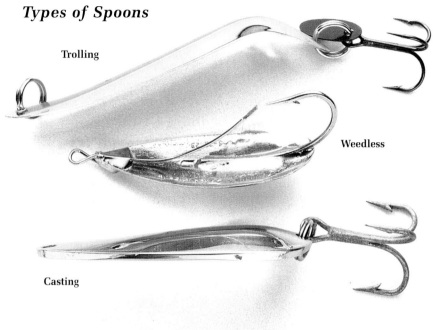

Understanding Wobble

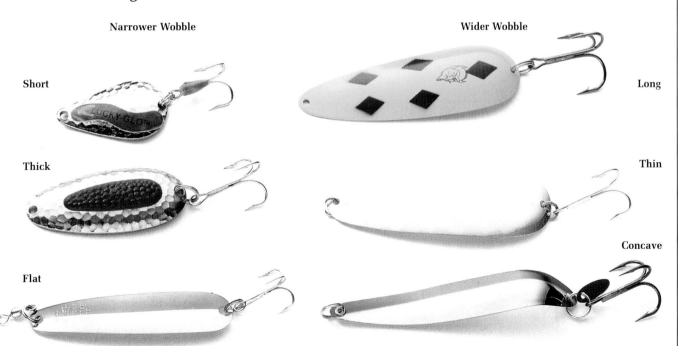

All other factors being equal, a long spoon will have a wider wobble than a short one (top); a thin spoon has a wider wobble than a thick one (middle) and a deeply concave spoon has a wider wobble than a flattened one (bottom).

CASTING SPOONS

Casting spoons include any spoons with metal thick enough to provide the weight necessary for good casting performance. If you attempt to cast into the wind with a spoon that is too thin, it will blow right back into your face.

But casting spoons aren't always used for casting. They also work well for trolling, and extra-thick models are a good choice for vertically jigging in deep water.

A spoon of medium thickness ($3/8$ to $1/2$ ounce for the average 3-inch model) works well for casting and trolling in shallow water or over shallow cover.

A thicker spoon ($5/8$ to $3/4$ ounce) is the best all-purpose selection.

Casting spoons are ideal for covering a large expanse of water.

Popular Casting Spoons

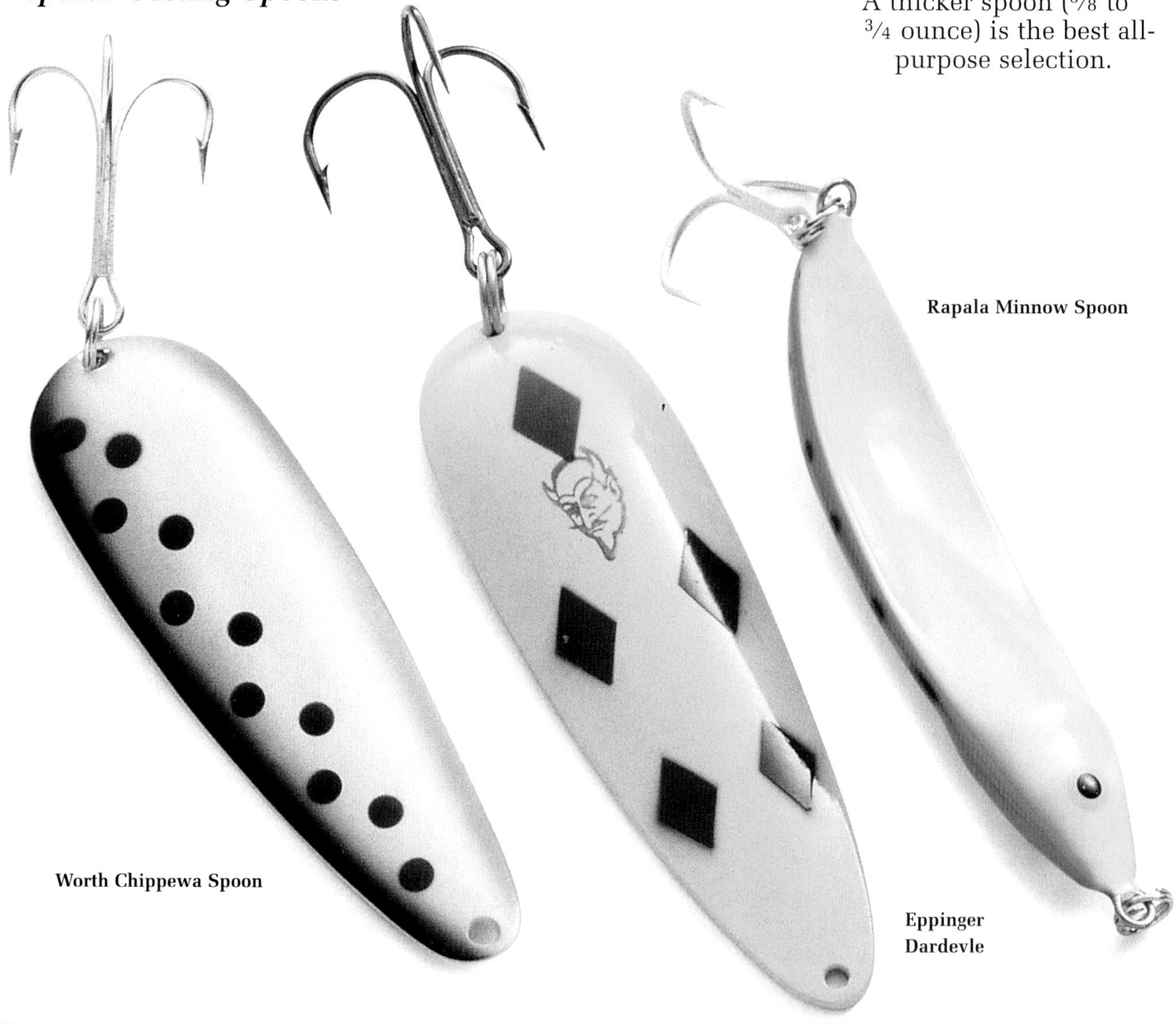

Rapala Minnow Spoon

Worth Chippewa Spoon

Eppinger Dardevle

You can fish it shallow by holding your rod tip high and reeling a little faster than normal, or slow down and let it run deep. It also has enough heft to stay down in slow to moderate current.

An extra thick spoon (1 to 1½ ounce) is needed for casting or trolling in deep water or strong current. You can also use it as a jigging lure, hopping it vertically off bottom in water as deep as 100 feet.

Casting spoons can be retrieved steadily, but are often more effective with a stop-and-go retrieve. If you're casting, stop reeling every few seconds, allow the spoon to flutter down, and then resume reeling. If you're trolling, periodically drop your rod tip back to throw some slack into the line.

Fish often grab the spoon as it is sinking.

Anglers use casting spoons as much as a foot long for big pike, muskies and lake trout. At the other extreme, crappie and stream-trout anglers sometimes use spoons only an inch long.

If your spoon doesn't come with an attachment ring, be sure to add a split-ring or use a rounded snap. This prevents break offs caused by the sharp edge of the metal damaging your line and gives the spoon more action.

Although a spoon wobbling properly will not twist your line, it's a good idea to use a snap-swivel instead of a plain snap. That way, should you retrieve a little too fast, you don't have to worry about line twist.

> ### Recommended Tackle
>
> A medium-power spinning or baitcasting outfit with 8- to 12-pound mono is adequate for most spoon fishing. For spoons weighing less than ¼ ounce, however, use a light spinning outfit with 4- to 6-pound mono; more than 1 ounce, a medium-heavy-power baitcasting outfit with 12- to 15-pound mono.

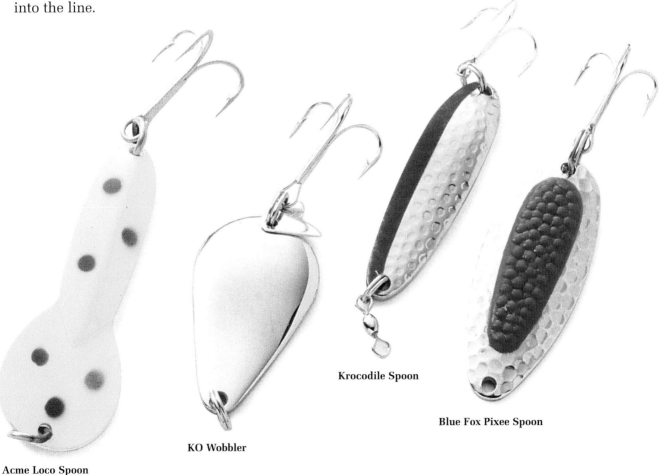

Krocodile Spoon

Blue Fox Pixee Spoon

KO Wobbler

Acme Loco Spoon

How to "Buzz" the Weed Tops

Keep your rod tip high and reel as fast as necessary to keep your spoon buzzing the weed tops. When you come to a pocket in the weeds, slow down and let the spoon drop. A spoon of medium thickness works best for this type of retrieve.

The Stop-and-Go Retrieve

Reel steadily, periodically stopping to let the spoon sink and then resuming your retrieve. The change in action often triggers fish to strike, usually while the lure is sinking. This retrieve is effective with any kind of casting spoon.

Five Tips for Fishing with Casting Spoons

If you're losing too many fish, replace the treble hook with a Siwash hook. The long, thin point penetrates more deeply and makes it more difficult for fish to throw the hook.

Use a long rod and make lengthy upward sweeps when vertically jigging a heavy spoon in deep water. Throw slack into the line as the spoon sinks to give it an erratic flutter.

Use an extra-thick spoon and quarter your casts upstream when fishing in strong current. This way, the spoon will sink into the fish zone before the current (arrow) sweeps it past you and starts to lift it.

Add a soft-plastic curlytail for extra attraction. Just push one prong of the treble hook through the end of the grub.

Restore the finish of a tarnished spoon by rubbing it with metal polish. If the polish won't remove the tarnish, try fine steel wool.

TROLLING SPOONS

Trolling spoons have long been the number-one choice of Great Lakes trout and salmon anglers, but these lures are effective for any kind of open-water predator fish. They're a favorite of many big-lake walleye anglers, for example, and are popular among striper fishermen in southern reservoirs.

Trolling spoons, which are made of thin metal, are very light for their size. The typical 3-inch spoon weighs only ⅛ ounce and some models weigh only half that much. Their light weight makes them nearly impossible to cast, but is a big advantage for trolling.

With most trolling spoons, you can move very slowly (1 to 2 mph) yet the lure will have good action and stay at a consistent depth. The slow, fluttering motion is often just what the fish want. If you trolled that slowly with a casting spoon, it wouldn't wobble as much as it should and its running depth would vary greatly as the boat's speed changed. Some trolling spoons, however, are designed for faster speeds.

They have the best action at speeds of 2.5 to 3.5 mph.

If you'll be trolling with more than one line, as most spoon trollers do, it's important to choose spoons that are compatible, meaning that they attain their best action at approximately the same speed. Otherwise, one spoon may have an enticing wobble while another may have practically no action at all. Always check your spoons for compatibility by trolling them at boatside.

A trolling spoon, by itself, will run no more than a few feet deep. To reach the desired depth, you'll need downriggers, diving planers or 3-way rigs. Be sure to use light line; heavy line will restrict the spoon's action. Always tie or clip your line directly to the spoon's attachment ring. A heavy snap-swivel will also restrict the action.

The fact that a trolling spoon doesn't sink much on its own means that you can troll it just above a snaggy bottom without constantly hanging up. A casting spoon, on the other hand, would sink to the bottom and possibly snag whenever the boat loses speed.

Recommended Tackle

For downrigger fishing, use a 7$\frac{1}{2}$ to 8-foot, medium-power, slow-action trolling rod and a high-capacity trolling reel spooled with 10- to 14-pound-test monofilament. A slow-action rod helps cushion a strong run, so a big fish won't break the light line.

For fishing with diving planers or 3-way rigs, use a 6$\frac{1}{2}$- to 7-foot, medium-heavy- to heavy-power trolling rod. The heavier rod is needed to withstand the strong resistance of these rigs. Select a high-capacity trolling reel, fill it with 20- to 30-pound-test mono or 30- to 40-pound-test superline and add a 10- to 14-pound-test mono leader.

Popular Trolling Spoons

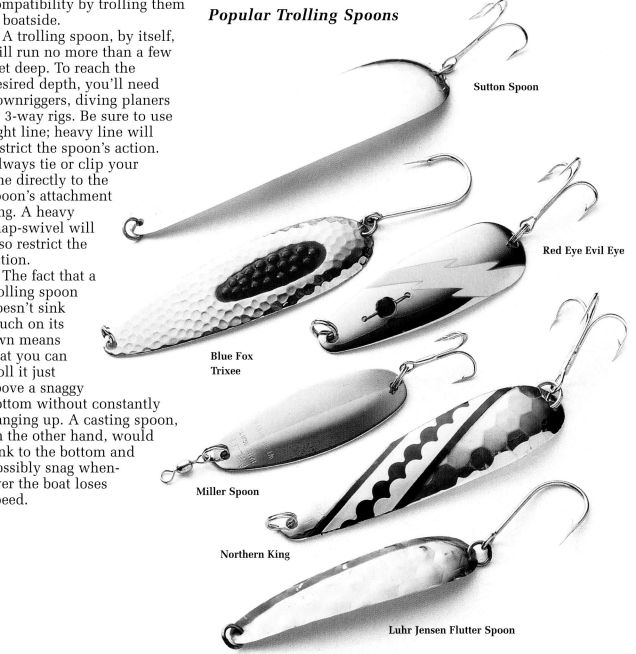

Sutton Spoon

Red Eye Evil Eye

Blue Fox Trixee

Miller Spoon

Northern King

Luhr Jensen Flutter Spoon

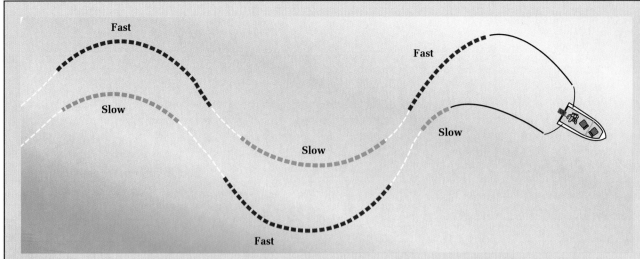

Troll in an S-shaped path to vary the action of your trolling spoons. As you turn, the spoons on the outside will speed up (red) and those on the inside will slow down (blue). The change in action often triggers strikes.

Use a 3-way rig to troll a spoon in deep water. Tie your line to a large 3-way swivel, attach an 18- to 24-inch dropper with a 6- to 12-ounce lead ball and a 6-foot leader. This rig keeps a trolling spoon well off bottom, minimizing snags.

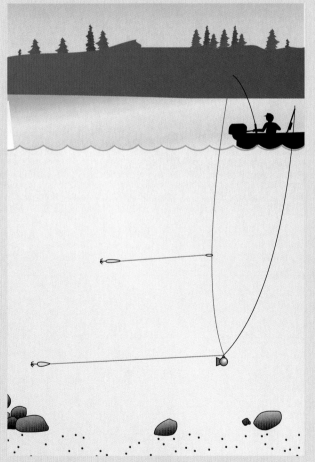

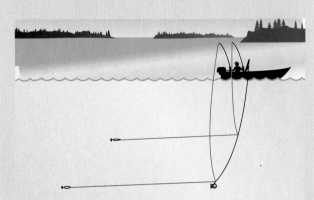

When "stacking" spoons on a downrigger, be sure to put the lightest spoon on top, This way, should the boat slow down, the top spoon won't sink rapidly and catch the bottom line.

Use a "cheater" when trolling with downriggers. Make a 6-foot leader with a clip on one end and a spoon on the other, and attach the clip to a line already set on a downrigger. The cheater will slide down the line and run at mid-depth.

Add colored tape to your spoons to match productive color patterns. You can cover the entire side of a spoon with a wide strip or use a narrow diagonal strip to add a splash of color.

If line twist is a problem, splice a small barrel swivel into your line about two feet ahead of the spoon. This way, the weight of the swivel won't impede the spoon's action.

Increase the bend of a trolling spoon to give it a wider wobble. Be sure the bend is smooth and gradual, with no kinks.

Use a trolling-speed indicator to maintain the right speed despite wind and current. This model has a sensor (inset) that attaches to your downrigger cable, giving you speed and water temperature readings at the depth you're fishing.

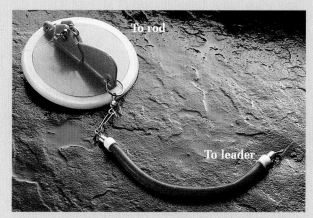

Attach a rubber "snubber" to your leader when using a diving planer. A planer has a great deal of water resistance and, without a snubber, a big fish could easily snap the leader.

Weedless spoons are the perfect choice for extracting bass from dense weeds.

WEEDLESS SPOONS

In summer, when bass are buried in matted weeds or other dense, shallow-water cover, few lures are as effective as a weedless spoon.

These baits also work well for northern pike and pickerel in heavy cover.

Most weedless spoons have some type of wire, plastic or bristle weedguard. There are three basic types of weedless spoons. Each type of spoon is intended for a different purpose:

- **Standard weedless spoons** - These metal spoons sink rapidly, so they are a good choice for subsurface retrieves in submergent vegetation. Some have an upturned nose or lip to help them slide over surface vegetation.
- **Spinner spoons** - A spinner or propeller attached to the spoon creates extra vibration and adds lift, so you can retrieve very slowly. The vibration helps fish zero in on the lure in extremely dense cover.

Recommended Tackle

A 6 1/2- to 7-foot, heavy-power baitcasting outfit and 17- to 20-pound abrasion-resistant monofilament is recommended for horsing fish from the dense cover before they have a chance to tangle your line around the weed stems. The long rod helps pull the fish upward and keep it on top of the weeds.

The Ultimate Guide To Freshwater Fishing

- **Plastic spoons** - These lightweight spoons are designed to slide across surface weeds with the hook pointing up. They can be retrieved very slowly without sinking.

Most weedless spoons come with a plastic, live-rubber or feather trailer that adds action and buoyancy. If your spoon doesn't have a trailer, add a pork strip or a soft-plastic curlytail.

The biggest problem in fishing weedless spoons is short strikes. Fish may have trouble clearly seeing the lure in the heavy cover, so they often swirl next to it, missing it completely. And even when you get a solid strike, the stiff weedguard causes you to lose some fish.

You can minimize the problem by making short casts and using a steady retrieve. That way, fish can track the lure more easily. And with less line out, you'll get a stronger hookset.

Types of Weedless Spoons

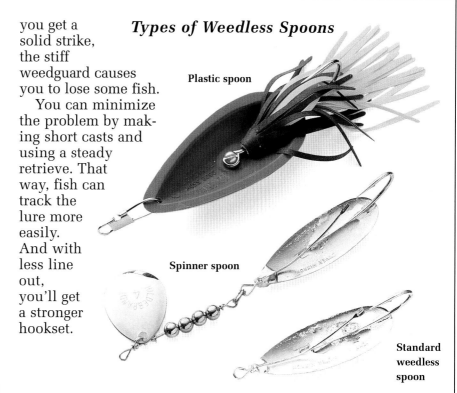

Plastic spoon

Spinner spoon

Standard weedless spoon

Popular Weedless Spoons

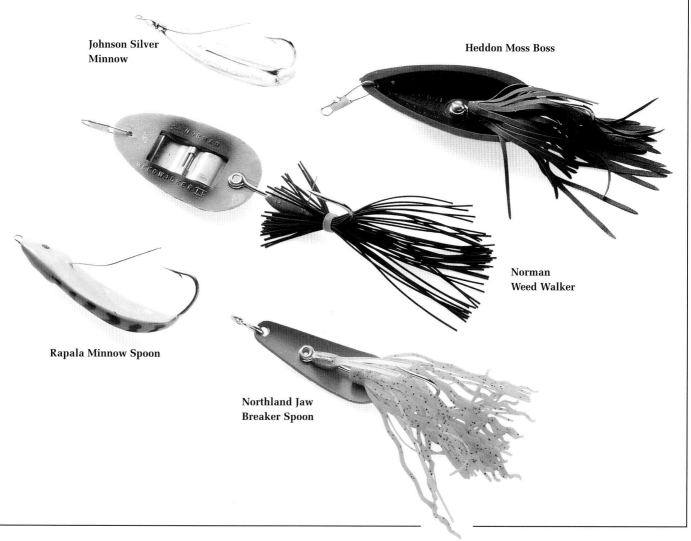

Johnson Silver Minnow

Heddon Moss Boss

Norman Weed Walker

Rapala Minnow Spoon

Northland Jaw Breaker Spoon

How to Retrieve Weedless Spoons

Slowly retrieve a standard weedless spoon or a spinner spoon through emergent weeds or the tops of submergent weeds. Reel steadily, keeping the lure just a few inches beneath the surface.

Work pockets in floating-leaved weeds by steadily reeling a standard weedless spoon up to the opening, pausing to let it sink a few feet and then resuming the retrieve until the lure reaches the next opening.

Skim a plastic spoon over matted weeds that are too thick for a subsurface retrieve. Keep your rod tip high, moving the lure slowly and steadily, and try to direct it toward any good-sized hole in the vegetation.

Tips for Fishing Weedless Spoons

Use a plastic spoon for skimming over the tops of shallow weeds. This way, you can retrieve slowly, yet the spoon won't sink into the vegetation.

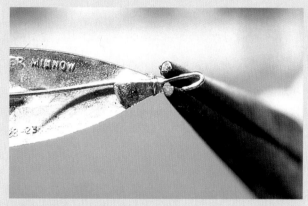

When fishing in stringy algae, squeeze the attachment eye with a pliers to give it a sharp point. This way, sticky filaments won't collect on the eye.

Trim the skirt of a weedless spoon to reduce the number of short strikes. With a trimmed skirt, the lure has a smaller profile, so fish are more likely to strike the hook.

Point your rod directly at the spoon on a subsurface retrieve. This way, you'll have much more hook-setting power than you would if you held the rod tip high.

Don't use a trailer that is too large for the bait. A big trailer has too much water resistance, so it prevents the lure from wobbling as it should.

FLIES

*T*he skyrocket-
ing popularity
of fly fishing
should come as
no surprise – it is
not only a relax-
ing retreat from
hectic city life, it
is a deadly fish-
catching method.

FLIES

The Ultimate Guide To Freshwater Fishing

In the hands of a knowledgeable fly fisherman, a well-stocked fly box is a highly potent weapon – not just for trout, but for many other kinds of gamefish as well.

It's no wonder flies are so effective; they mimic insects or other foods that most gamefish consume at some stage in their life.

Much has been written about "matching the hatch" – choosing a fly that closely imitates the real thing. But unless you're trying to catch "educated" fish, super-realistic flies are seldom necessary. Normally, an *impressionistic* fly – one of the general size, shape and color of the natural, will do the job.

Flies are categorized as follows, based on the type of food item they imitate:

- **Dry Flies** - These floating flies resemble the adult forms of common aquatic insects, such as mayflies, stoneflies and caddisflies. Most have hair or feather wings and a hackle collar that keep them floating on the surface.
- **Wet Flies** - These subsurface flies don't imitate any particular insect, but bear a general resemblance to a variety of fish foods including drowned adult insects, emerging aquatic insects and baitfish. Some wet flies are simply attractors, appealing to fish with their color and flash.
- **Nymphs** - Designed to be fished beneath the surface, these flies imitate the juvenile stages of aquatic insects. Nymphs are tied on heavy hooks, some of which are wrapped with wire for extra weight.
- **Streamers** - Intended to imitate baitfish rather than insects, streamers have an elongated body tied on an extra-long hook. They are often weighted with lead wire so they can be fished deep.
- **Bugs** - These big floating flies resemble frogs, mice, large insects or injured baitfish. Some have hard wooden or plastic bodies while others are made of sponge or clip-ped deer hair.
- **Specialty Flies** - In addition to the types already described, flies have been devised to represent practically any item in a fish's diet.

Common types of specialty flies include egg flies, which look like trout or salmon eggs; terrestrials, which simulate crickets, grasshoppers, beetles and other land-dwelling insects; leech and crayfish imitations; and trolling flies, baitfish imitations most often used by big-lake trout and salmon trollers.

Common Types of Flies

Dry fly

Nymph

Wet fly

Streamer

Bug

Specialty fly
(Crayfish)

DRY FLIES

So much has been written about the difficulty of fishing with dry flies that many anglers are too intimidated to give them a try. But, in fact, fishing dry flies is one of the simplest fly-fishing methods.

When fish are taking insects on the surface, you know precisely where the fish are and what they're eating, so you know what fly to tie on and where to cast it. And you can see the fish take the fly, so you know exactly when to set the hook.

Hundreds of different dry fly patterns are available. The majority fall into one

A dry fly has a head consisting of a mound of thread; a body of yarn, hair or fur, tinsel or feather quills; a hackle collar; a tail of hair or feather fibers; and, usually, hair or feather wings. Dry flies are tied on light-wire hooks.

Styles of Dry Flies

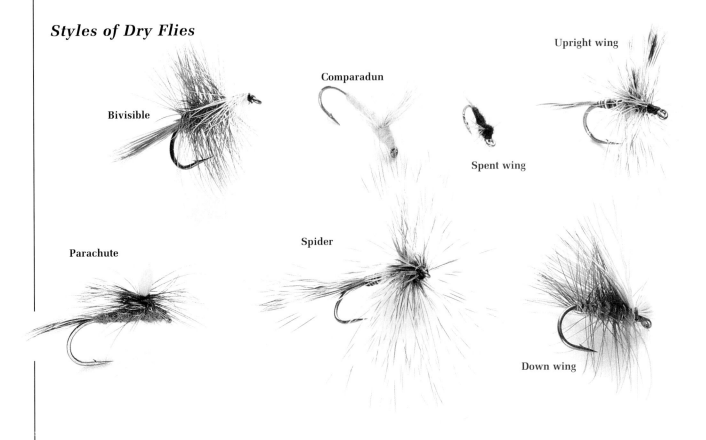

of the following eight categories:

- **Upright wing** - The wings, which are made of feathers, hair or fabric, point straight up like those of a live mayfly.
- **Down wing** - These flies, with hair or feather wings that are swept back or lie tight to the body, resemble stoneflies or caddisflies.
- **Spent wing** - With their feather wings spread, these flies float on the water like a dead mayfly.
- **Comparadun** - There is no hackle collar to provide flotation, so these flies ride lower in the water than most other dries. They have a realistic look but are difficult for the angler to see.
- **Spider** - The hackle collar on these wingless flies is much longer than normal, so they land softly and float high.
- **Bivisible** - Another wingless high floater, the bivisible has hackle along the length of its body. The front of the fly is white and the back dark, making it easy for the angler to see.
- **Parachute** - The hackle is wound horizontally around the upright wing, creating a "parachute" effect as the fly settles to the water. Not only does the fly land very softly, it floats low in the water and has a realistic look.

Popular Dry Flies

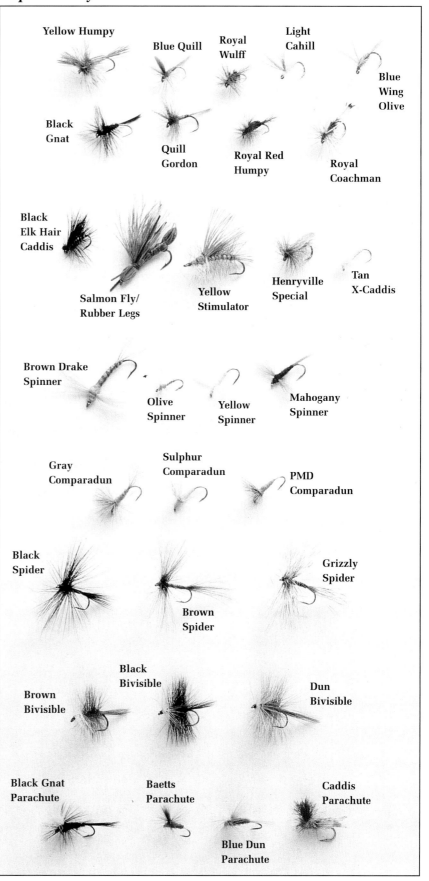

Yellow Humpy
Blue Quill
Royal Wulff
Light Cahill
Blue Wing Olive
Black Gnat
Quill Gordon
Royal Red Humpy
Royal Coachman

Black Elk Hair Caddis
Salmon Fly/ Rubber Legs
Yellow Stimulator
Henryville Special
Tan X-Caddis

Brown Drake Spinner
Olive Spinner
Yellow Spinner
Mahogany Spinner

Gray Comparadun
Sulphur Comparadun
PMD Comparadun

Black Spider
Brown Spider
Grizzly Spider

Brown Bivisible
Black Bivisible
Dun Bivisible

Black Gnat Parachute
Baetts Parachute
Blue Dun Parachute
Caddis Parachute

Fishing with Dry Flies

When you see fish rising, try to determine what insects they're taking. Sometimes there is more than one hatch in progress at the same time, and the most apparent insects aren't always the ones the fish are eating.

The number-one consideration in selecting the right fly is matching the size of the natural. Most fly-fishing authorities agree that size is more important than shape or color. If you cannot match the size exactly, it's better to choose a fly that is slightly smaller rather than larger.

As a rule, bushy, high-floating flies work best in turbulent water; delicate, sparsely tied, low-floating flies, in clear water.

Durability is a concern when fishing for large, hard-fighting fish like steelhead and salmon. Flies with hair wings and tails are generally more durable than those with feather wings or tails.

Another important consideration is visibility. If you can't see your fly, you won't see the take and know when to set the hook. A light-colored fly is the best choice under low-light conditions, but a dark fly is easier to see when the sun is in your eyes.

Selecting the right fly is one matter; presenting it so it looks like a naturally drifting insect is another. It's important to use a long leader with a light tippet. And don't allow your fly line to pull on the fly, creating *drag* that will cause fish to turn up their nose at your offering.

Drag is normally not a problem in still water, but it can be a major headache in current. When the moving water catches your line, it forms a belly that speeds up your fly and causes it to make a wake as it skids unnaturally across the surface.

The easiest way to avoid drag is to cast upstream, not across the current. But don't cast straight upstream or your line will float over the fish and spook it before the fly gets there. If a belly does form, you can solve the problem by *mending* your line (p. 300).

You can also avoid drag by casting downstream, but then you'll have to feed line at the same speed as the current.

There are times, however, when you don't want to fish your dry fly with a drag-free drift. For example, when the fish are feeding on stoneflies or caddisflies that are skittering across the surface, you'll want your fly to do the same. Hold your rod tip high and gently shake it as you strip in line, periodically twitching your rod tip to make the fly skip.

When fishing in a stream, always cast well upstream of any rise. When a fish spots a floating insect, it normally follows it downstream a few feet before grabbing it and then returning to its lie. If you cast to the rise, your fly will be well downstream of the spot where the fish is holding.

In a lake, cast directly to the rise. If the fish doesn't take in a few seconds, pick up your line and cast to another rise. If the pattern of rises indicates that a fish is moving, you may be able to intercept it by casting well ahead of the last rise.

Although most dry-fly fishing involves casting to rises, don't assume that you won't catch fish if you're not seeing them surface. Most gamefish are opportunists; they won't pass up the chance for an easy meal. Make a few casts in a likely spot even if you don't see surface activity.

One of the most common mistakes in dry-fly fishing is setting the hook too hard and snapping the light tippet. You don't need to rear back and bring the rod over your shoulder; all that's needed for a firm hookset is to lift the rod smoothly, keeping it parallel to the water (opposite).

Recommended Tackle and Fly Sizes

For the majority of trout fishing in streams or lakes, you'll need a 2- to 6-weight fly rod with a weight-forward or double-taper floating line and an 8- to 12-foot leader with a 4X to 8X tippet. Most of the dry flies used for trout are sizes 8 to 16, although some patterns come in sizes as small as 28.

For Atlantic salmon, steelhead and other large trout, choose a 7- to 11-weight fly rod with a weight-forward or double-taper floating line and a 10-foot leader with an 8- to 15-pound-test tippet. Most anglers use size 2 to 8 flies.

For panfish, use a 2- to 5-weight fly rod and a weight-forward or double-taper floating line. The leader should be between 7 1/2 and 9 feet long with a 4X to 8X tippet. Most panfish anglers use dry flies in sizes 8 to 12.

For smallmouth bass, anglers commonly use a 6- to 8-weight fly rod and a weight-forward or bass-bug taper line. The 6- to 9-foot leader should have a 2X to 5X tippet. Size 4 to 8 dry flies work well for smallmouth.

Dry Flies—How to Set the Hook

Wrong Way – A strong backward sweep of the rod causes a lot of disturbance when you rip the line out of the water, and will often snap a light tippet.

Right Way – A smooth lift of the rod, keeping it parallel to the water, will set the hook firmly and won't disturb the water enough to spook any remaining fish.

Tips for Fishing with Dry Flies

Apply a powdered dessicant to your fly to make sure it is completely dry. Rub the dessicant in with your fingers and then blow it away.

Rub your fly with a paste floatant to keep it riding high in the water. If the fly starts to sink, reapply dessicant and floatant.

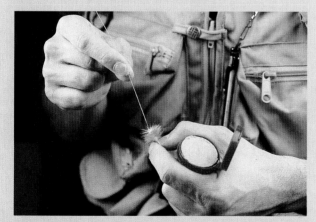

Rub leader sink on your tippet; a sunken leader is less visible to fish than one floating on the surface.

Make several backward and forward strokes to dry your fly before allowing it to land. This technique is called "false casting".

WET FLIES

Wet flies are proof positive that a fly need not look like real food in order to catch fish.

These subsurface flies, intended to resemble drowned insects or baitfish, have been around for centuries. But in the mid 1900s, as realistic dry flies and nymphs came into vogue, wets began to lose favor.

That trend has been reversed, however, as fly fishermen came to realize that some of the old wet fly patterns were outproducing the newer, more "sophisticated" offerings.

Wet flies are made with soft, absorbent materials such as wool or chenille, tied around heavy hooks. They include the following types:

- **Feather wings** - The swept-back wings, usually made of hackle tips, resemble the wings of adult aquatic insects, like caddisflies and stoneflies. Feather wings

sink more rapidly than hair wings and have more action, but they are more easily damaged.

Most wet flies have a head made of a mound of thread; short, swept-back hair or feather wings; wool or floss body on a heavy wire hook; sparse hackle collar or hackle throat and feather-fiber tail.

Types of Wet Flies

Salmon fly

Feather wing

Soft hackle fly

Palmer-hackle fly

Hair wing

- **Hair wings** - These durable flies are used mainly for steelhead and other large gamefish. The hooks are often wrapped with wire to sink the buoyant hair wings. Some have a brass bead for a head.
- **Soft hackle flies** - These wingless flies have a bushy hackle collar. They sink quickly and, when the fly is retrieved with a twitching motion, the hackle collar "breathes" like the gills of a mayfly nymph.
- **Palmer-hackle flies** - With hackle wound over the full length of the body, these flies pulsate enticingly when retrieved with a series of twitches. Wooly worms are the most popular type of palmer-hackle fly.
- **Salmon flies** - Tied with colorful (and often rare) materials, these flies look like nothing a fish would normally eat. Although they are still used by some salmon anglers, these flies are more often tied for collectors.

Popular Wet Flies

Black Gnat

March Brown

Light Hendrickson

Royal Coachman

Skykomish Sunrise

Green Butt Skunk

Purple Peril

Max Canyon

Hare's Ear Soft Hackle

Orange Soft Hackle

Comet

Boss

Olive Wooly Worm

Black Wooly Worm

Yellow Wooly Worm

Yuk Bug

Silver Doctor

Jock Scott

Black Dose

Green Highlander

Fishing with Wet Flies

Wet flies are easier to fish than most other types of flies; in fact, it's nearly impossible to fish them the wrong way.

You can present a wet fly with a drag-free drift, in the same manner as you would fish a dry fly. You can also retrieve a wet fly across stream with a series of twitches, let it hang in the current to fish a pocket behind cover, or even retrieve it upstream.

When you're using a wet fly to imitate a drowned insect, you should obviously fish it with a drag-free drift, mending the line as necessary to avoid drag (below). But if you want it to resemble a baitfish, use a cross-stream or upstream retrieve and strip in line to achieve an erratic, darting action. This type of retrieve also works well in still water.

While dry flies are usually aimed at a specific rise, wets are normally fished at random. The idea is to cover a large expanse of water likely to hold fish. Use the wet-fly drift technique (below) for thorough coverage.

Another effective wet-fly method is dabbling. Just drop the fly into an opening in brushy or weedy cover, then repeatedly dip it into the water and pull it back out to imitate an aquatic insect attempting flight.

A wet fly can be fished with a floating or sinking fly line. When the fish are shallow, a floating line works best, because you can pick up the line more easily to make another cast. But when the fish are deep, you'll need a sink-tip or full-sinking line.

When fishing with a sinking line, be sure to use a short leader. With a long one, a sinking line would not pull the fly down to the desired depth. A delicate tippet is usually not necessary; because the entire leader is under water, fish don't seem to pay as much attention to the diameter of the tippet as they do in dry-fly fishing.

Strikes are sometimes difficult to detect when you're fishing a wet fly in current. A large belly in the line damp- ens your feel, so try to keep the belly to a minimum by following the drifting fly with your rod tip and mending line as needed. Pay close attention to the spot where the line enters the water, watching for any twitch or hesitation that signals a strike. Set the hook with a smooth lift of the rod.

Recommended Tackle and Fly Sizes

You can use the same tackle for fishing wet flies as you would for dry flies (p. 296) but, when you're using a sinking line, your leader should only be 3 to 5 feet long. Tippets used with wet flies can be a little heavier than those used with dries.

For most trout fishing, use wet flies in sizes 8 to 16; for salmon, steelhead and other large trout, sizes 2 to 8; for smallmouth bass, sizes 4 to 8 and for panfish, sizes 8 to 12.

The Wet-Fly Drift

Make a cross-stream cast, then allow the fly to swing downstream. Follow the line with your rod tip and periodically mend line (throw a curve of line upstream) on the drift.

After the fly swings downstream, retrieve it with short strips. Then move downstream a few feet and make another cast. This process allows you to cover a lot of water quickly.

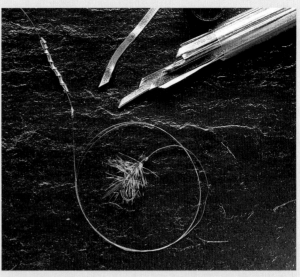

Fish a wet fly with a spinning rod by attaching a plastic "bubble" for weight two or three feet ahead of the fly. The bubble floating on the surface usually won't spook the fish.

For extra depth, add a strip of lead leader wrap a few inches ahead of the fly. You can also add a split shot or two or use a bead-head fly.

Use a tandem wet-fly rig to fish two flies at once. To make a tandem set-up, cut 2 or 3 feet off your leader and then splice the sections with a blood knot, leaving a 4-inch dropper. Then tie a wet fly to the dropper and the end of the leader (top). Fish a tandem rig by angling your cast downstream and then holding your rod tip high as the flies swing below you, one skittering along the surface and the other running deep (right).

STREAMERS

These long-bodied flies are intended to imitate baitfish. They are tied on extra long hooks and have a long wing that "streams" back over the body.

Although some streamers are fairly realistic, most do not attempt to mimic any particular type of baitfish. Instead, they rely on color, flash and a darting action to draw the fish's attention.

Most streamers have a single open hook, but a few have mono weedguards for fishing in heavy cover, and some extra-long-bodied patterns have an upturned trailer hook to reduce the number of short strikes. There are eight basic styles of streamers:

- **Muddlers** - These popular streamers have feather wings and a large head made of clipped deer hair. Most muddler patterns float or sink slowly, and are fished on the surface to imitate terrestrial insects. Others are wrapped with wire and sink quickly; these patterns are often fished deep to simulate bottom-dwelling baitfish, such as sculpins.
- **Marabous** - Because of the fluffy marabou wing, these flies have a seductive breathing action when retrieved with a twitching motion. Marabous sink slowly and are effective in current or still water.
- **Hackle-wings** - The stiff hackle-feather wings have the best action in moving water. Because the feathers have little buoyancy, these flies

Most streamers have a head made of thread, or clipped deer hair; long hackle-feather, bucktail or marabou wing; long body tied on extra-long-shank hook; hackle collar and tail.

Wing

Butt

Body

Head

Assorted Streamer Types

Muddler

Hackle-wing

Jigging fly

Matuka

Marabou

sink rapidly and are a good choice for fishing in fast current.

- **Matukas** - These flies also have a hackle-feather wing, but it is wrapped with thread or tinsel over the full length body. This way, the wing stands upright, providing a keel effect so the fly doesn't tip or spin in fast water. Like hackle-wings, matukas sink rapidly.

- **Bucktails** - With a wing of bucktail or other buoyant hair, these flies sink more slowly than hackle-wings. Bucktails pulsate slightly in still water, but have the best action in current.

- **Combination flies** - With a wing consisting of a combination of feathers and hair, these flies sink at a moderate rate. Because the wing has little action, combination flies are best suited to moving water.

- **Jigging flies** - The head is wrapped with wire or otherwise weighted to make these flies sink rapidly in a head-first position. They have an attractive jigging action when retrieved with a twitch-and-pause motion, and work well in still water and current.

- **Trolling streamer** - These flies feature an extra-long hackle-feather or bucktail wing and a dressed trailer hook. Used primarily by lake trollers seeking trout and salmon, these flies are not a good choice for casting because the long wing tends to foul on the main hook.

Popular Streamers

Marabou Muddler

Spuddler

Popsicle

Brown Marabou

Dark Spruce Fly

Black Ghost

Olive Matuka

Black Matuka

Royal Coachman

Black Nose Dace

Gray Ghost

Black Hare Sculpin

Clouser Deep Minnow

Fish a deep run by making a short cast to point A, then following the streamer with your rod until it reaches point B. Then make a slightly longer cast to Point C and drift the fly to point D. Continue making longer casts until you cover the full width of the run. If you cannot cover the length of the run from one position, start at the upstream end, make a series of drifts, then take a few steps downstream and repeat the process. Continue working downstream until the entire length has been covered. Mend the line as necessary to avoid drag.

Fishing with Streamers

There is one major reason for the popularity of streamers: they catch big fish.

Trout anglers catch good numbers of fish on dry flies and nymphs, which imitate adult and immature insects, but the biggest trout seldom fall for these flies. Good-sized trout, particularly browns, feed primarily on baitfish, explaining why streamers are the number-one choice of trophy hunters.

Streamers also work well for other baitfish eaters including salmon, crappies, white bass and stripers, pike, muskies, pickerel and all species of black bass.

Most flies are effective only in water that is relatively clear. But streamers,

because of their size and bulk, create enough water disturbance that fish can detect them with their lateral-line sense, even in muddy water. This also explains why streamers work so well for night fishing.

Because streamers imitate baitfish rather than insects, they're effective even in cold water or at other times when there is no hatch in progress.

A streamer can be fished with a drag-free drift, much the same way you would fish a wet fly. By varying the length of your casts and allowing the streamer to swing with the current (above), you can quickly cover a large expanse of water. But a streamer can also be retrieved cross-stream with a series of long, fast strips.

Some anglers use a streamer as a searching lure, rapidly covering water in an attempt to get a fish to swirl at the fly and reveal its location. Then, they tie on a different fly or use some other type of lure to catch the fish.

You can use a streamer on a sinking line when trolling or drifting for suspended fish in still water. Long-bodied trolling streamers (p. 303) are popular for landlocked salmon and brook trout, but you can use other types of streamers as well. Small marabou streamers are a good choice for suspended crappies.

Streamers have larger, stronger hooks than most other types of flies, so once you hook a fish, you're not likely to lose it. This is especially important in landing big fish, which could easily bend or shake a tiny fly hook.

The weight of the hook also helps get the fly down in deep water or fast current. Some streamers are wrapped with wire so they sink even faster. If you're having trouble getting your fly deep enough, pinch a few small split shot onto your line.

Recommended Tackle and Fly Sizes

The rods, reels, lines, leaders and tippets used in streamer fishing are much the same as those used in wet-fly fishing. For most trout fishing, use streamers in sizes 6 to 12; for crappies and white bass, 4 to 8; for smallmouth and spotted bass, 2 to 6; for largemouth bass, salmon and large trout, 1/0 to 4 and for northern pike, muskies and striped bass, 2 to 3/0.

Tips for Fishing with Streamers

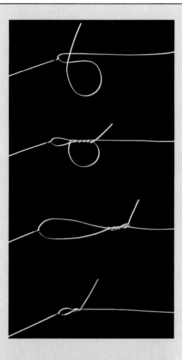

Use a loop knot to attach a streamer (plain hook used for clarity). A loop knot, such as this Duncan loop, gives the fly more action than a clinch knot, so it can easily swing from side to side or jig up and down.

Retrieve a streamer by holding the line against the grip with the index finger of your rod hand and then stripping in line with your other hand.

Use a stripping basket when making long casts. Otherwise, the line you strip in may tangle around your legs or catch on a rock.

To fish deep water with a streamer, pinch on three or four small split shot a few inches apart. Several widely spaced shot are easier to cast than one large one.

NYMPHS

When you see fish rising, they're normally feeding on adult insects. But it's far more common for fish to feed beneath the surface on immature insects. Nymphs imitate these juvenile forms.

Because juvenile insects are always present in a lake or stream, nymphs are effective year-round. Fish sometimes root in the bottom mud to find immature insects but, at other times, they intercept them as they drift with the current or swim from the bottom toward the surface prior to hatching.

Nymphs differ from wet flies in that they more closely represent the real thing. Some nymphs are ultrarealistic, with jointed legs and segmented bodies, but that degree of realism is usually not necessary. Many nymph patterns have lead wire wrapped on the hook or a

Most nymphs have a thorax (an enlargement near the front of the fly, which often has a wing case on the back); abdomen that is often wrapped with ribbing; sparse tail and throat or "beard".

metal bead on the head to make them sink faster. Following are the most common types of nymphs:

- **Mayfly nymphs** - Most of these flies have a wing case on the back and legs made of picked-out dubbing. The tail, made of feather fibers or hair, often has two or three filaments, like that of the natural.

- **Stonefly nymphs** - The wing case of a stonefly nymph is usually segmented, the tail consists of two stiff feathers and the antennae are prominent.

- **Caddisflies** - Larval caddisflies live in sand or stick cases, which they shed when they reach the pupal stage. Nymphs are tied to imitate the larvae, with

Types of Nymphs

and without the case, and the pupae.

- **Dragonfly/Damselfly nymphs** - Dragonfly imitations have a wide, flat abdomen; damselflies, a thin, extra-long tail. Many patterns have beads for eyes to represent the large eyes of the natural.
- **Emergers** - These flies imitate nymphs that are just about ready to hatch.

Emergers have large wing cases made of polypropylene yarn or other buoyant materials. They are tied on light-wire hooks and fished, mostly submerged, in the surface film.

- **Scuds** - Although scuds are tiny crustaceans rather than insects, they are normally classified as nymphs. Scud patterns are tied on short-shank

hooks and usually have a plastic or epoxy shellback and picked-out dubbing for legs. Some realistic patterns also have antennae and tails made of hackle fibers.

Popular Nymphs

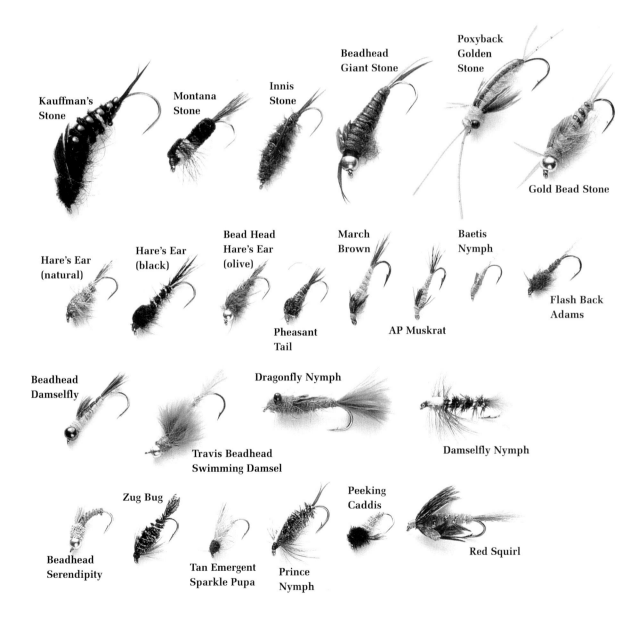

Kauffman's Stone

Montana Stone

Innis Stone

Beadhead Giant Stone

Poxyback Golden Stone

Gold Bead Stone

Hare's Ear (natural)

Hare's Ear (black)

Bead Head Hare's Ear (olive)

Pheasant Tail

March Brown

AP Muskrat

Baetis Nymph

Flash Back Adams

Beadhead Damselfly

Travis Beadhead Swimming Damsel

Dragonfly Nymph

Damselfly Nymph

Beadhead Serendipity

Zug Bug

Tan Emergent Sparkle Pupa

Prince Nymph

Peeking Caddis

Red Squirl

When fishing an emerger pattern, dress all but the last few inches of your leader with paste floatant to keep the fly drifting in the surface film or just beneath it.

Fishing with Nymphs

Food-habit studies often show that the majority of a trout's diet consists of immature insects. So it's not surprising that nymphs, which imitate these immature forms, are so consistently effective. Nymphs catch fish when there is no hatch in progress and they may, in fact, be the best choice even when there is a hatch.

Many anglers assume that trout feed only on adult insects during a hatch. But, in many cases, the fish are taking the immatures before they reach the surface, explaining why a nymph often outproduces a dry fly when the air is full of insects.

While most anglers think of nymphs as trout flies, they also work well for largemouth, smallmouth and spotted bass and most kinds of panfish.

Fish feeding on immature insects are normally not as selective as those feeding on adults, so you may be able to catch fish on a variety of nymph patterns. But it helps to choose flies that represent immature forms present in the water you're fishing.

Some nymph fishermen stir up the bottom, then use a fine-mesh net to collect organisms that drift downstream. Others just turn over rocks or sift through bottom debris to determine the most common immature forms.

Because fish commonly feed on immature insects that

Nymph-Fishing Tips

Turn over rocks to check for the most abundant forms of insect life. Then, tie on a nymph that looks like one of the common forms.

When you see trout "tailing," they're probably rooting immature insects from the bottom and are likely to take a well-presented nymph.

are dislodged from the bottom and drift with the current, any nymph can be fished with a drag-free drift, just as you would fish a wet fly. Most nymphs work best when drifted near the bottom, but emerger patterns are normally drifted in the surface film or just beneath the surface.

Some immature forms, including mayfly, dragonfly, and damselfly nymphs, swim with a darting motion, so you can best imitate them with a twitching retrieve. To mimic an insect making its way to the surface prior to hatching, lift your rod just before the nymph reaches a probable lie. The pressure of the current against your fly line will lift the fly.

Nymphs are also effective in still water. Experiment with different retrieves ranging from short, fast pulls to long, slow ones, until you find the action the fish want on a given day.

The biggest problem in nymph fishing is detecting strikes. Don't expect to see a swirl or feel a definite jerk. You may just notice a hesita-tion in your drift or feel a slight nudge. When that happens, set the hook by firmly lifting your rod as you would in dry-fly fishing.

A strike indicator makes detecting a take much easier. Nymph fishermen use a wide variety of indicators, ranging from tiny floats to fluorescent yarn to buoyant putty (opposite).

Long casts are counterproductive in nymph fishing. With a long line, detecting strikes is nearly impossible.

Popular strike indicators include (1) fluorescent yarn tied into knot connecting leader sections; (2) styrofoam float pegged on with toothpick; (3) adhesive foam tab that pinches onto your line; (4) float putty, which can be molded around your leader and (5) slotted, twist-on type, which can be put on or taken off without removing the fly.

Recommended Tackle and Fly Sizes

The tackle used in nymph fishing is the same as that used in fishing wet flies. Be sure to use a floating line, however, when fishing emergers. For most trout fishing, use nymphs in sizes 6 to 18; for panfish, 6 to 12; for smallmouth and spotted bass, 2 to 6 and for largemouth bass and large trout, 1/0 to 4.

Splice a dry fly into your leader in place of a strike indicator. It will telegraph strikes on the nymph, and it's possible to catch fish on either fly.

To detect strikes more easily, keep your casts short and attach the strike indicator as close to the fly as the water depth allows.

BUGS

Although many anglers refer to any large topwater fly as a "bug," the term is misleading because many bugs bear no similarity to an insect. Some look like mice and others like frogs, but the majority resemble nothing in a fish's diet. They're effective primarily because of the surface disturbance they create. The most popular types of bugs include:

- **Divers** - As their name suggests, these flies are designed to dive and make a gurgling sound when pulled forward. As long as you keep pulling, they stay under water. But when you pause, they float back up. This frog-like action, combined with the gurgling noise, explains why these flies are so effective for large predator fish like bass, pike, muskies and stripers.

- **Poppers** - These hard-bodied lures, made of plastic, cork or balsa wood, have a cupped or flattened face, so they make a popping sound when you twitch them. Many have hair or feather tails, rubber legs or hackle collars. Small poppers work well for sunfish; larger ones for bass.

- **Sliders** - A slider, with its bullet-shaped head, creates less surface disturbance than a popper. But that may be an advantage when fish are not in an aggressive feeding mood. Sliders are easier to cast than poppers, and they work especially well for skittering over matted or floating-leaved weeds to catch largemouth bass and sunfish. They can also be used for small-mouth bass and trout in fast current.

- **Hair bugs** - Used mainly for bass, pike and large trout, these bugs have a head and/or body of clipped deer or elk hair. Some hair bugs resemble frogs or mice, but realism is not much of a consideration because the hollow fibers make them float so high that fish don't get a clear look at them. Hair bugs are more wind-resistant and difficult to cast than hard-bodied bugs, but they feel more natural, so fish hold on to them longer.

- **Sponge bugs** - These small soft-bodied bugs, used mainly for panfish and trout, have long rubber legs and resemble spiders. Because of their sponge body, they feel like real food, so fish won't eject them as quickly as they would a hard-bodied bug. The sponge material soaks up water, so most of these flies barely float.

If you'll be fishing around weeds, brush, logs or other snaggy cover, be sure to use a bug with a mono or light-wire weedguard.

One of the most common mistakes in fishing with bugs is selecting one with a hook that is not large enough. A small hook may not provide enough weight to keep the bug upright, and the narrow gap will cause you to miss numerous strikes.

Recommended Tackle and Fly Sizes

Large, wind-resistant bugs require a 7- to 9-weight fly rod, a weight-forward or bass-bug-taper floating line and a 6- to 9-foot leader with a 0X to 4X tippet. Pike and muskie anglers should use a 10- to 14-pound-test leader with a 15- to 30-pound-test braided-wire tippet.

Smaller bugs can be fished with a 4- to 6-weight rod, a weight-forward floating line and a 2X to 6X tippet.

For pike, muskies and stripers, use bugs in sizes 4/0 to 1/0; for largemouth bass and large trout, 1/0 to 2; for smallmouth and spotted bass, 1 to 4; for sunfish and crappies, 4 to 8 and for smaller trout, 8 to 12.

Types of Bugs

Slider

Sponge Bug

Diver

Popper

Hair Bug

How to Retrieve Bugs

Retrieve a diver by sharply stripping in line and then pausing. When you strip, the fly will dive under, making a gurgling sound and emitting an air bubble.

Retrieve a popper by stripping in line to create the popping action and then waiting for the ripples to subside. Experiment with the intensity of the pops and duration of the pauses.

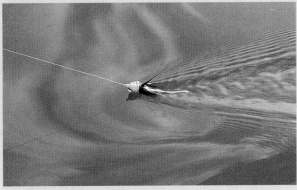

Skitter a slider across the surface by steadily stripping in line. Some anglers fish a slider fast enough that it kicks up spray. You can also use a twitch-and-pause retrieve.

Fish a hair bug by casting to rises or obvious cover and working the fly slowly, with light twitches followed by long pauses.

Tips for Using Bugs

Watch your bug closely to detect subtle strikes. Sometimes a fish will slowly swim up to the lure and gently suck it under, leaving only a light swirl. When that happens, set the hook.

Free a bug from a snag by making a roll cast to pull it off from the opposite direction. Just raise your rod tip and make a hard downward stroke to roll the line out.

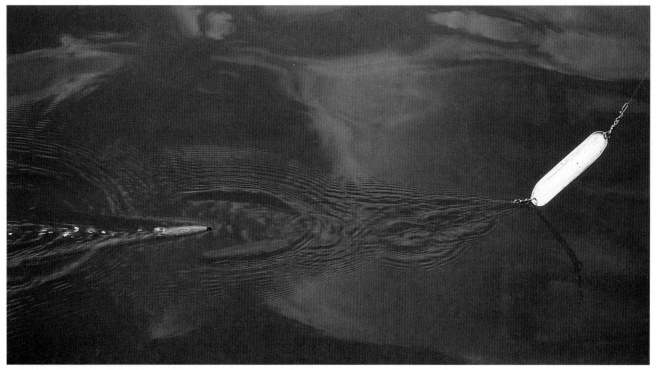

A dodger swings widely from side to side, giving a trolling fly more action and providing flash that helps attract fish.

SPECIALTY FLIES

Hundreds of fly patterns don't fit into any of the categories previously mentioned and are intended for a very specific purpose.

When coastal streams or Great Lakes tributaries are full of spawning salmon, for example, resident trout and migrating steelhead often gorge themselves on salmon eggs. Then, a fly that looks like a salmon egg or a cluster of eggs will greatly outproduce an insect imitation.

Common types of specialty flies include:

• **Leech flies** - Used mainly for bass, pike, panfish and trout, leech flies have a long tail made of marabou, chamois, latex or rabbit fur. When retrieved with a moderate jigging motion, these flies have an undulating, leech-like action.

• **Crayfish flies** - Crayfish imitations are deadly for smallmouth and spotted bass, as well as large

brown trout. The flies can be fished on a drag-free drift or with a twitch-and-pause retrieve.

Types of Specialty Flies

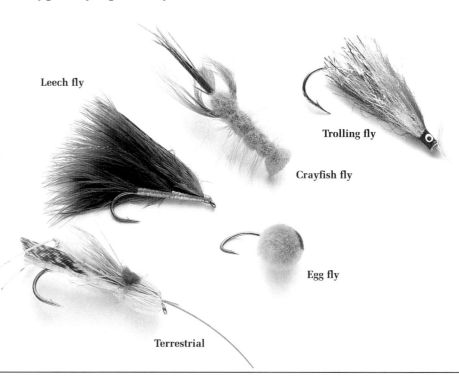

Leech fly

Trolling fly

Crayfish fly

Egg fly

Terrestrial

- **Egg flies** - These flies are nothing more than a little fluorescent yarn or synthetic material tied on a short-shank hook and trimmed to resemble a single salmon egg or an egg cluster. Some egg imitations, called corkies, have a bouyant cork or balsa body; others are made of molded plastic. Egg flies are fished on a drag-free drift, so they tumble naturally with the current, like a real egg.

- **Terrestrials** - Intended to imitate crickets, grasshoppers, beetles, ants or other terrestrial insects, these flies are a favorite of trout anglers, especially when no aquatic insects are hatching. They also work well for bass and panfish. Terrestrials are fished on or beneath the surface, using a drag-free drift.

- **Trolling Flies** - Used mainly when deep-trolling for lake trout and salmon, these flashy flies have a long body made of mylar, tinsel, hair, soft plastic, or a combination of these materials. Some have a small spinner blade to provide even more flash. Trolling flies are normally fished behind some type of attractor, usually a dodger.

Skimpy Linda

Twinkle Trolling Squid

Popular Specialty Flies

Leadeye Leech

Woolly Bugger

Marabou Leech

Buckskin Crawdad

Clouser's Crayfish

Crayfish

Travis Trout Egg Cluster

Moe Egg

Apricot Supreme Omelette

Orange Egg

Chartreuse Egg

Schroeder's Parachute Hopper

Dave's Cricket

Letort Cricket

Crowe Beetle

Joe's Hopper

Henry's Fork Hopper

Flying Black Ant

Cinnamon Ant

Quick Sight Ant

Hi Vis Foam Beetle

Black Fur Ant

PART III

LIVE BAIT

INTRODUCTION

Most of us love artificial lures. We pick up all the latest baits, and if they work, buy them by the dozen so we have them in every size and color.

But when fishing is tough—and that's often—it's time to shelve the artificials ... and reach for live bait!

Worms. Minnows. Leeches. Adult insects and larvae. Frogs. Live bait catches fish, even when artificial lures don't. It's that simple.

It is estimated that 75 percent of all fish caught are fooled by live bait. And that's why information like this is so important. It will help you fish effectively with the best live baits available. You'll see how to create the rigs, present the offerings ... everything.

If you want to catch fish when the fishing is good *or* tough ... this part of the book is for you.

BASIC RIGGING METHODS

*G*amefish will turn up their noses at even the freshest, liveliest bait if it isn't rigged properly.

BASIC RIGGING METHODS

According to some estimates, natural bait accounts for three-fourths of all game-fish caught in fresh water. And when the going gets tough, even the staunchest lure chuckers dig into their bait boxes.

While natural bait has a look, smell and action that can't be duplicated by artificials, even the most enticing bait is practically worthless if it isn't rigged properly. It may tear off the hook when you cast, it won't have the right action and, even if a fish grabs it, you probably won't get a good hookset.

Luckily, you don't have to learn a separate rigging method for every different kind of bait. The rigging techniques shown on the following pages (with minor modifications) can be used for a wide variety of baits, for many different fish species and over a broad range of conditions. For example, you can use a slip-bobber rig to catch everything from farm-pond bluegills on waxworms to big-river flatheads on foot-long suckers. All you have to do is change the size and style of float, hook and sinker.

We'll show you all the most popular rigs for presenting natural bait. But before discussing these rigs, you need to understand the components that go into those rigs. Only then will you be able to modify the basic rigs to suit your style of fishing.

Yet the basic rigging methods shown here are not suitable for all types of baits in all situations. You'll have to learn how to make many specialty rigs as well. You'll find these rigs in the chapters dealing with each specific type of bait.

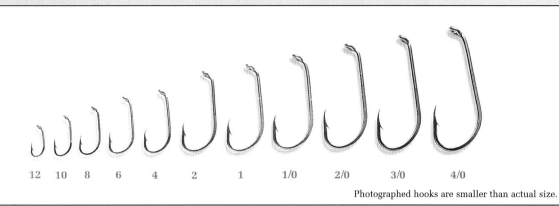

12   10   8   6   4   2   1   1/0   2/0   3/0   4/0

Photographed hooks are smaller than actual size.

Size. *Hook size is designated by a number that reflects the size of the hook's gap, which is the distance between the point and the inside of the shank. For smaller hooks, the number increases as the hooks decrease in size. Larger hooks are measured with a number and an "aught" designation (1/0, 2/0, etc.); the numbers increase as the hooks increase in size.*

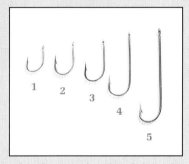

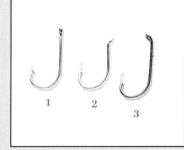

Selecting Hook Size

Fish Type	Hook Size
Largemouth Bass	2–2/0
Smallmouth Bass	6–1
Panfish	12–4
Pike/Muskie	2–8/0
Walleye/Sauger	8–2
Catfish/Sturgeon	1–6/0
Stream Trout	12–2
Lake Trout	2–2/0
Pacific Salmon	4–1/0

Shank Length. *Shank length is designated as (1) extra-short, (2) short, (3) standard, (4) long and (5) extra-long. The length you need depends mainly on the size and shape of your bait. An extra-short shank would be ideal for a salmon egg; a long-shank would be better for a grasshopper or gob of worms.*

Type of Eye. *Most bait fishermen prefer a (1) straight-eye hook, but hooks with a (2) turned-up eye are better for snelling. Some anglers swear by hooks with a (3) turned-down eye which they say improves hooking by directing the hook point into the fish.*

Hook Style. *(1) Round bend, for general-purpose use; (2) Aberdeen, with a thin shank for hooking delicate baits; (3) baitholder, with barbs to prevent bait from sliding down hook shank; (4) claw, with a turned-in point for better hooking; (5) keel, which rotates on the hookset for better penetration; (6) double-needle, for threading on dead baitfish; (7) wide-bend, with a point that is directed toward the eye for stronger hooksets; (8) weedless, for fishing in weedy or brushy cover; (9) sneck, to keep more of the hook point exposed when using large baitfish; (10) Swedish hook, mainly for rigging dead baitfish in ice fishing.*

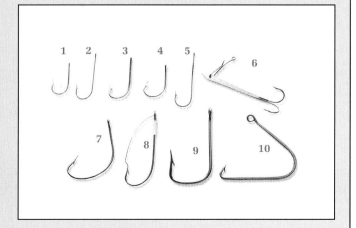

Selecting Sinkers

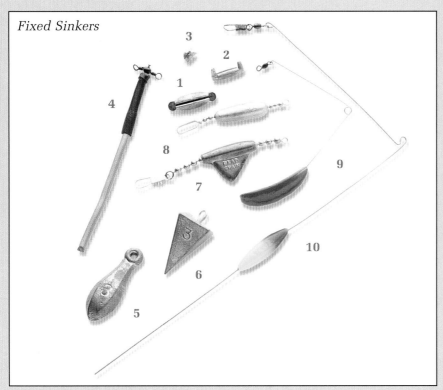

Fixed Sinkers

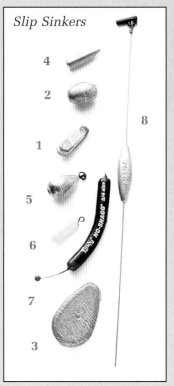

Slip Sinkers

Fixed Sinkers. *(1) Rubbercor, which twists onto your line; (2) dog-ear and (3) split-shot, which pinch onto your line; (4) surgical tubing with lead insert that can pull out in snaggy cover; (5) bell sinker and (6) pyramid sinker, for dropper rigs; (7) bead chain with keel and (8) bead chain, to minimize line twist; (9) baitwalker and (10) bottom-bouncer, for rocky bottoms.*

Slip Sinkers. *(1) Walking sinker and (2) egg sinker, for general-purpose use; (3) disk sinker, which resists drifting or rolling in current; (4) bullet sinker, for weedy cover; (5 & 6) clip-on sinkers, which enable you to change weights easily; (7) No-Snagg sinker and (8) Slip-Bouncer, for snaggy bottoms.*

Selecting Stops

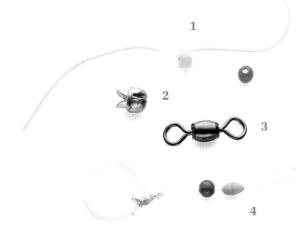

Selecting Floaters

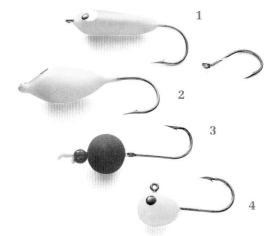

Stops. *(1) slip-knot and bead, (2) split shot, (3) barrel swivel, (4) rubber stop.*

Floaters. *(1) Soft-body floating jig with stinger hook to catch short biters; (2) soft-body floating jig, which has a lifelike feel; (3) Styrofoam ball, which is held in front of the hook by a stop; (4) hard-bodied floating jig.*

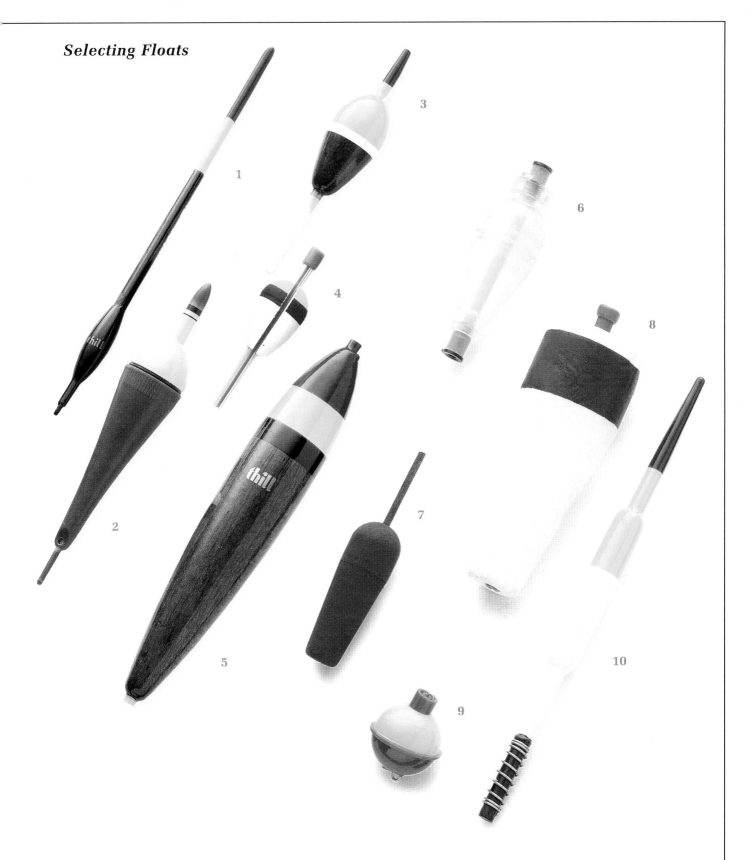

Slip-Bobbers. *(1) European-style, for extra delicacy; (2) lighted slip-bobber, for night fishing; (3) tube-style slip-bobber, which can be adjusted by moving a stop on the line; (4) removable slip-bobber, with a slot that enables you to quickly remove it from your line; (5) cigar float, a slip-bobber for large gamefish.*
Fixed Bobbers. *(6) Casting bubble, which can hold water for extra casting distance; (7) peg-on; (8) weighted casting float, with an internal lead weight; (9) clip-on; (10) spring-lock.*

SLIP-SINKER RIGS

The idea behind a slip-sinker rig is that a fish can pick up your bait and swim away without feeling much resistance. The fish detects nothing out of the ordinary so it is not as likely to drop the bait as it would be if it were towing a heavy sinker.

Another advantage to a slip-sinker rig: Because the sinker is not affixed to the line, you can change weights very easily. This explains why many anglers use slip-sinkers even when fishing with a bobber or using other rigs in which the sinker does not slip.

The basic slip-sinker rig and variations on it are shown below. Functions of the various components are explained on page 320.

When you detect a bite, release the line. As the sinker rests on the bottom, the fish can swim off without feeling much resistance.

Slip-Sinker Rig Variations

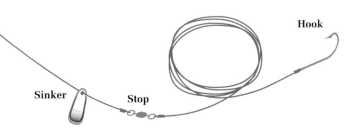

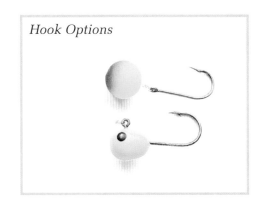

Hook Options

Sinker Options

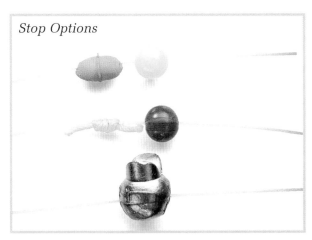

Stop Options

How a Slip-Sinker Rig Works

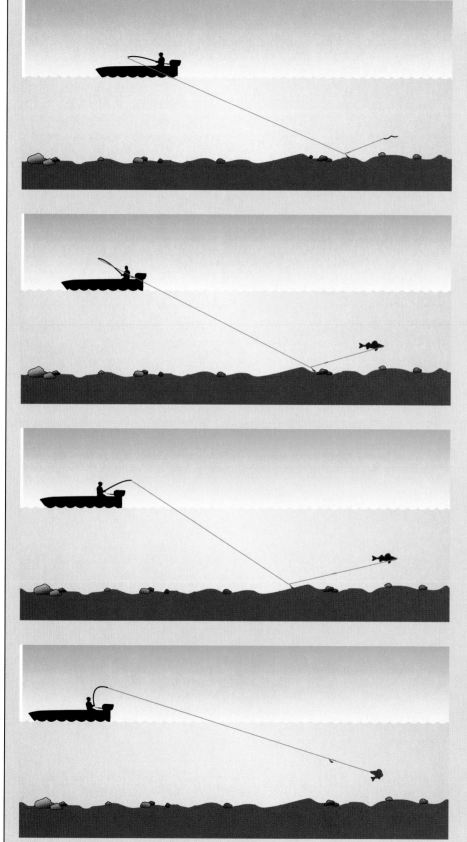

1 Feed line until you feel your sinker hit bottom, then open your bail and hold the line with your finger as you start to troll or drift slowly. You may have to feed a little more line as the boat starts moving, in order to maintain contact with the bottom.

2 When you feel a bite, release the line from your finger so the fish can run without feeling resistance. Before releasing the line, however, you may want to "test" the bite by holding onto the line for a second or two to feel some life. This way, you know you haven't hooked a weed or stick.

3 When you're sure the resistance you feel is a fish, feed line until the fish stops running. Be sure your spool is nearly full and there are no nicks on the rim; otherwise, the line may hang up while the fish is running, causing it to drop the bait.

4 When the fish stops running, rapidly wind up slack until you feel the fish's weight, then set the hook with a sharp upward snap of the wrists. Often, the fish does not swim off in a straight line and in some cases may actually double back on you. If you don't wind up the slack, you probably won't get a firm hookset.

FIXED-SINKER RIGS

With a sinker that is tied in or pinched or twisted onto your line, the rig is not intended to slip when a fish swims off with your bait. This type of rig is most commonly used for large fish that don't mind feeling a little resistance, or fish that bite so aggressively that there is no need to wait for them to swim off before setting the hook. Split-shot rigs are weighted so lightly that fish usually don't notice the slight resistance.

Fixed-sinker rigs offer one big advantage over slip-sinker rigs. Because they don't require a stop, fixed-sinker rigs are easier to tie, and some don't require any tying at all (other than adding a hook). You simply pinch or twist a sinker onto your line and start fishing.

Towing a little extra weight doesn't bother a large and aggressive biter, such as a catfish.

Fixed-Sinker Rig Variations

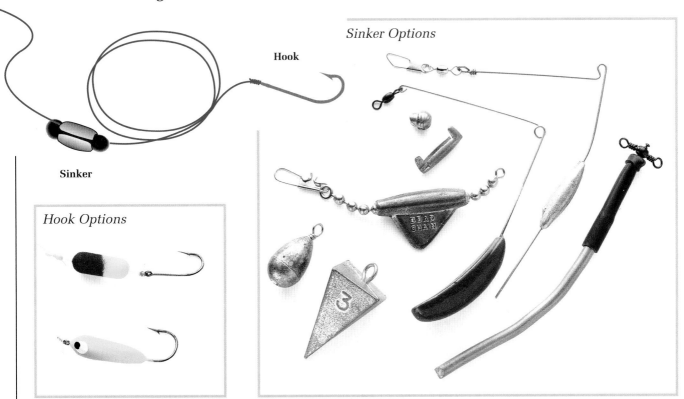

Hook

Sinker

Sinker Options

Hook Options

The Ultimate Guide To Freshwater Fishing

Fixed-Bobber Rig Variations

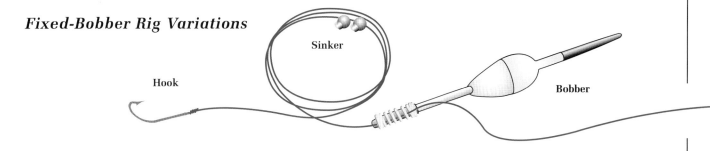

Hook   Sinker   Bobber

Hook Options

Bobber Options

Sinker Options

FIXED-BOBBER RIGS

There's nothing complicated about fishing with a fixed-bobber rig. Just attach a float to your line and balance it with a sinker or enough split shot so it barely floats. This way, a fish can pull it under without feeling much resistance.

Anglers using this technique often make the mistake of using a float that is way too big. Not only does this make it harder to detect bites, it increases the likelihood that a fish will drop the bait.

Because of its simplicity, a fixed-bobber rig is not as likely to tangle as a slip-bobber

A fixed-bobber rig is ideal for fishing pockets in shallow weeds.

rig. And you can cast it a long distance without having to worry about the line catching

on the bobber stop and tearing off your bait.

SLIP-BOBBER RIGS

With a bobber affixed to your line, you're limited to fishing only about 6 feet deep, because you can't cast with more than that much line dangling from the end of your rod. But with a slip-bobber rig, there is no limit on how deep you can fish. You can reel your bait to within a short distance of the rod tip for easy casting, then the line will slip through the float until it reaches a depth determined by where you position the bobber-stop.

Slip-bobber rigs can be used for everything from quarter-pound sunfish to 100-pound catfish. The size of the float you use depends not only on the size of the fish, but on the size of the bait it must support.

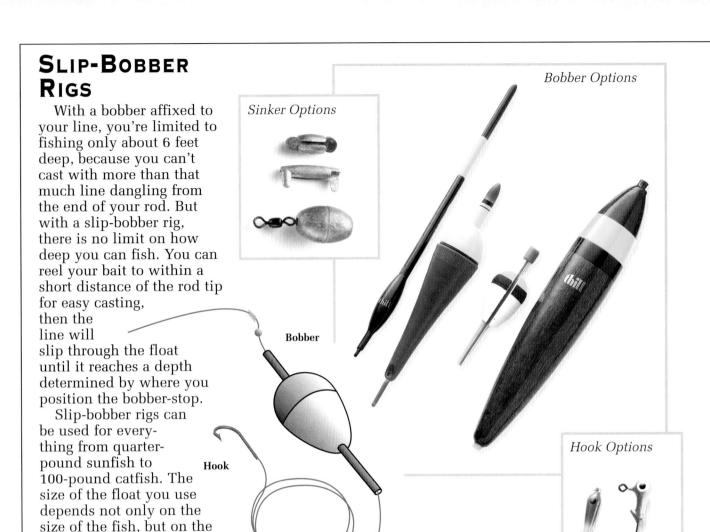

Sinker Options

Bobber Options

Bobber

Hook

Sinker

Hook Options

Slip-Bobber Rig Variations

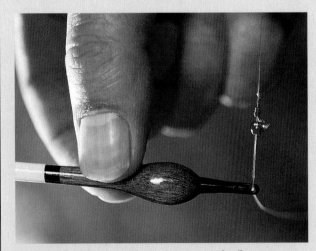

Lighted bobbers and European-style floats are threaded on through a hole in the bottom. In most cases, the hole is fairly large, so you must use a bead ahead of the bobber stop to prevent it from slipping through the hole.

If you do not have a slip-bobber, substitute a clip-on or peg-on float rigged with a bead and bobber stop. To rig a clip-on, push in the button and turn the wire clip so it rests on the surface of the float as shown.

How a Slip-Bobber Rig Works

1 Reel up enough line so your bait is only 12 to 18 inches from the rod tip. Then, using a sidearm motion, lob the rig gently so the bait does not tear off. Lob-casting also prevents losing your bait should the bobber stop hang up on your spool or in your line guides.

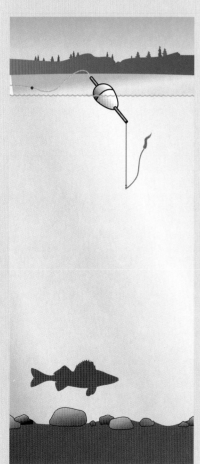

2 Feed line as the bait sinks. The bobber stop will move toward the bobber, which is resting on its side.

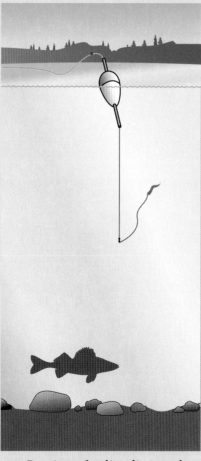

3 Continue feeding line as the stop approaches the bobber. If you stop feeding line too soon, the rig will pull back toward you.

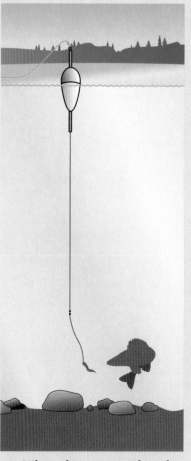

4 When the stop reaches the bobber, the weight will stand it upright and the bait will be at the desired depth.

LURE/BAIT COMBOS

Many kinds of artificial lures are much more effective when tipped with natural bait. The bait not only adds realism, it leaves a scent trail that fish can follow to the lure. But tipping does not work for all lures, because the extra weight of the bait can interfere with the lure's action.

But not all types of bait lend themselves to tipping. Delicate insect baits, for example, are difficult to keep on the hook when casting; and nibbling fish can easily pick them off the hook. And some wiggly baits, such as

Tipping an artificial lure with a leech may not be a good idea.

leeches, tend to wrap themselves around hooks (espe-

cially trebles) so the bait doesn't trail properly.

Lures Commonly Tipped with Bait

Leadhead Jig. Tip leadheads with baitfish, worms, leeches, grubs, frogs, salamanders, crayfish, shrimp and cut bait.

Floating Jig. Floaters are commonly tipped with baitfish, worms or leeches. Floaters do not have the buoyancy necessary to lift heavy baits like crayfish or salamanders.

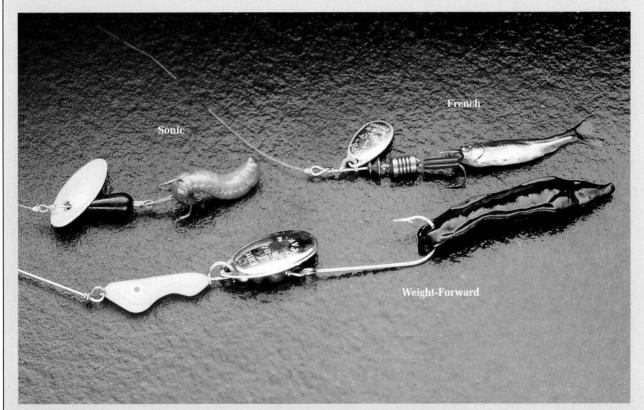

In-Line Spinner. French-style and sonic spinners can be tipped with baitfish or worms. Because of their single hook, weight-forward spinners can also be tipped with leeches.

Spinnerbait. *Spin-rigs (left) and jigs with clip-on spinnerbait arms (right) are usually tipped with baitfish, worms or leeches.*

Spinner Rig. *Single-hook spinner rigs (top) are commonly tipped with baitfish, worms or leeches. Multiple-hook rigs (bottom) are designed for nightcrawlers.*

Spin-n-Glo. *Most often, these floating spinner rigs are tipped with fresh spawn, but they can also be tipped with baitfish or nightcrawlers.*

Spoon. Large spoons have enough "kick" to retain their action when tipped with minnows or strips of cut bait.

Trolling Plug. You can tip wide-wobbling plugs, such as a Flatfish, with one or more nightcrawlers.

Tear Drop. Tip these tiny lures with grubs, scuds, grass shrimp, small baitfish, or pieces of worms or leeches.

Jigging Spoon. Prone to tangling, these lures are often tipped with baitfish, baitfish heads or bait-fish eyes.

BAITFISH

*T*he flash and vibration from a struggling bait-fish is a magnet to practically every kind of gamefish.

BAITFISH BASICS

Many kinds of gamefish feed almost exclusively on smaller fish. And as they grow larger, their liking for small fish grows even stronger. So it should come as no surprise that baitfish are the favorite bait of millions of freshwater and saltwater anglers.

The term "baitfish" refers to any small fish that serve as forage for larger fish. Coincidentally, many of the most common baitfish are also popular fishing baits.

To eliminate any confusion as to what the term baitfish means, why not just call any small fish used for bait a "minnow"? That is, in fact, what many anglers do, but the term minnow technically refers only to members of the minnow family, *Cyprinidae*. While many of the most popular baitfish (like chubs and shiners) are minnows, many are not.

How a baitfish is classified, of course, means absolutely nothing to a fish that is about to eat it. What does matter is how the bait looks, smells and swims. Here are the most important bait-selection criteria:

• **Liveliness.** The predatory nature of many gamefish demands that a baitfish look alive. If it's hanging lifelessly on your hook, the fish may swim up to look at it or may even take a nip at it, but probably won't strike aggressively. A baitfish struggling to escape, however, usually

Hardiness of Common Baitfish

Very Hardy	Hardy	Delicate	Very Delicate
Fathead Minnow	Dace (all species)	Common Shiner	Emerald Shiner
Rosy Red	Creek Chub	Golden Shiner	Spottail Shiner
Eel	Redtail Chub	Red Shiner	Cisco
Madtom	Stoneroller	Yellow Perch	Shad
	White Sucker	Killifish	Smelt
	Goldfish		
	Sculpin		
	Bluntnose Minnow		
	Bluegill		

Note: Check your state and local regulations regarding the use of panfish such as bluegill or yellow perch, or exotics such as goldfish, as bait.

draws a vicious strike.

Some types of bait, like emerald shiners, look good at the bait shop; but by the time you get them to the lake, half of them are dead.

Others, like fathead minnows, are extremely hardy and will stay alive even if you abuse them. The hardiness of various baitfish species is shown in the chart above.

• **Size.** Predator fish generally prefer a bait of approximately the same size as their natural prey. In fact, size is often the most important consideration.

For example, in early summer when striped bass are feeding on young-of-the-year shad from 2 to 3 inches long, they're not likely to take a 6-inch baitfish. By fall, however, when the year's crop of shad have reached 6 or 7 inches in length, 6-inch baitfish are ideal.

Although shape is not as important as size, it can be a factor as well. When the fish are feeding on deep-bodied forage, deep-bodied baitfish generally work better than long, thin ones.

• **Color/Flash.** As a rule, a bright-colored, flashy baitfish works better than a dark, drab one. In clear water, predators spot the flash from a swimming baitfish from as much as 20 feet away, while they may not even notice a dull-colored baitfish.

But there are exceptions. There will be times when dark-colored baitfish that emit a strong odor will out-produce even the flashiest shiners.

BUYING BAITFISH

It's certainly a lot more convenient to buy baitfish than to collect your own and, in most cases, store-bought baitfish will do the job.

The main drawback to buying your bait is that only a small fraction of the baitfish species shown on the following pages are likely to be available at bait shops in your area. So if you need some other kind of baitfish to appeal to fussy biters, you'll have to learn how to catch your own.

Here are some important baitfish-buying tips:

• Be sure you're getting the kind of baitfish you want, because bait shops do not adhere to any type of standard nomenclature. For example, fathead minnows may be called "tuffies"; ciscoes, "herring"; madtoms, "willow cats"; etc.

• Make sure the baitfish you buy are healthy (opposite page). If they're sick when you buy them, they'll probably be dead by the time you get them to the water.

• Don't overcrowd your bait bucket. If you buy too many baitfish for the size of your bucket, they will use up the oxygen before you get to your destination. If you need a lot of bait, ask for an oxygen pack or use an aerated bucket.

• Be careful about temperature changes. Bait dealers keep their baitfish in very cold water (less than 55°F). If you allow the water to warm rapidly on the way to your destination, you could lose most of your bait. To prevent this problem, some anglers add ice to their bait. But over-icing can be just as detrimental as overwarming. As a rule, you should try to keep the water temperature within a few degrees of that at the bait shop.

Bait-Buying Tips

Baitfish that form tight clumps near the bottom of the bait tank are healthier than those swimming about in loose formations or near the surface.

Don't buy your bait from a tank with any dark or otherwise discolored baitfish. They may be carrying a disease that has already been transmitted to other baitfish in the tank, weakening them.

Don't buy baitfish with red snouts, missing scales, damaged fins or noticeable patches of white, cottony fungus on the body. These signs of overhandling mean that the bait has been in the tank too long and is not in top condition.

The males of some baitfish, such as fathead minnows (shown) and most chubs, turn dark and develop breeding tubercles on their heads at spawning time. As a rule, the dark-colored males (top) are less effective than the lighter-colored females (bottom).

Fathead Minnow (also called tuffie, mudminnow). *Most common in small lakes, ponds and sluggish creeks, fatheads are found throughout most of North America. The first ray of the dorsal fin is very short and the lateral band, unlike that of the bluntnose minnow, does not reach the eye.*

Rosy Red. *The rosy red is a commercially-reared variety of fathead minnow that has been bred to have an orangish or pinkish color.*

Bluntnose Minnow. *The bluntnose prefers larger waters than its close relative, the fathead, but it is found in a wide variety of lakes, ponds and rivers throughout the eastern United States. Like the fathead, it has a short first ray on the dorsal fin, but the lateral band extends to the eye.*

Creek Chub. *As its name suggests, the creek chub resides in creeks and smaller rivers, mainly in the eastern U.S. One of the most common stream minnows, it can be easily distinguished from the hornyhead chub by the black spots at the front of the dorsal fin and base of the tail.*

Hornyhead Chub (also called redtail). *Most common in medium-sized, clearwater streams in the northeastern U.S., the hornyhead chub gets its name from the prominent tubercles on the head of the breeding male. The hornyhead chub resembles the creek chub, but the fins and tail are more reddish.*

Blacknose Dace. *The blacknose dace gets its name from the black lateral band which extends all the way to the nose. The sides are brownish with scattered black scales. Found mainly in the eastern half of the U.S., the blacknose dace inhabits small, fast-moving streams.*

Redbelly Dace (also called rainbow). *Together, the range of the northern and southern redbelly dace covers an area west of the Rockies, from Hudson Bay to Oklahoma. Found mainly in boggy lakes and small- to medium-sized streams, redbellies have a distinct dark lateral band, a second, less-distinct band just above it and a reddish to yellowish belly.*

Golden Shiner. *This deep-bodied baitfish, which is not really a shiner at all, often grows to a foot in length. The sides have a golden hue and the belly has a sharp keel. Although there are scattered pockets of golden shiners in the West, they're found mainly in weedy lakes and ponds in the eastern U.S. and southeastern Canada.*

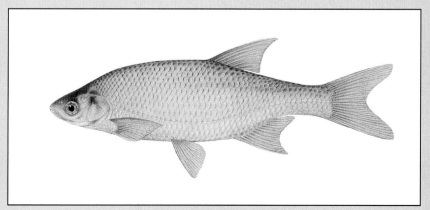

Popular Kinds of Baitfish (Continued)

Emerald Shiner. *It's easy to see where the emerald shiner gets it name—it has an iridescent blue-green back and silvery sides. Found throughout central Canada and the eastern U.S., the emerald shiner inhabits large lakes, reservoirs and rivers.*

Spottail Shiner. *Found in big rivers and big lakes throughout most of Canada and the northeastern U.S., the spottail shiner gets its name from the prominent black spot at the base of the tail. The back is pale olive and the sides are silvery.*

Common Shiner. *This shiner has a deeper body and larger scales than most other shiners. Mainly a stream dweller, the common shiner also inhabits some clearwater lakes. It ranges from southern Saskatchewan to Colorado and then eastward to the Atlantic coast.*

Red Shiner. *Named for the reddish-tinged head, sides and fins of the breeding male, the red shiner has a very deep body—even deeper than that of the common shiner. The red shiner inhabits small streams throughout much of the central and southern U.S. and into northeastern Mexico.*

Goldfish. *This Asian native, a close relative of the carp, has been introduced throughout most of the U.S., mainly by people discarding unwanted aquarium fish. The goldfish thrives in shallow, weedy lakes, reservoirs and streams. It has a deep body that varies in color from green to gold to orange, often with black mottling.*

White Sucker. *Found throughout the northern two-thirds of the U.S. and most of Canada, the white sucker is one of our most common baitfish. Some anglers use suckers weighing more than a pound to catch large catfish, pike and muskies. Suckers have an underslung mouth with large, fleshy lips and drab olive sides with scales that get larger toward the tail.*

Madtom (also called willow cat). *This small, brownish catfish has one continuous fin extending from the middle of the back to the anal fin. The pectoral fins are coated with venom and can inflict a painful sting. Madtoms are most common in medium- to large-sized rivers in the eastern U.S. but are also found in parts of the Northwest.*

Sculpin (also called bullhead, muddler). *Easily identified by its broad head and large pectoral fins, the sculpin is primarily a resident of small streams, but it is also found in large lakes. Sculpins prefer cold water and are most common in the northern half of the U.S., up into Canada and Alaska.*

Shad. *The gizzard shad is hardier than its close relative, the threadfin shad, so it is more commonly used as bait. Gizzard shad inhabit rivers and reservoirs throughout most of the eastern U.S. They have a deep, silvery body, a long ray at the rear of the dorsal fin and a dark spot behind the head.*

Skipjack Herring. *Found primarily in the Mississippi River drainage system, the skipjack herring is easily identified by its protruding lower jaw. It has a bluish to greenish back, silvery sides and a whitish belly. Its extremely oily flesh makes it a favorite of catfish anglers.*

Cisco (also called herring, tullibee). *A resident of large, deep lakes of the northern U.S. and Canada, the cisco makes ideal food for gamefish because of its long, sleek shape. Ciscoes have a greenish back, silvery sides and a small adipose fin behind the dorsal fin.*

Smelt. *This marine species entered the Great Lakes through the St. Lawrence Seaway and has spread to many deep, cold inland lakes in the northern U.S. and Canada. Smelt resemble ciscoes, but their snout is more pointed and they have large teeth.*

Killifish. Many species of killifish live in fresh and brackish waters from southeastern Canada into South America. They are easily identified by their turned-up mouth and dorsal fin positioned far back on the body.

Bluegill. Found throughout most of the U.S., this sunfish inhabits practically all types of warmwater lakes, reservoirs and streams, particularly those with abundant weed growth. The bluegill gets its name from its powder-blue gill cover. It has a black ear lobe and a dark spot at the base of the dorsal fin.

Yellow Perch. Native to most of the northern U.S. and Canada, yellow perch have been widely stocked throughout the South. They thrive in a variety of warmwater and coolwater lakes and streams with sparse to moderate vegetation. Yellow perch have a yellowish coloration with 6 to 8 dark vertical bars on the sides.

American Eel. Eels spawn at sea, but the females spend most of their life in fresh water. They enter rivers along most of the Atlantic and Gulf coasts of North America and often migrate great distances to reach the upstream sections of these waters. Eels are easily identified by the long fin bordering the rear two-thirds of their snakelike body.

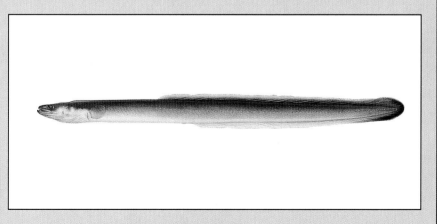

FISHING WITH BAITFISH

Anglers use baitfish to catch practically every kind of freshwater gamefish, from 6-inch perch to 10-foot sturgeon. And there are just about as many ways to rig and fish baitfish as there are kinds of gamefish that will take them.

The rigging method depends mainly on the size and shape of the baitfish and whether you're fishing them alive or dead. The most popular rigging methods are listed on the opposite page.

Your hooking method is of utmost importance. A baitfish that is small in comparison to the size of the fish being targeted can be hooked most anywhere—through the lips, roof of the mouth, back or tail. But a comparatively larger baitfish is much harder to swallow, so the hooking options are more limited.

Most gamefish catch baitfish however they can—by the head, sideways or by the tail. But they almost always swallow them head-first. This way, their meal slides down easily and the fins fold back neatly so they don't catch in the fish's throat. This explains why anglers using very large baitfish often hook them in the head or use some sort of harness, with one hook near the front and another farther back.

Tail-hooking large baitfish is risky; unless the fish happens to grab the bait tail-first and you set the hook right away, you probably won't hook up.

A long, thin-bodied baitfish gives you more hooking options than one with a deep body. If you tried to hook a deep-bodied baitfish, like a bluegill, in the lips, you'd probably pull it out of the

fish's mouth. With a thin-bodied baitfish, the barb is more likely to catch in the mouth. As a rule deep-bodied baitfish should be hooked

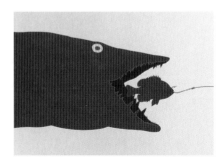

It's easy to see why deep-bodied baitfish shouldn't be lip-hooked.

through the back.

Most anglers use live baitfish, because that's what the majority of gamefish prefer. But baitfish can also be fished dead to catch scent-feeders like catfish and lake trout. Or, they can be used as cut bait.

Popular Baitfish–Rigging Methods

Species of Gamefish	Size/Type of Baitfish	Popular Rigging Methods
Panfish (crappies, sunfish, rock bass, warmouth, yellow perch, white perch, white bass)	1½- to 3-inch fathead minnows, shiners and redbelly dace (rainbows).	• Bobber rig with plain hook, small jig or tear drop • Welding-rod rig (crappie stick) • Jig and minnow or inch-long strip of cut bait • Tandem-hook (tightline) rig • Beetle-Spin and minnow • Jigging spoon and minnow head
Walleye, sauger, smallmouth bass	2½- to 4-inch fathead minnows, bluntnose minnows, shiners, chubs, dace and madtoms.	• Slip-bobber rig with plain hook or small jig • Slip-sinker rig with plain hook or floater • Split-shot rig • Jig and minnow • Spinner rig with slip-sinker or bottom bouncer • Jigging spoon with whole minnow or minnow head • Spin-rig and minnow
Northern pike, muskie	4- to 12-inch suckers, chubs, shiners, goldfish, yellow perch, smelt and ciscoes. For trophy fish, some anglers use baitfish up to 15 inches long.	• Slip-bobber rig with wire leader and plain hook, Swedish hook or quick-strike rig • Slip-sinker rig with wire leader and plain or weedless hook • Off-bottom rig with wire leader • Jig and minnow with wire leader • Strip-on spinner and minnow with wire leader
Largemouth bass	4-8 inch golden shiners, shad, chubs, dace and killifish; eels up to 12 inches long.	• Freelining with weedless hook • Peg-on float with weedless hook • Slip-sinker rig with plain or weedless hook • Slip-bobber rig with plain hook
Catfish	4- to 12-inch suckers, chubs, shiners, shad, skipjack, goldfish, carp and bluegills; mackerel and bonito for cut bait.	• Slip-sinker rig with egg or disk sinker and plain hook • Slip-sinker floating rig • 3-way swivel rig with bell sinker or bottom bouncer • Tandem-hook dropper rig • Slip-bobber rig
Striped bass	6- to 12-inch shad, skip-jack, golden shiners, bluegills, chubs and frozen anchovies; eels up to 18 inches long.	• Jig tipped with minnow or "pencil" eel • Casting bobber with jig and minnow • Balloon or slip-bobber rig with plain hook
Trout	3- to 12-inch smelt, ciscoes, shiners, chubs, suckers and sculpins.	• Slip-sinker rig and plain hook with minnow or cut bait • Jig tipped with minnow or cut bait • Heavy spoon tipped with cut bait • Needle-hook rig
Salmon	4- to 8-inch smelt, ciscoes and shiners. Coastal anglers use herring; Great Lakes anglers, alewives.	• Slip-sinker rig with floater • Trolling harness • Mooching rig

Basic Baitfish-Hooking Methods

Through Lips. *Push your hook through the lips of a thin-bodied baitfish from the bottom up. The bait will stay lively, and trail naturally when you're casting or trolling.*

Through Snout. *Also used for thin-bodied baitfish, this hooking method leaves more of the hook point exposed, increasing your chances of the barb penetrating when you set the hook.*

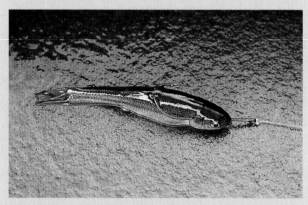

Out Gill and Through Back. *Using a long-shank hook, push the hook point through the mouth, out the gill and through the back. This method holds the baitfish securely but usually kills it.*

Through Nostrils. *Commonly used for shad, this hooking method directs the hook point to the side, rather than the top, of the head. This way, when the bait is lying flat in a fish's mouth, the hook is pointing toward the top or bottom of the fish's mouth.*

Through Tail. *This is the best way to hook baitfish for freelining, but it also works well for slow-trolling or casting; when pulled backward, the baitfish struggles more than it otherwise would.*

Through Back. *This method works well for still-fishing with either deep- or thin-bodied baitfish. Try to position the hook so the baitfish balances horizontally.*

Tips for Rigging & Fishing Live Baitfish

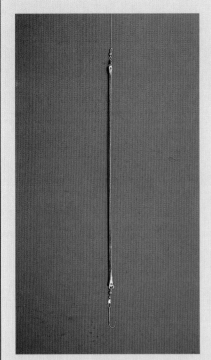

To prevent crappies or other panfish from tangling your line in brushy cover, use a "crappie stick." Flatten the ends of a welding rod and drill holes in each end. Add a split ring and long-shank, light-wire hook to one end and a split ring or snap-swivel to the other (left). The rod makes it much more difficult for a fish (or your minnow) to tangle your line in the brush (right). Should you get snagged, just let the rod drop freely; the downward force of the weight is usually enough to free the hook.

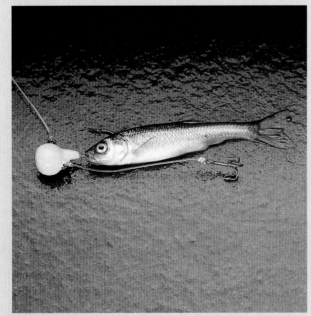

A jig and minnow is a deadly bait for walleyes, bass, pike and panfish, but there will be times when the fish strike short. To solve the problem, use a jig head with an extra eye and attach a treble "stinger hook." Let it trail free rather than hooking it in the minnow's tail.

Use a quick-strike rig to fish large baitfish (live or dead) for pike and muskies. Push one hook into the body near the pectoral fin and the other in front of the dorsal. When a fish strikes, set the hook immediately.

Freeline a large bait-fish in heavy vegetation to catch big large-mouths. Hook the bait just above the anal fin with a size 2/0 to 4/0 weedless hook and feed line as it swims through the weeds.

A wire leader is a must when using large baitfish to catch pike and muskies. But ordinary wire leaders tend to kink. To solve the problem, substitute a titanium leader, which is nearly impossible to kink.

Used mainly for pike, an off-bottom rig keeps a large baitfish close to, but not on, the bottom. A sinker maintains bottom contact while the bait is held above the bottom by a float and wire arm.

 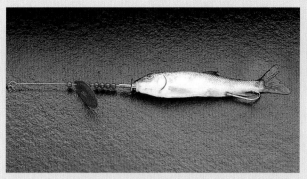

Strip-on Spinner. *Remove the double hook and then push the wire through the mouth of a large bait-fish and out the vent (left). Then replace the double hook by pushing it through the opening in the wire with the points up (right). Strip-ons are most commonly used for pike and muskies but are also effective for big bass, stripers, lake trout and other large predator fish.*

Needle Hook. *Popular for fishing sculpins for trout in western streams, the needle hook can be used for rigging practically any kind of dead baitfish. Push the "needle" through the vent and out the mouth (left). Then attach the clip to the hole in the needle (right). This way the bait can swing freely on the clip.*

Mooching Rig. *Popular for salmonids in coastal waters of the Pacific Northwest, mooching rigs are also used in the Great Lakes and other inland waters. The rig consists of a pair of single hooks, one of which slides on the line so the rig can be adjusted to the length of the bait. Push the rear hook through the tail and the front hook through the head (top). Then adjust the position of the front hook to snug up the line (bottom).*

Swedish Hook. *These unusual hooks are used mainly for fishing smelt, ciscoes or other dead baits for pike. With the hook shank down, push the hook into the vent up to the bend (left). Then rotate the hook so the shank is up and push the point through the back (right). Rigged properly, the bait should ride horizontally in the water.*

Threading On. *Use a bait needle to push your line through the mouth of a baitfish and out the vent (left). Remove the needle then tie on a treble hook; pull on the line to draw the shaft of the hook into the vent (right).*

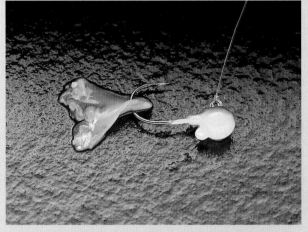

Throat Latch. *Should you run out of bait, remove the throat latch from a walleye or perch you've already caught by cutting along the dotted line (left). Fish the throat latch on a plain hook or use it to tip a jig (right). The throat latch emits scent, wiggles enticingly and is remarkably durable.*

Plug-Cut Baitfish. *"Plug-cutting" means slicing off the head of a baitfish at an angle so the bait rolls slowly when you're drifting or slow-trolling for salmonids. First, angle your cut from top to bottom and from side to side (1). Remove the innards. Then push the rear hook of a mooching rig (2) into the body and out the side above the vent (3). Finally, push the front hook through the back so it pierces the backbone, and adjust the position of the hook to take up most, but not all, of the slack.*

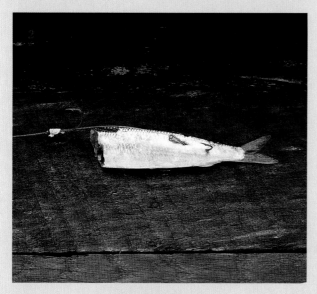

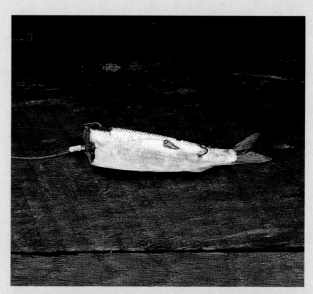

Chunk Bait. *Cut a good-sized shad, skipjack herring or other oily baitfish into inch-wide chunks (left) to catch catfish. Push the hook through the back (right), leaving plenty of the hook point exposed.*

WORMS

Worms are the oldest known fish bait, and they are no less effective today than they were centuries ago.

The Ultimate Guide To Freshwater Fishing

WORM BASICS

Worms are a near-universal bait for freshwater gamefish. They will catch everything from sunfish to sturgeon, and even toothy predators, like pike, don't hesitate to gobble up a lively nightcrawler.

Besides their amazing fish appeal, there are many other reasons for the popularity of worms:

• They are one of the easiest baits to find. After a good rain you can probably find enough worms for several fishing trips by picking them up on your lawn or a nearby golf course.

• Worms are easier to keep alive than most other kinds of bait. Most species of worms will live for weeks in a can of black dirt kept in a cool spot.

• Many species of worms are surprisingly easy to raise. Avid worm fishermen often have a "worm box" in their basement or backyard to give them a permanent supply.

Most kinds of worms thrive in fertile, loamy soil. But some can be found in soil consisting mainly of sand or clay. Worms feed by eating their way through the ground, leaving a trail of castings that further enrich the soil.

Worms are *hermaphrodites*, meaning that each individual possesses male and female sex organs, which are found in the dark band, or collar, near the head. An individual cannot fertilize its own eggs but, when two individuals breed (right), both are impregnated and produce a cocoon filled with eggs that is deposited in the soil. In about 2 or 3 weeks, tiny worms emerge from the cocoon to begin life on their own.

Worms have another unique property: They can be broken into pieces without killing them. When you're fishing for small gamefish, just break off a small piece of a worm—it will stay alive and wiggly for quite awhile. If you're after big fish, thread several worms onto the hook to create a writhing gob that fish find hard to resist.

Although worms do not have eyes or ears, they can sense the presence of predators (or humans attempting to catch them) by detecting subtle ground vibrations. Their body is also equipped with light-sensitive cells, explaining why they seldom come out of their burrows during the day and why they rapidly dart back into them when struck by the beam of a flashlight.

Nightcrawlers and some other kinds of worms breed on rainy nights, lying side by side on the ground and joining at the collar to fertilize each other's eggs.

Common Nightcrawler. *One of the most widely distributed worms, the common night-crawler is sometimes called the "dew worm" because it comes out of its burrow on cool, dewy or rainy nights. These big worms are 6 to 10 inches long, varying in color from brownish to pinkish to purplish, with a darker collar.*

European Nightcrawler. *These worms, available from many commercial growers, resemble common night-crawlers but have a much slimmer body.*

African Nightcrawler. *Like gray nightcrawlers, African nightcrawlers are grown commercially and are exceptionally lively. But they are more heat-tolerant and can be kept at room temperature. Similar in color to common night-crawlers, they range from 3 to 5 inches in length.*

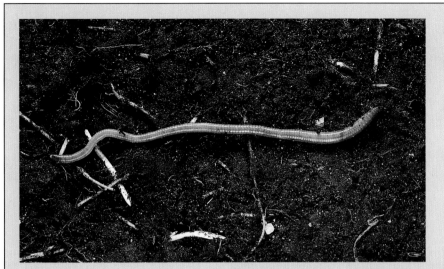

Grunt Worm. The term "grunt worm" refers to any of several large worms commonly taken by "grunting" or "fiddling". These worms vary in color from pinkish to brownish to grayish, with no distinct collar, and range in length from 5 to 8 inches.

Garden Worm. Perhaps the most common of all fishing worms, the garden worm is commonly called the "angle-worm." Garden worms are usually 3 to 4 inches long and vary in color from pinkish to grayish to bluish, with a collar only slightly darker than the rest of the body.

Red Wiggler. A favorite of panfish anglers, these lively, commercially grown worms run only 1½ to 3 inches in length. Dark reddish in color, red wigglers are also called "manure worms" because they thrive in compost piles.

Leaf Worm. Commonly found under leaves and logs, these worms resemble miniature common nightcrawlers. They range in length from 3 to 4 inches.

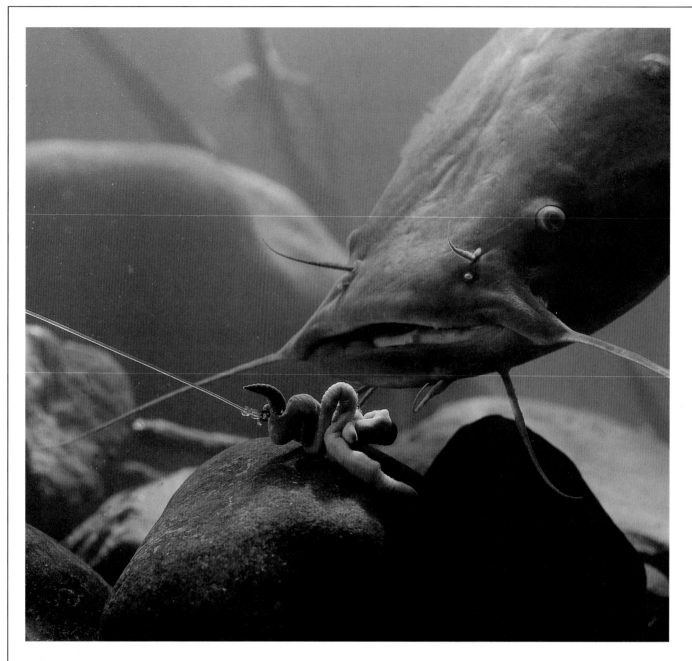

FISHING WITH WORMS

Other than the rare occasions when heavy rains wash earthworms into lakes and streams, gamefish seldom encounter earthworms in their natural environment. Nevertheless, earthworms will catch practically every kind of gamefish that swims in fresh water. Even large fish eaters, like northern pike or striped bass, will occasionally take a nightcrawler.

The most likely reason that fish bite on earthworms is that the fish feed on aquatic insect larvae that resemble worms. Walleyes, for example, commonly eat midge larvae or "bloodworms" that look like miniature red wigglers.

One important consideration in choosing worms is size. A single nightcrawler is the best choice for most large gamefish, but for giant catfish and sturgeon, some anglers gob on as many as 6 crawlers. Panfish and other small gamefish will take a whole crawler, but they'll probably just nip off the end. A 2- or 3-inch garden worm or red wiggler is a better choice.

Equally important is freshness of your bait. A lively, squirming worm will draw more strikes than a squishy, lifeless one. Even if a fish takes a dead worm, there's a good chance it will spit it out before you can set the hook.

Popular Worm-Rigging Methods

Species of Gamefish	Size/Type of Worm	Popular Rigging Methods
Panfish (sunfish, rock bass, warmouth, yellow perch, white perch)	Garden worms, red wigglers, leaf worms and other worms from 1¹/₂ to 4 inches in length; pieces of nightcrawler.	• Small float (fixed, slip or casting bubble), split shot and plain hook • In-line spinners and small spinnerbaits tipped with pieces of worm • Plain hook and split shot fished on a cane pole or extension pole • Plain hook on a "hanger" rig (yellow perch) • Small jig tipped with piece of worm
Walleye and sauger	4- to 8-inch nightcrawlers (plain or inflated).	• Slip-sinker rig with plain short-shank hook or floater • Slip-bobber rig with plain short-shank hook or ¹/₁₆-ounce jig head • Split-shot rig and plain hook • Weight-forward spinner or spin-rig tipped with nightcrawler • Bottom-walker rig with spinner and double- or triple-hook crawler harness • Trolling plug tipped with crawlers
Smallmouth and largemouth bass	4- to 8-inch nightcrawlers (plain or inflated).	• Slip-sinker rig with plain short-shank hook or floater • Split-shot rig and plain hook • Slip-bobber rig with plain short-shank hook or ¹/₁₆-ounce jig head • Spin-rig tipped with nightcrawler
Catfish	4- to 8-inch nightcrawlers.	• Fixed or slip-sinker rig with 2 to 6 worms gobbed onto plain or treble hook • Slip-bobber rig with 2 or 3 worms gobbed onto plain hook • Plain hook with gob of worms on jug-fishing rig
Sturgeon	4- to 8-inch nightcrawlers.	• Fixed or slip-sinker rig with 2 to 4 crawlers gobbed onto plain hook
Bullheads	Garden worms, red wigglers, leaf worms and other worms from 1¹/₂ to 4 inches in length; pieces of nightcrawler.	• Fixed or slip-sinker rig with 1 to 3 worms gobbed onto plain hook
Trout	Garden worms, red wigglers, leaf worms and other worms from 1¹/₂ to 4 inches in length; crawler pieces, whole crawlers (large trout).	• Split-shot rig and plain hook • In-line spinner tipped with worm • Small jig tipped with worm or half a crawler • Small float (fixed, slip or casting bubble), split shot and plain hook • "Cowbells" tipped with a worm

For panfish and other small fish that tend to nibble at the bait, hook a small worm several times, letting only about ½ inch of the tail dangle. A long-shank hook makes unhooking the fish easier because you can grab the hook more easily.

For trout or other fish that tend to "inhale" the bait, hook a worm through the middle so both ends dangle for maximum action.

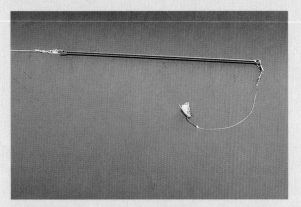

Lower a worm to the bottom on a "hanger" rig, which consists of a metal rod and an 8- to 12-inch dropper with a plain hook. You can also bait the rig with a minnow head. Bounce the rig on the bottom to "mud up" the water and attract perch.

Gob several worms (or crawlers) onto the hook to create a writhing mass that appeals to bullheads, catfish and sturgeon. Add new worms as needed to keep plenty of exposed ends wiggling. Some catfish anglers prefer treble rather than single hooks.

Add a single garden worm, red worm or leaf worm to a "cowbell" rig consisting of a series of large spinner blades. Cowbells, also called "pop gear" or lake trolls, are extremely popular among trollers because they produce flash that can be seen from a great distance in clear-water trout lakes.

Walleyes and bass often favor the natural look of a night-crawler hooked through the head. To make the worm trail straight without spinning, push a short-shank hook into the tip of the head and out the side about $1/4$ to $3/8$ inch back from the tip.

Use a "worm blower" to inflate a nightcrawler and make it float up off the bottom where fish can see it more easily. Insert the needle just behind the collar and squeeze a small bubble of air into the head. Inflating the tail makes the worm look unnatural.

Rig up a half crawler when the fish are striking short. For best results, hook the crawler through the broken end as shown. Most anglers report better success with the head section than the tail section but either will work.

Hook a nightcrawler onto a 2- or 3-hook worm harness to reduce the number of short strikes. When hooking the worm, remember that it will contract when you handle it, so you must leave a little slack between the hooks. This way, the worm can stretch out naturally without being restricted by the harness.

LEECHES

*E*ven the fussi-est gamefish find it hard to resist a leech squirming right in their face.

LEECH BASICS

Biologists who study the food habits of freshwater gamefish know that leeches are a common item in the diets of many fish species. Yet leeches are nowhere near as popular as other common food items as fishing bait.

In the last few decades, leeches have gained popularity among walleye, sunfish and smallmouth bass anglers throughout much of the Midwest, and many consider them the premier bait for these species. But they have not caught on to that degree in other parts of the country, probably because many anglers consider them "bloodsuckers" and are reluctant to handle them.

In truth, the popular bait leeches are not bloodsuckers; they feed on small worms and other aquatic organisms, but they will not bore

ature, they tend to curl up into a tight ball and refuse to swim. The warmer the water, the more active a leech becomes.

Whether you buy leeches or trap your own, it's important to know which species work well for bait and which do not (below).

Good Leeches

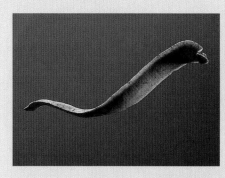

Ribbon Leech. *These common leeches may be brown, black, olive or mottled. Their body is firmer than that of a horse leech and the crosswise grooves are less distinct. They range in length from 2 to 6 inches when stretched out.*

Tiger Leech. *Much less common than the ribbon leech, the tiger leech is one of the most active leech species. Tiger leeches, which usually measure 2 to 4 inches in length, get their name from the 4 parallel black stripes on their back.*

Bad Leeches

Horse Leech. *Ranging in length from 3 to 12 inches, horse leeches may be black or mottled brown. They have very distinct grooves, a "squishy" feel and a powerful sucking disk that enables them to crawl out of a bait bucket.*

Medicine Leech. *Once used for sucking blood from sick humans, medicine leeches are easy to identify because of the row of red spots down the back and their rust-colored belly. Like horse leeches, they have a squishy feel and distinct grooves.*

through the skin of live animals to suck their blood. When a bait leech attaches to your skin with the powerful suction cup on its tail (wide end), it is only trying to hold on, not suck your blood. The mouth is actually located on the narrow end.

As a rule leeches work best at water temperatures of 50°F or higher. Below that temper-

FISHING WITH LEECHES

If you've ever watched a leech swim through the water, you know why it makes such an irresistible target for many kinds of gamefish. A leech swims slowly, undulating wildly as it moves along, so all a fish has to do is leisurely cruise up to the morsel and inhale it.

But when a leech does not undulate as it normally would, it loses its near-magical attraction. That's why it's important to use hooking techniques that give the leech freedom of movement and to replace any leech that has been injured by nibbling panfish.

The importance of this intense action also explains why leeches work best in warm water. Northern anglers know that leeches are worthless as ice-fishing bait because they don't swim at all at near-freezing water temperatures. In fact, they usually wrap themselves around the hook, forming a hard ball. They will not swim normally until the water temperature rises into the 50s.

Even at warm temperatures, some leeches are more active than others. Savvy anglers spend some time sorting through their leech bucket, looking for the best swimmers.

Many fishermen make the mistake of using jumbo leeches that are more than 6 inches long when stretched out. These giant baits are sometimes referred to as "mud flaps." Although a good-sized fish won't hesitate to grab these baits, your hooking percentage may suffer. As a rule, you'll do better with a smaller leech that has an enticing action.

Popular Leech-Rigging Methods

Species of Gamefish	Size/Type of Leech	Popular Rigging Methods
Panfish (sunfish, rock bass, yellow perch)	Ribbon and tiger leeches from 1½ to 3 inches long (stretched out); pieces of leech.	• Small float (fixed, slip or casting bubble), split shot and plain hook • In-line spinners and small spinnerbaits tipped with small leeches • Plain hook and split shot fished on a cane pole or extension pole • Small jig tipped with piece of leech
Walleye and sauger	Ribbon leeches from 2½ to 5 inches long; tiger leeches from 2 to 4 inches long.	• Slip-sinker rig with plain short-shank hook or floater • Slip-bobber rig with plain short-shank hook or ¹⁄₁₆-ounce jig head • Split-shot rig and plain hook • Weight-forward spinner or spin rig tipped with leech • Bottom-walker rig with spinner and single hook
Smallmouth and largemouth bass	Ribbon leeches from 2½ to 5 inches long. Largemouth have been known to take 6- to 8-inch horse leeches.	• Slip-sinker rig with plain short-shank hook or floater • Split-shot rig and plain hook • Slip-bobber rig with plain short-shank hook or ¹⁄₁₆-ounce jig head • Spin-rig tipped with leech
Trout	Ribbon leeches from 2 to 4 inches long.	• Split-shot rig and plain hook • In-line spinner tipped with leech • Small jig tipped with leech • Small float (fixed, slip or casting bubble), split shot and plain hook

How to Hook Leeches

Through the tail. *In most situations where you're retrieving the leech, hook it just ahead of the sucker on the tail.*

Through the head. *When nibbling panfish are stealing your bait, hook the leech through the tough skin of the neck.*

Through the middle. *When float-fishing or using any vertical presentation, hook your leech through the middle.*

Select a lively leech by sorting through your bucket, looking for the most active swimmers. If you pick out a leech that wants to wrap itself around your hook, discard it and select a different one.

Should nibbling panfish injure your leech, causing it to lose its flattened shape, discard it and put on a new one.

Tip a tiny jig with a piece of leech to catch panfish. Any part of a leech will work, but many anglers prefer the head end because it is tougher. Hook the head section through the broken end.

When tipping a jig, choose a fairly small leech and hook it through the head end. This way, it's more difficult for a fish to pick it off the hook, and the leech is less likely to wrap itself around the lure.

Don't use leeches that are too large for the fish you're after. A leech that looks to be only 2 inches long in the hand may stretch out to a length of 6 inches or more in the water. An average-sized walleye or bass may grab a "mud flap," but it will probably strike short. A smaller leech is equally attractive and will significantly boost your hooking percentage.

When trolling with a spinner rig, choose one with a single hook rather than a 2- or 3-hook harness. This way the leech can wiggle more freely and won't wrap itself up in the harness.

Freeline a leech to catch walleyes, bass or panfish in shallow water. Just hook the leech ahead of the sucker with a short-shank hook, toss it out with light spinning gear and let it swim on its own.

INSECTS

*P*ractically all kinds of gamefish feed heavily on insects at some point in their lives, so it's easy to understand why these delicate baits are so effective.

The Ultimate Guide To Freshwater Fishing

AQUATIC INSECTS

Every kind of freshwater gamefish habitat supports some type of aquatic insect, and many waters hold hundreds of different types. Fly fishermen understand the importance of these insects more than other anglers, and have created a staggering array of fly patterns intended to "match the hatch."

Although there is a great deal of variation in aquatic insect life cycles, the cycle of the mayfly (below) is fairly typical. Like the mayfly, most aquatic insects have an immature stage that spends a year or more in the water. Their life as an adult, which lasts only a few days, is spent on land and in the air.

The immature forms of aquatic insects are much more widely used as bait because they're available throughout the year. They're also more appealing to gamefish and considerably easier to keep on the hook.

Despite the obvious appeal of aquatic insects to many kinds of gamefish, few anglers have taken the time to learn how to use live insects to their best advantage. On the following pages, we'll show you how to identify the aquatic insects most commonly used for bait, where and how to collect them and keep them in good condition, and the best techniques for using them to catch various kinds of gamefish.

Life Cycle of a Mayfly

1 Adult mayflies mate in flight and then the female deposits her fertilized eggs in the water. The eggs stick to plants, rocks and debris on the bottom.

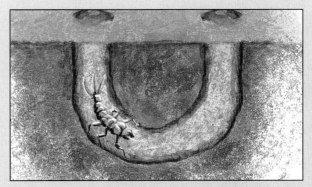

2 The nymphs hatch in about 6 months. Burrowing mayflies (the largest types), tunnel into a firm mud bottom where they feed for several more months while undergoing numerous molts.

3 The full-grown nymph swims to the surface and sheds its skin. A dun or subimago, which has cloudy wings, then emerges and flies off to nearby vegetation where its wings can dry.

4 Within a day or two, the dun molts into a mature adult, called a spinner or imago, which has clear wings. The spinners deposit their eggs within a few days and then die.

Mayflyies. *Often called "wigglers," mayfly nymphs (left) have a single pair of wingpads, gills on the abdomen and two or three long tail filaments. The adults or spinners (right), have clear, upright wings.*

Stoneflies. *The nymphs (left) have two pairs of wingpads, two short, thick tail filaments and gills on the underside of the thorax. Adults (right) are dull brownish or grayish and their wings lie flat rather than stand upright.*

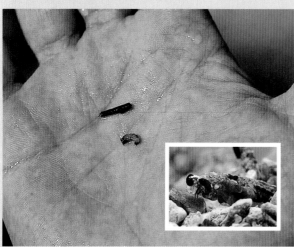

Caddisflies. *Caddisfly larvae or caddisworms (left) have a segmented, tan or cream-colored body with three pairs of legs near the front. Most live in a case made of sand or sticks, but some are free-living. The adults (right), are brownish and have tentlike wings.*

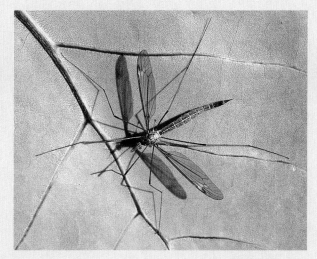

Craneflies. *Cranefly larvae, called waterworms (left), may be up to 2½ inches in length. The soft, segmented body is grayish or brownish and has several hairy projections on the tail. The adults (right) resemble giant mosquitoes.*

Dragonflies. *The stout-bodied nymphs (left) vary in color from dark brown to pale green. They can be identified by their large labium (lower lip) which is used to grasp prey. Adults (right) have a pair of large, usually multicolored, wings.*

Dobsonflies. *The larvae, called hellgrammites (left), measure up to 3 inches in length and have a forbidding look, with large pincers on their head. Adult males (right) may be as much as 5 inches long and have extremely long jaws.*

FISHING WITH AQUATIC INSECTS

Although larval aquatic insects are used primarily for trout, they're also popular for smallmouth bass, yellow perch and even walleyes. During a hatch, some anglers use the adult forms of mayflies and stoneflies, but these insects are extremely delicate and difficult to keep on the hook.

Even many of the larval forms are quite delicate, so it's important to hook them properly. Otherwise they'll fly off the hook when you cast, or nibbling fish will strip them off the hook.

Because of the delicacy issue, you should use a light-wire hook. If you attempt to push a heavy wire hook through the dainty body, you may damage the bait so it won't stay on the hook. If you're threading the bait on lengthwise, the hook should have an extra-

long shank.

A rod with a soft tip reduces the chances of losing the bait on the cast. Instead of "throwing" the bait, you can gently lob-cast it, letting the rod do the work and reducing the strain on the bait.

Popular Methods for Rigging Aquatic Insects

Species of Gamefish	Size/Type of Insect	Popular Rigging Methods
Yellow perch and walleye	Mayfly nymphs from 1 to 2 inches long.	• Small float (fixed or slip), split shot and light-wire, extra-long-shank hook • 1/8- to 1/4-ounce jigging spoon tipped with mayfly nymph • Jigging spoon with mono dropper and light-wire, extra-long-shank hook
Smallmouth and largemouth bass	Hellgrammites from 2 to 3 inches long; dragonfly nymphs from 1 to 1 1/2 inches long.	• Split-shot rig and plain hook • Fixed- or slip-bobber rig with split shot and plain hook
Trout	Stonefly and mayfly nymphs from 1 to 2 inches long, hellgrammites from 1 1/2 to 2 inches long, waterworms, 2 or 3 caddis larvae.	• Split-shot rig and plain hook • Small float (fixed, slip or casting bubble), split shot and plain hook

How to Hook Aquatic Insects

Mayfly Nymph. *Thread the nymph onto a size 10 or 12 long-shank, light-wire hook. Most anglers thread the nymph head first, but some thread it tail first.*

Stonefly Nymph. *Hook the nymph under the collar using a size 8 or 10 light-wire hook.*

Caddis Larvae. *Hook 1 to 3 larvae through the head using a size 12 to 16 light-wire hook. Some anglers hook on the case and the worm.*

Hellgrammite. *Hook a hellgrammite under the collar with a size 4 to 8 light-wire hook. Grab it behind the head to avoid the pincers.*

Waterworm. *Push a size 8 or 10 light-wire hook through the tough skin just ahead of the projections on the tail.*

Dragonfly Nymph. *Hook the nymph under the collar using a size 8 or 10 light-wire hook.*

Tips for Fishing with Aquatic Insects

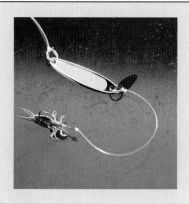

Make a dropper rig for yellow perch and walleyes by replacing the treble hook on a jigging spoon with a long-shank single hook on a 4- to 6-inch mono dropper. Thread on a mayfly wiggler.

Lob-cast delicate insect baits using a smooth sidearm motion. The rod tip must be soft enough to "load" on the backcast so the "recoil" can propel the bait on the forward cast.

TERRESTRIAL INSECTS

The term, "terrestrial insect" means any insect that completes its entire life cycle on land. Besides well-known adult forms like crickets and grasshoppers, many anglers use immature forms including caterpillars (butterfly and moth larvae), maggots (fly larvae) and grubs (beetle larvae).

Terrestrial insects are not a staple in the diet of most gamefish. In fact, few gamefish ever see the immature forms and they feed on the adults only on rare occasions in summer, usually when strong winds blow them into the water.

Nevertheless, terrestrial insects rank among the most effective baits for many kinds of gamefish. Although they are used most commonly for smaller fish, like stream trout and panfish, some types also work well for big fish. Catalpa worms, for example, are widely considered to be one of the finest catfish baits.

Common Adult Terrestrials

Grasshoppers. *There are hundreds of different kinds of grasshoppers, most of which inhabit grassy or weedy fields. They range in color from grayish to brownish to greenish. Those used for fishing are usually 1 to 2 inches long.*

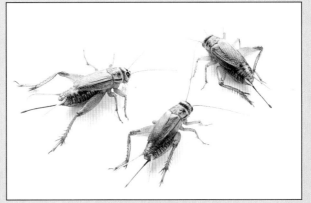

Crickets. *Gray crickets (shown) are grown commercially and are readily available at many bait shops or pet-supply stores. But anglers also use a variety of other crickets that they catch themselves, usually in grassy or weedy fields.*

Common Terrestrial Insect Larvae

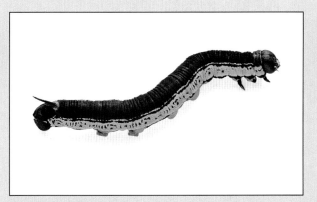

Catalpa Worm. *These large worms (up to 3 inches long) are the larval stage of the catalpa sphinx moth; they feed on the leaves of catalpa trees. They have prominent black stripes down the back and a black spine on the tail.*

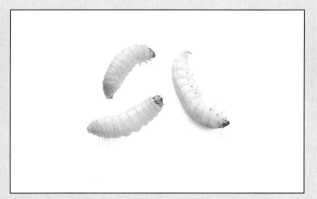

Waxworm. *Measuring from ¹/₂ to 1 inch in length, waxworms are larvae of the bee moth. They have a cream-colored body with distinct segments and a brownish head.*

Goldenrod Grub. *These small, whitish maggots, which are only about ¹/₄-inch long, are the larvae of the goldenrod gall fly. They burrow into the stems of goldenrod plants, making the characteristic swellings or "galls."*

Mousee. *These small larvae, also known as rat-tailed maggots, are the immature form of the bee fly. Their tannish body is about ¹/₂ inch long, with a tubelike tail at least that long. They live in stagnant water and use the tube to breathe.*

Spike. *Housefly and blowfly maggots are often sold as "spikes" or "silver wigglers." Most varieties are light tan in color and measure about ¹/₂ inch in length.*

Eurolarvae. *Maggots of the European blowfly are fed dyed food and sold as "Eurolarvae." The tough-bodied larvae come in a variety of colors and are ³/₈ to ¹/₂ inch long.*

Mealworm. *Commonly sold as "golden grubs," these inch-long larvae are the immature form of the darkling beetle. The yellowish to tannish body has distinct segments; the head is dark brown.*

FISHING WITH TERRESTRIAL INSECTS

For centuries, freshwater anglers have been catching fish on crickets and grasshoppers. And ice fishermen have long known that waxworms and other small terrestrial insect larvae are dynamite panfish baits. Until recently, however, these larvae were not widely used for open-water fishing.

Trout anglers, for example, are now discovering that larval terrestrials often work just as well as immature aquatic insects. And panfish anglers who previously swore by worms and small minnows have found that there are times when larval

baits work better.

One big advantage to larval baits: They seem to work better after fish have bitten them and broken the skin, releasing their body fluids. So there is no need to replace mangled bait; just add new bait as needed.

Popular Methods for Rigging Terrestrial Insects

Species of Gamefish	Type of Insect	Popular Rigging Methods
Panfish (sunfish, crappies, rock bass, warmouth, yellow perch)	Cricket, grasshopper, waxworm, mealworm, spike, Eurolarvae, mousee, goldenrod grub.	• Small float (fixed or slip), split shot and light-wire, extra-long-shank hook with cricket or hopper • Small float (fixed or slip), split shot and light-wire hook or tear drop with larvae • 1/16- to 1/4-ounce jigging spoon tipped with larvae • Jigging spoon with mono dropper and light-wire, extra-long-shank hook
Smallmouth and largemouth bass	Cricket, grasshopper.	• Split-shot rig and extra-long-shank hook • Insect floated on surface with extra-long-shank hook (no extra weight)
Trout	Cricket, grasshopper, waxworm, mealworm, spike, Eurolarvae, mousee, goldenrod grub.	• Split-shot and extra-long-shank hook with cricket or hopper • Split-shot and short-hank hook with larvae • Small float (fixed or slip), split shot and extra-long-shank hook with cricket or hopper or short-shank hook with larvae • Insect floated on surface with casting bubble and extra-long-shank hook
Catfish	Catalpa worm, grasshopper.	• Slip-sinker rig and plain hook • Slip- or fixed-bobber rig and plain hook • Plain hook on trotline

Grasshopper/Cricket. *Thread a grasshopper or cricket onto a light-wire, extra-long-shank hook either (1) head first or (2) tail first. Trout fishermen often hook grasshoppers (3) under the collar with a light-wire hook for a more natural presentation.*

Waxworm, Mealworm & Mousee. *Using a light-wire hook or tear drop, push the hook point through the head and out the side about ¼ inch down. The bait should hang straight down, not stick out to the side.*

Spike & Eurolarvae. *These baits have very tough skin so they can be hooked lightly through the head with most of the body left dangling. Put 2 or 3 larvae on a light-wire hook or tear drop.*

Goldenrod Grub. *Put 2 or more of these tiny larvae onto a light-wire hook or tear drop. Push the hook through the middle of the body.*

Catalpa Worm. *Push the hook point into the back about ⅓ body length from the tail end. Bring the hook out the back midway up the body (left). Or thread the worm onto the hook tail first so the body lies straight (right).*

FROGS

*T*he number of frog-imitating lures on the market is testament to the tremendous fish appeal of these common amphibians.

FROG BASICS

If you hang around a north-country bait shop in the fall, you'll most likely hear the old-timers talking about the "frog migration." As the weather begins to cool, the frogs start moving from shallow marshes (that will soon freeze solid) to deeper lakes where they will hibernate in the muddy bottom.

Accordingly, that's the best time to toss out a lively frog to catch bass, walleyes, pickerel and other hungry predators patrolling the lakeshore for an easy meal as they try to fatten up for winter.

Decades ago, frogs were a much more popular bait than they are today. That's because modern anglers can buy a wide variety of soft-plastic frog imitations and many kinds of hard-bodied, frog-imitating topwaters.

Another reason for the

frog's declining popularity as bait: Widespread disease (particularly redleg disease) has decimated frog populations in many parts of the country. Wetland drainage and pesticides have also taken their toll as well.

Nevertheless, many experienced anglers know that a fake frog is no match for a live one kicking its way through the water. That explains why these anglers are willing to spend hours slogging along marshy shorelines with dip net in hand.

The leopard frog, by far the most common North American frog species, is also the most common bait species. But practically any kind of small frog can be used for bait. Surprisingly, tadpoles do not make good bait. It's not that fish won't eat them; they're just too delicate and nearly impossible to keep alive on the hook.

Bullfrogs, which may be more than a foot long, are rarely used as live bait, but they make good cut bait, especially for catfish.

Popular Bait Frogs

Leopard Frog. *The body is greenish to light brown with numerous irregular dark spots and distinct ridges running the entire length of the back. Leopard frogs measure up to 4 inches in length and are found throughout North America, with the exception of the West Coast.*

Green Frog. *These unspotted frogs, found in the eastern U.S. and southeastern Canada, vary in color from pale greenish to brownish and measure up to 3½ inches in length. They have ridges that extend from the head just past the middle of the back.*

Bullfrog. *These giant frogs are greenish to brownish with mottled undersides and no ridges on the back. The body itself measures 4 to 6 inches in length, and the legs add another 7 to 10 inches. Bullfrogs are found throughout the U.S. with the exception of the Rockies and northern plains.*

Use a stout cane pole or extension pole to dabble a frog into openings in the vegetation. Dabbling enables you to place the frog exactly where you want it and, because you can set the frog down gently, it stays livelier than it would if you were casting.

FISHING WITH FROGS

A frog kicking its way through a shallow weedbed has a short life expectancy. The surface disturbance is almost sure to attract hungry gamefish.

Most anglers think of frogs as good bait for largemouth bass, but they work equally well for smallmouth. They're also effective for northern pike, pickerel and even catfish.

Frogs will catch fish most any time, but they seem to work best in fall. Some anglers claim that gamefish move into the shallows in fall to feed on frogs migrating from shallow marshes to deeper lakes. But it's more likely that the fish are in the shallows to gorge themselves on baitfish in preparation for winter, and they just happen to encounter the frogs.

Here are some things to keep in mind when using frogs for bait:

• Frogs are more delicate than you may think. Repeated casting will weaken or kill them. Always cast with a gentle, sidearm lob so the frog doesn't splash down too hard.

• Replace your bait frequently. When a frog tires and stops kicking, it is much less effective.

• Hooking fish may be difficult when using frogs. If you're missing too many fish, switch to a smaller frog and wait longer before setting the hook.

Popular Frog-Rigging Methods

Species of Gamefish	Size/Type of Frog	Popular Rigging Methods
Largemouth bass, smallmouth bass, walleye	Leopard frog or green frog no more than 3 inches long.	• Slip-sinker rig with plain or weedless hook • Split-shot rig with plain or weedless hook • Freelining or dabbling with plain hook and no extra weight
Northern pike, pickerel	Leopard frog or green frog no more than 4 inches long.	• Slip-sinker rig with wire leader and plain or weedless hook • Split-shot rig with wire leader and plain or weedless hook
Catfish	Large leopard frog or pieces of bullfrog.	• Large slip-float rig with plain hook • Slip-sinker rig with plain hook • 3-way-swivel rig with plain hook

Tips for Rigging & Fishing Frogs

Hook a live frog through the lips with either a (1) plain hook or weedless hook. When float fishing or freelining, you can also hook a frog (2) through the hind leg.

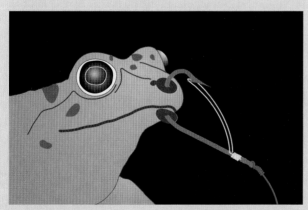

Keep a frog on the hook with plastic tabs punched from the lid of a coffee can. Push one tab onto the hook bend, hook the frog through the lips, then secure it with another tab.

Freeline a frog by feeding line as it swims over the vegetation. Keep your line taut, but not tight, so you can get a solid hookset when a fish strikes.

SALAMANDERS

These tough, lively amphibians have long been the "secret weapon" of Southern bass anglers.

SALAMANDER BASICS

Flip through the pages of your latest fishing tackle catalog and you'll see dozens of soft-plastic "lizards" and maybe a few "waterdogs." The popularity of these sala-mander imitations—and their real-life counterparts—stems from the common belief that salamanders are "nest robbers," so fish are quick to attack them to protect their eggs and young.

Live salamanders have long been a favorite of Southern bass anglers, but are used much less commonly in the North. They are popular,

may live on land or in the water, depending on the species.

Both adult and larval salamanders are used for bait. The most popular types fall into the 3 categories discussed here.

MOLE SALAMANDERS

These reclusive salamanders get their name from their habit of living in the underground tunnels of moles and other small mammals.

In spring, the adults emerge from the tunnels and migrate to small, fishless ponds to breed. The young reach full size by fall and then leave the water to begin their life as land-dwelling adults.

By far the most common mole salamander species is the tiger salamander (below).

Adult Tiger Salamander. *These large salamanders range from 6 inches to more than a foot in length; most anglers use 6- to 8-inchers for bait. Several species of tiger salamanders, all which have a distinctive yellow and black coloration, are found in the United States, southern Canada and northern Mexico.*

Larval Tiger Salamander. *Often called "waterdogs," larval tiger salamanders are generally considered to be much better bait than the adults. Waterdogs have external gills, tiny legs and a long fin extending around the rear of the body. They range in length from 4 to 8 inches.*

however, among some north-country anglers who target trophy walleyes and northern pike.

Although anglers refer to some kinds of salamanders as "lizards," they are amphibians, not reptiles. Most salamanders have an aquatic larval form, but the adult form

LUNGLESS SALAMANDERS

This is by far the most common salamander group, with almost 100 species found in North America. As their name suggests, they do not have lungs; instead, they absorb oxygen through their skin.

Anglers refer to some members of this group as "spring lizards" because they're commonly found in the vicinity of springs, brooks or small streams. Other types live in damp woodlands, taking cover under rocks or logs or burrowing into leaf litter and other debris on the forest floor.

Lungless salamanders have sleek bodies and are good swimmers, accounting for their popularity as fishing bait. Most anglers prefer the adult form.

Spring Salamander. The back and sides of the spring salamander are grayish to brownish with rows of darker spots that end at or above the legs. Adults range in length from 5 to 6½ inches. During the day, these salamanders hide beneath pieces of rock or wood in caves or along the banks of streams or springs. They can often be found feeding along stream-banks on rainy nights.

Dusky Salamander. The back of the dusky salamander is yellowish-brown to dark gray, sometimes with an irregular dark lateral band. Averaging just under 5 inches in length, dusky salamanders are normally found along the banks of springs and streams. They prefer moist soil but can survive in tiny, leaf-filled trickles and even in creek beds that are practically dry.

Redback Salamander. As their name suggests, redback salamanders have a reddish dorsal stripe. The back is dark gray to black and the belly is mottled with black and white. These small salamanders range from 2½ to 5 inches in length. They're normally found under rocks, logs and leaf litter in damp deciduous, evergreen or mixed forests.

GIANT SALAMANDERS

This group of large salamanders includes some species that reach more than 2 feet in length. The hellbender, for example, grows to a length of 30 inches and is capable of inflicting a painful bite. The giant salamanders used for bait, however, are generally no more than 12 inches long. Some giant salamanders take several years to mature, so it's possible to find bait-sized individuals even in waters inhabited by the larger species.

Giant salamanders differ from other kinds of salamanders in that they spend their entire life in water. Most have external gills that persist through life. One type, the siren (below), looks more like an eel than a salamander because it has only tiny front legs and no hind legs.

Siren. Found mainly in the coastal plain of the southeastern and south-central U.S., sirens favor the quiet, weedy waters of shallow ditches, swamps and ponds. Sirens vary in color from black to olive-green. The lesser siren ranges in length from 6 to 15 inches, but the greater siren (shown) has been known to reach lengths exceeding 3 feet.

Mudpuppy. These common amphibians have a broad head, thick body and paddlelike tail. The common mudpuppy (shown), found mainly in large, sluggish rivers, reaches lengths of nearly 20 inches. The dwarf mudpuppy has a slate-gray to purplish-black back with a few small, lighter spots and is 4½ to 7½ inches long. Dwarf mudpuppies are found in small, sluggish streams, mainly in coastal areas.

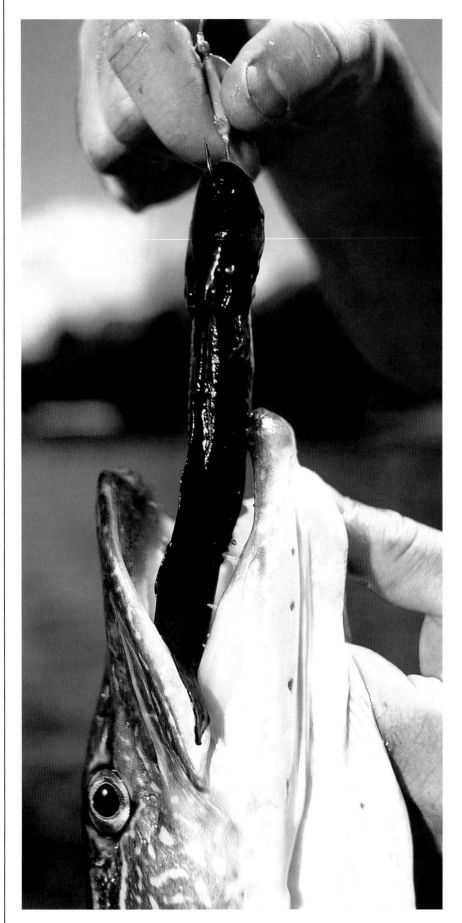

FISHING WITH SALAMANDERS

Innovative anglers throughout the country have discovered that salamanders are not just a bass bait. They also catch catfish, northern pike and even walleyes.

Big fish like big baits, so it's not surprising that large salamanders are considered prime fare for trophy fishing. An 8-inch waterdog, for example, makes an excellent bait for big walleyes and northern pike, and a foot-long siren is a premier bait for hefty largemouths.

Not all salamanders, however, are equally effective as bait. As a rule, the more active the salamander, the better fish like it. This explains why a waterdog, which swims with an enticing wiggle, usually works better than an adult tiger salamander, which swims lethargically or crawls along the bottom. Spring lizards are also active swimmers, but they tend to tire quickly.

Perhaps the liveliest salamander of all is the siren. Used mainly by bass anglers in the southeastern states, these snakelike amphibians swim with an irresistible motion unlike that of any other salamander.

The biggest problem in fishing with salamanders is getting a solid hookset. Fish tend to grab them by the tail and when you try to set the hook, all you get is a scuffed-up salamander. To solve the problem, use smaller salamanders or rig them with a stinger hook (next page).

Popular Salamander-Rigging Methods

Species of Gamefish	Size/Type of Salamander	Popular Rigging Methods
Walleye, pickerel	Waterdog from 4 to 6 inches long.	• Slip-sinker rig with plain hook • Split-shot rig and plain hook
Northern pike	Waterdogs and "spring lizards" from 5 to 8 inches long.	• Slip-sinker rig with wire leader and plain or weedless hook • Split-shot rig with wire leader and plain or weedless hook
Largemouth bass, smallmouth bass	Waterdog from 4 to 8 inches long; adult salamander from 5 to 8 inches long (up to 12 inches for trophy largemouth).	• Slip-sinker rig with plain or weedless hook • Split-shot rig and plain or weedless hook • Freelining or dabbling with plain hook and no extra weight
Catfish	Waterdog from 5 to 8 inches long; adult salamander from 5 to 12 inches long.	• Large slip-float rig with plain hook • Slip-sinker rig with plain hook • 3-way-swivel rig with plain hook

Tips for Rigging & Fishing Salamanders

Hook a salamander through the lips, from the bottom up. If you're having problems keeping the bait on the hook, use plastic tabs as you would with frogs (p. 387).

Spring lizards and other adult salamanders are often hooked just in front of the back leg. Hooked this way, the bait stays alive longer and is not as likely to get off the hook.

Make a stinger-hook rig by tying a short length of mono to your main hook and then adding a size 8 or 10 treble. Push the treble into the body behind the rear legs.

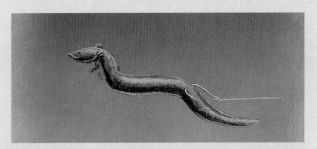

When bass are in heavy weeds, freeline a siren by hooking it through the back as shown and then feeding line as it slithers through the vegetation.

CRUSTACEANS

Crustaceans may look forbidding to anglers. But they're like candy to many kinds of gamefish.

CRUSTACEAN BASICS

Crustaceans are an important part of the diet of almost all gamefish, so it's not surprising that they make excellent bait. In the first months of their life, juvenile fish of all kinds feed on tiny planktonic crustaceans, such as water fleas. Later in life the fish eat larger crustaceans, such as freshwater shrimp and crayfish. Here are the types of crustaceans most commonly used as bait:

CRAYFISH

More than 500 species of crayfish inhabit North American waters. They're found in every conceivable type of freshwater habitat, including shallow, stagnant ponds, roadside ditches, natural and man-made lakes, fast-flowing coldwater streams and sluggish warmwater rivers.

Most fishermen don't attempt to distinguish one species of crayfish from another. The main consideration in selecting crayfish is size. Anglers targeting trophy largemouth bass use crayfish up to 4 inches long, while panfish anglers prefer those less than 2 inches long.

SHRIMP

Freshwater fishermen use both freshwater and saltwater varieties of shrimp for bait. Anglers in coastal areas can purchase live saltwater shrimp in bait shops or catch their own in coastal estuaries. They can also catch mud shrimp and ghost shrimp along the mud flats of estuaries. Inland anglers can buy chilled or frozen saltwater shrimp at grocery stores.

Several types of freshwater shrimp, called grass shrimp, are popular among panfish anglers. Saltwater varieties of grass shrimp are also used for bait.

River shrimp—large freshwater shrimp found in some major river systems—also make good bait. But their limited availability restricts their popularity to specific areas, mainly the lower Mississippi River region.

SCUDS

Fishermen commonly refer to these small crustaceans as "freshwater shrimp," but the term is a misnomer. Scuds are considerably smaller than true freshwater shrimp and lack the distinctive fanlike tail.

Scuds are found in a variety of freshwater environments ranging from small coldwater streams to shallow, fertile natural lakes.

Scuds are seldom sold at bait shops, but they're fairly easy to catch.

When threatened, a large crustacean propels itself backward with a flip of its powerful, fan-shaped tail.

Crustaceans Commonly Used for Bait

Crayfish. These large crustaceans have powerful claws, or pincers, and hard, thick shells. Most are brownish or greenish, but they may be reddish or bluish. Most species are 2 to 4 inches long when fully grown, excluding the pincers.

Saltwater Shrimp. Many species of saltwater shrimp, ranging from 3 to 5 inches in length, are used for bait. Saltwater shrimp have very small claws and short antennae and are tannish to pinkish in color.

Mud Shrimp. Found mainly on intertidal flats along the Pacific and Gulf coasts, mud shrimp have large pincers that resemble those of crayfish. They vary in color from pinkish to tannish to bluish and range in length from 4 to 7 inches.

Ghost Shrimp. *These pale-colored shrimp are found mainly on intertidal flats along the Gulf coast. Ghost shrimp have one pincer that is considerably larger than the other, explaining why some anglers call them "one-armed bandits." They vary in color from pinkish to off-white and range in length from 4 to 7 inches.*

Grass Shrimp. *These diminutive shrimp, which are only 1 to 2 inches in length, have a light greenish to tannish color and a translucent, almost glassy look. Saltwater varieties are most common in estuaries along the Atlantic and Gulf coasts; freshwater types, in ditches, ponds and small lakes in the southeastern U.S.*

Scuds. *Smaller than any other crustaceans used for bait, scuds range from ½ to ¾ inch in length. Unlike crayfish and shrimp, they do not have a fanlike tail. Scuds have the unusual habit of swimming on their side, explaining why they are sometimes called "sideswimmers."*

FISHING WITH CRUSTACEANS

Crustaceans have one big advantage over other kinds of natural bait: They emit a strong scent that attracts fish from a considerable distance.

Despite this fact, crustaceans, with the notable exception of crayfish, are not widely used among freshwater fishermen. They are extremely popular in certain areas, however, and their popularity is increasing as more and more anglers are discovering their virtues.

Here are some guidelines for fishing with each type of crustacean:

Crayfish

Although crayfish are widely known as an excellent bait for smallmouth bass, they also work well for largemouth bass, catfish and large trout, including steelhead. And small crayfish (less than 2 inches long) are an underrated bait for yellow perch, rock bass, shellcrackers, longear sunfish and even crappies. Peeled crayfish tails are another good option for panfish.

Although some anglers

insist that softshell crayfish catch more fish than hardshells, others say it makes little difference—as long as the crayfish is the right size for the fish you're targeting. A good-sized crayfish in defensive posture with pincers outstretched may look too intimidating for all but the largest gamefish.

Shrimp

Grass shrimp have long been a favorite of panfish anglers in Florida and other southeastern states. And their popularity is growing as they are being offered by more and more bait shops in other parts of the country.

The larger species of shrimp have not gained widespread popularity among freshwater fishermen, but anglers in coastal areas use them to catch largemouth bass, catfish, sturgeon, steelhead and salmon.

Scuds

Scuds are an excellent trout bait, as evidenced by the dozens of fly patterns intended to imitate them. Although they work equally well for panfish, few panfishermen have ever heard of them.

The main reason scuds are not more popular is their delicacy. Fish can easily pick them off the hook, and they may tear off when you cast. It helps to use small, light-wire hooks and lob cast with a soft-tipped rod.

Popular Methods for Rigging Crustaceans

Species of Gamefish	Size/Type of Crustacean	Popular Rigging Methods
Panfish	Scuds, grass shrimp, crayfish less than 2 inches long, crayfish tails, pieces of saltwater shrimp.	• Split-shot rig and light-wire hook • Slip- or fixed-bobber rig with light-wire hook or teardrop • Jig tipped with scuds, grass shrimp or pieces of shrimp
Largemouth bass, smallmouth bass	Crayfish from 2 to 4 inches long, shrimp from 3 to 5 inches long (primarily for largemouth).	• Slip-sinker rig with plain or weedless hook • Split-shot rig with plain or weedless hook
Catfish	Crayfish from 3 to 4 inches long, shrimp from 3 to 5 inches long.	• Slip-sinker rig with plain hook • 3-way-swivel rig with plain hook • Large slip-float rig with plain hook
Sturgeon	Mud shrimp and ghost shrimp from 4 to 7 inches long.	• Slip- or fixed-sinker rig with plain hook
Trout	Scuds, grass shrimp, crayfish no more than 3 inches long, crayfish tails.	• Split-shot rig and regular or light-wire hook • Slip- or fixed-bobber rig with regular or light-wire hook • Casting bubble with plain hook (scuds and grass shrimp)
Salmon, steelhead	Mud and ghost shrimp from 3 to 5 inches long. Crayfish up to 3 inches long (steelhead only).	• Slip-sinker rig with plain hook • Split-shot rig with plain hook • Surgical-tubing rig with plain hook • Fixed-bobber rig to float shrimp • Floating spinner tipped with piece of shrimp

Crayfish. *Hook a crayfish by pushing the hook through the bony "horn" on its head (left). Hooked this way, a crayfish is not likely to scoot backward, crawl under a rock and get you snagged. If the horn is too fragile, hook the craw through the side of the next-to-last segment of the tail (right). The latter method is also a better choice in very clear water, because the hook is less apparent.*

Crayfish Tail. *Push the hook into the broken end of a crayfish tail and bring the point out through the top of the shell.*

Grass Shrimp. *When fishing with a float, hook a grass shrimp through the back (left) so it hangs level in the water. To tip a jig, push the hook through the head and out the back (right).*

Saltwater Shrimp. *Hook a whole shrimp (1) through the tail, or cut it in half and hook it through the broken end with either a plain hook (2) or a jig (3). For panfish, hook a small piece of peeled shrimp onto a plain hook (4).*

Scuds. *Thread several scuds onto a light-wire hook (left) or teardrop (right) so that only the tails dangle. Inspect the bait often and add more scuds as needed.*

Tips for Fishing with Crustaceans

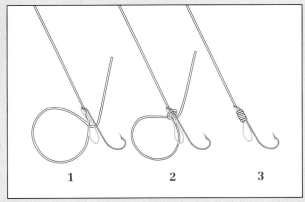

Snell a rubber band onto a long-shank hook (left) to secure mud shrimp or other fragile crustaceans. Lay the rubber band on the hook shank, then (1) push the line through the hook eye and make a loop in the line. (2) Wrap the free end through the loop and around the hook shank and rubber band; continue wrapping about 6 times. (3) Snug up the knot by pulling on the standing line and the free end. Then thread the middle of the shrimp onto the hook and then pull the rubber band over the tail (right).

Another way to keep fragile crustaceans on the hook is to thread them on as shown above and then wrap the tail with a piece of soft copper wire or a pipe cleaner.

To attract panfish or trout, mash a few dozen scuds in a small container and then dip a small jig with a hair, feather or soft-plastic tail into the juice so it absorbs the scent. Redip the jig frequently.

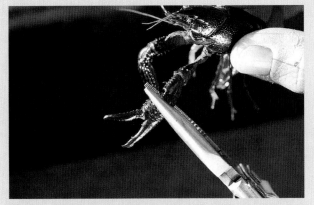

Remove the pincers of a large crayfish to make it look smaller and less formidable. Using needlenose pliers, squeeze the claw firmly and it will neatly detach from the body without injuring the craw.

Use a float to keep a mud or ghost shrimp from dragging on a rocky streambed. It's difficult to keep these delicate crustaceans on the hook if they're allowed to tumble along the bottom.

POTPOURRI

*V*eteran anglers know that there are times when these unusual baits will greatly outproduce the standard offerings.

EGG BAITS

During the spawning run, salmon and trout gorge themselves on a natural food not present at other times of the year: Their own eggs. Normally, the eggs they eat are those that have drifted from their redds and have no chance to survive.

Serious fishermen know that eggs are a can't-miss bait for practically all species of trout and salmon. They work especially well during the spawning run, but will catch fish anytime. Some anglers rely on fake eggs and egg clusters, but these imitations are seldom as effective as the real thing.

Real eggs produce a strong scent that fish can detect from a considerable distance. Fresh eggs "milk" when dropped into the water, leaving a visible trail that clearly marks the path of the scent. When the eggs stop milking, it's time to put on some fresh ones.

Anglers use single eggs, egg chunks and spawn bags for bait (right). Any kind of trout or salmon eggs can be used, but the eggs of most trout are much smaller than those of salmon, so they are difficult to fish individually.

Egg chunks must be cut

The Ultimate Guide To Freshwater Fishing

Popular Types of Egg Baits

Single Egg. *An individual egg on an egg hook is an excellent bait for any kind of trout or salmon.*

Spawn Bag. *Wrap loose eggs in a piece of mesh that allows the scent to escape. Spawn bags work well for salmon and good-sized trout.*

Egg Chunk. *For salmon or large trout, cut a chunk from a fresh skein and push the hook through the membrane several times to secure the eggs.*

from a fresh *skein*, or egg sac. The membrane covering the skein is needed to keep the eggs on the hook. When the eggs mature, the membrane weakens and you'll need a spawn bag to hold the eggs together.

Whatever eggs you use, make sure they are clear and firm. Cloudy or mushy eggs have been dead too long and are seldom as effective.

RIGGING & FISHING EGG BAITS

Spawn bags and chunks are normally used to catch salmon and large trout, while single eggs work better for smaller trout. But a trophy chinook will pick up a single egg and a pan-sized rainbow will inhale a spawn bag that barely fits into its mouth. The main consideration in selecting egg baits is the type of water—not the type of fish.

For example, when you're drift-fishing in strong current, a spawn bag is a better choice than a single egg or spawn chunk because the bag stays on the hook much longer. But when the stream is low and clear, a single salmon egg works better because of its natural look. A fresh spawn chunk is the best bet in slow or still water; it emits more scent than a spawn bag, yet stays on the hook fairly well.

Although drift-fishing while wading a stream is the most popular way to present egg baits, some anglers prefer to float-fish from a boat or fish with a fixed- or slip-bobber rig, either in still or moving water.

Whatever type of egg bait you prefer, be sure it's fresh. When the eggs start to look washed out, replace them. Washed out eggs emit very little scent and attract few fish.

How to Hook Egg Baits

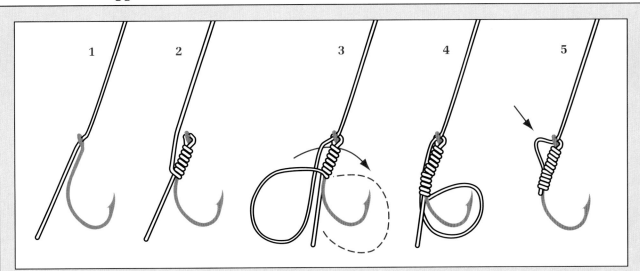

Egg Chunk. To hold an egg chunk on the hook, make an egg loop. Using a hook with a turned-up eye and a 2-foot piece of mono: (1) push your line through the eye; (2) make 6 wraps around the shank and tag end and hold the wraps with your fingers; (3) push the other end of the line through the eye, leaving a loop; (4) wrap one leg of the loop over the other leg and the tag end about 6 times, as shown; (5) snug up the knot by pulling on the line, then open the loop (arrow) by pushing on the line. Finally, cut a chunk of eggs from a fresh skein, put them into the loop and snug up the line.

Single Egg. (1) Push the hook through the side of the egg, (2) turn the hook 180 degrees and (3) bury the point in the opposite side of the egg.

Spawn Bag. You can tie a spawn bag as small as ³/₈ inch in diameter for stream trout or as large as ³/₄ inch for steelhead or salmon. Select a short-shank hook that suits the size of the spawn bag and then push the point in one side of the bag and out the other, leaving the hook point exposed as shown. The hook eye should barely protrude from the bag.

Drift-Fishing with Egg Baits

Add a pinch-on sinker or enough split shot to your line (inset) so your bait bumps naturally along the bottom at the same speed as the current. If you do not use enough weight, the current will lift your bait off the bottom; if you use too much, the bait will catch on the bottom and won't drift fast enough. Angle your cast upstream to (a) the closest part of a likely riffle or run. Hold your rod tip high as your bait drifts, keeping the line taut until the bait is well downstream of your position. Make several drifts through the same zone. Then reel up and make (b) a slightly longer cast at the same angle. Repeat the procedure until the entire riffle or run has been thoroughly covered (c and beyond).

Float-Fishing with Egg Baits

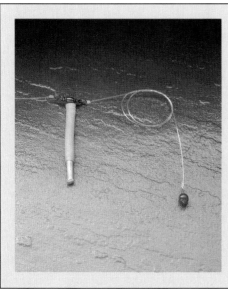

A surgical-tubing rig is ideal for float-fishing on a snaggy bottom. Just push a piece of pencil lead into the tubing. Then, should the pencil lead get snagged, it will pull out so you don't lose the whole rig.

Control the boat with oars or a small motor to keep it drifting at the same speed as the current. This way your line stays vertical, enabling you to easily feel the bottom and detect bites.

Tips for Fishing with Egg Baits

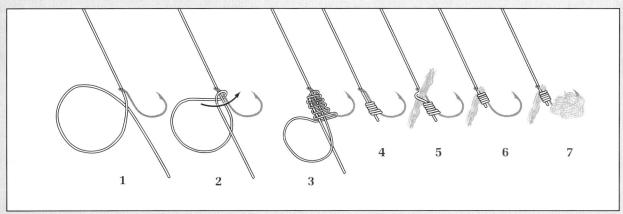

Snell a piece of yarn onto your hook for extra attraction. To make a snell: (1) push the line through the hook eye; (2) make a loop in the line; (3) wrap the free end through the loop and around the hook shank 6 times; (4) snug up the knot by pulling on the standing line and the free end; (5) insert a short piece of yarn under the standing line; (6) pull on the standing line until the snell abuts the hook eye. Finally, (7) push your hook into a spawn bag so the point is barely exposed.

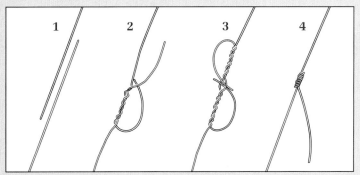 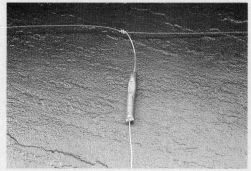

When drift-fishing on a snaggy bottom, use a dropper rig instead of pinching the sinker directly onto your line. To make a dropper, cut your line and then retie it using a blood knot (left): (1) Hold the lines alongside each other, with the ends facing opposite directions; (2) wrap one line around the other 4-5 times, and pass the free end between the two lines, as shown; (3) repeat step 2 with the other line; (4) pull on both lines to snug up the knot and leave one tag end untrimmed. Pinch pencil lead or split shot onto the dropper (right). When the sinker snags, a sharp tug will pull it off of the line and free the rig. Then all you have to do is pinch on a new sinker.

Thread a floater, such as a "corkie," onto your line before tying on your hook. A floater not only reduces the number of snags, it acts as an attractor. Some floaters are designed to spin for even more attraction.

For a day of fishing, carry spawn bags or preserved egg chunks in a flip-top egg dispenser that attaches to your belt.

FISHING WITH CLAM MEAT

Given the opportunity, many kinds of gamefish feed on clams and other molluscs. In fact, the shellcracker (redear sunfish) gets its name from its habit of eating small clams and snails.

Although clam meat is a favorite of some sunfish anglers, it is used more commonly by river fishermen in search of larger quarry, particularly catfish and sturgeon.

You can find clams in practically any body of unpolluted water. In clear lakes and rivers, all you have to do is wade through the shallows and pick them up. If the water is not clear enough to see them, just take off your shoes and feel for them with your bare feet. They're most numerous on a clean, sandy bottom.

Clams are easy to keep alive. They'll live for a few days in a bucket of water kept in a cool spot, and for several weeks in a submerged live box.

The biggest problem in fishing with clam meat is keeping it on the hook. Although the meat is somewhat rubbery, it tears off quite easily, especially when you cast. But you can secure it just as you would fresh spawn, enclosing it in a mesh bag or holding it on with a loop of mono. Gobbing it onto a treble hook also works well (opposite).

Most anglers use fresh clam meat. But for catfish you may want to try soaking the meat in sour milk for a few days. Catfish are attracted to the strong smell of spoiled clams and the soaking process firms up the meat.

Clam meat is usually fished on the bottom, using a fixed- or slip-sinker rig. But sunfish anglers and a few catfishermen prefer to suspend it from a float.

Tips for Rigging & Fishing Clam Meat

Pry open a live clam and look for the firm muscle, called the "foot" (arrow). This is the part that makes the best bait.

Save the rest of the clam meat, dice it into small pieces and then use it for chum. Spread it around your fishing spot at least ½ hour before you start fishing.

For sunfish, cut the foot into small pieces and push one or two of them onto a long-shank hook.

For larger fish, tie the meat into (1) a mesh bag or secure it with (2) an egg loop. Where legal, gob the clam meat onto (3) a treble hook, pushing each barb through the meat.

FISHING WITH BLOOD BAIT

Many catfish experts swear by blood bait, especially for catching channels and blues. Blood bait leaves an intense scent trail, drawing catfish from a long distance.

You can make blood bait from the blood of most any warm-blooded animal, but most anglers use beef or chicken blood because it's readily available at slaughter houses and processing plants.

Most anglers still-fish with blood baits, waiting for the scent to draw catfish. This technique works best in big rivers and reservoirs that have enough current to create a scent trail.

In still waters, blood baits are effective when bumped along the bottom from a drifting boat. Catfish combing the bottom for food are quick to detect the scent trail and follow it to your bait.

You can buy prepared blood baits, but most serious catfishermen prefer to make their own using fresh blood. Some anglers use chicken or beef liver instead of blood. These baits, when fresh, also emit a bloody scent trail but it is less intense than that of pure blood.

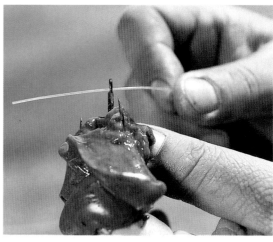

Push some liver over the shank of a treble hook, impale it onto the 3 points and then tie your line to the hook.

How to Make Blood Bait

1 *Obtain some fresh blood from a slaughter-house and pour it into a large baking pan at least 1 inch deep.*

2 *Refrigerate the pan for about 5 days or until the blood congeals into a firm, rubbery mass.*

3 *Set the pan in the sun for a few hours until the blood forms a tough skin, which helps keep it on the hook. Then cut the bait into 1- to 3-inch squares and refrigerate them in resealable plastic bags.*

How to Hook Blood Bait

1 *Make a foot-long leader with a size 1 to 2/0 treble hook on one end and a barrel swivel on the other.*

2 *Push a piece of wire with a sharp bend on the end through the blood bait, hook an eye of the barrel swivel and then pull the leader through the bait.*

3 *Slide the bait down to the hook and impale it with all 3 points of the treble. Attach the leader to a clip at the end of your line.*

INDEX

Y